MW01700435

Nectar

Trans Femme & Non Binary Erotic Comics Anthology

Edited by Tab Kimpton
& Harry-Anne Bentley

ISBN 978-1-9162243-2-2

First Printing November 2021

Published by Khaos as part of Discord Comics

Find out more at DiscordComics.com

A Note from the Editors

Erotica is incredibly subjective, so we've done our best to tag each story as appropriate. If something is not to your taste just look at the tags in the peach for the page number to skip ahead to the next story.

It would be impossible to cover the breadth of tastes, delights and desires that span the trans femme and non binary spectrum, however we hope that this book is a refreshing cocktail to whet your appetite.

We'd like to thank Eve Greenwood for their lettering skills, and all our kickstarter backers who believed in the project and made it our best one yet. We'd also like to thank Gwen Barr, Cody F, Sam Orchard, Laura Blake and Amy Whitington, you know what you did.

We are forever grateful to everyone who submitted to our open call for this anthology, along with our final contributors. You made this the sweetest experience editors could hope for.

- Tab & Harry-Anne

Contents

Last Call

Story by Emily Riesbeck - Art by Dominique Duong

Two Galli Priests drink a hydria filled with delicious but strange smelling wine (because they're idiots) and the love making that follows is... transformative to say the least.

Writer's Note

" The galli really are a fascinating piece of transfeminine-adjacent history, and I'm so glad I was able to write a story featuring two galli characters. Their ritual castration is obviously quite eye-catching, but the galli were also known for wearing women's clothing and long, bleached hair.

*While experiences like the galli are far removed from our contemporary understanding of gender, I think it's important to see the through-lines from past cultural experiences to our own, if only to understand that the history of humanity is *our* history, too, despite claims to the contrary. If I get to write some transformation smut along the way, then all the better. "*

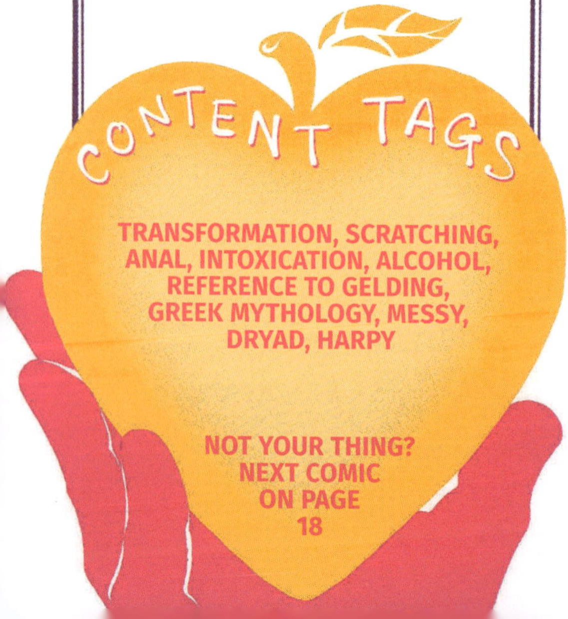

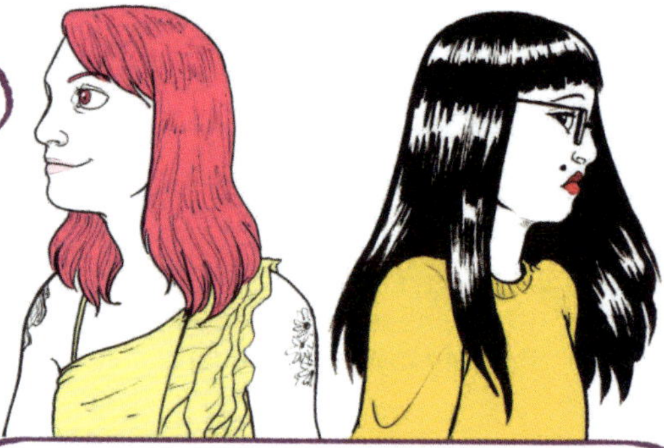

About the Creators

Emily (they/them) is a queer author who enjoys allegorical world-building and unlikely pairings. Their work includes It's Your Funeral (Iron Circus Comics), Mountain (Cow House Press) and The Pirate and the Porcelain Girl (2022, Simon and Schuster). They live in Chicago with their two partners and cat, Yuri.

EmilyRiesbeck.com

Dominique (she/her) is a bisexual Chinese/Vietnamese illustrator and comic artist based in the UK. She enjoys creating queer horror and fantasy stories, and loves surreal, conceptual imagery. Her work has appeared in a number of anthologies, including Come Together and Turning Roads, and she's published her own comics, such as queer Chinese Zodiac romance, The Dog & the Cat, and supernatural horror, The Flower Maiden.

DomDuong.com

LAST CALL

Story by Emily Riesbeck
Art by Dominique Duong

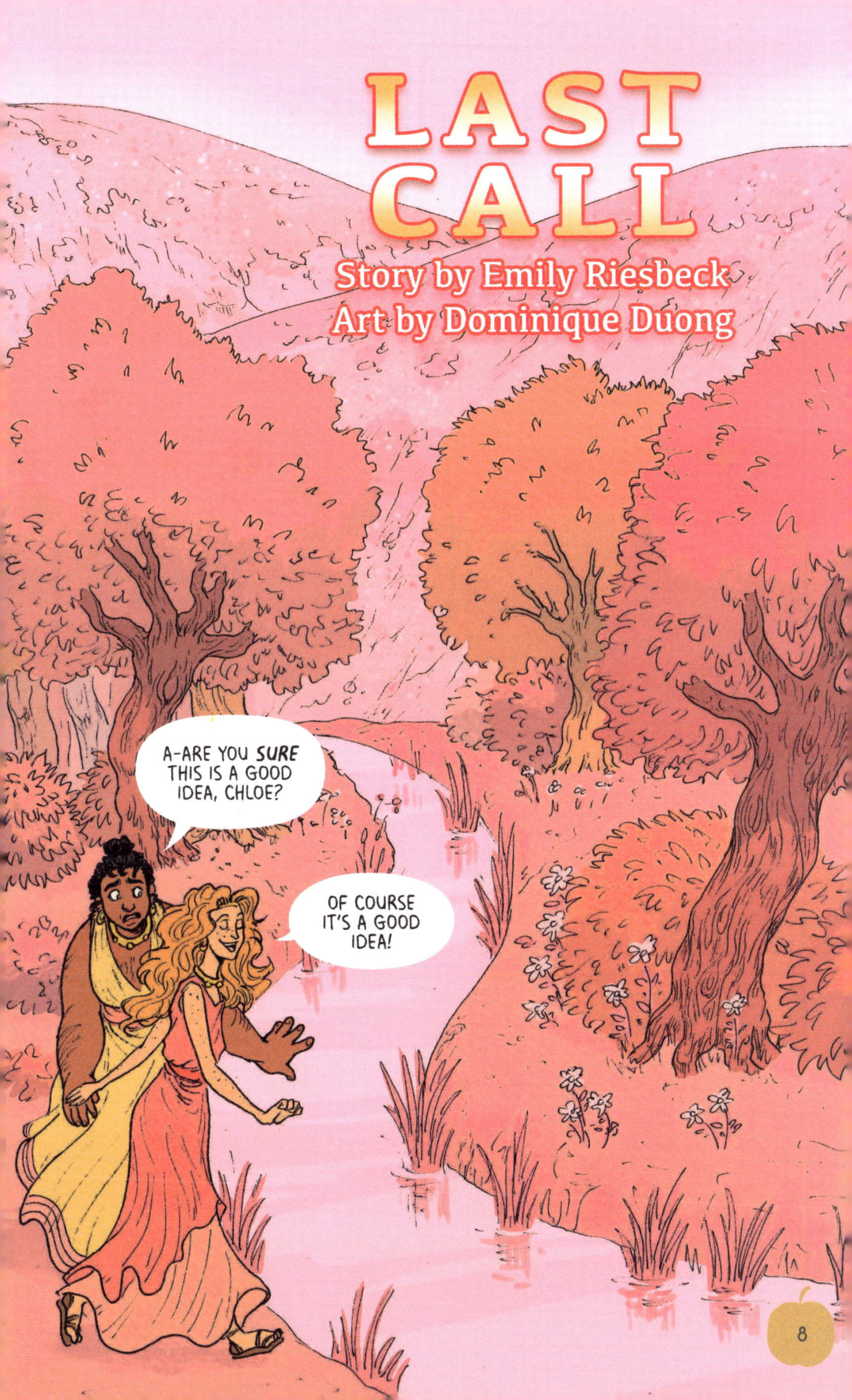

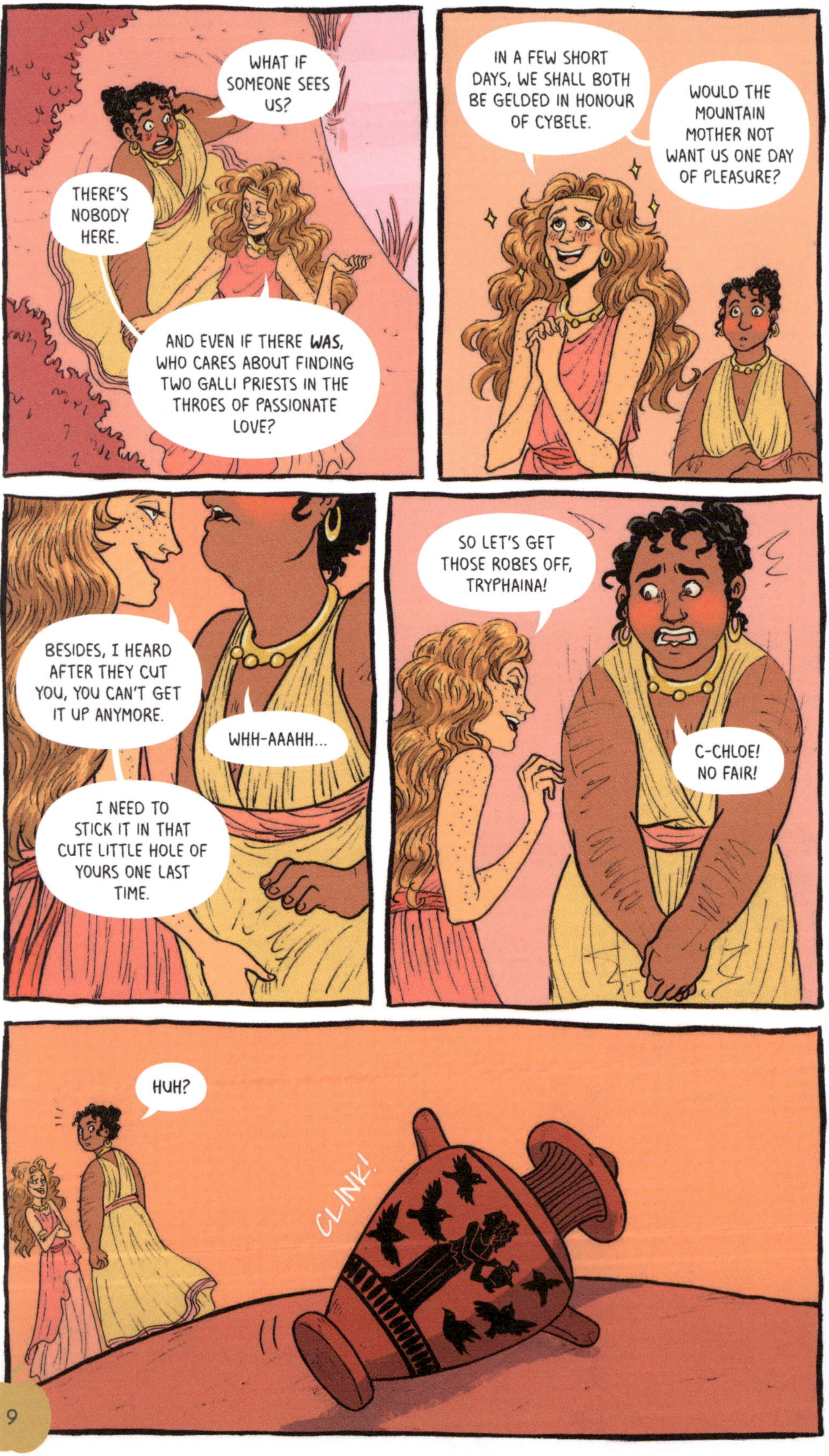
WHAT IF SOMEONE SEES US?
THERE'S NOBODY HERE.
AND EVEN IF THERE WAS, WHO CARES ABOUT FINDING TWO GALLI PRIESTS IN THE THROES OF PASSIONATE LOVE?
IN A FEW SHORT DAYS, WE SHALL BOTH BE GELDED IN HONOUR OF CYBELE.
WOULD THE MOUNTAIN MOTHER NOT WANT US ONE DAY OF PLEASURE?
BESIDES, I HEARD AFTER THEY CUT YOU, YOU CAN'T GET IT UP ANYMORE.
WHH-AAAHH...
I NEED TO STICK IT IN THAT CUTE LITTLE HOLE OF YOURS ONE LAST TIME.
SO LET'S GET THOSE ROBES OFF, TRYPHAINA!
C-CHLOE! NO FAIR!
HUH?
CLINK!

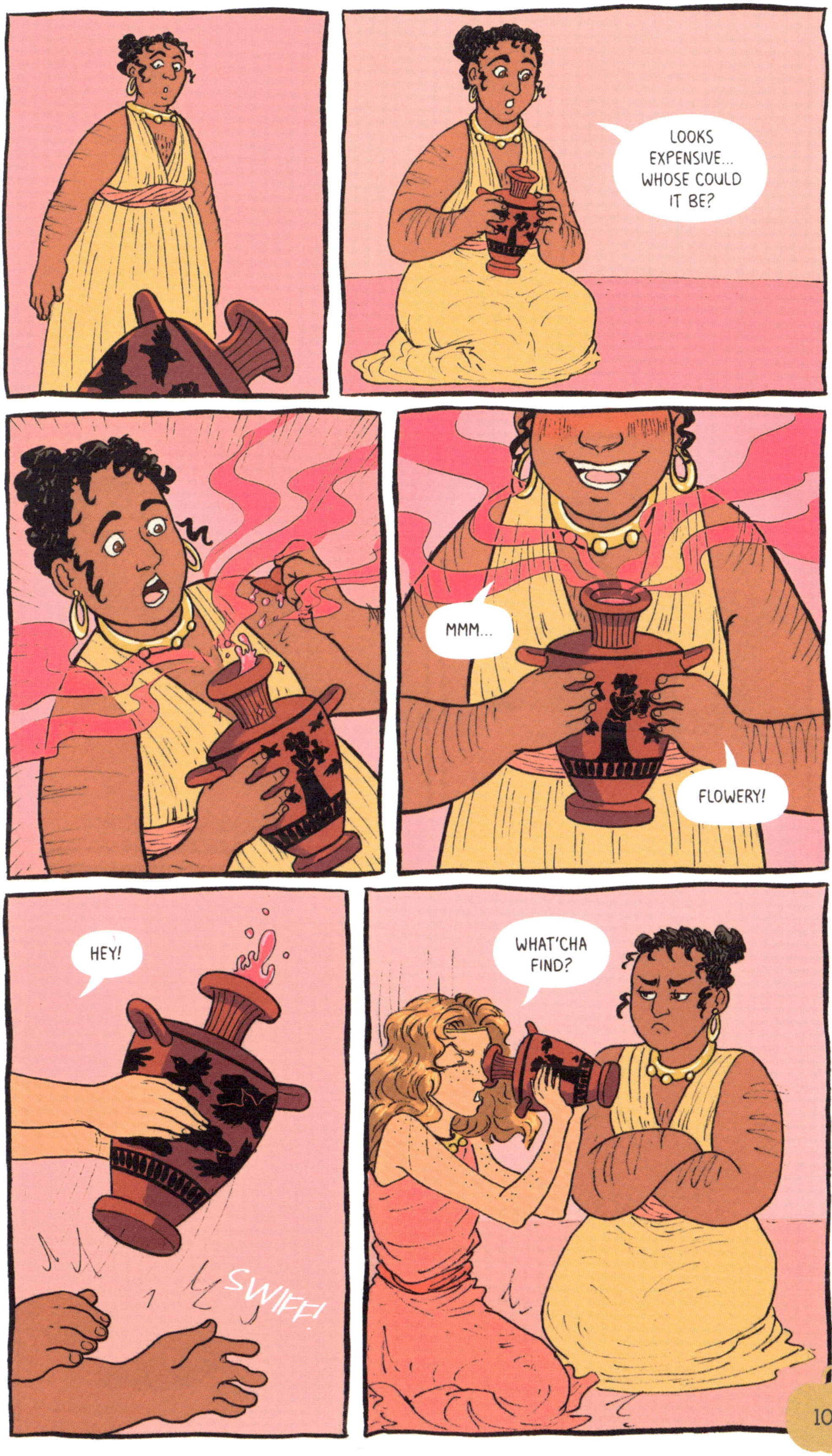

LOOKS EXPENSIVE... WHOSE COULD IT BE?
MMM...
FLOWERY!
HEY!
SWIFF!
WHAT'CHA FIND?

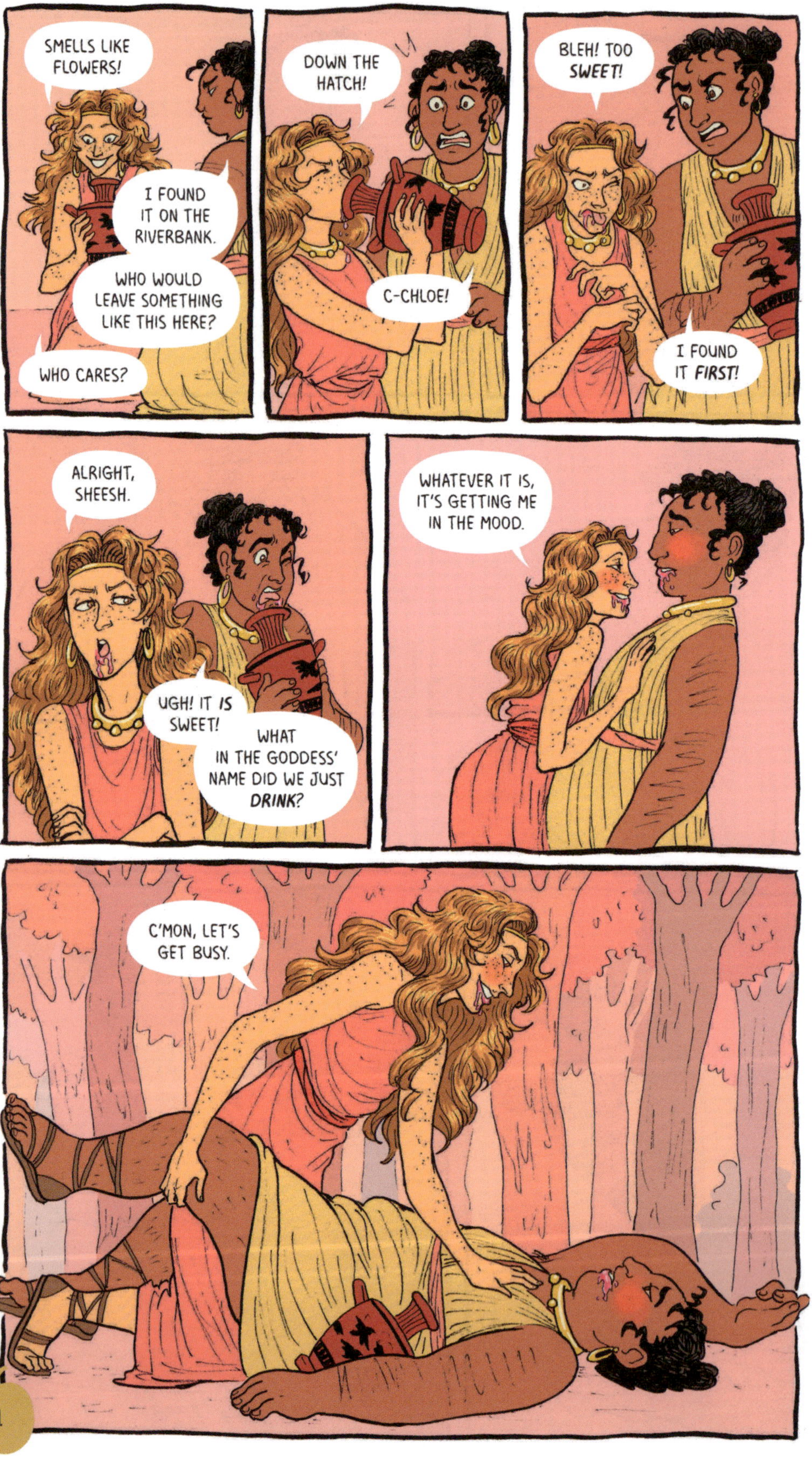
SMELLS LIKE FLOWERS!
I FOUND IT ON THE RIVERBANK.
WHO WOULD LEAVE SOMETHING LIKE THIS HERE?
WHO CARES?
DOWN THE HATCH!
C-CHLOE!
BLEH! TOO **SWEET!**
I FOUND IT **FIRST!**
ALRIGHT, SHEESH.
UGH! IT ***IS*** SWEET!
WHAT IN THE GODDESS' NAME DID WE JUST ***DRINK?***
WHATEVER IT IS, IT'S GETTING ME IN THE MOOD.
C'MON, LET'S GET BUSY.

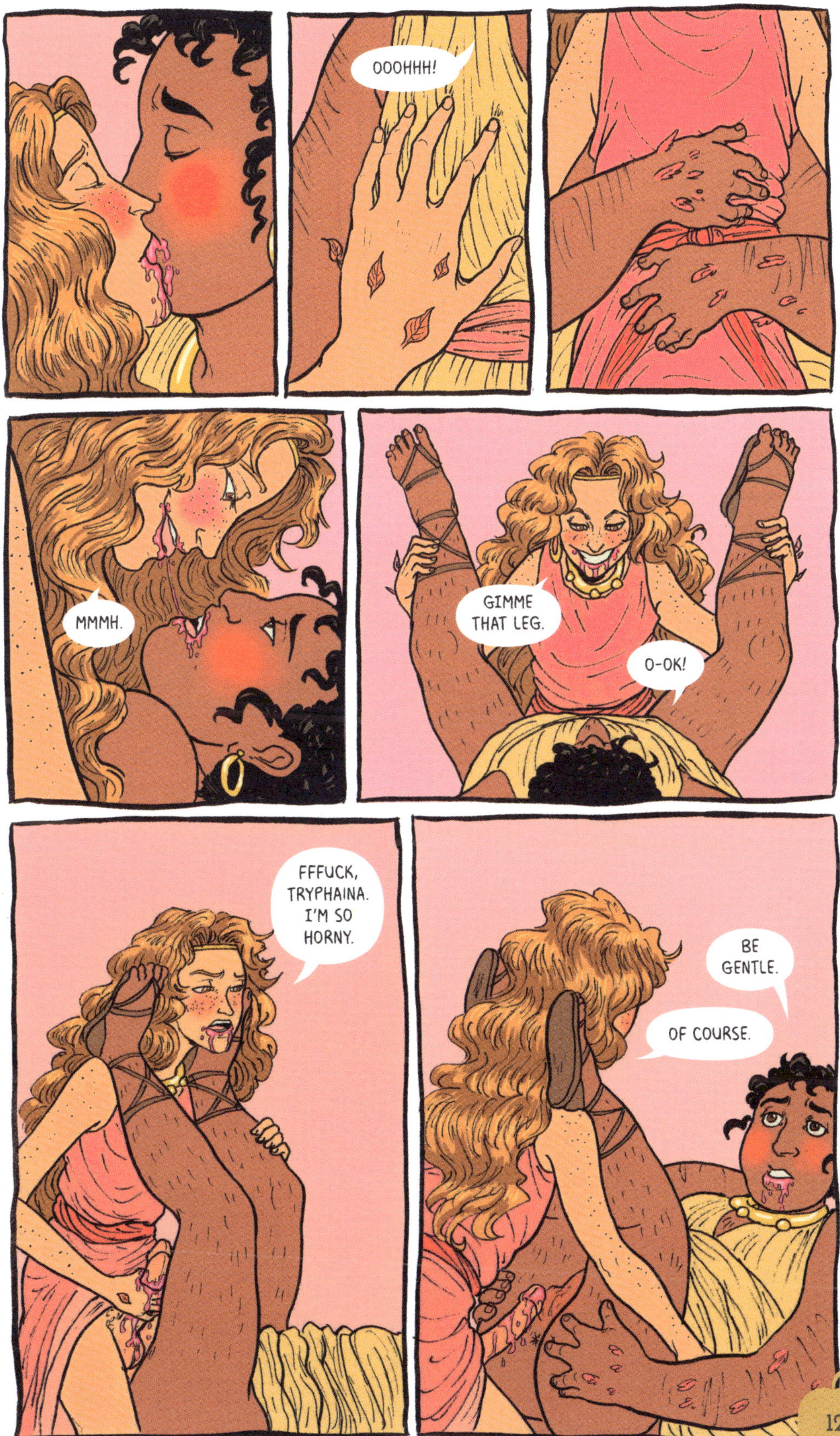
OOOHHH!
MMMH.
GIMME THAT LEG.
O-OK!
FFFUCK, TRYPHAINA. I'M SO HORNY.
BE GENTLE.
OF COURSE.

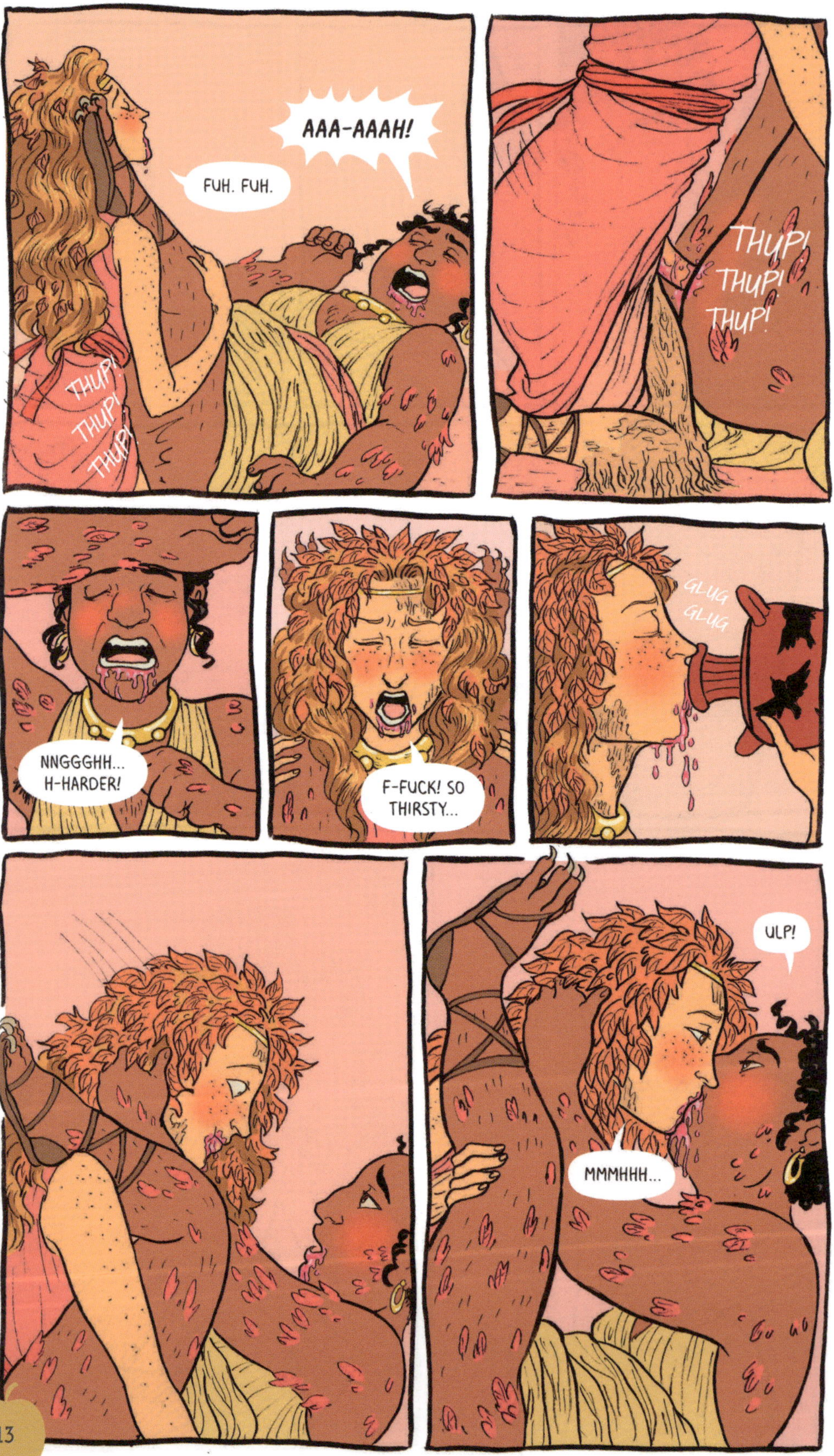
FUH. FUH.
AAA-AAAH!
THUP! THUP! THUP!
THUP! THUP! THUP!
NNGGGHH... H-HARDER!
F-FUCK! SO THIRSTY...
GLUG GLUG
ULP!
MMMHHH...

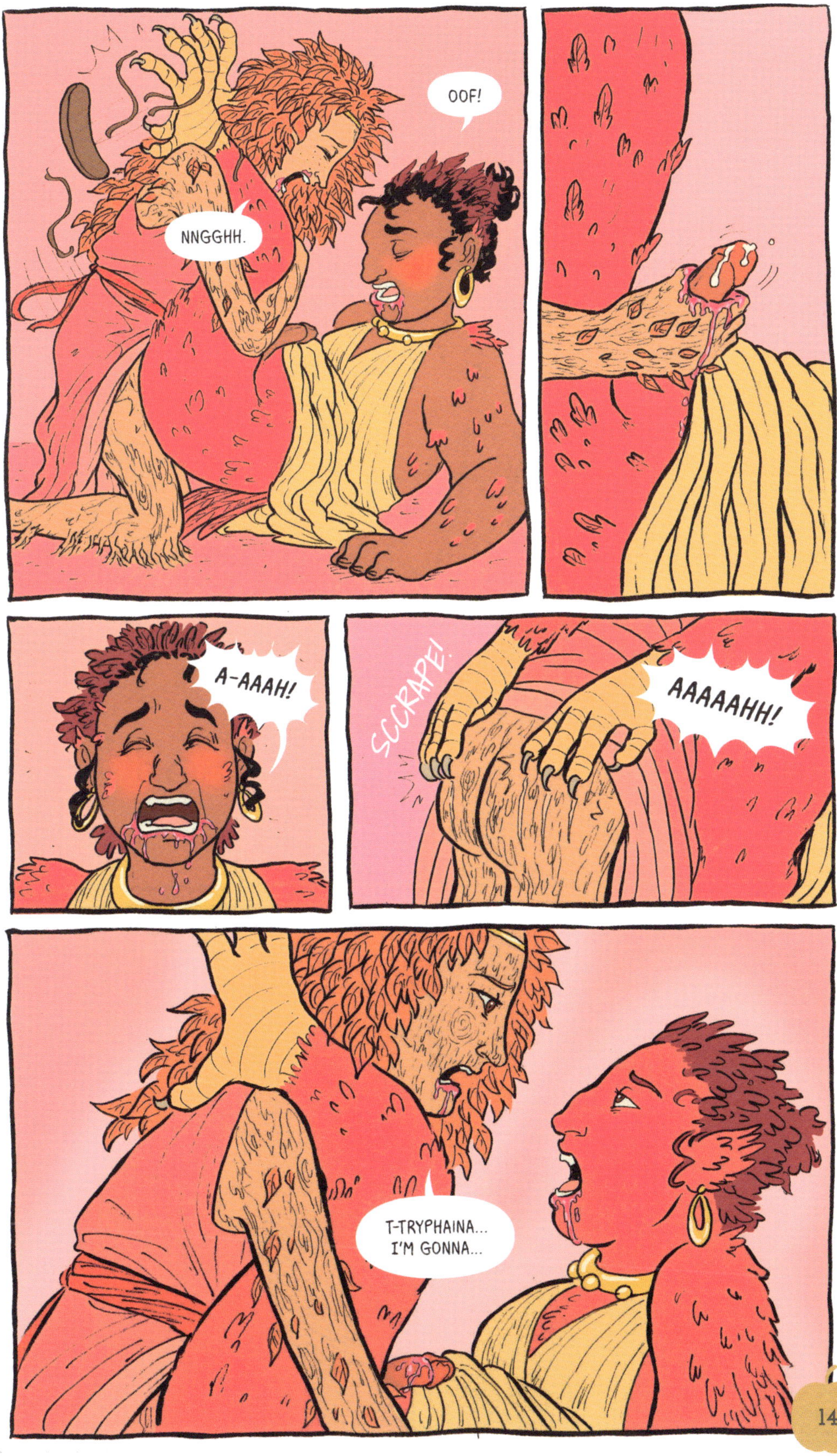
OOF!
NNGGHH.
A-AAAH!
SCCRAPE!
AAAAAHH!
T-TRYPHAINA...
I'M GONNA...

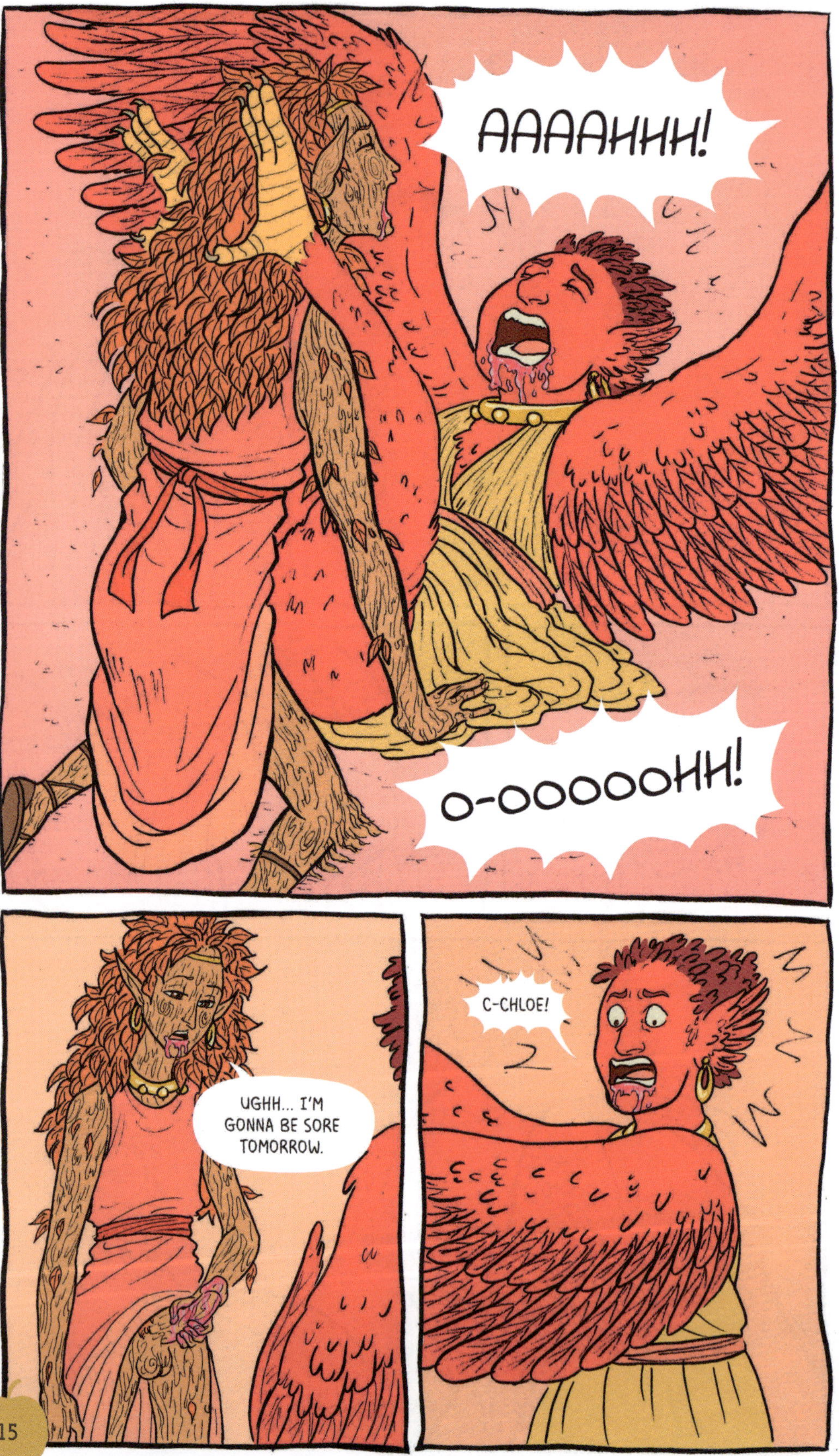
AAAAHHH!
O-OOOOOHH!
UGHH... I'M GONNA BE SORE TOMORROW.
C-CHLOE!

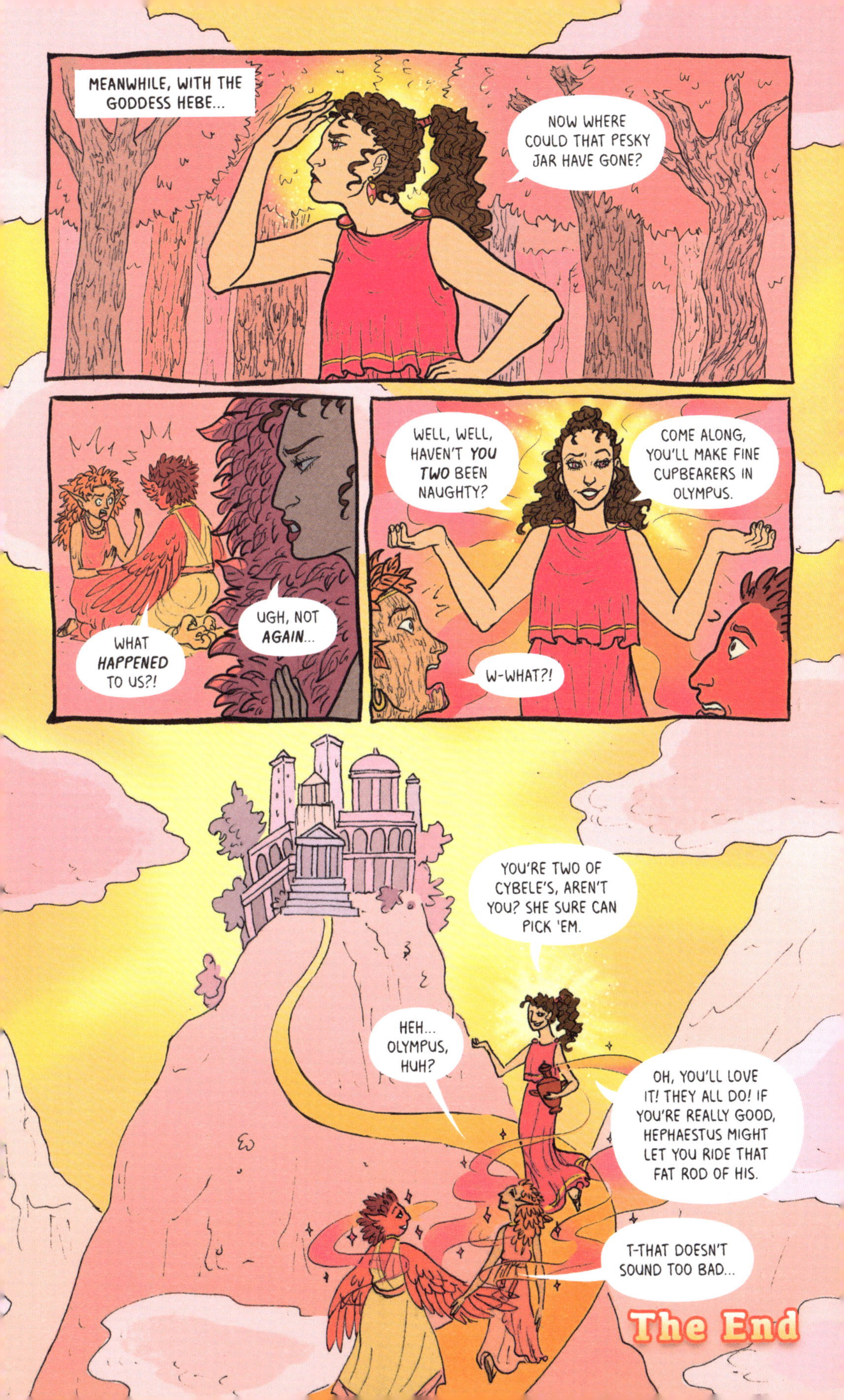
MEANWHILE, WITH THE GODDESS HEBE...
NOW WHERE COULD THAT PESKY JAR HAVE GONE?
WHAT **HAPPENED** TO US?!
UGH, NOT **AGAIN**...
WELL, WELL, HAVEN'T **YOU TWO** BEEN NAUGHTY?
COME ALONG, YOU'LL MAKE FINE CUPBEARERS IN OLYMPUS.
W-WHAT?!
YOU'RE TWO OF CYBELE'S, AREN'T YOU? SHE SURE CAN PICK 'EM.
HEH... OLYMPUS, HUH?
OH, YOU'LL LOVE IT! THEY ALL DO! IF YOU'RE REALLY GOOD, HEPHAESTUS MIGHT LET YOU RIDE THAT FAT ROD OF HIS.
T-THAT DOESN'T SOUND TOO BAD...
The End

Fey

Story by Atla Hrafney - Art by Ariel Vittori

Long distance partners meet and get busy under the aurora borealis, though one must be careful as Icelandic Fey Elves are very good at tempting locals into staying in their realm forever.

Creators' Notes

" I wanted boobies and rope in my story, and I got both of these things. I have also gotten 'do a porno comic with a stellar Italian artist' off my bucket list, which is always nice. " -Atla

" My goal was to have the representation of nature acting much like the fey people: bringing you in, each detail of the natural landscape a morsel of food or small drink that just keeps you unable to escape its beauty. This way nature - just like passionate love - becomes a rope you don't want to get untangled from. " -Ariel

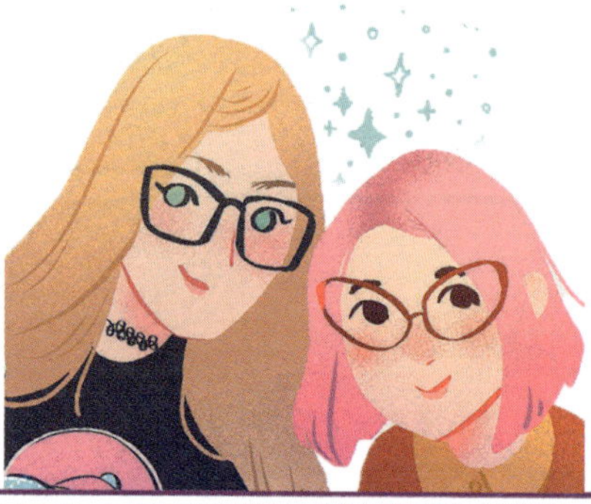

About the Creators

Atla Hrafney (she/her) is a comics writer, editor and organizor. Atla works at the lovely Hiveworks Comics as editor, and is the current chairman of the Icelandic Comics Society.

She also writes Gzhel Guardian, and does smut like this in her spare time.

AtlaTheWriter.com

Ariel Vittori (she/her) is a queer Italian illustrator, and comic maker. She also works as an editor for the award-winning indie comic label she co-founded, Attaccapanni Press, and as art director for London-based creative agency Book on a Tree.

In her work and her life she loves to explore intimacy, nature and food.

ArielVittori.com

Content Tags

BONDAGE, ORAL SEX, OUTDOORS, MAGICAL REALISM, LONG DISTANCE ROMANCE, CUM SWALLOWING, REFERENCE TO BOOB JOB, CUTE ENDING

NOT YOUR THING? NEXT COMIC ON PAGE 28

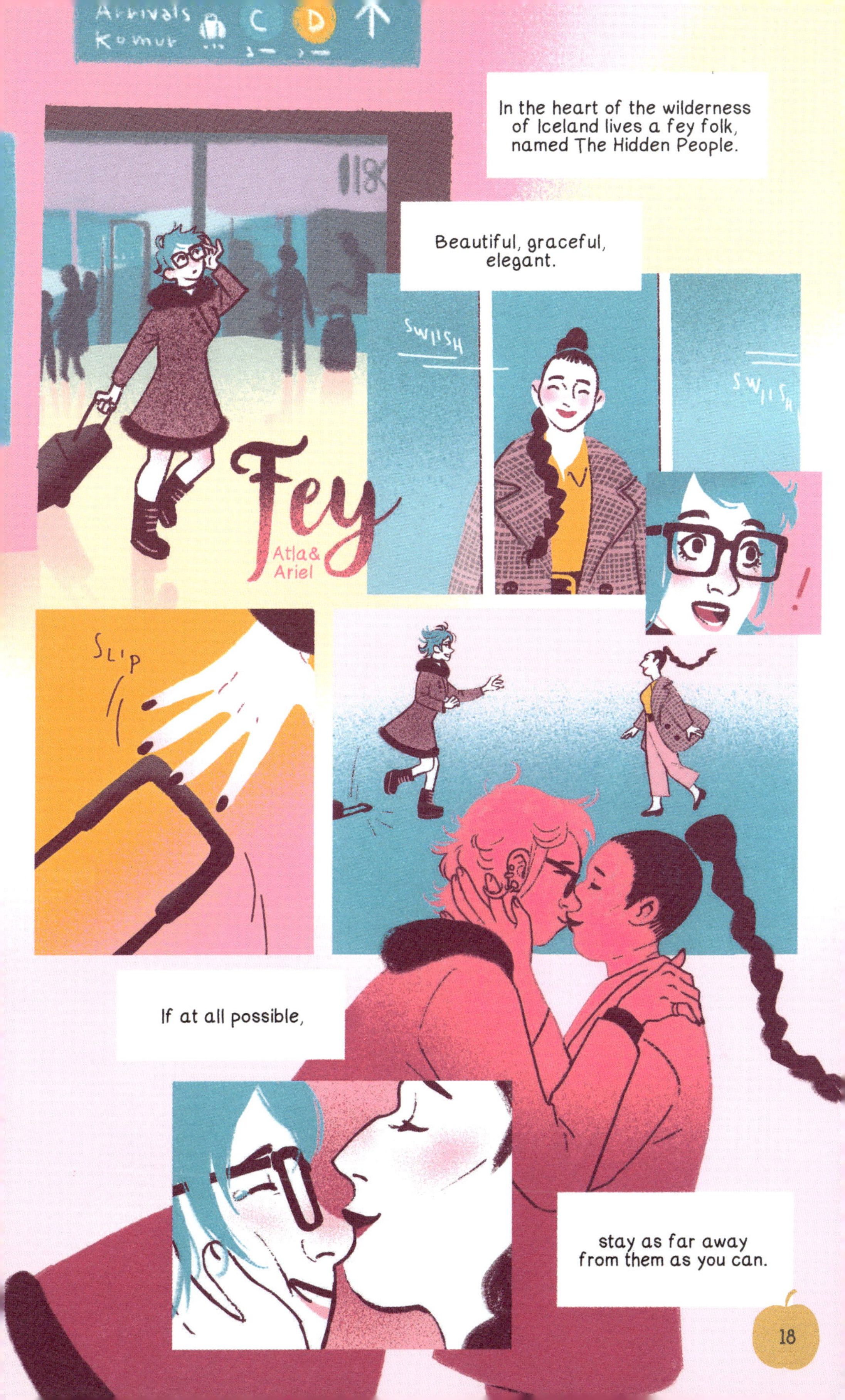
Arrivals
Komur
C
D
In the heart of the wilderness of Iceland lives a fey folk, named The Hidden People.
Fey
Atla & Ariel
Beautiful, graceful, elegant.
SWISH
SWISH
!
SLIP
If at all possible,
stay as far away from them as you can.

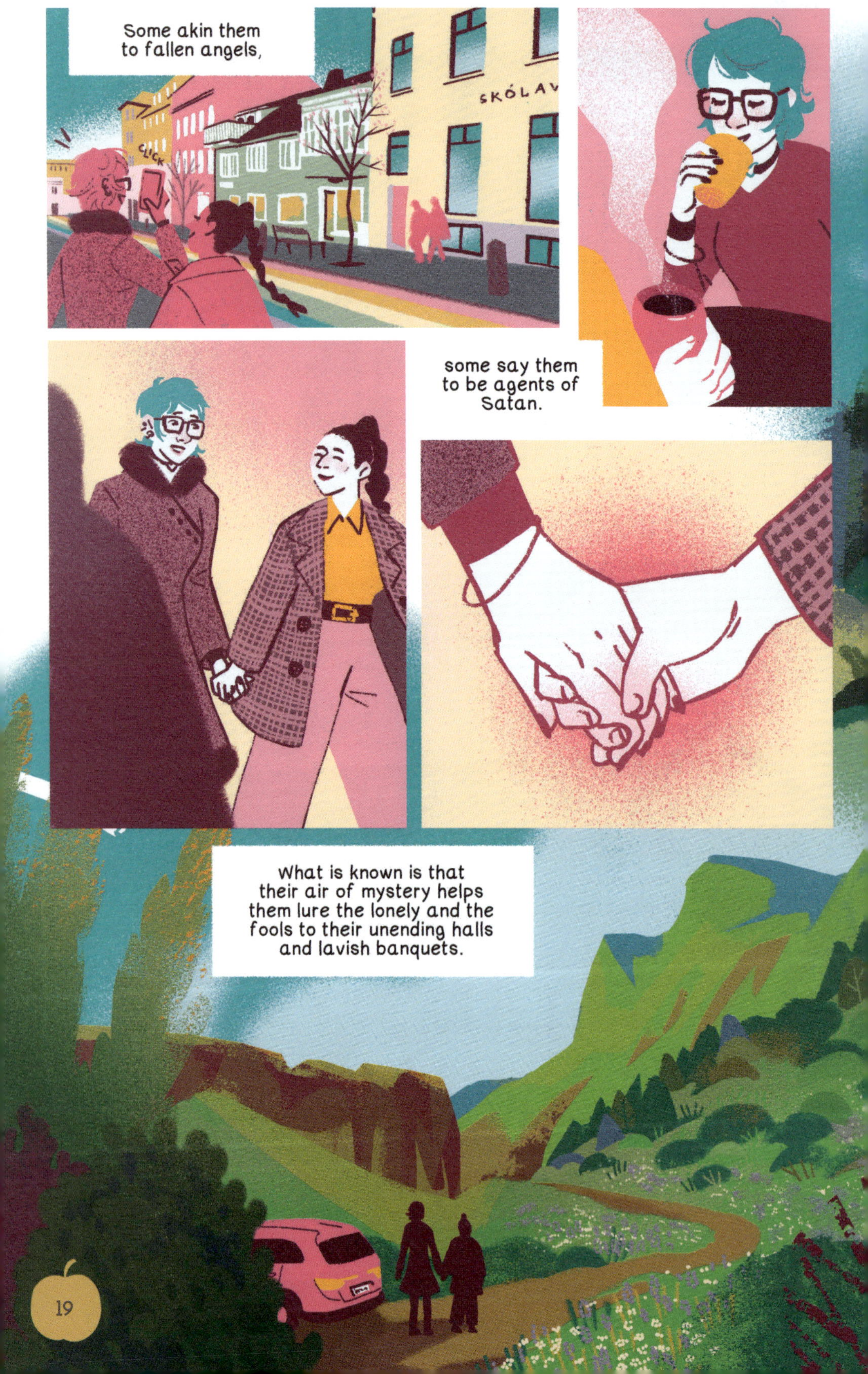
Some akin them to fallen angels,
CLICK
SKÓLAV
some say them to be agents of Satan.
What is known is that their air of mystery helps them lure the lonely and the fools to their unending halls and lavish banquets.

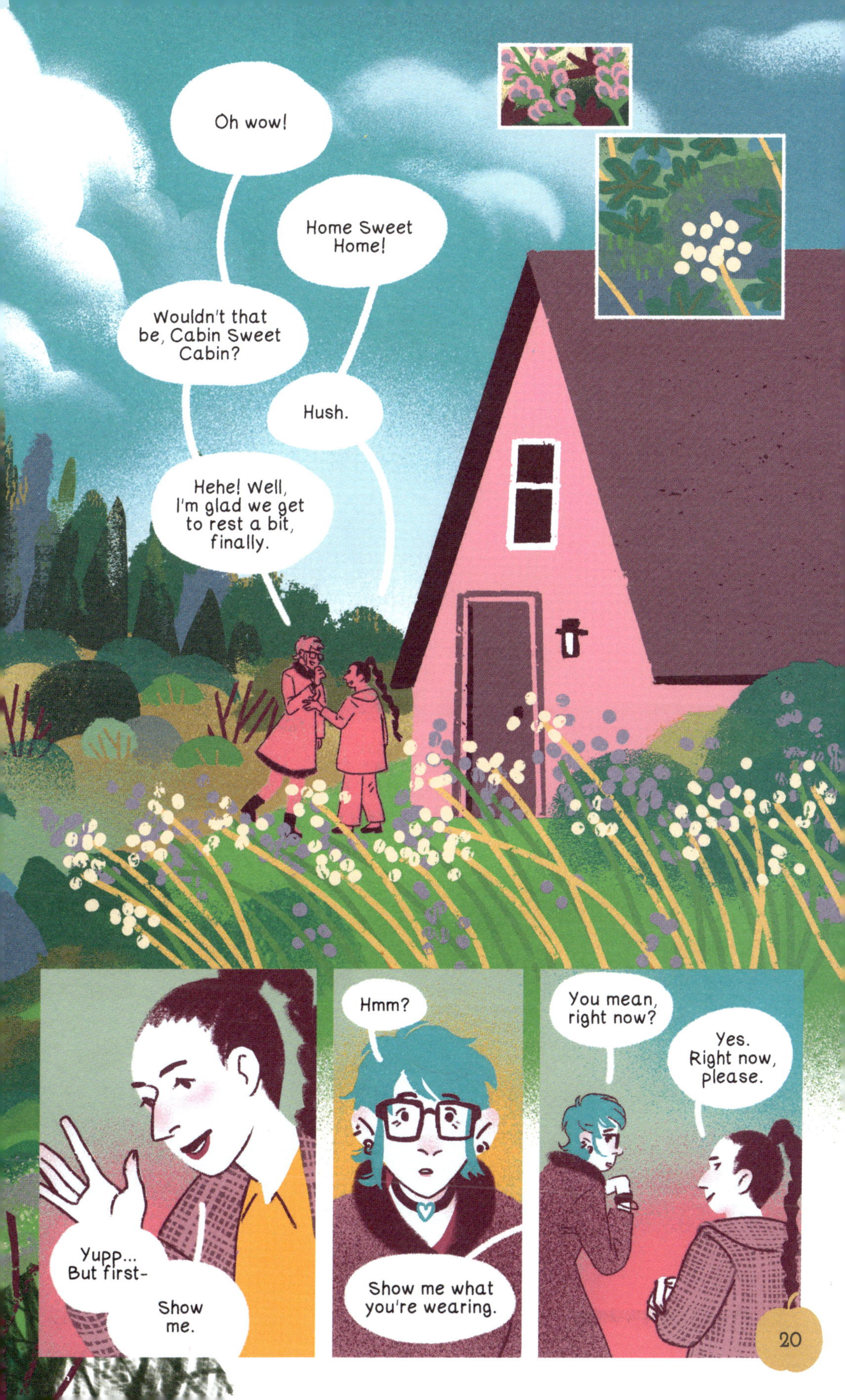
Oh wow!
Home Sweet Home!
Wouldn't that be, Cabin Sweet Cabin?
Hush.
Hehe! Well, I'm glad we get to rest a bit, finally.
Yupp... But first-
Show me.
Hmm?
Show me what you're wearing.
You mean, right now?
Yes. Right now, please.

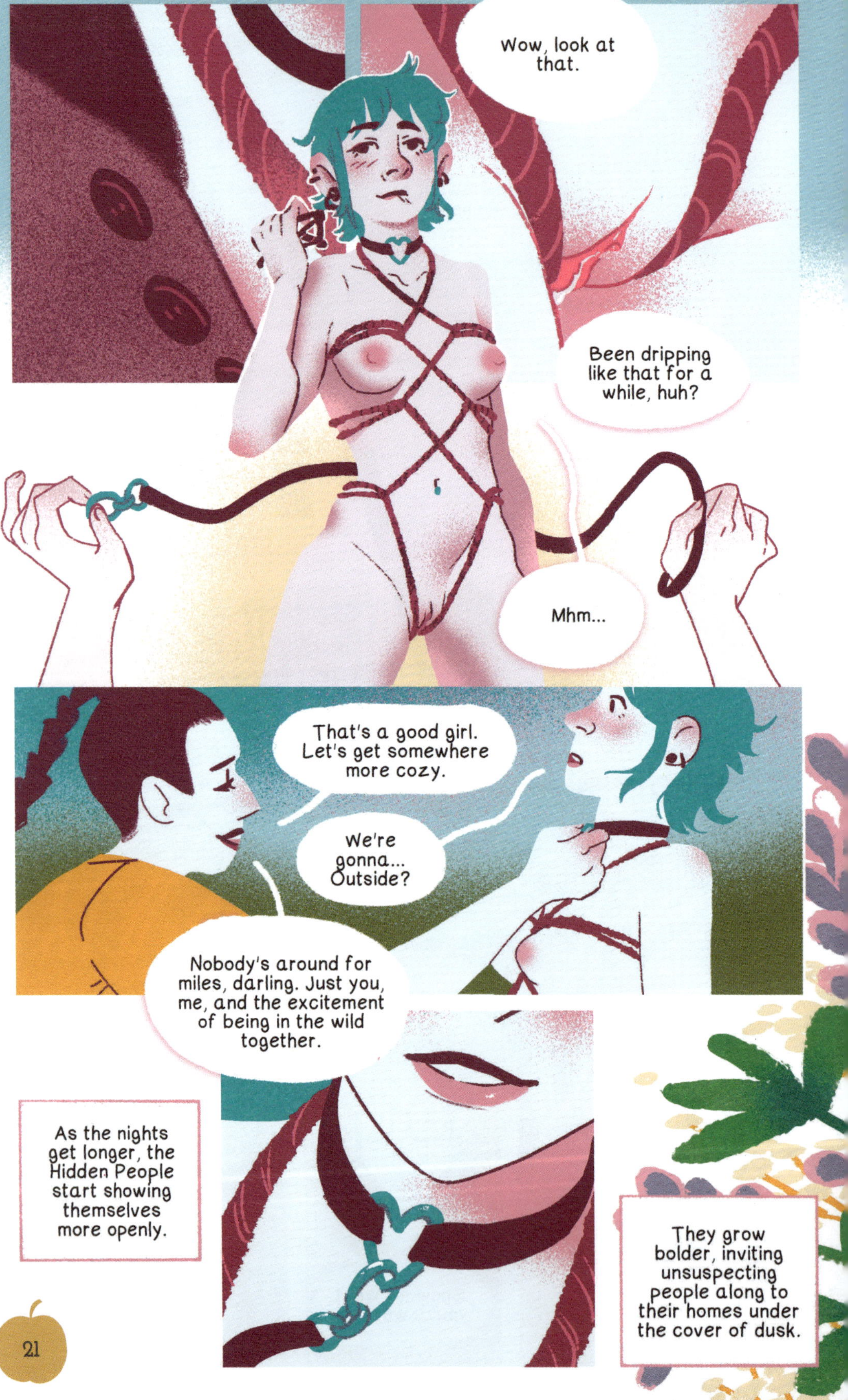
Wow, look at that.
Been dripping like that for a while, huh?
Mhm...
That's a good girl. Let's get somewhere more cozy.
We're gonna... Outside?
Nobody's around for miles, darling. Just you, me, and the excitement of being in the wild together.
As the nights get longer, the Hidden People start showing themselves more openly.
They grow bolder, inviting unsuspecting people along to their homes under the cover of dusk.

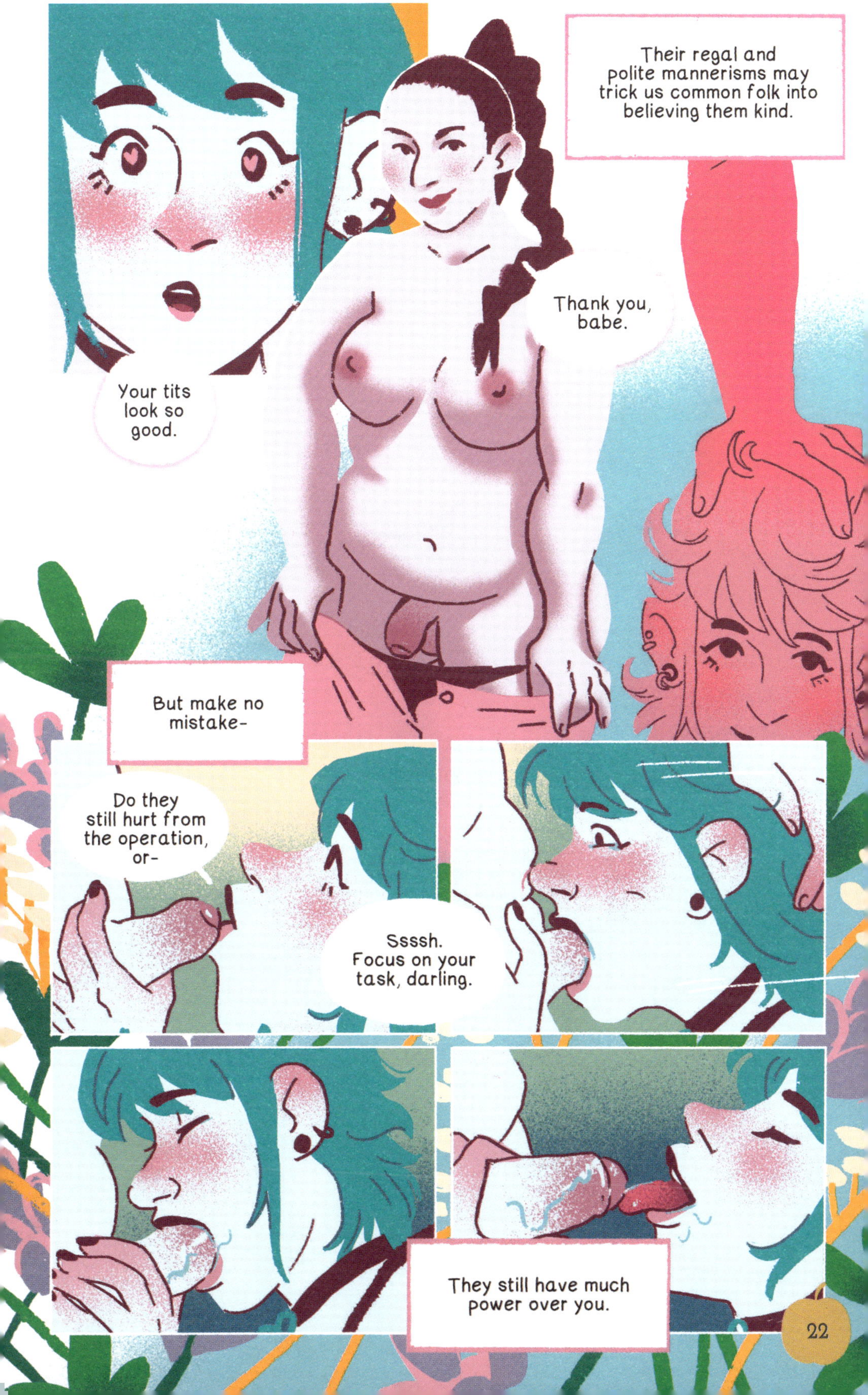
Their regal and polite mannerisms may trick us common folk into believing them kind.
Your tits look so good.
Thank you, babe.
But make no mistake-
Do they still hurt from the operation, or-
Ssssh. Focus on your task, darling.
They still have much power over you.

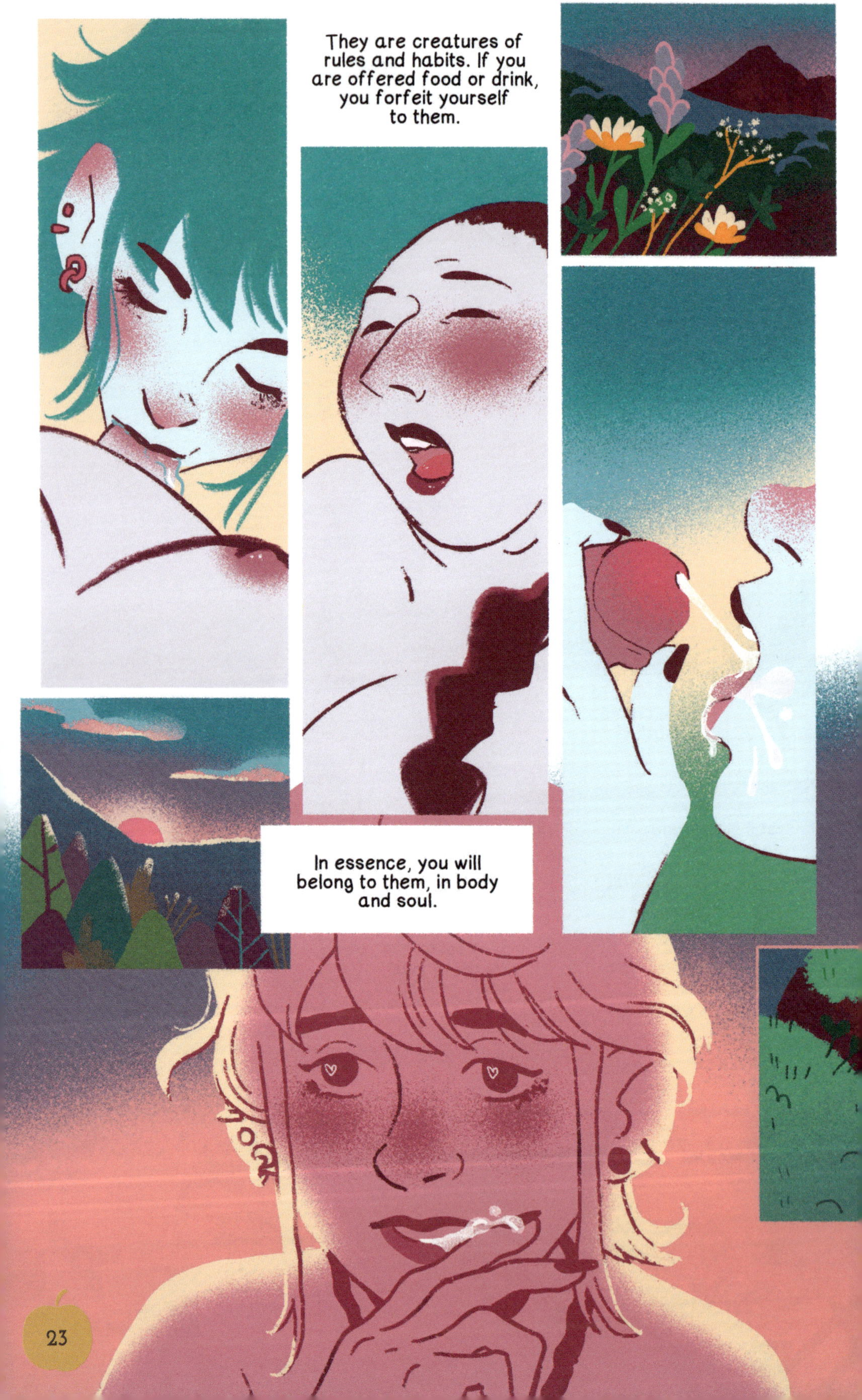
They are creatures of rules and habits. If you are offered food or drink, you forfeit yourself to them.
In essence, you will belong to them, in body and soul.

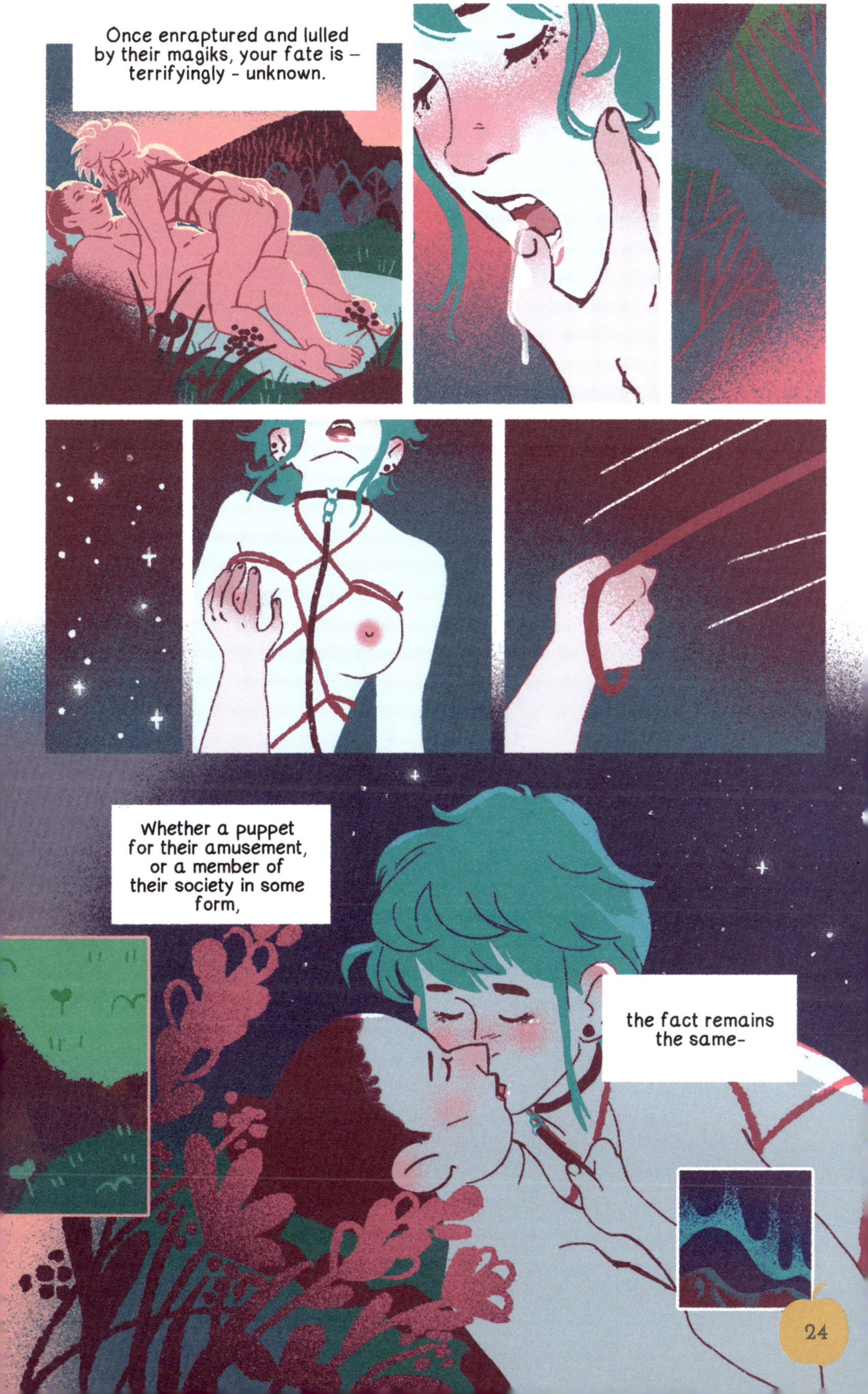
Once enraptured and lulled by their magiks, your fate is – terrifyingly - unknown.
Whether a puppet for their amusement, or a member of their society in some form,
the fact remains the same-

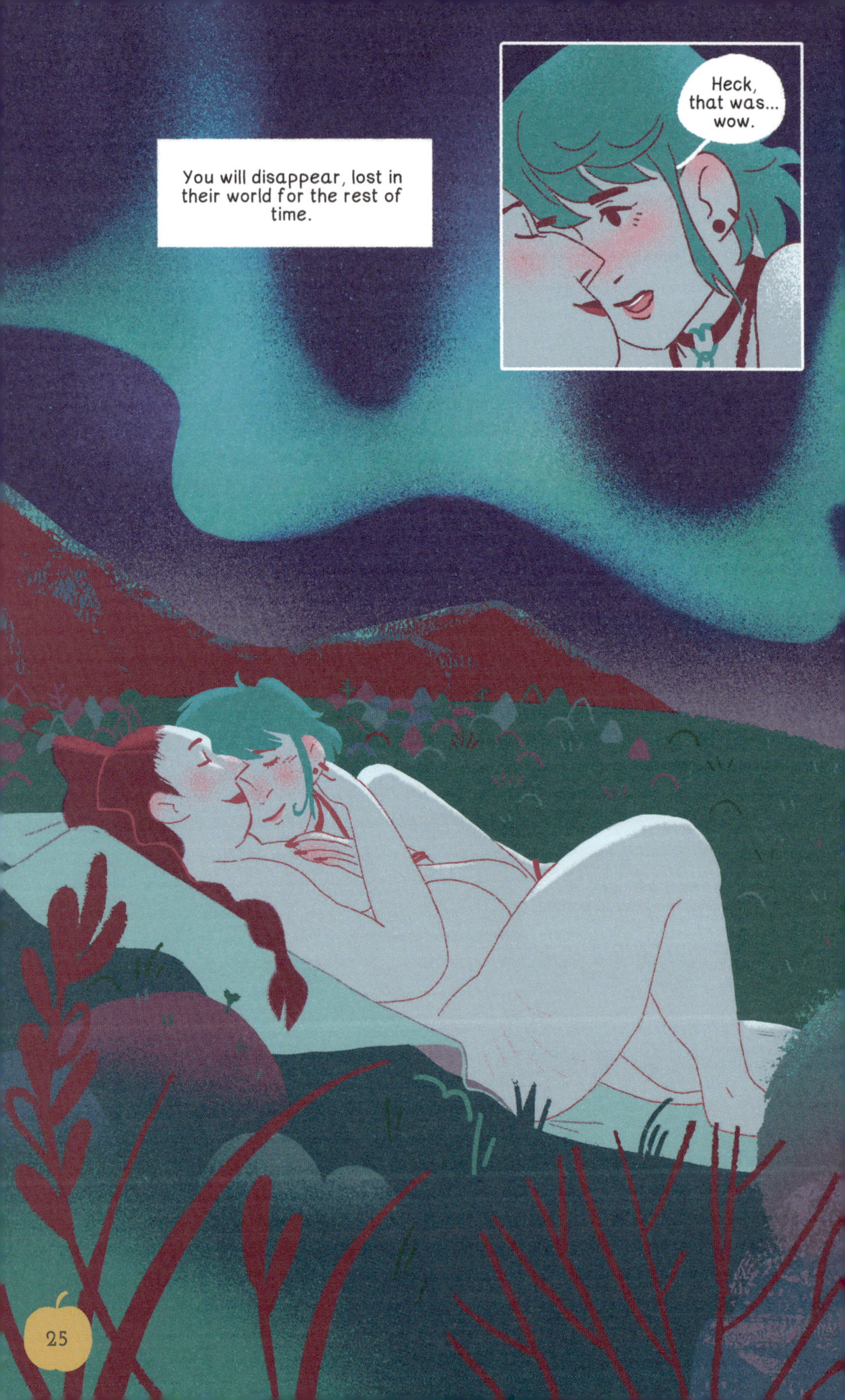
You will disappear, lost in their world for the rest of time.
Heck, that was... wow.

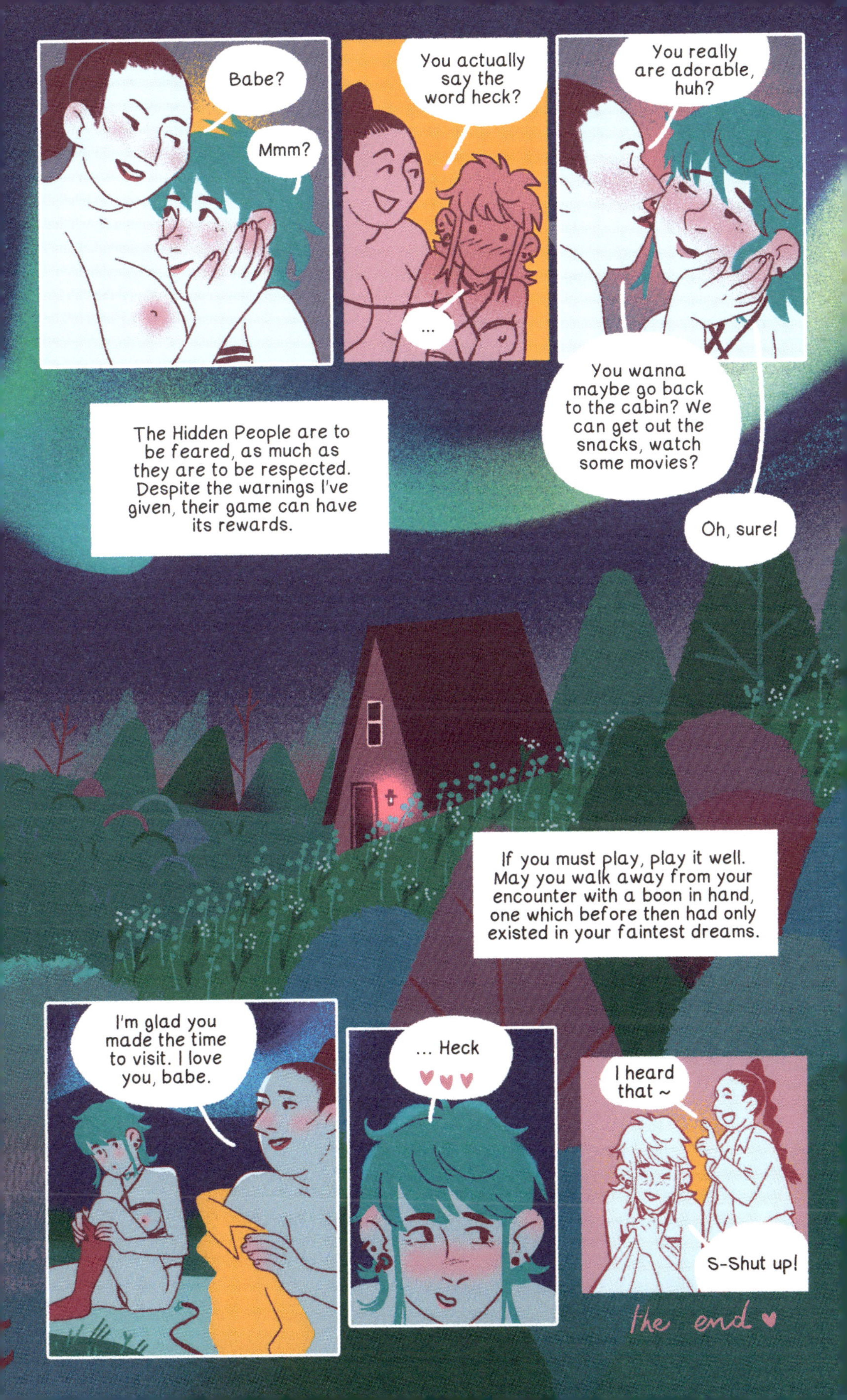
Babe?
Mmm?
You actually say the word heck?
...
You really are adorable, huh?
You wanna maybe go back to the cabin? We can get out the snacks, watch some movies?
The Hidden People are to be feared, as much as they are to be respected. Despite the warnings I've given, their game can have its rewards.
Oh, sure!
If you must play, play it well. May you walk away from your encounter with a boon in hand, one which before then had only existed in your faintest dreams.
I'm glad you made the time to visit. I love you, babe.
... Heck
I heard that ~
S-Shut up!
the end

Homecoming

by Raysdrawlings

Long distance lovers Roux and Rain, can only see each other once a year when the Over and Underworlds get together for a grand one night long celebration. They move heaven and earth to slow time down and bask in each other while they can.

Creator's Note

" This was my first time writing for an adult audience, as someone who usually writes romances for all ages.

It was a great experience and I learned so much; pushing my panel use, page flow, and focus on senses.

I hope you enjoy! "

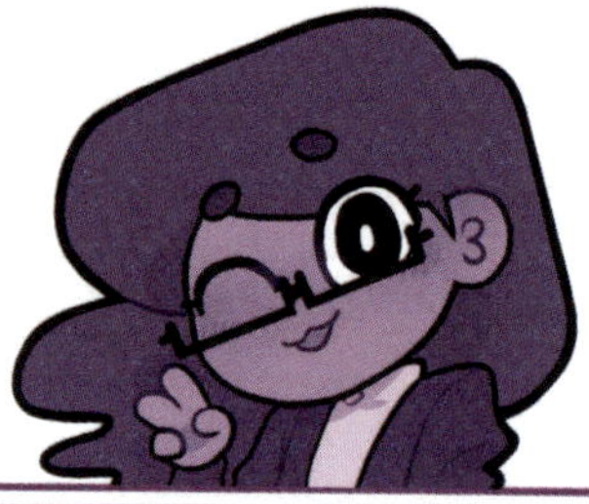

About the Creator

Raysdrawlings (she/he/they) is an Animator & Comic Artist from Canada!

They enjoyed making this comic as their first dive into adult comics!

Twitter.com/Raysdrawlings

Content Tags

UNPROTECTED SEX, VAGINAL SEX, ORAL, STRAP ON, REDUCTION SCARS, GRATUITOUS AMOUNTS OF SPARKLES & HEARTS, BITTERSWEET

NOT YOUR THING? NEXT COMIC ON PAGE 40

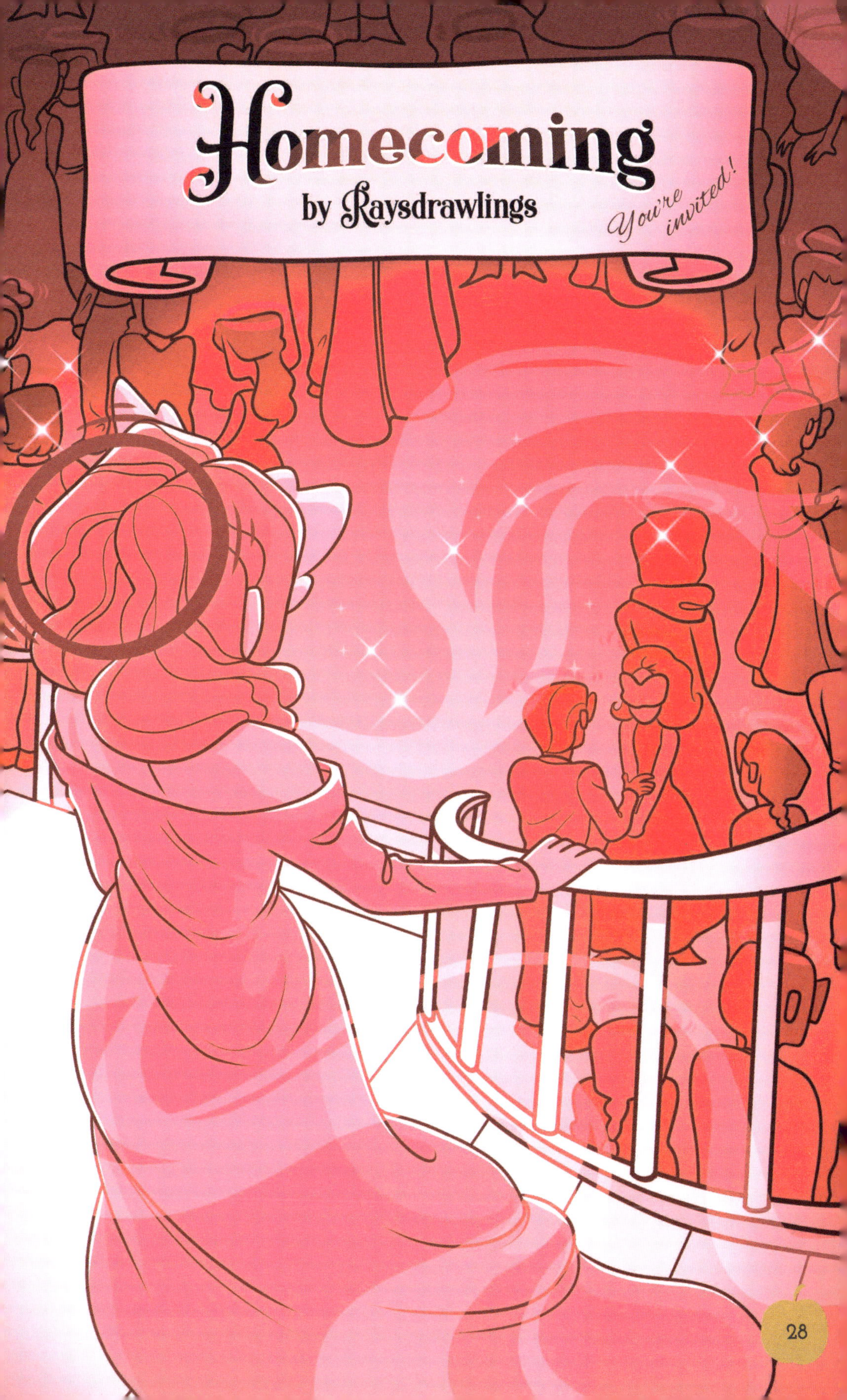
Homecoming
by Raysdrawlings
You're invited!

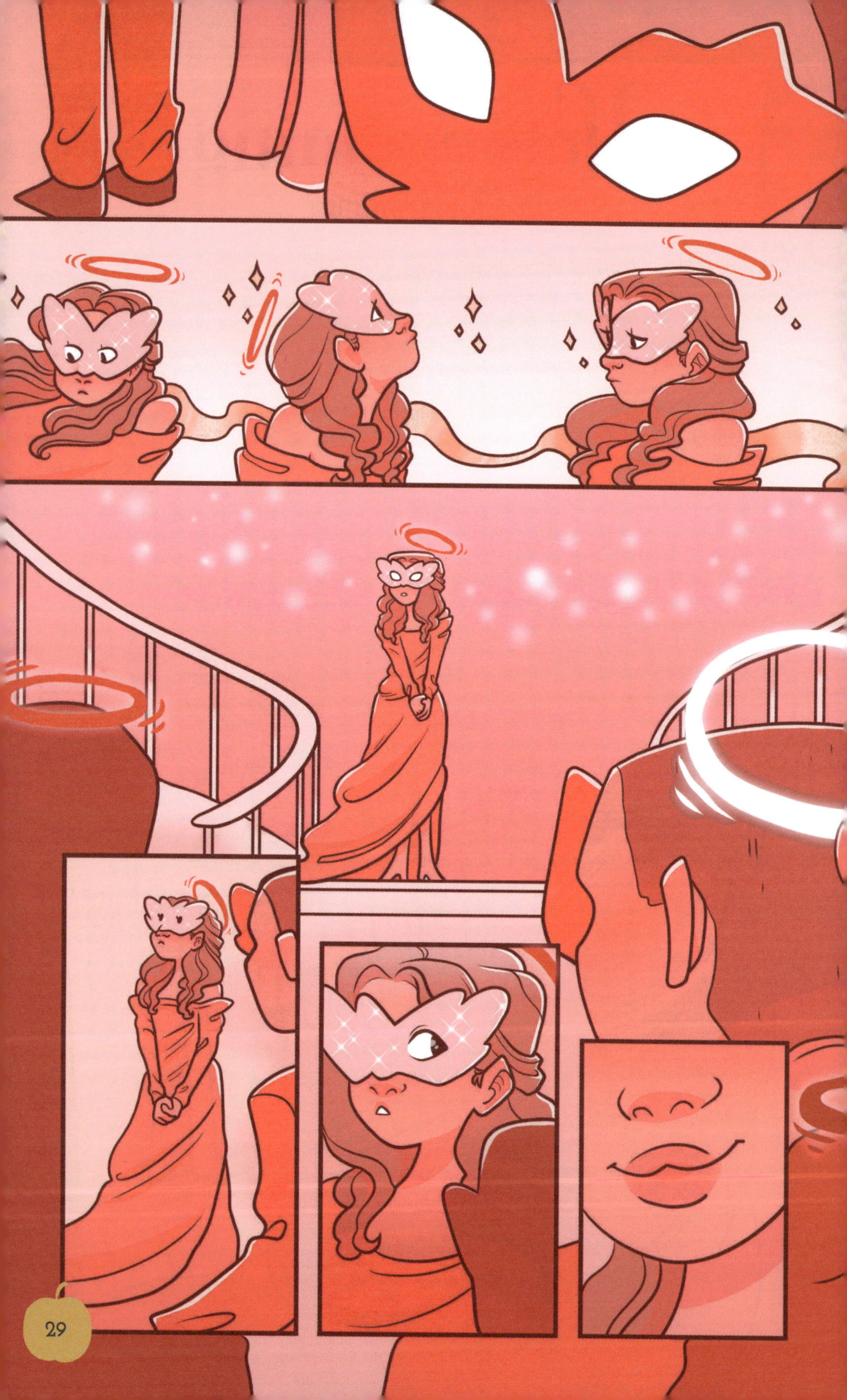

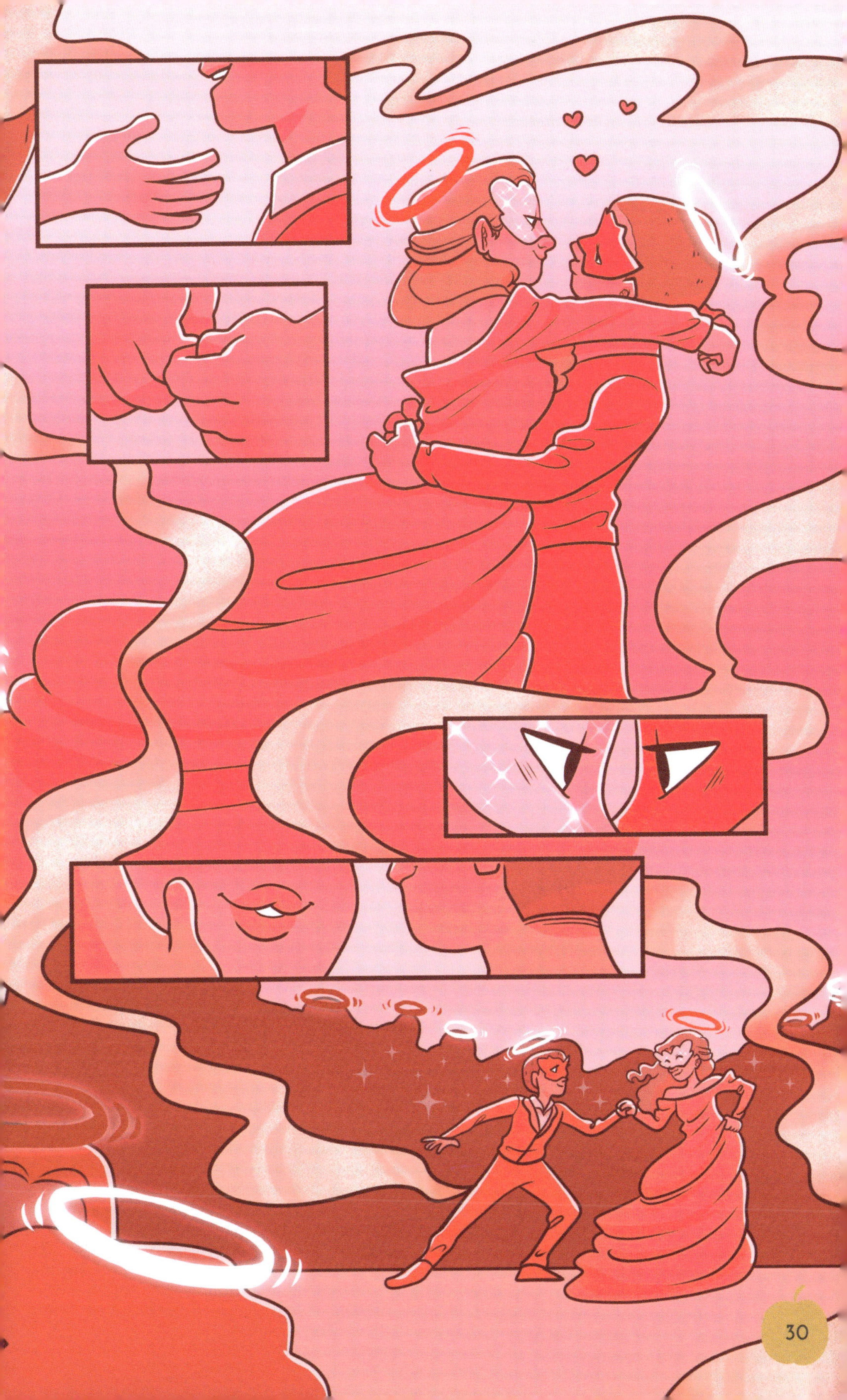

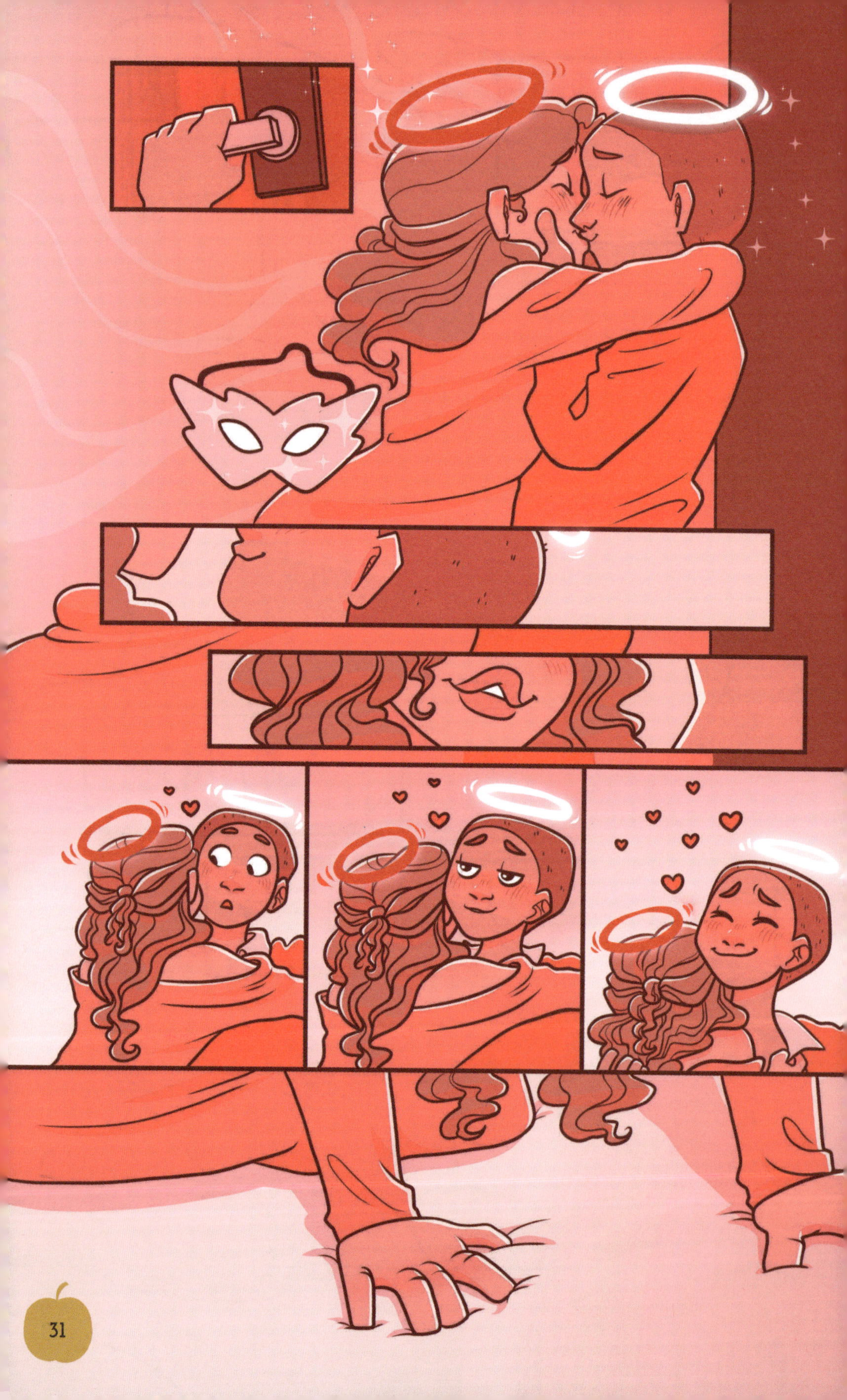

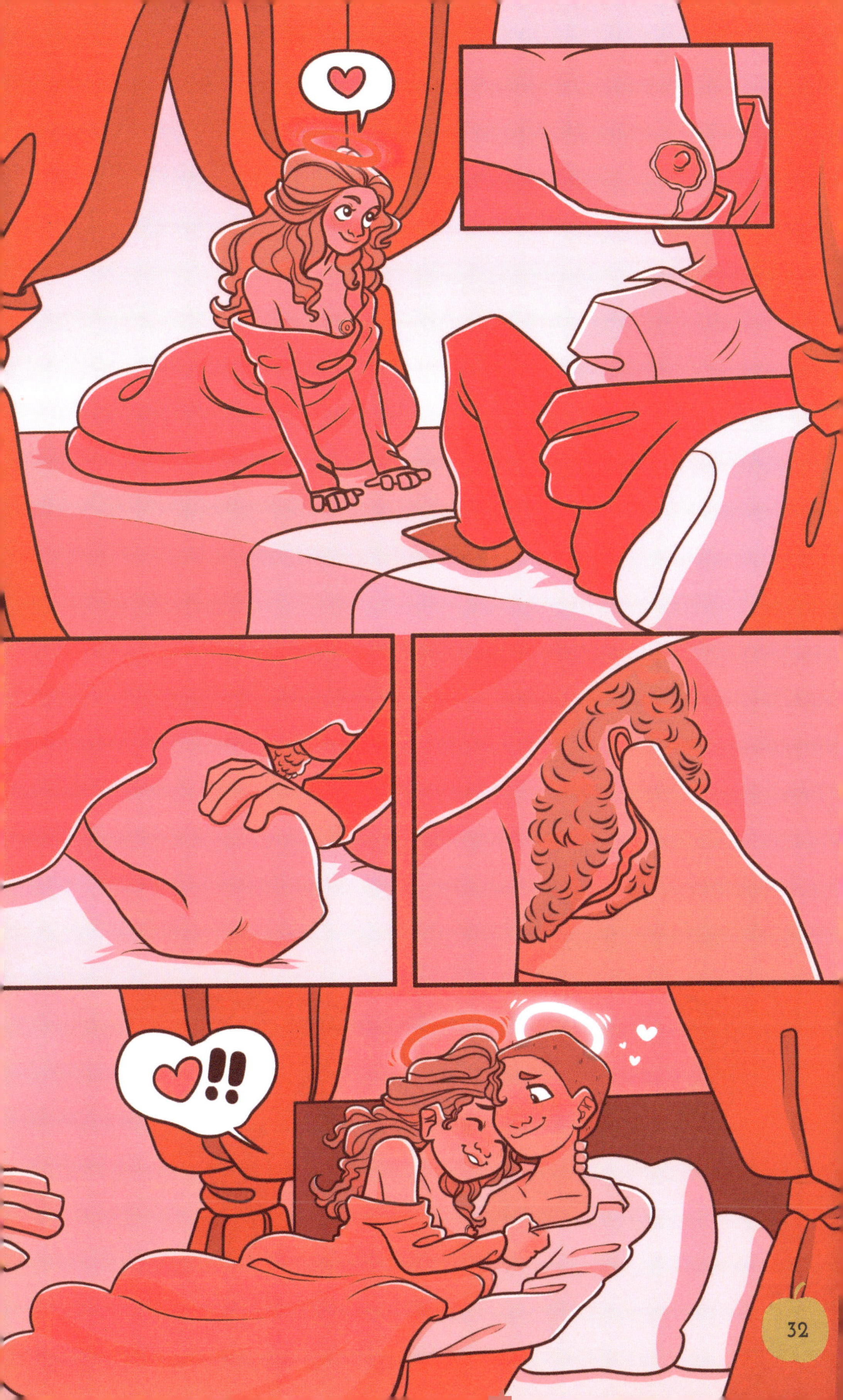

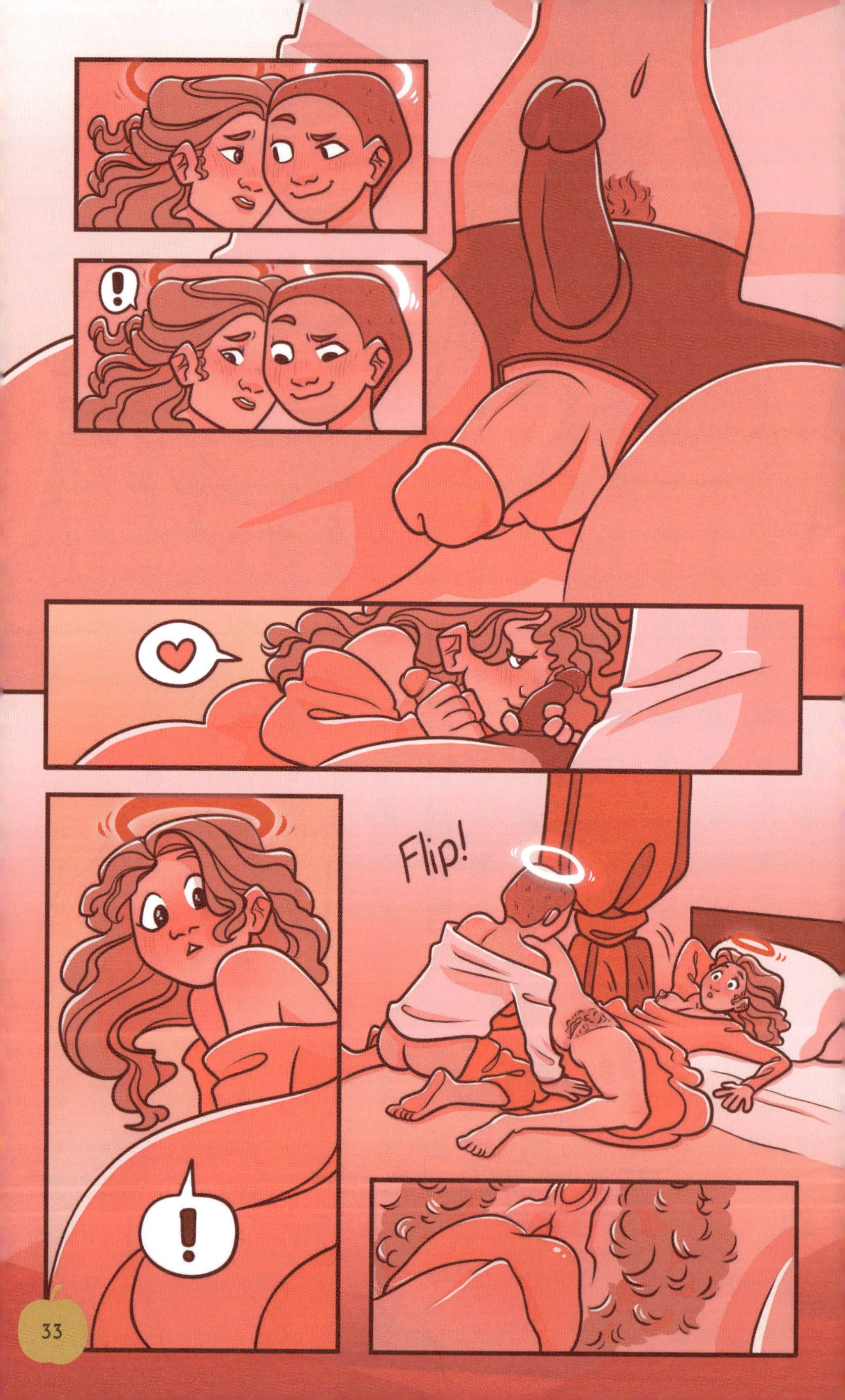
!
!
Flip!

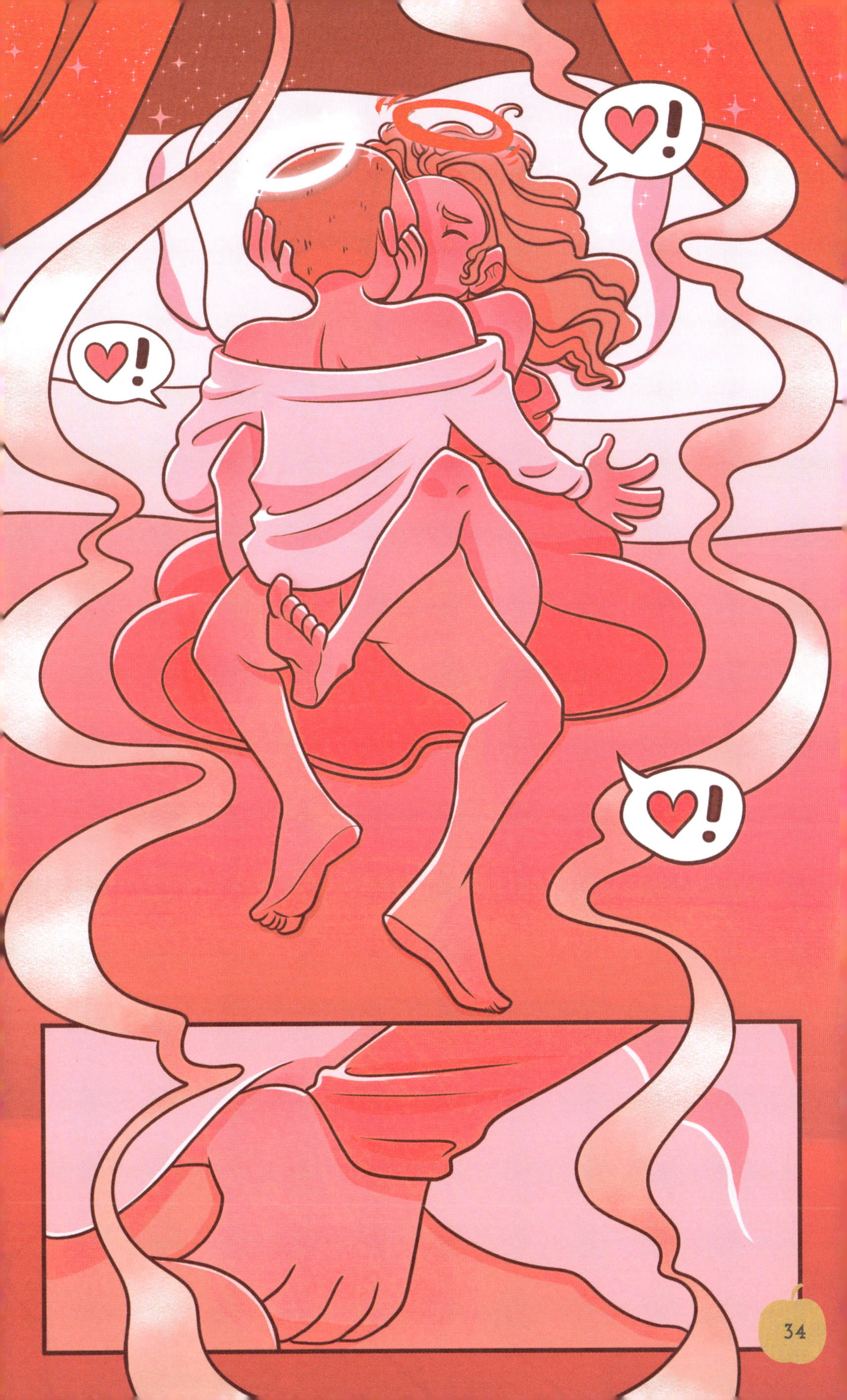

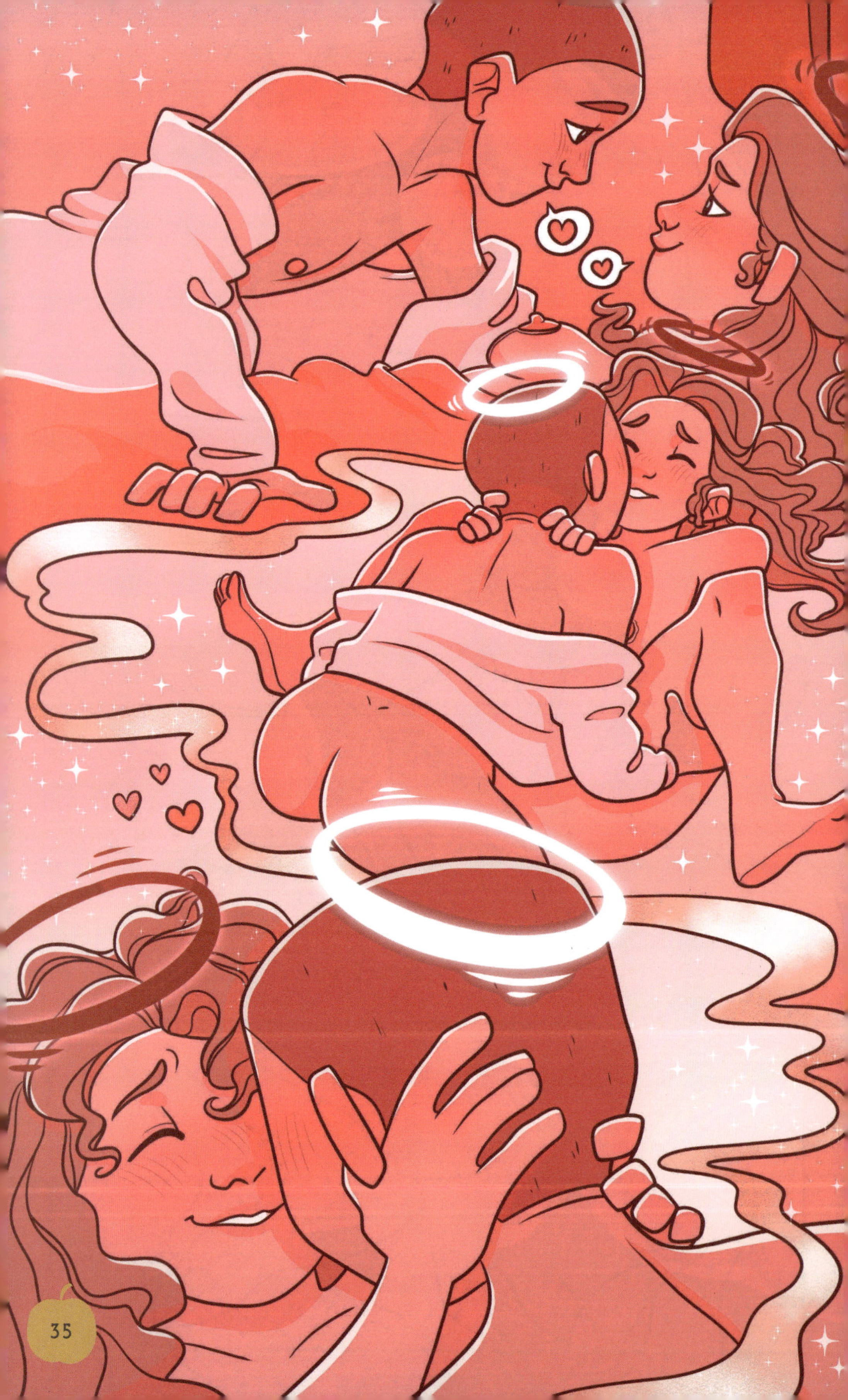

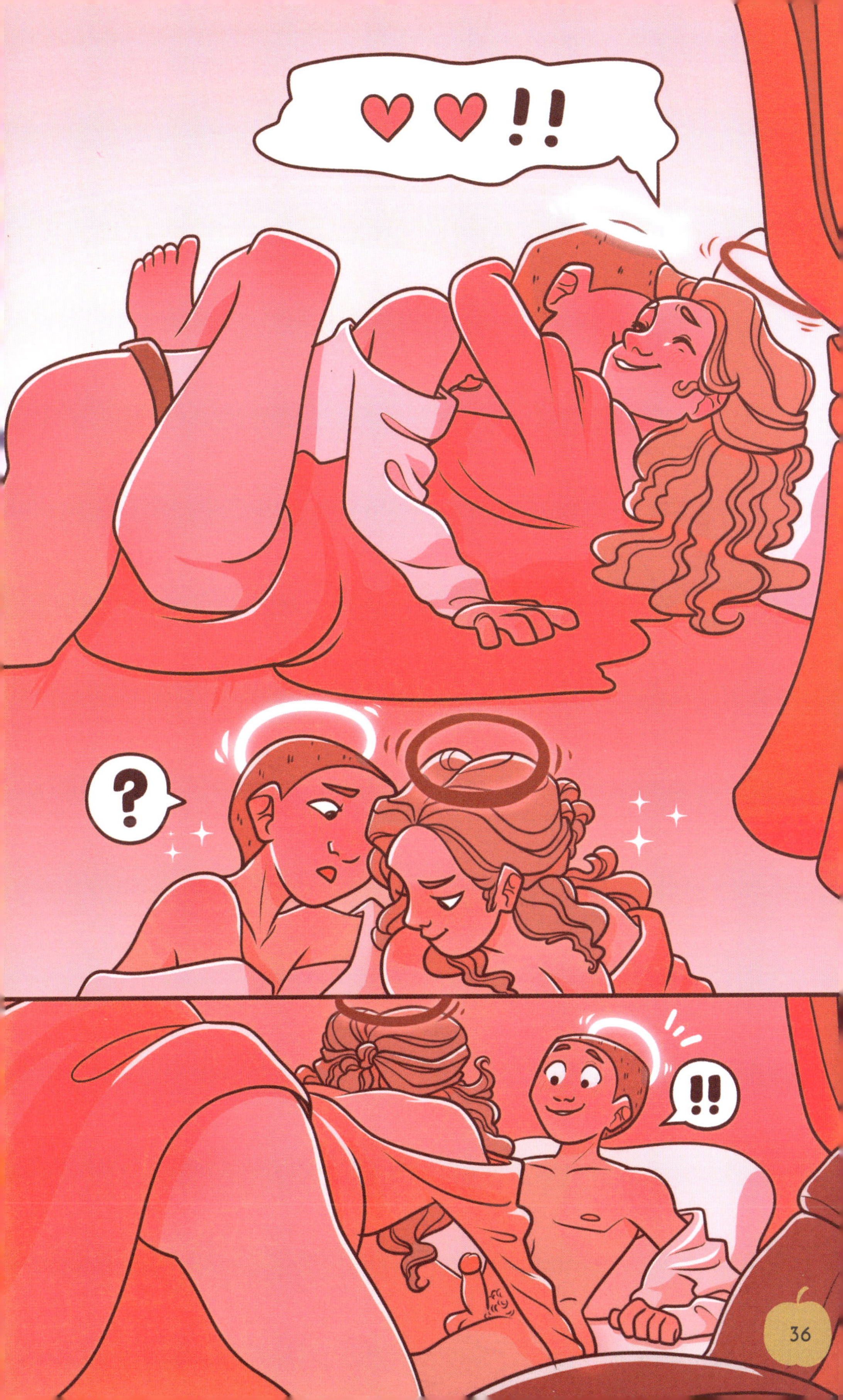

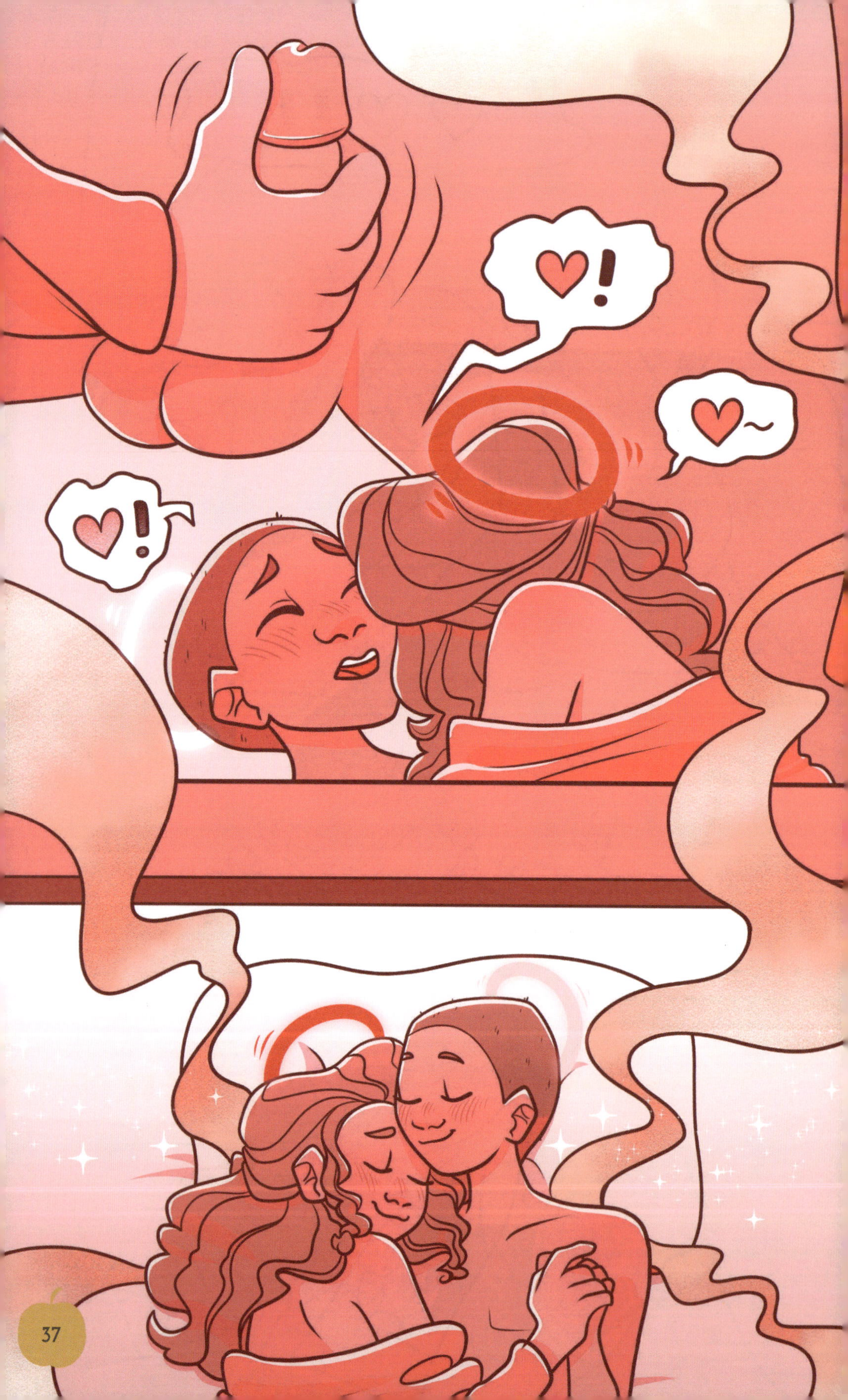

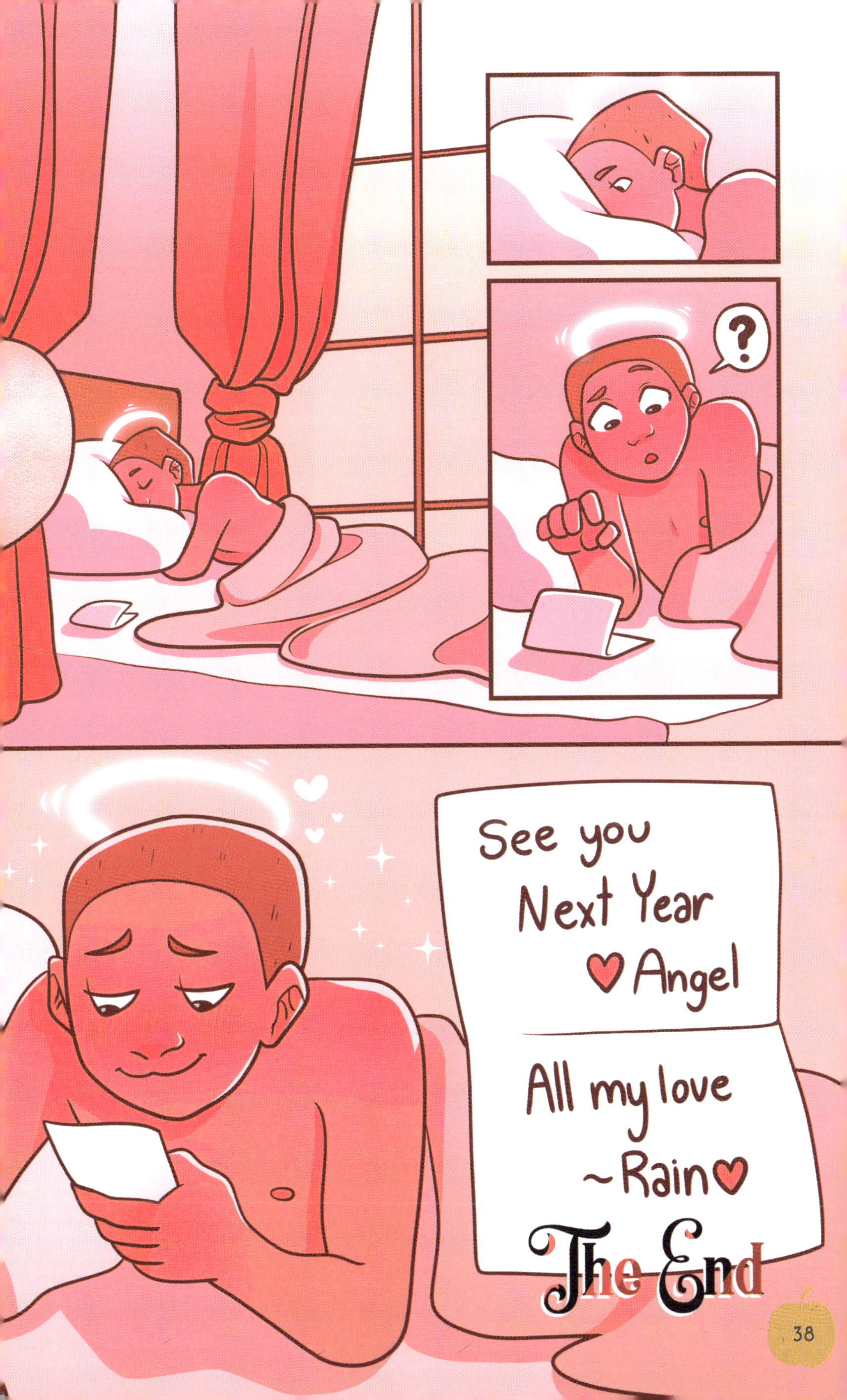
?
See you
Next Year
♥Angel
All my love
~Rain♥
The End

Please, Priestess!

by Yhasmin W.

Farmer Slate wants to help his partner, Priestess Aspen, to clean up the village temple, but they get swept up in memories of their first kiss.

Creator's Note

" Please, Priestess! is a fun, fluffy and sexy story about Farmer Slate helping (and pleasing) their partner, Priestess Aspen. "

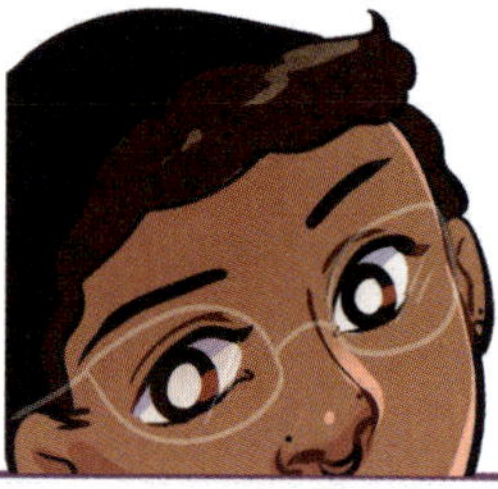

About the Creator

Yhasmin (they/them) is a zine maker and comic illustrator based out of Michigan.

BoyMonsta.com

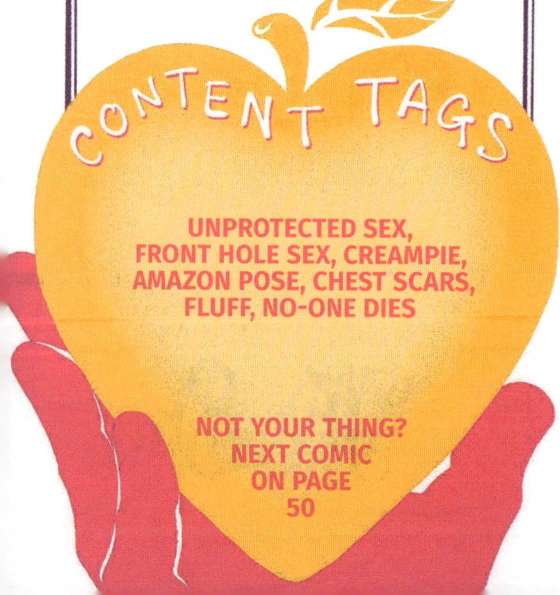

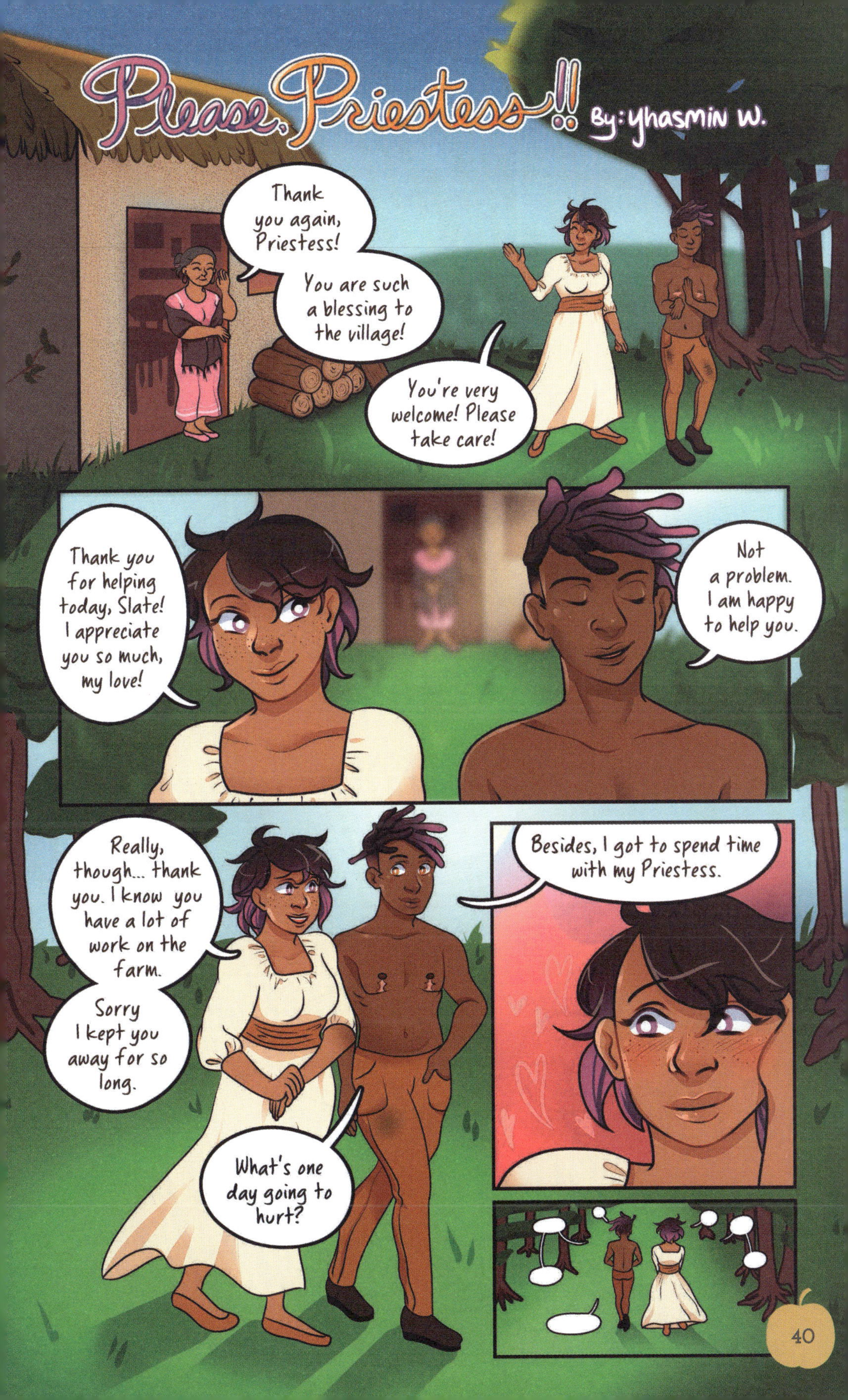
Please, Priestess!! By: Yhasmin W.
Thank you again, Priestess!
You are such a blessing to the village!
You're very welcome! Please take care!
Thank you for helping today, Slate! I appreciate you so much, my love!
Not a problem. I am happy to help you.
Really, though... thank you. I know you have a lot of work on the farm.
Sorry I kept you away for so long.
What's one day going to hurt?
Besides, I got to spend time with my Priestess.

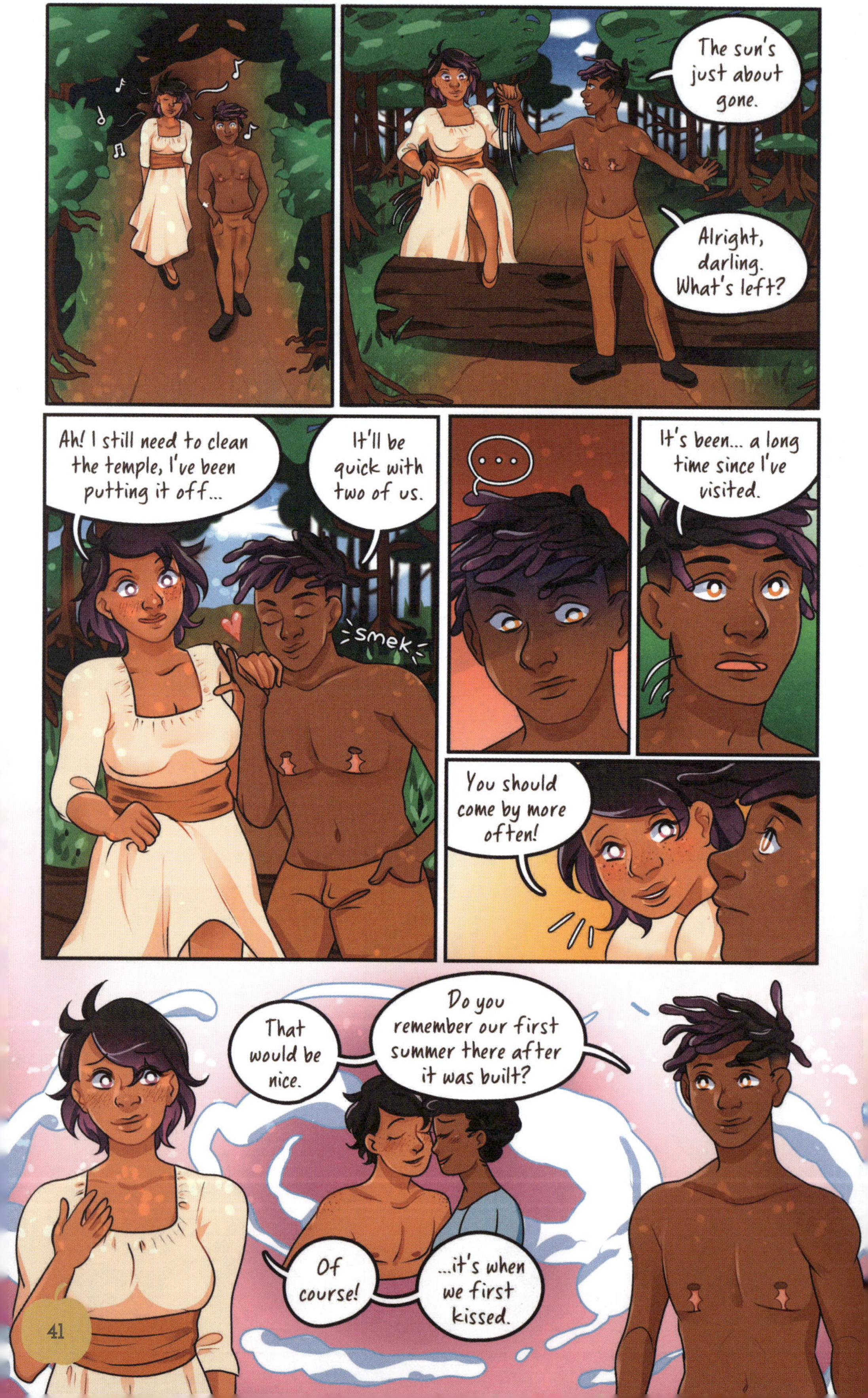

The sun's just about gone.
Alright, darling. What's left?
Ah! I still need to clean the temple, I've been putting it off...
It'll be quick with two of us.
smek
...
It's been... a long time since I've visited.
You should come by more often!
That would be nice.
Do you remember our first summer there after it was built?
Of course!
...it's when we first kissed.

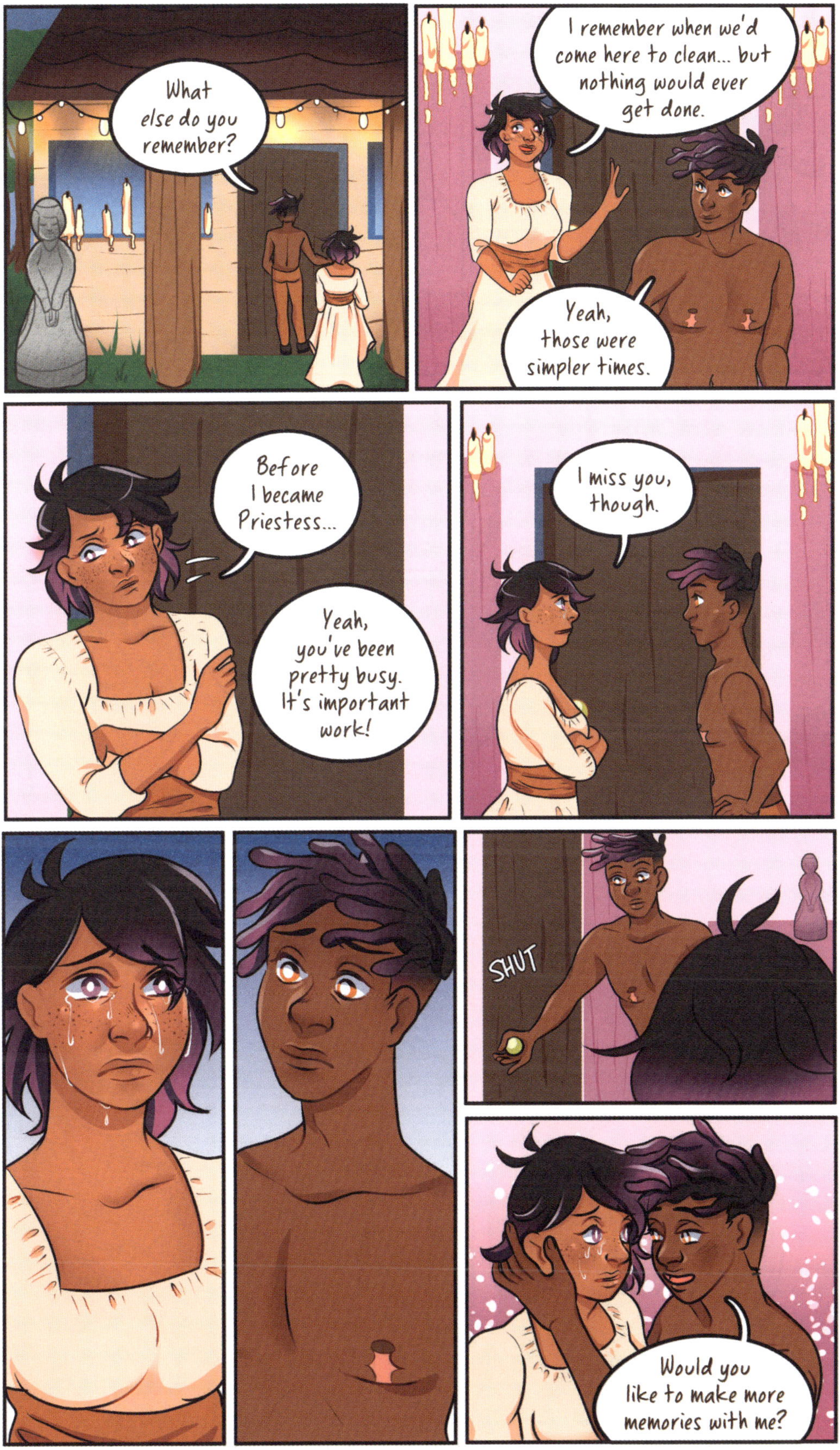
What else do you remember?
I remember when we'd come here to clean... but nothing would ever get done.
Yeah, those were simpler times.
Before I became Priestess...
Yeah, you've been pretty busy. It's important work!
I miss you, though.
SHUT
Would you like to make more memories with me?

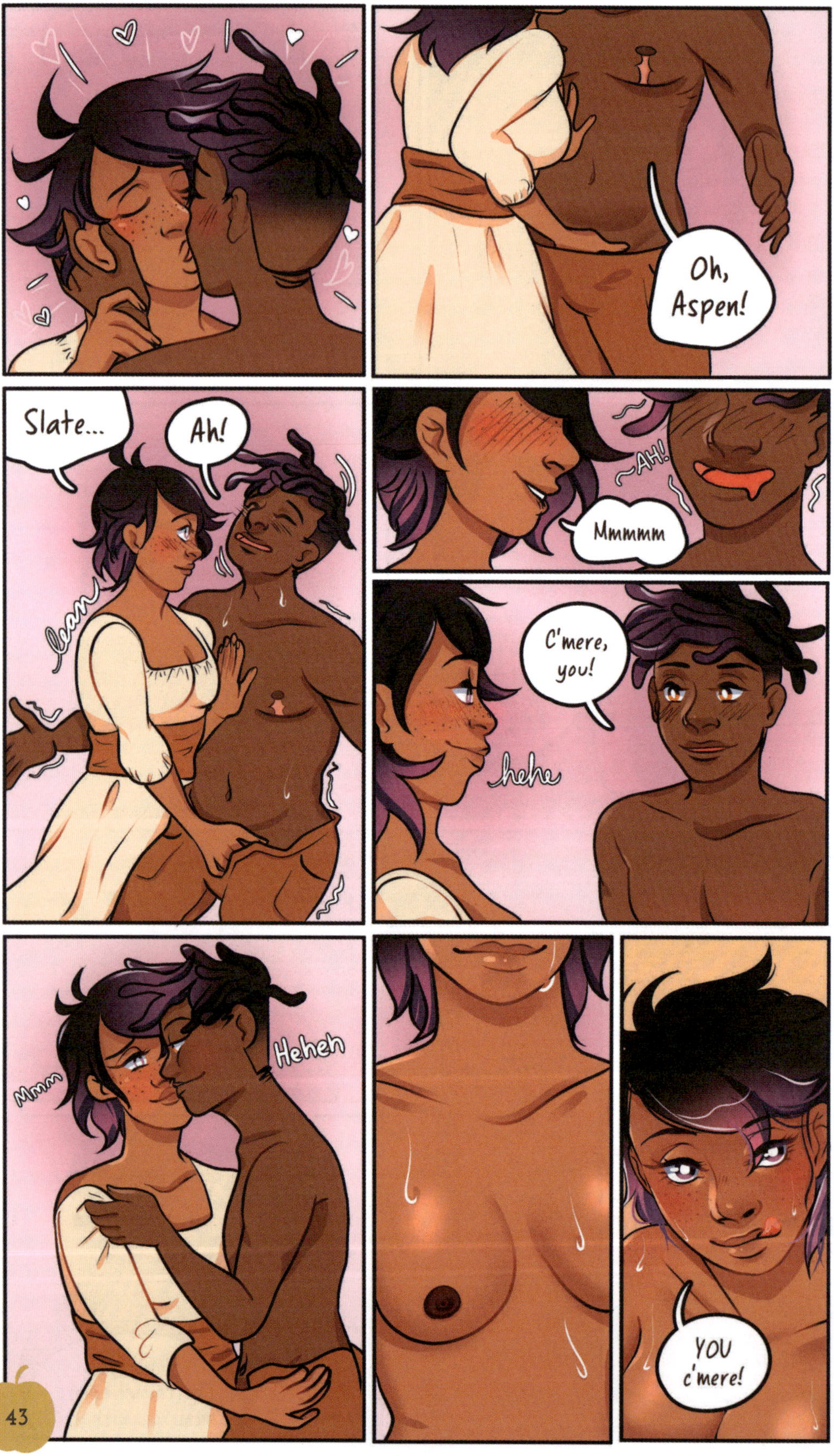

Oh, Aspen!
Slate...
Ah!
lean
~AH!
Mmmmm
C'mere, you!
hehe
Mmm
Heheh
YOU c'mere!

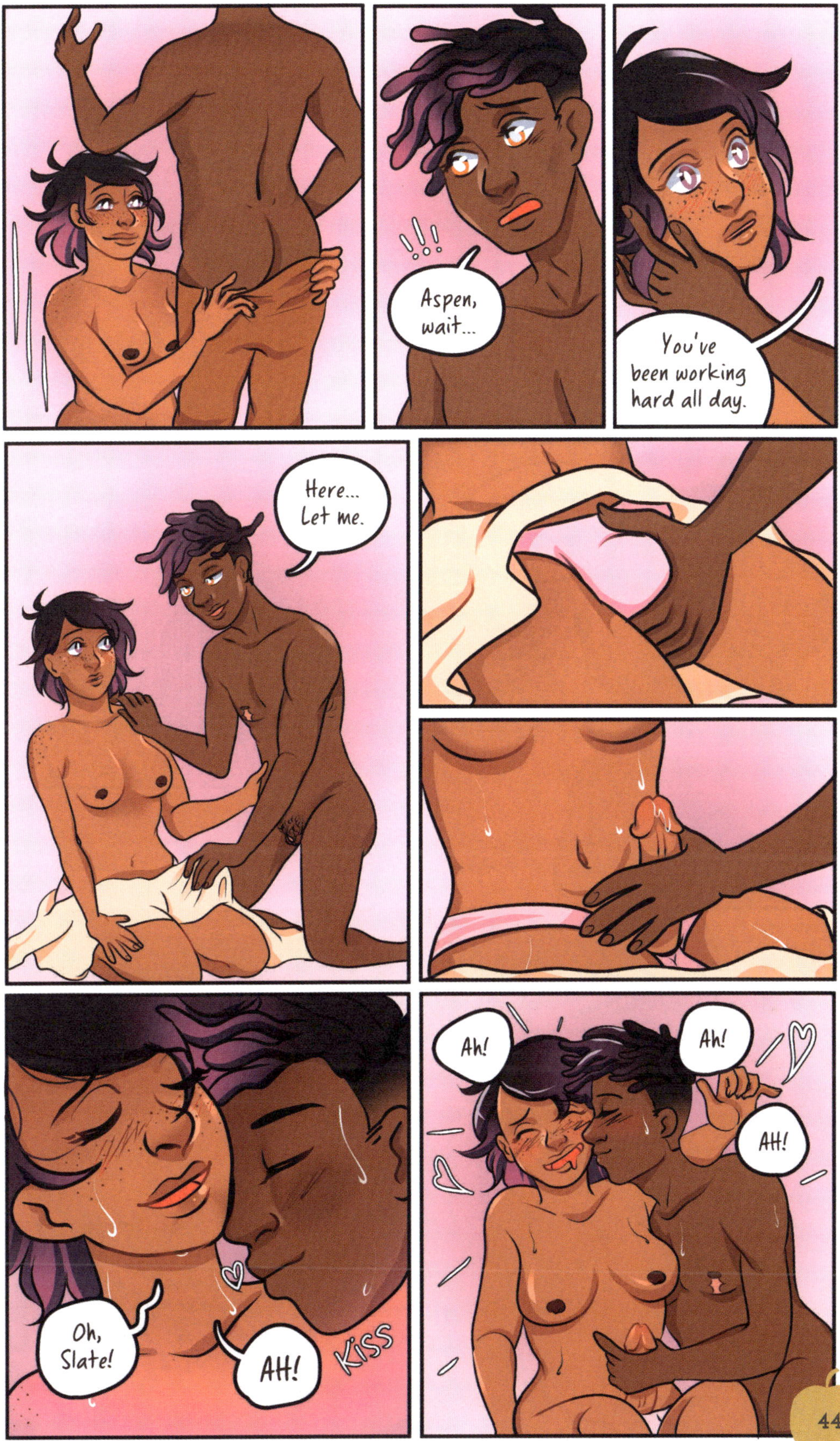
Aspen, wait...
You've been working hard all day.
Here... Let me.
Oh, Slate!
AH!
KISS
Ah!
Ah!
AH!

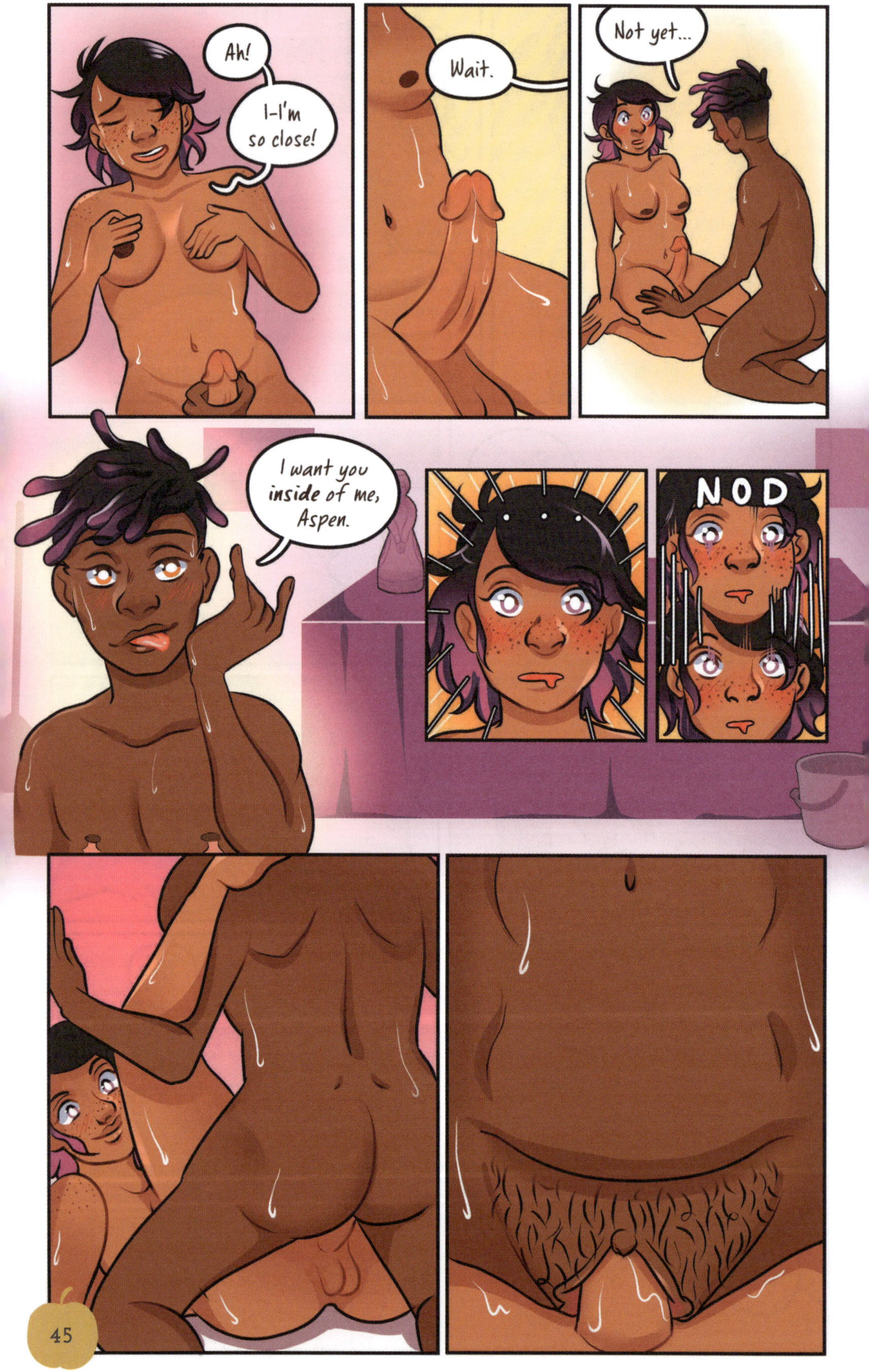
Ah!
I-I'm so close!
Wait.
Not yet...
I want you inside of me, Aspen.
NOD

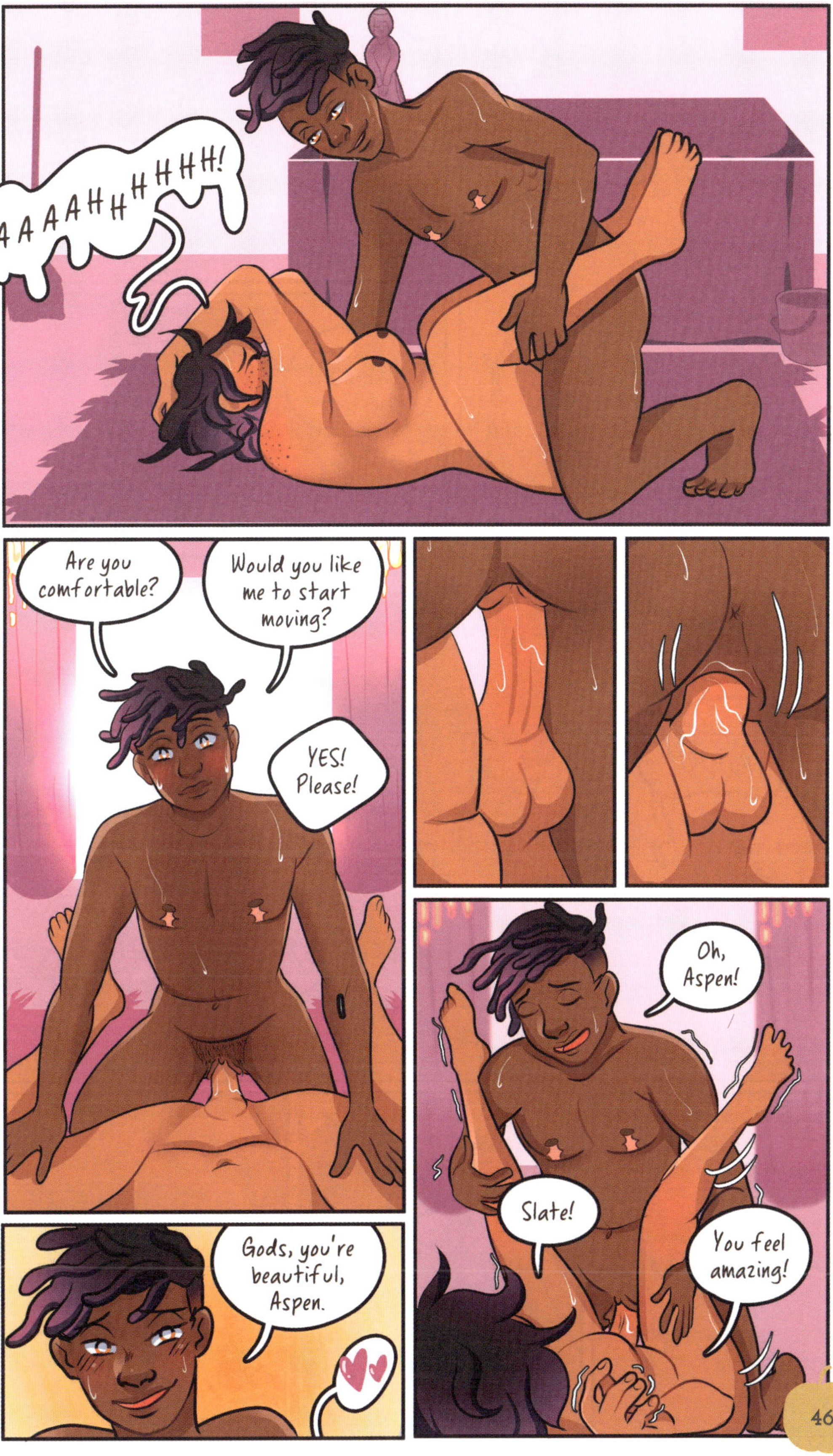

AAAAHHHHHHH!
Are you comfortable?
Would you like me to start moving?
YES! Please!
Gods, you're beautiful, Aspen.
Oh, Aspen!
Slate!
You feel amazing!

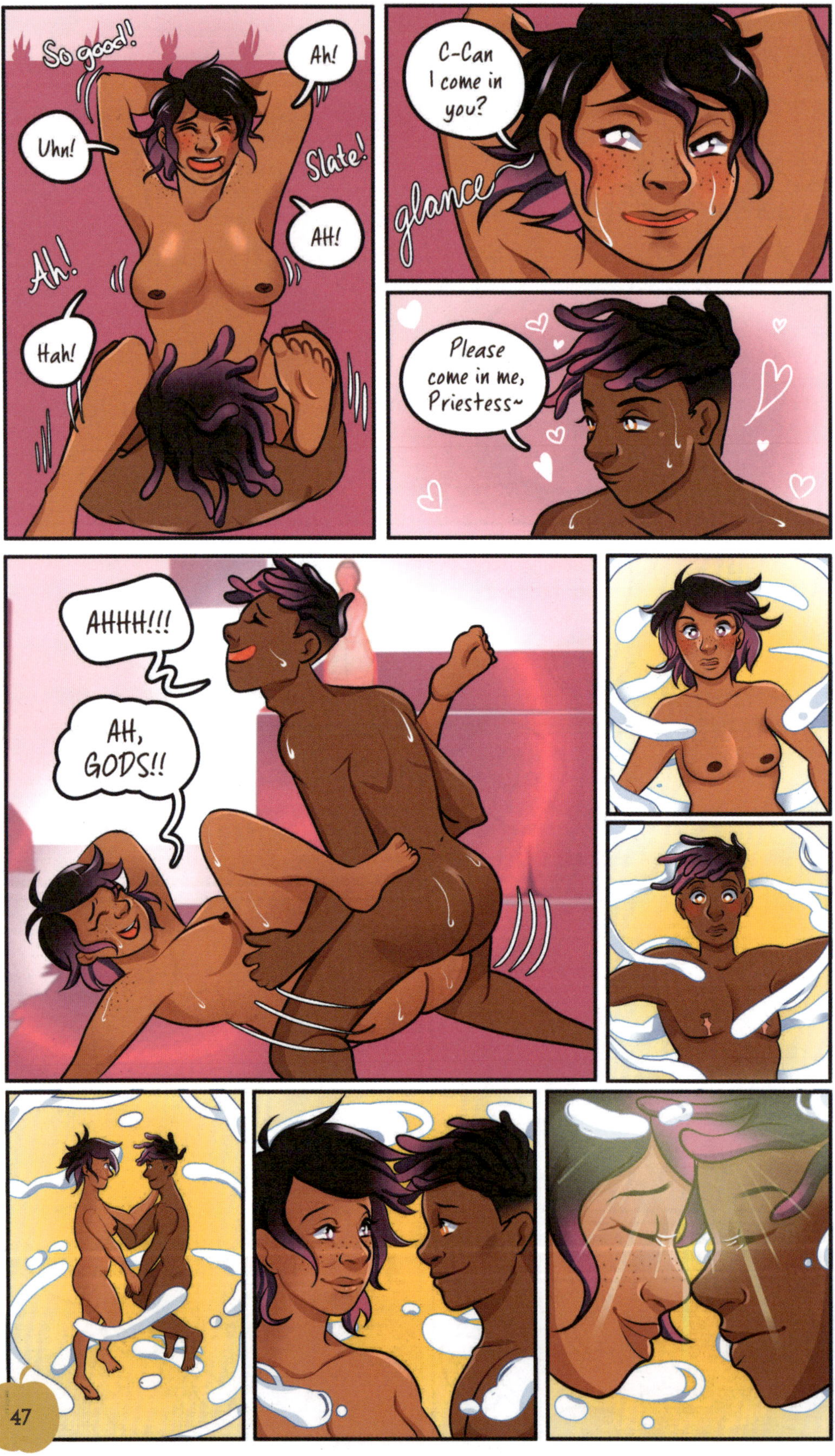
So good!
Ah!
Uhn!
Slate!
AH!
Ah!
Hah!
C-Can I come in you?
glance~
Please come in me, Priestess~
AHHH!!!
AH, GODS!!

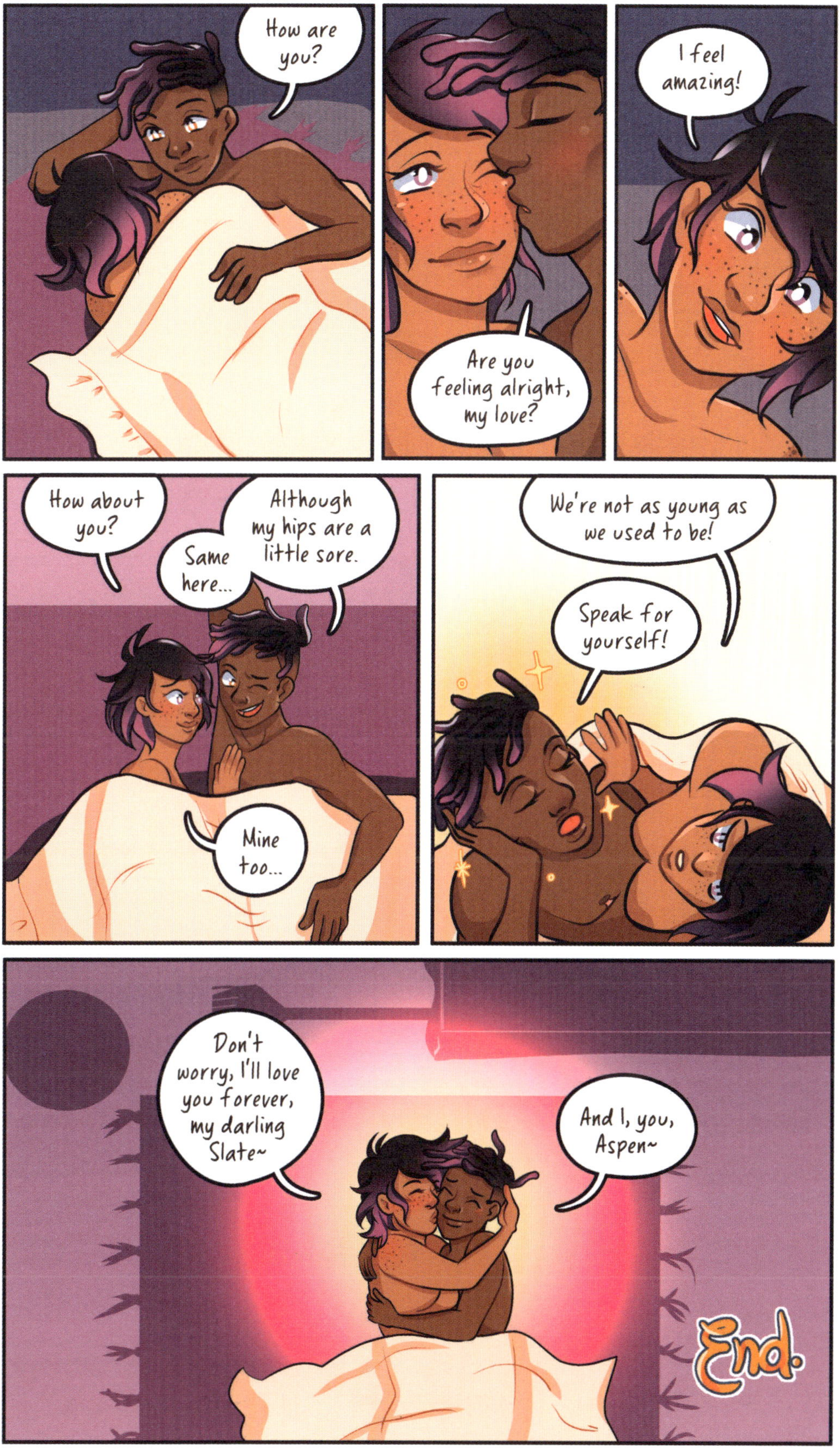
How are you?
Are you feeling alright, my love?
I feel amazing!
How about you?
Same here...
Although my hips are a little sore.
Mine too...
We're not as young as we used to be!
Speak for yourself!
Don't worry, I'll love you forever, my darling Slate~
And I, you, Aspen~
End.

Cream of the Crop

Story by Reinapepiada and Art by Fanfi

Maimará dreams of meeting the beautiful deity of corn Mama Sorca who has been her town's symbol of prosperity, fertility and harvest for centuries; only revealing themselves to humans at the fall festival in May.

Creators' Note

" We really wanted to make an erotic story set in Latin America and some brainstorming sessions later we came up with Cream of the Crop— A sweet and passionate story from ancient times, almost like a legend of a chosen one.

We put a lot of love in the story and the characters! To me, the most interesting trivia fact is that all the leaves, fruits, vegetables and flowers that appear in the comic are native plants from South America. "

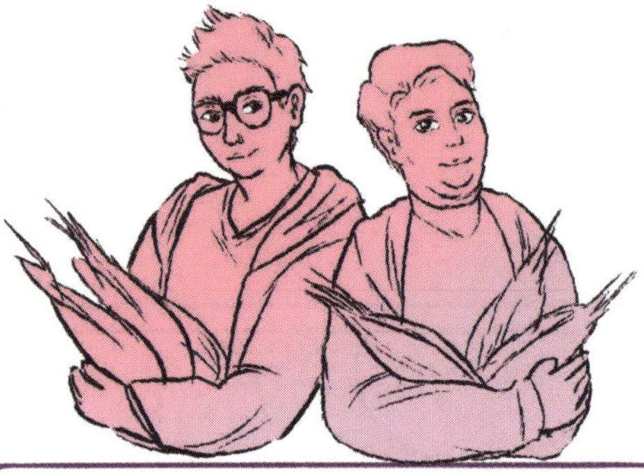

About the Creators

Reinapepiada (they/any) is a nonbinary venezuelan artist and writer living in Chile, they generally write and draw about original stories of LGBT urban fantasy, action, comedy and romance. While not usually on the erotic scene, they're interested in mixing in some magic and fantasy with queer themes, exploring unusual kinks and dynamics.

Reinapepiada.pb.gallery

Fanfi (he/him) is a visual artist and cartoonist based in Chile. He has a multidisciplinary background in fine arts that he incorporates into his work. He's mostly focused in creating queer+trans erotic work of intense intimacy.

Fanficciera.weebly.com

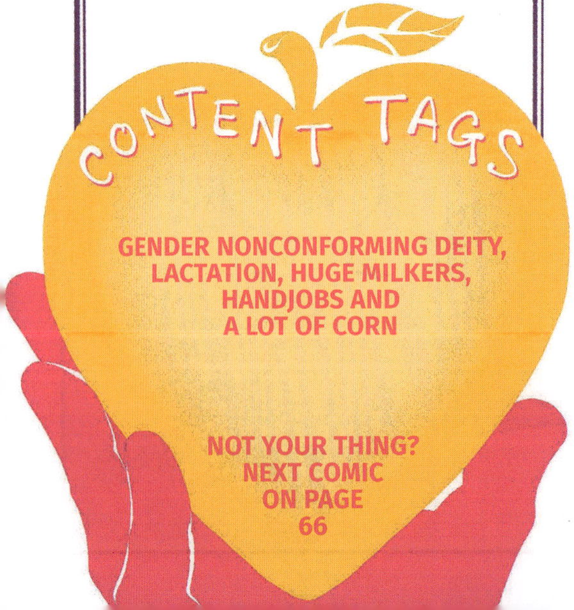

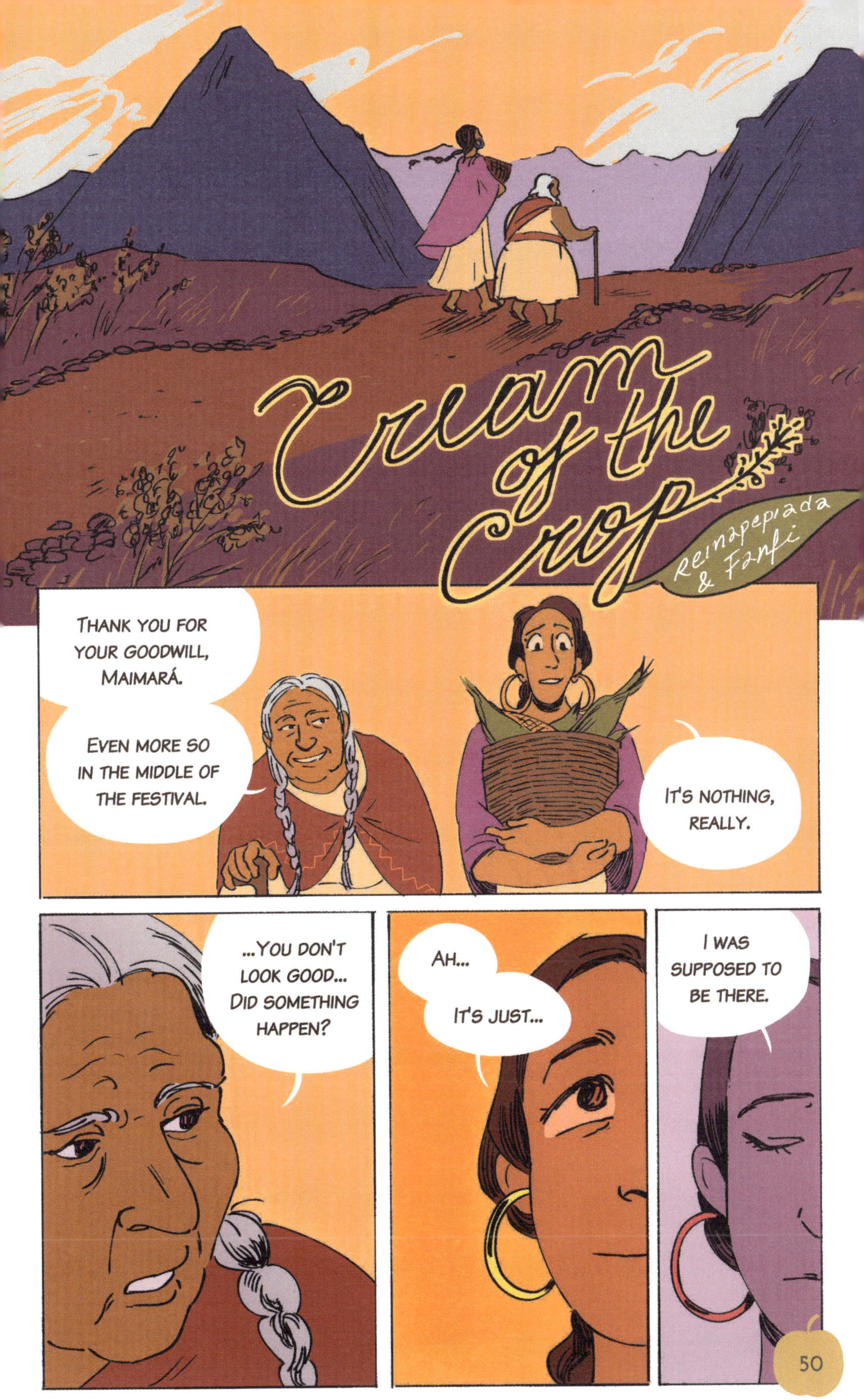
Cream of the Crop
Reinapepiada & Fanfi
THANK YOU FOR YOUR GOODWILL, MAIMARÁ.
EVEN MORE SO IN THE MIDDLE OF THE FESTIVAL.
IT'S NOTHING, REALLY.
...YOU DON'T LOOK GOOD... DID SOMETHING HAPPEN?
AH...
IT'S JUST...
I WAS SUPPOSED TO BE THERE.

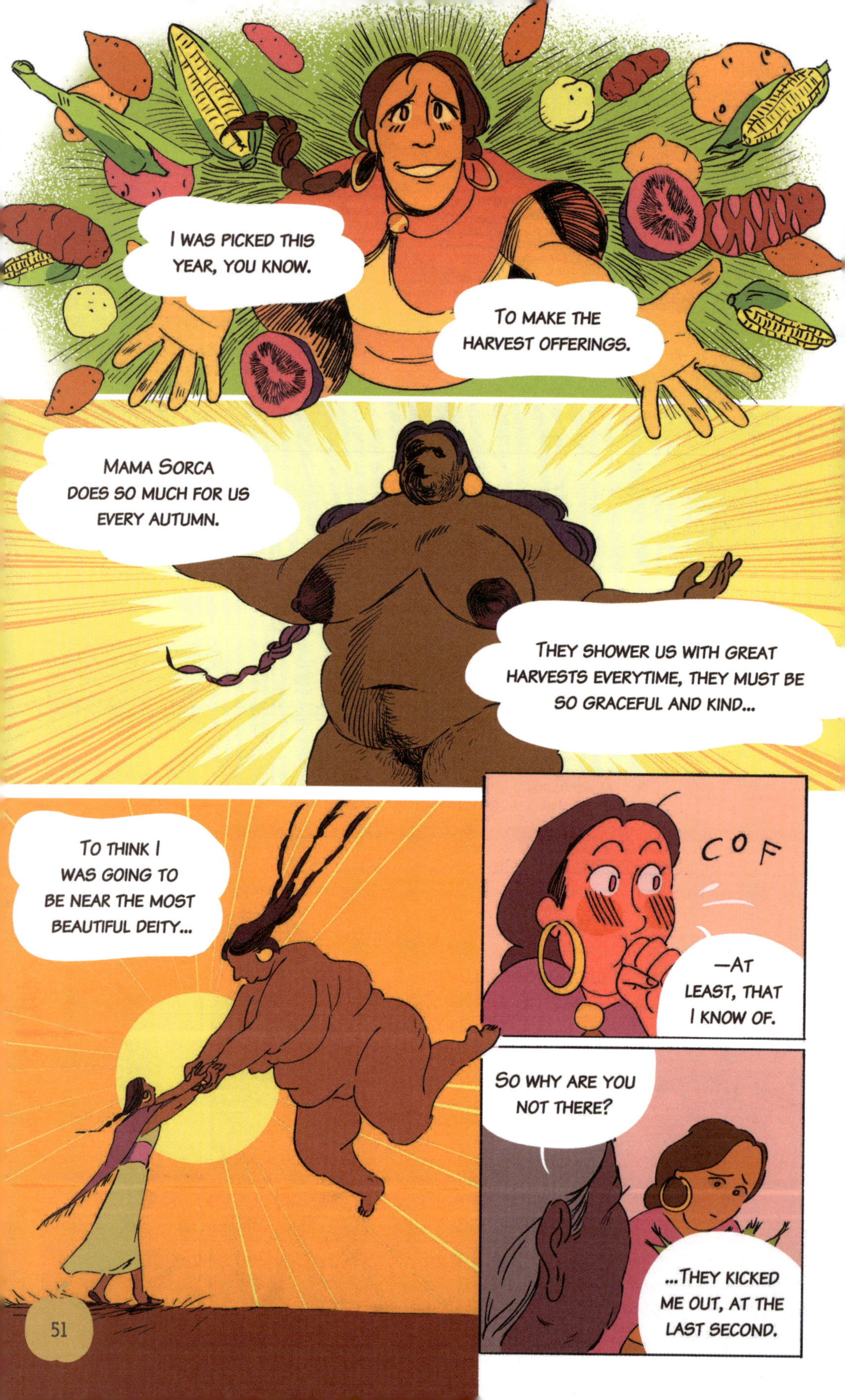
I WAS PICKED THIS YEAR, YOU KNOW.
TO MAKE THE HARVEST OFFERINGS.
MAMA SORCA DOES SO MUCH FOR US EVERY AUTUMN.
THEY SHOWER US WITH GREAT HARVESTS EVERYTIME, THEY MUST BE SO GRACEFUL AND KIND...
TO THINK I WAS GOING TO BE NEAR THE MOST BEAUTIFUL DEITY...
COF
—AT LEAST, THAT I KNOW OF.
SO WHY ARE YOU NOT THERE?
...THEY KICKED ME OUT, AT THE LAST SECOND.

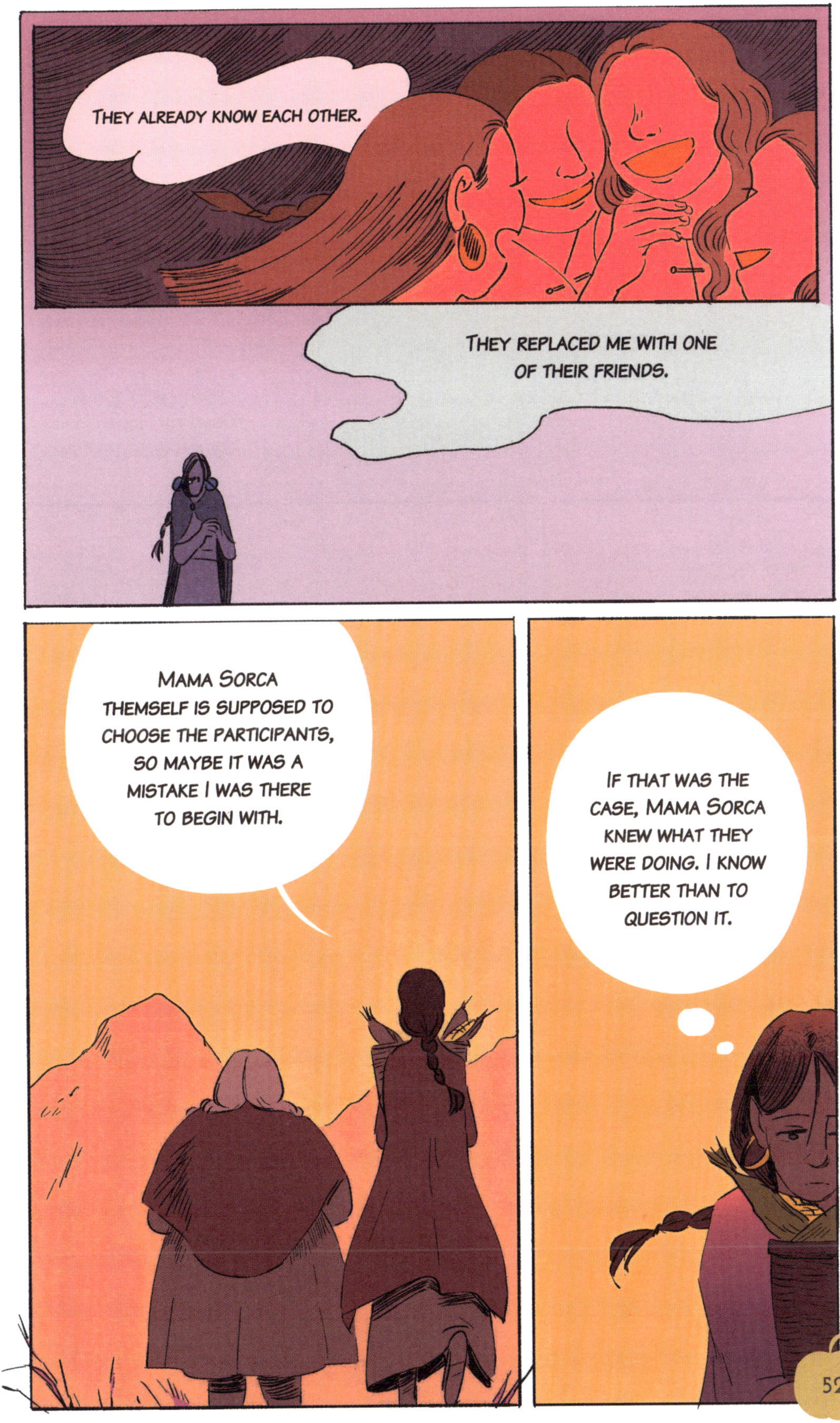
THEY ALREADY KNOW EACH OTHER.
THEY REPLACED ME WITH ONE OF THEIR FRIENDS.
MAMA SORCA THEMSELF IS SUPPOSED TO CHOOSE THE PARTICIPANTS, SO MAYBE IT WAS A MISTAKE I WAS THERE TO BEGIN WITH.
IF THAT WAS THE CASE, MAMA SORCA KNEW WHAT THEY WERE DOING. I KNOW BETTER THAN TO QUESTION IT.

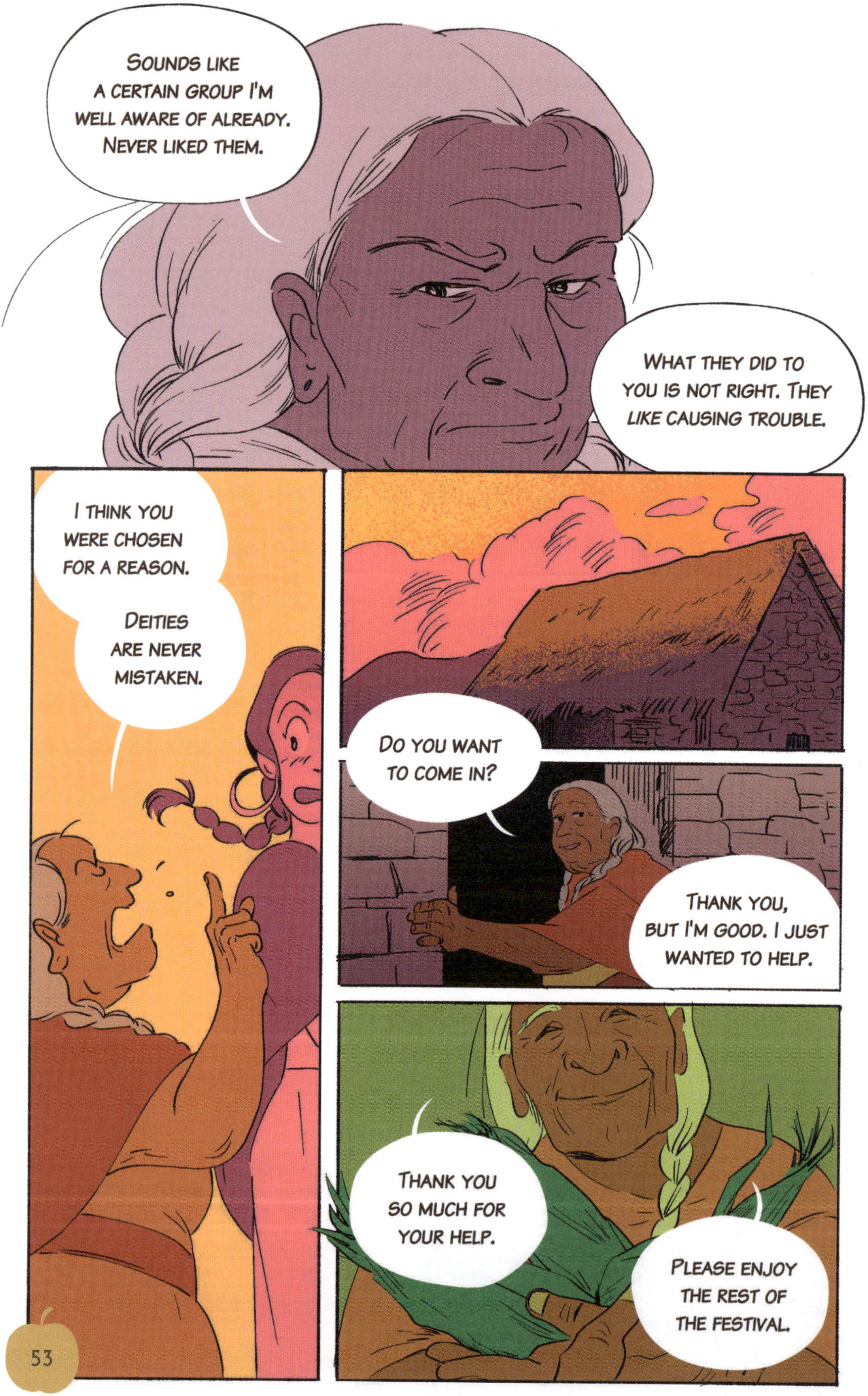
SOUNDS LIKE A CERTAIN GROUP I'M WELL AWARE OF ALREADY. NEVER LIKED THEM.
WHAT THEY DID TO YOU IS NOT RIGHT. THEY LIKE CAUSING TROUBLE.
I THINK YOU WERE CHOSEN FOR A REASON.
DEITIES ARE NEVER MISTAKEN.
DO YOU WANT TO COME IN?
THANK YOU, BUT I'M GOOD. I JUST WANTED TO HELP.
THANK YOU SO MUCH FOR YOUR HELP.
PLEASE ENJOY THE REST OF THE FESTIVAL.

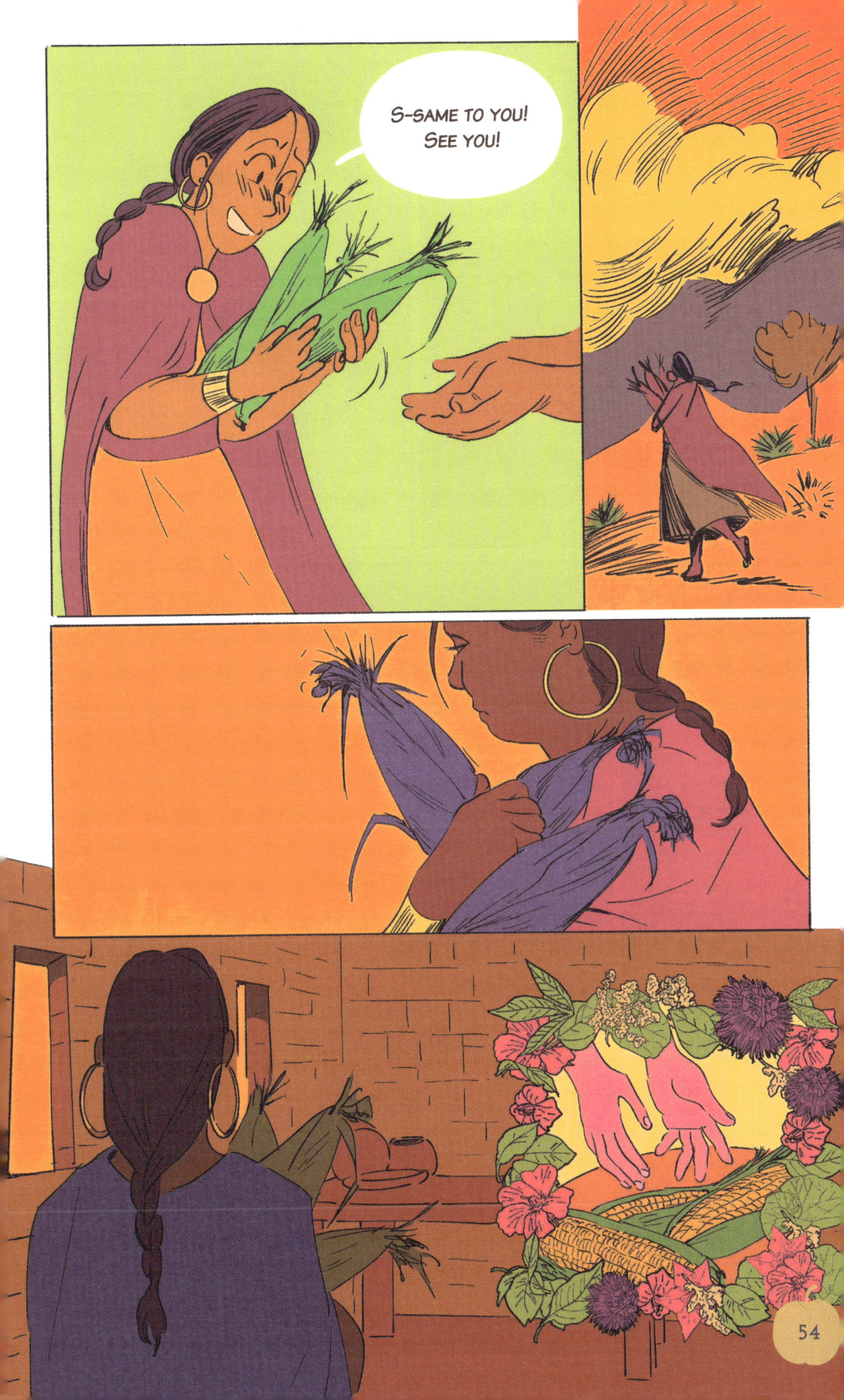
S-SAME TO YOU!
SEE YOU!

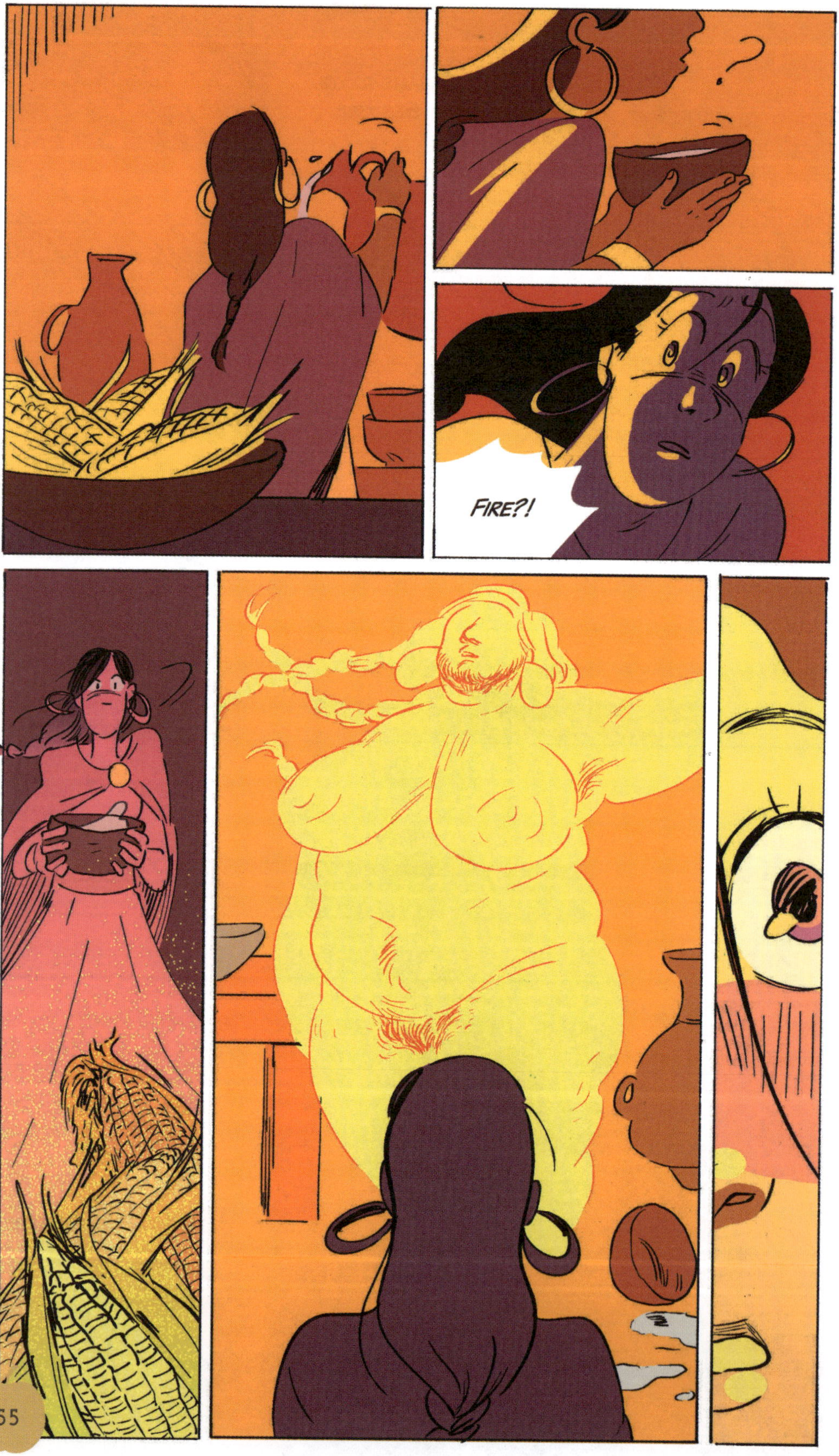
?
FIRE?!

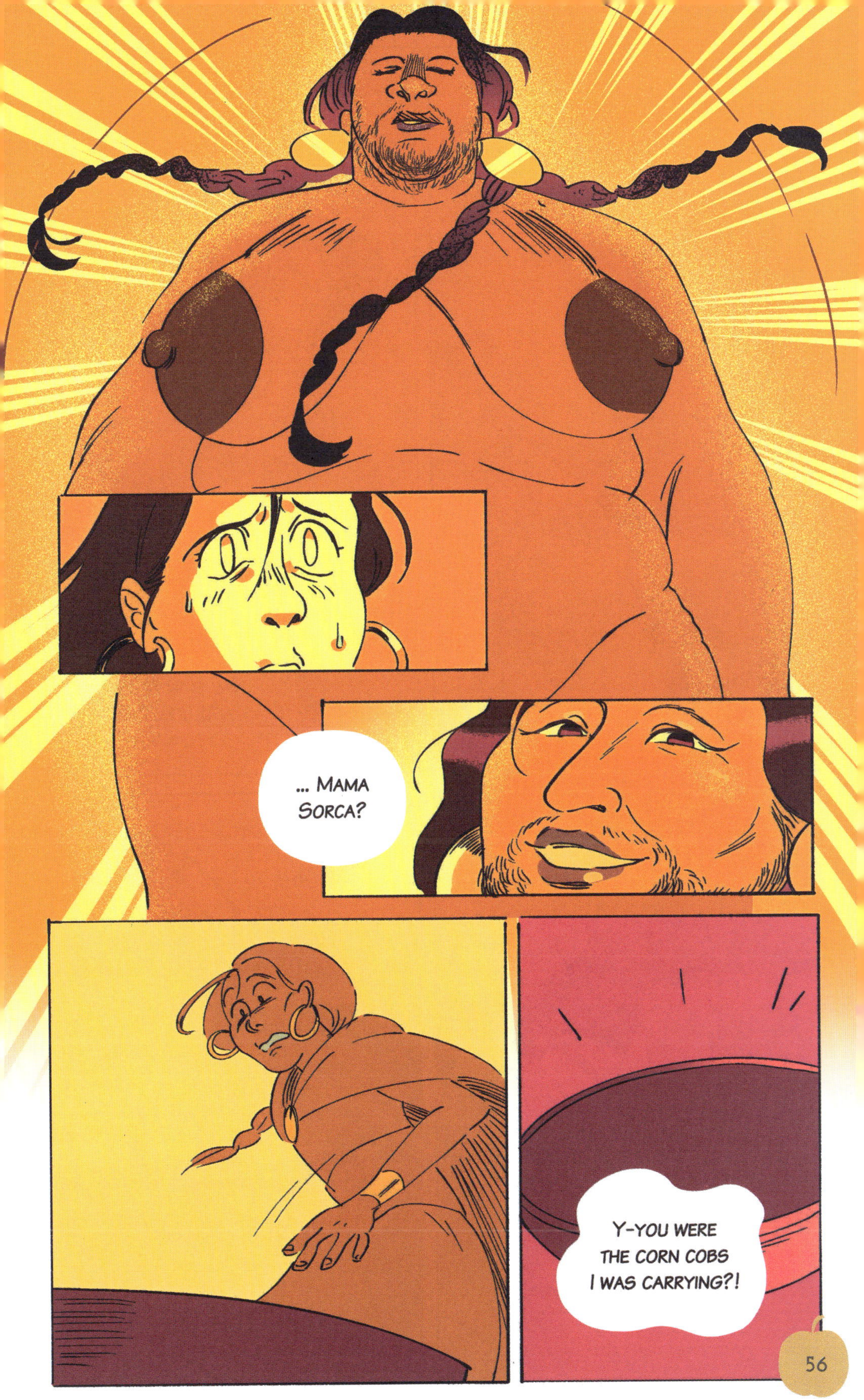
... MAMA SORCA?
Y-YOU WERE THE CORN COBS I WAS CARRYING?!

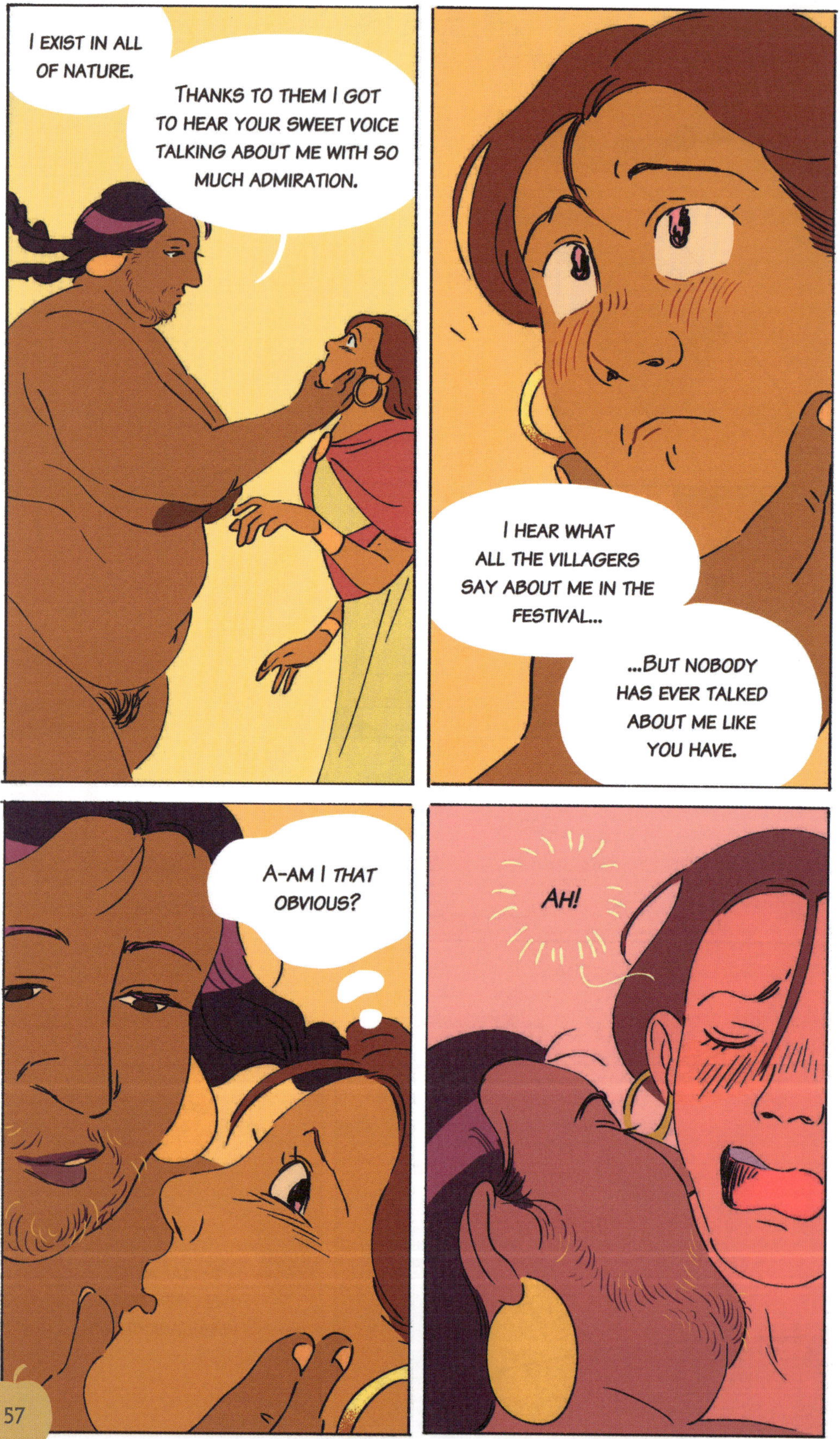
I EXIST IN ALL OF NATURE.
THANKS TO THEM I GOT TO HEAR YOUR SWEET VOICE TALKING ABOUT ME WITH SO MUCH ADMIRATION.
I HEAR WHAT ALL THE VILLAGERS SAY ABOUT ME IN THE FESTIVAL...
...BUT NOBODY HAS EVER TALKED ABOUT ME LIKE YOU HAVE.
A-AM I THAT OBVIOUS?
AH!

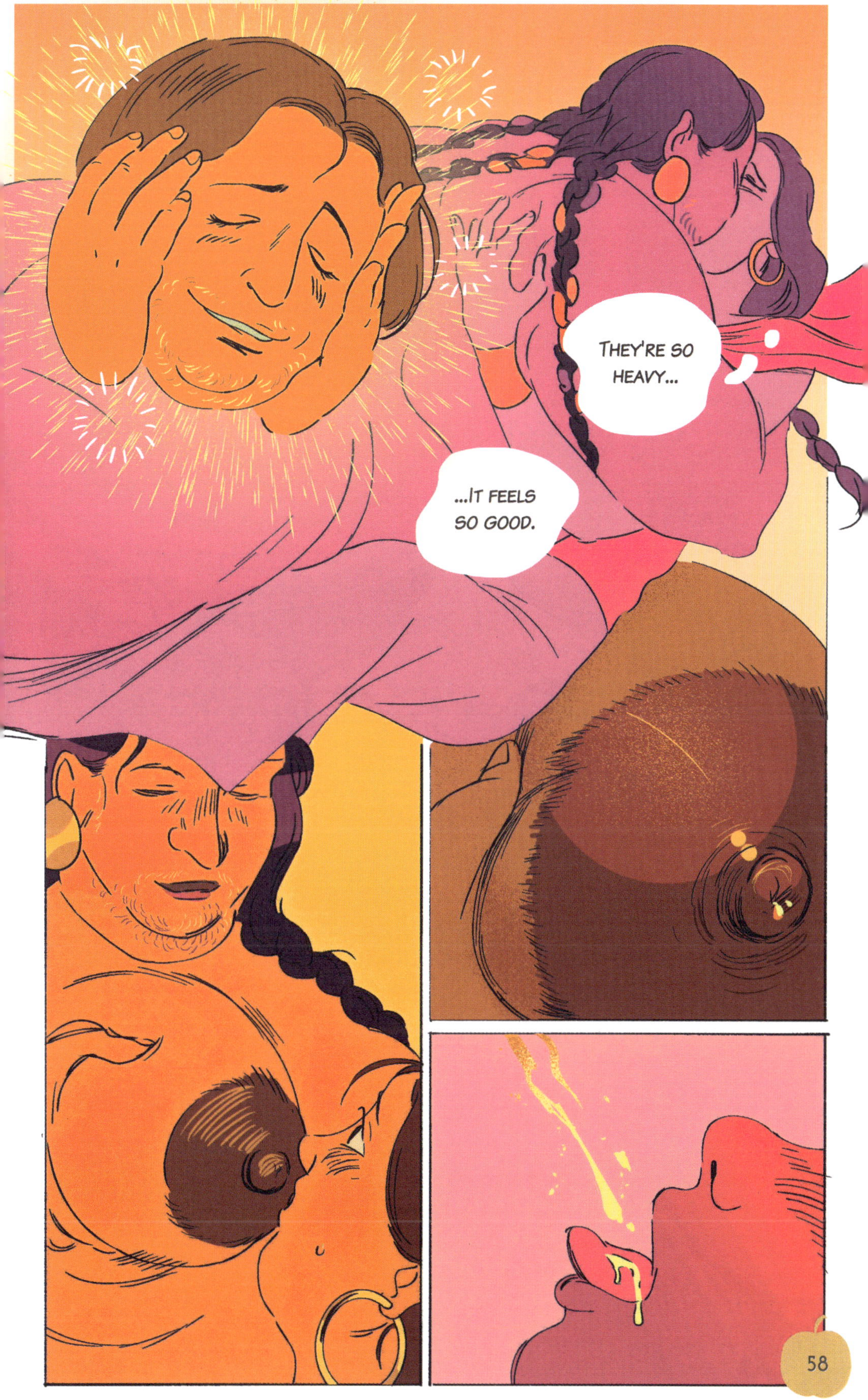
THEY'RE SO HEAVY...
...IT FEELS SO GOOD.

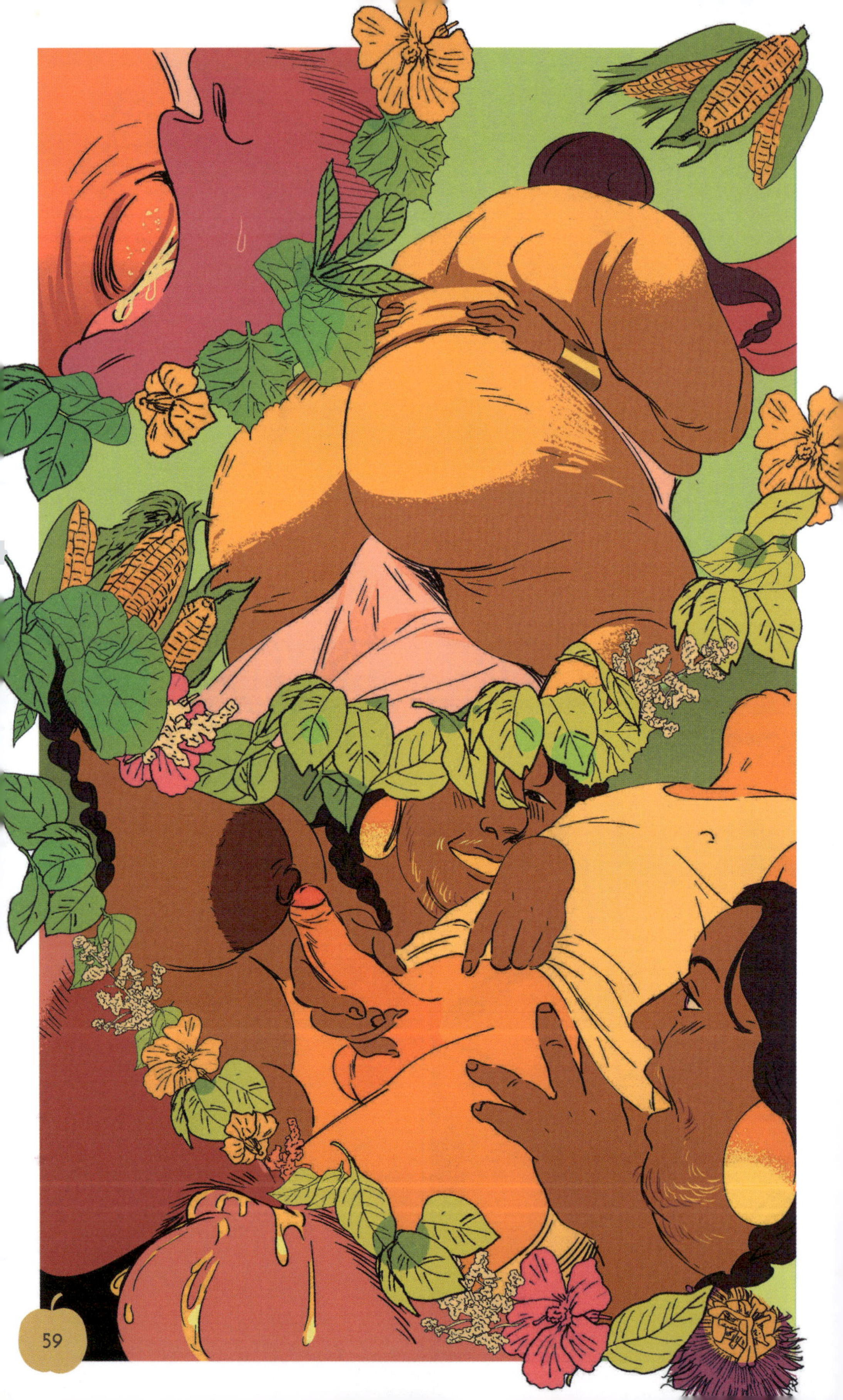

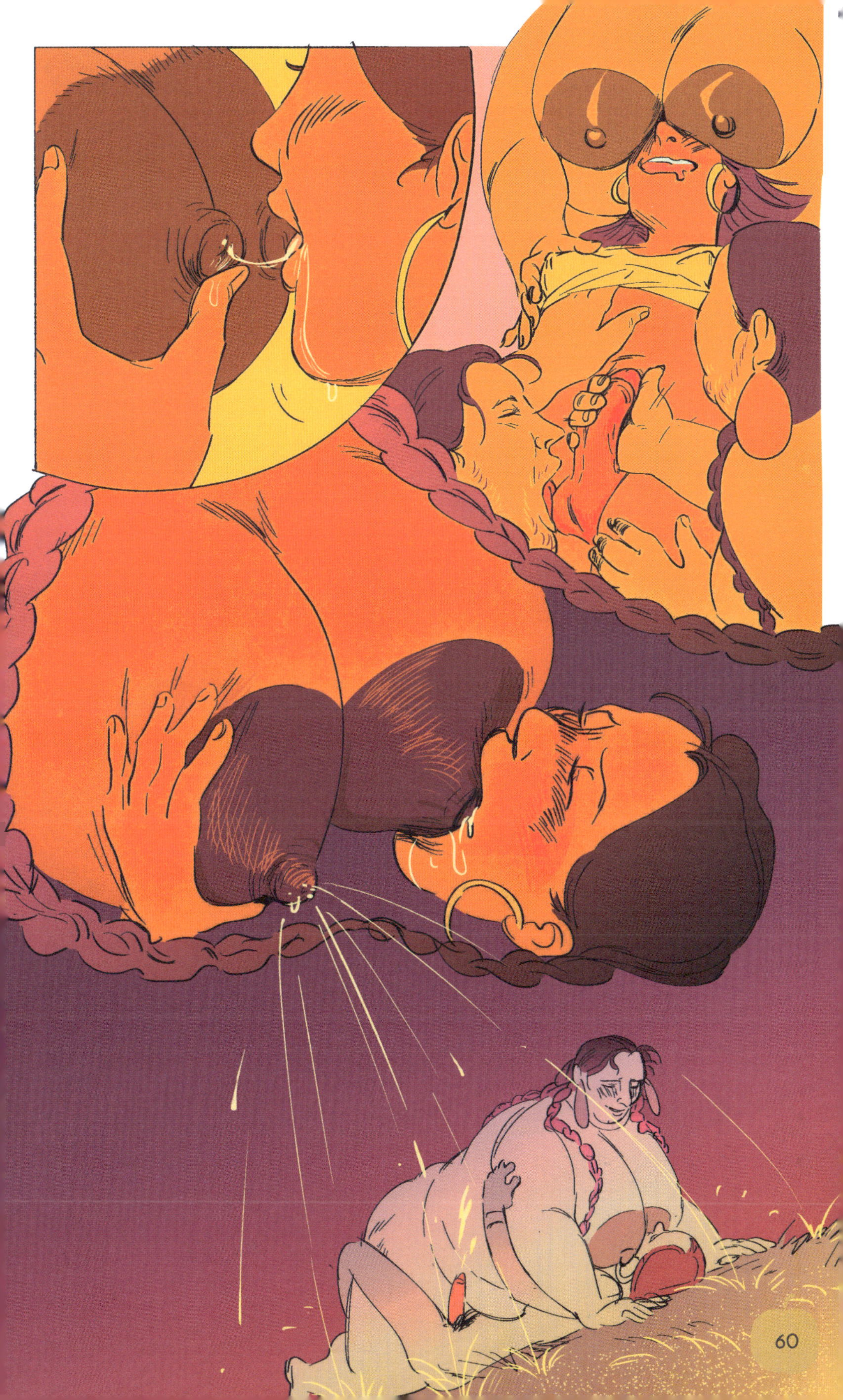

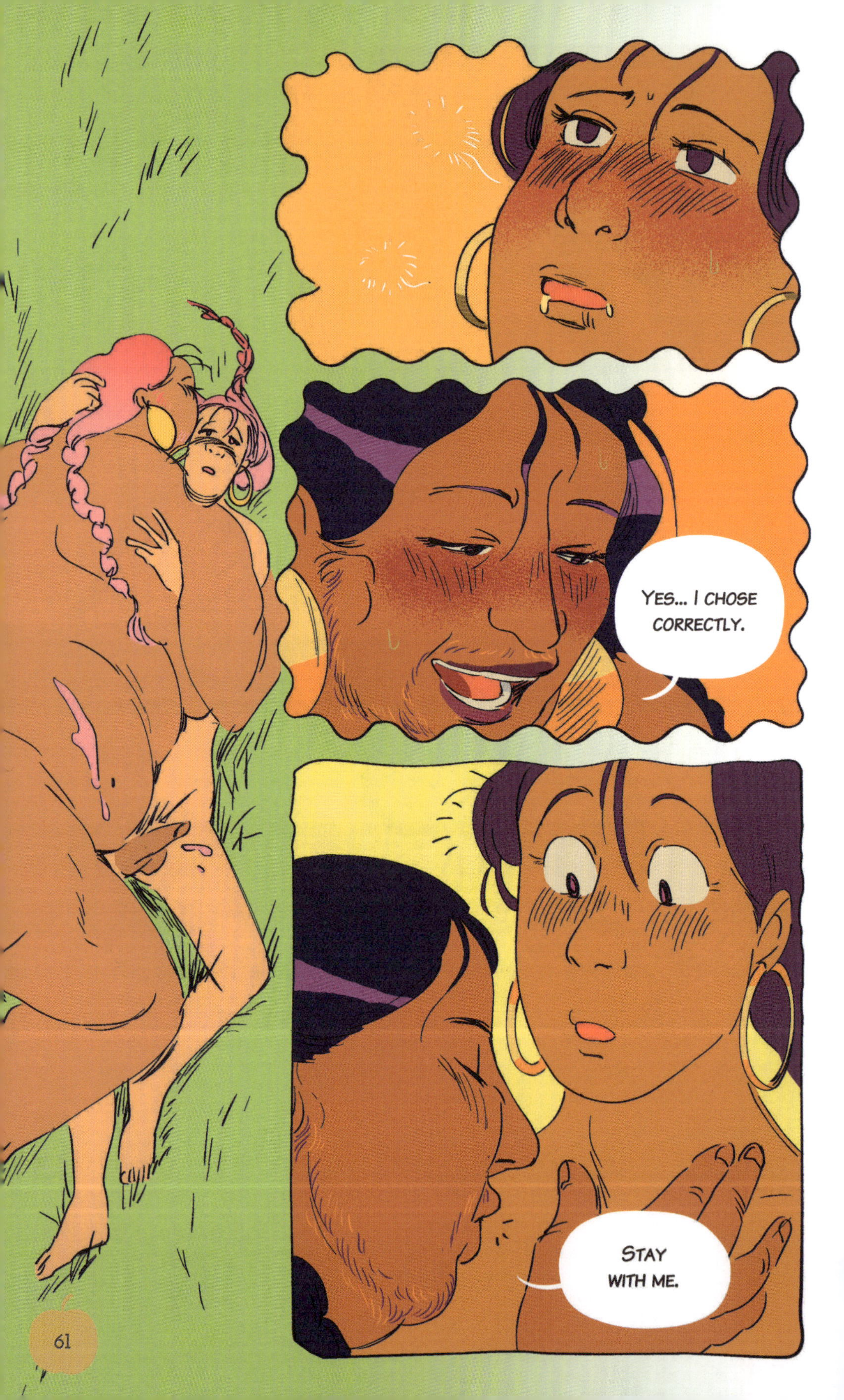
YES... I CHOSE CORRECTLY.
STAY WITH ME.

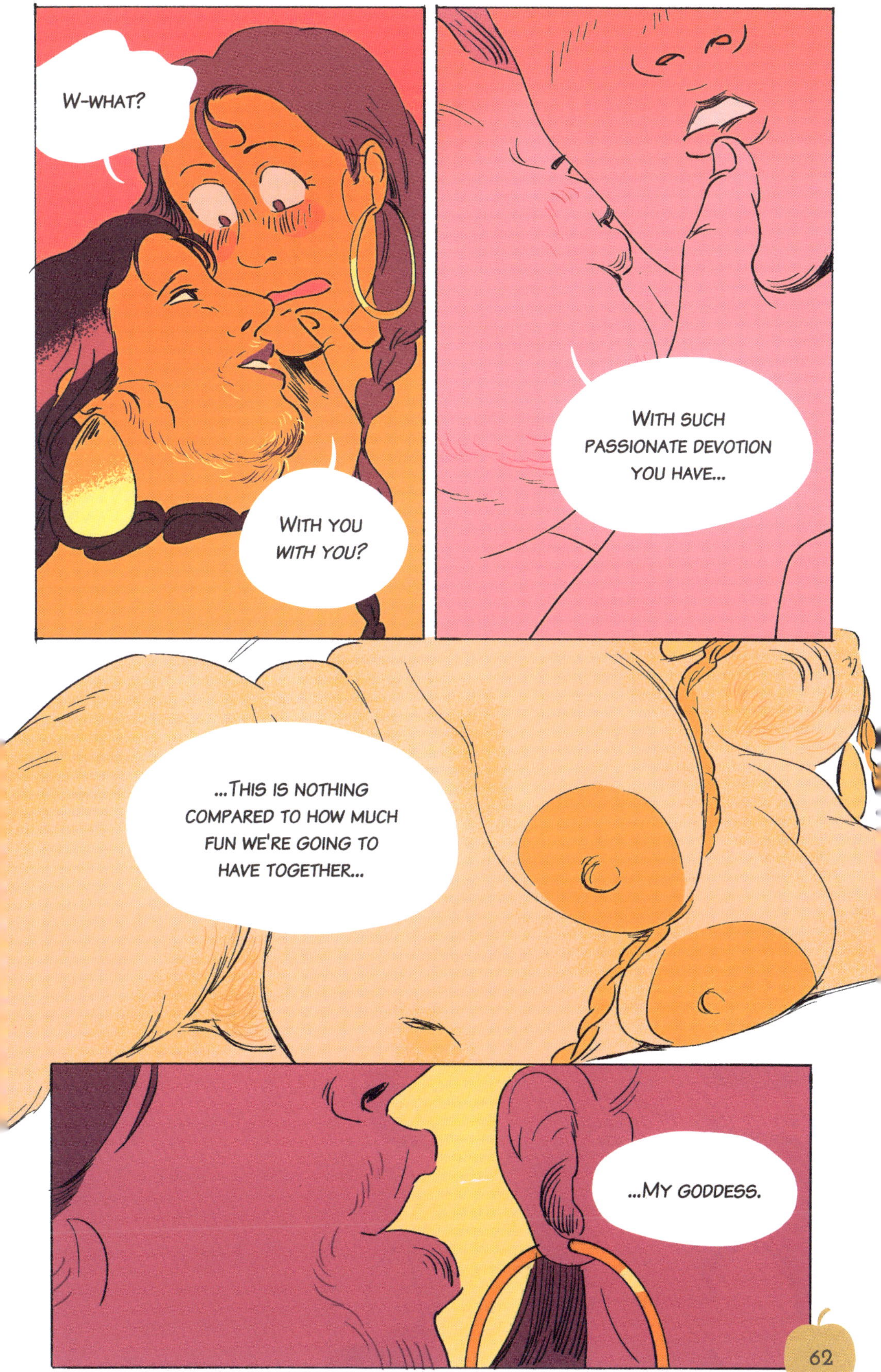
W-WHAT?
WITH YOU WITH YOU?
WITH SUCH PASSIONATE DEVOTION YOU HAVE...
...THIS IS NOTHING COMPARED TO HOW MUCH FUN WE'RE GOING TO HAVE TOGETHER...
...MY GODDESS.

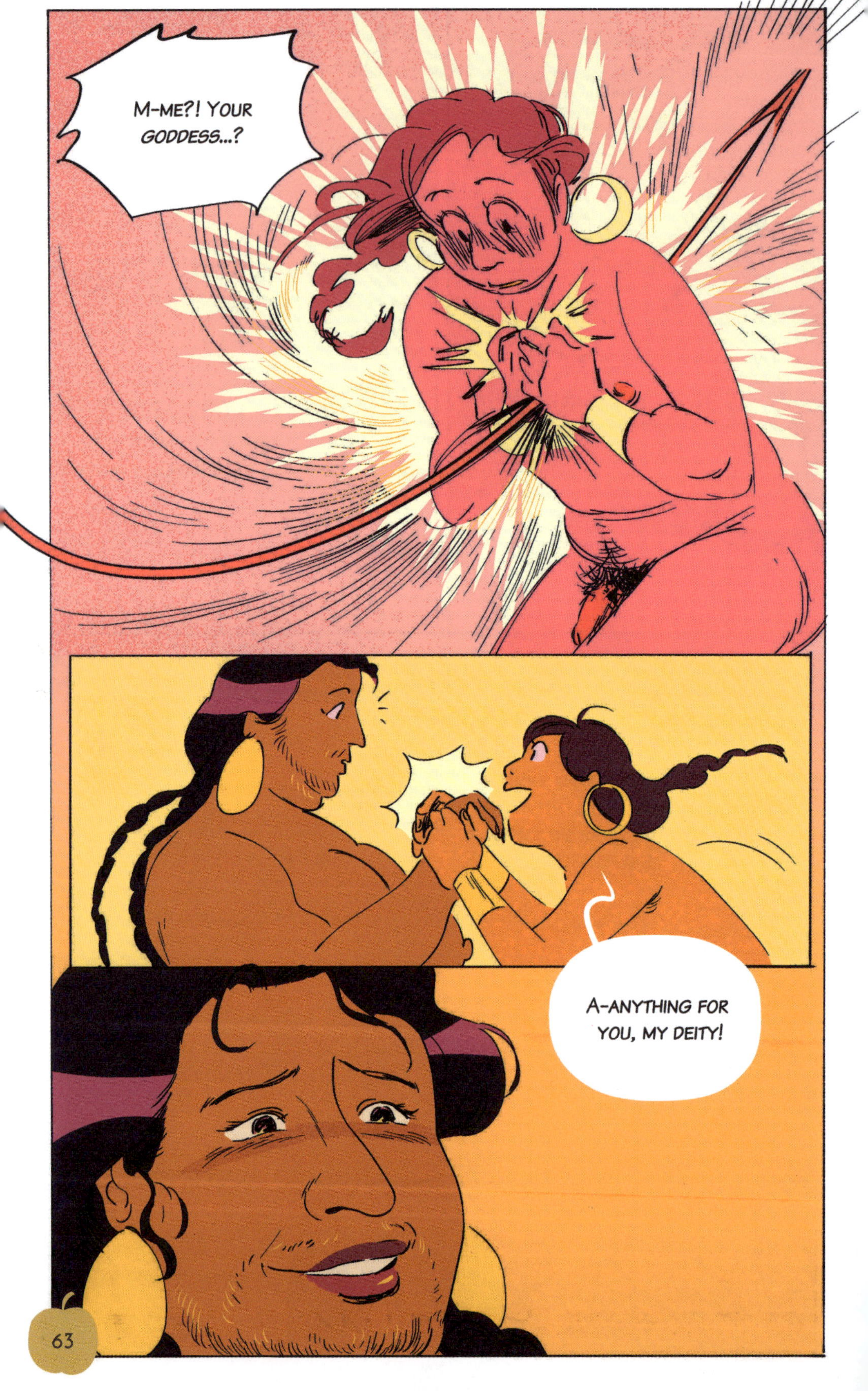
M-ME?! YOUR GODDESS...?
A-ANYTHING FOR YOU, MY DEITY!

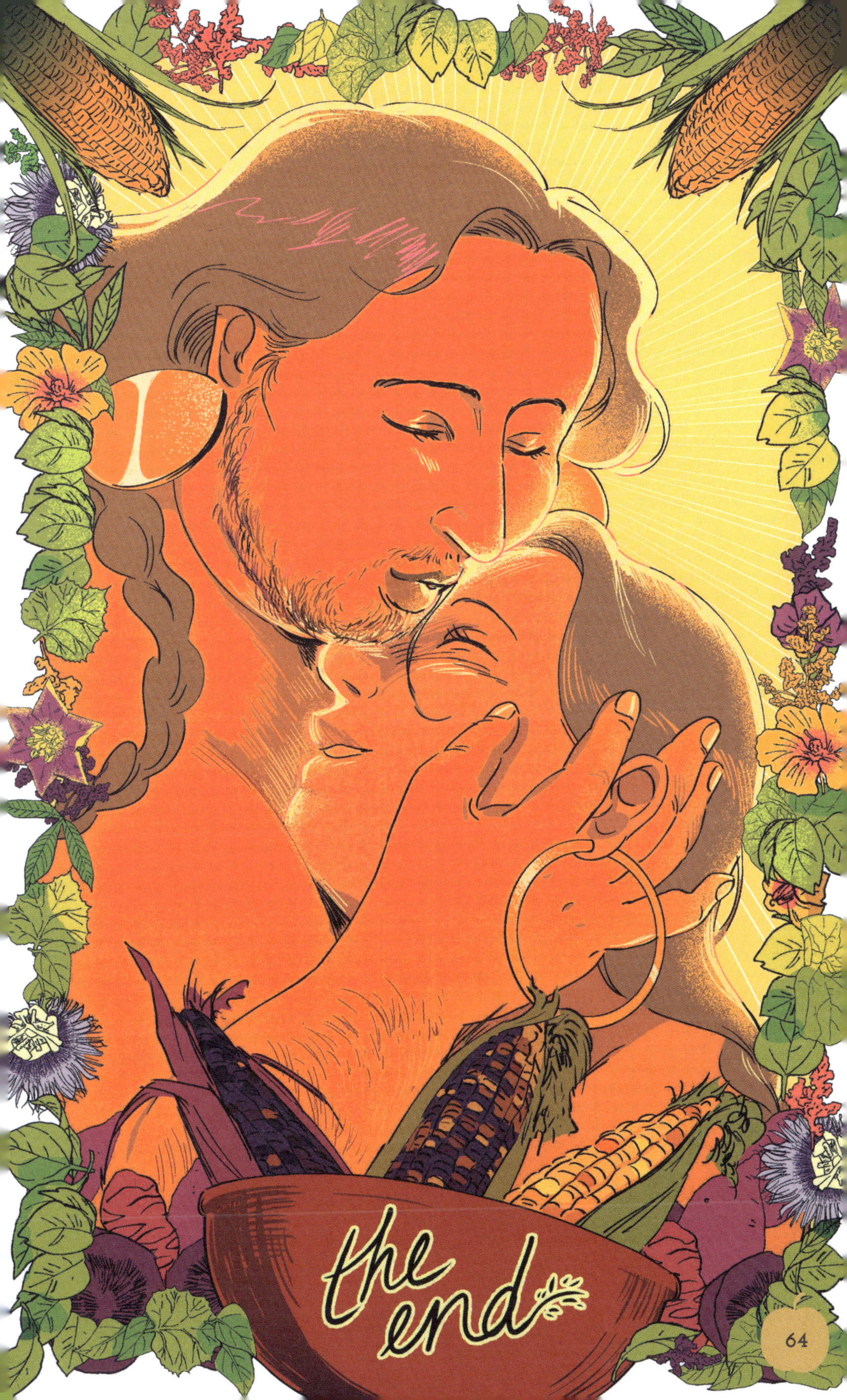
the end

Witch's Promise

by Zianne Benedict

A squire stumbles upon a witch bathing in a stream and realises the person who she has been told is an enemy, is instead living the body and life she wishes she could have. Unfortunately, the squire's master sees only a witch to be slain...

Creator's Note

" This story is a prequel to my story that appeared in the Prism Comics anthology.

Like that story, it's painted in watercolor on Fabriano Artistico paper, which should last a thousand years or so. No idea about the lifespan of the paint itself, though.

One particular inspiration for the story is the 2010 film Black Death directed by Christopher Smith.

I have a few of other stories I want to tell about my central character, based variously on murder ballads and folk songs. "

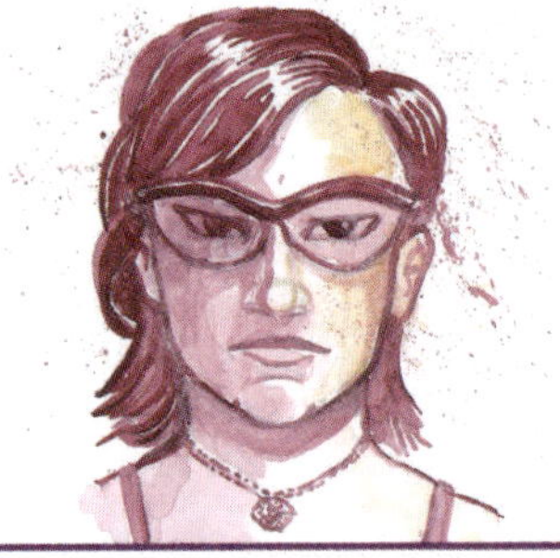

About the Creator

Christianne's (she/her) work has appeared in We're Still Here, the Prism Comics anthology, and Womantholgy, as well as several self published comics.

She also writes about film semi-professionally, with bylines at Indiewire, Filmmaker Magazine, Film and Fishnets, and a couple of out of print books.

She lives in rural Missouri with her partner and an expanding number of cats.

ChristiannesArt.blogspot.com

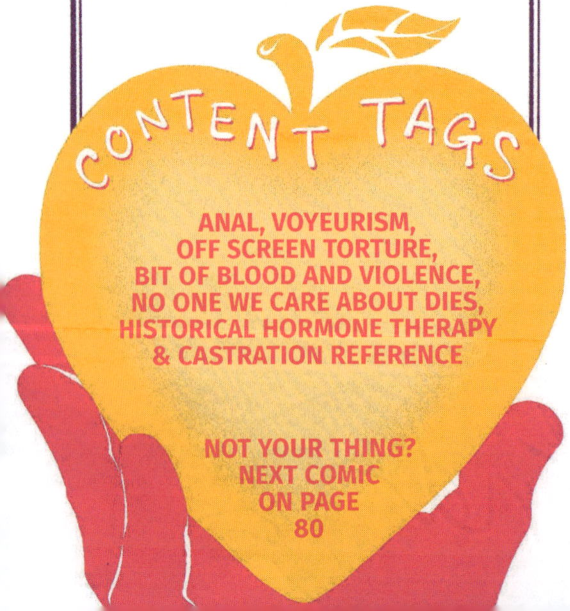

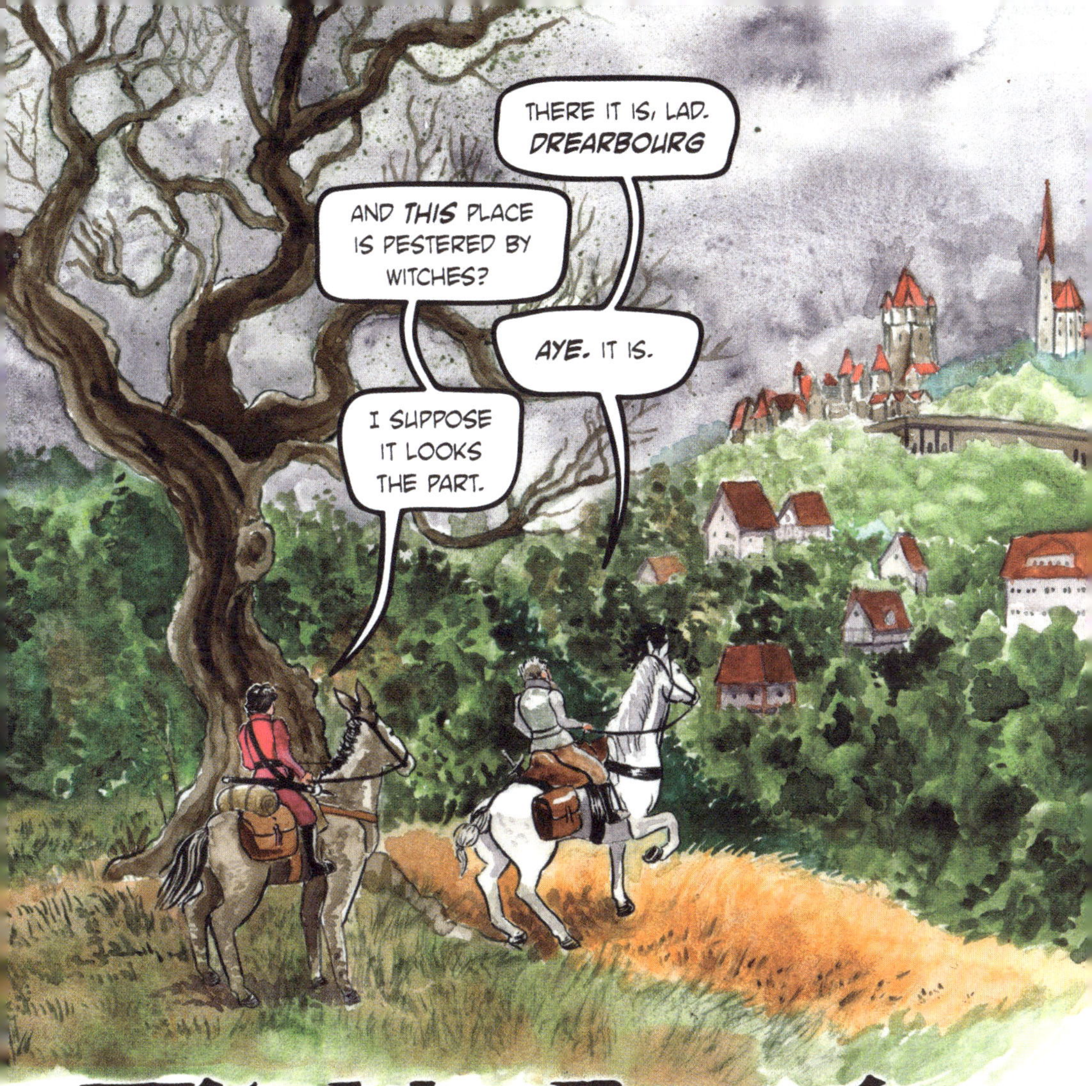

Witch's Promise

by Christianne Benedict

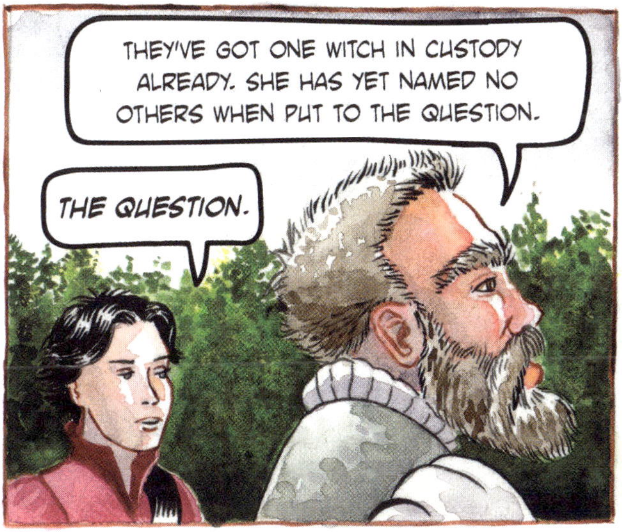

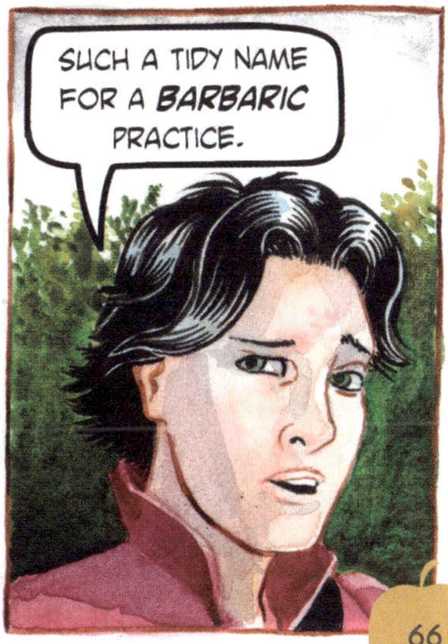

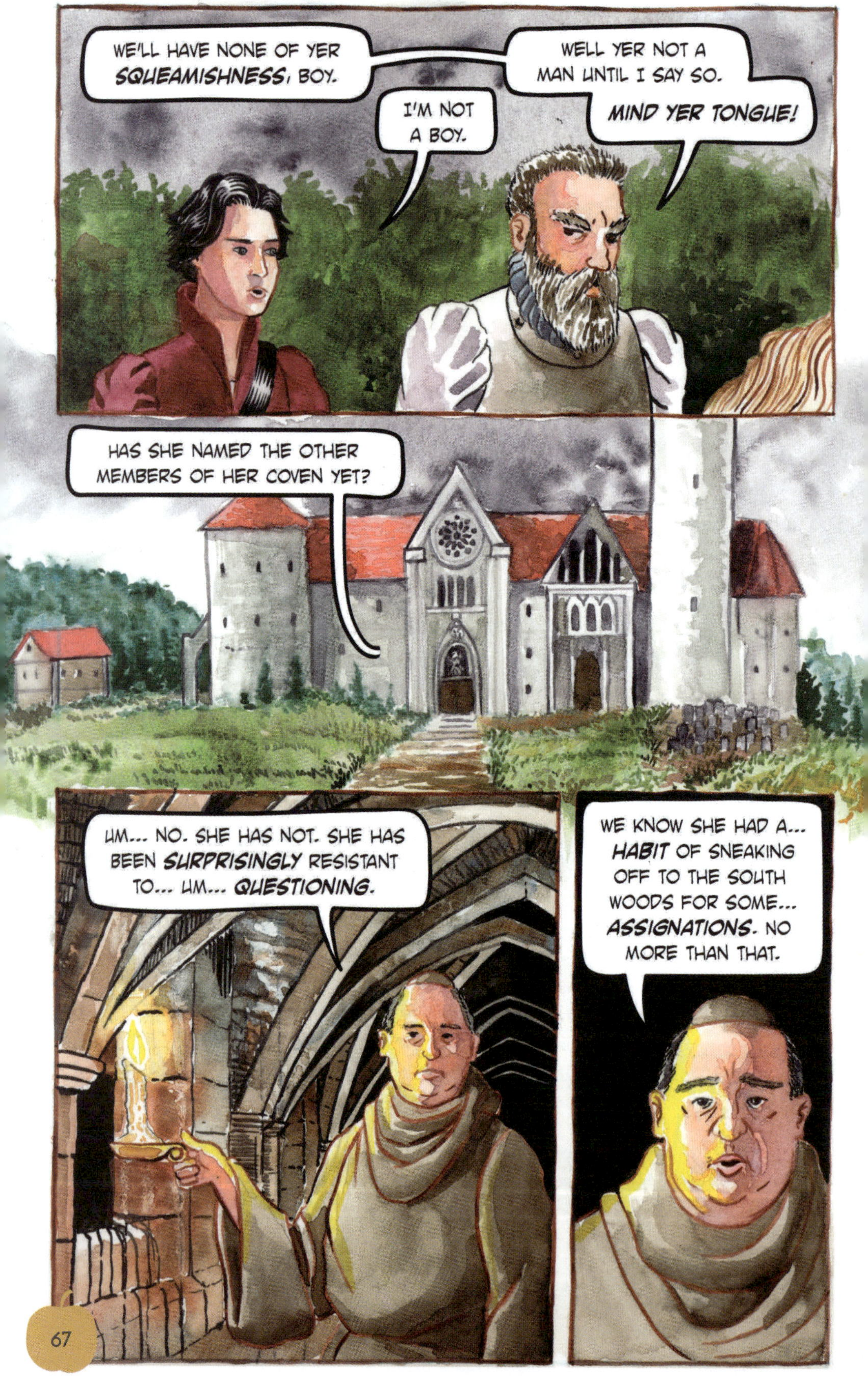
WE'LL HAVE NONE OF YER SQUEAMISHNESS, BOY.
I'M NOT A BOY.
WELL YER NOT A MAN UNTIL I SAY SO.
MIND YER TONGUE!
HAS SHE NAMED THE OTHER MEMBERS OF HER COVEN YET?
UM... NO. SHE HAS NOT. SHE HAS BEEN SURPRISINGLY RESISTANT TO... UM... QUESTIONING.
WE KNOW SHE HAD A... HABIT OF SNEAKING OFF TO THE SOUTH WOODS FOR SOME... ASSIGNATIONS. NO MORE THAN THAT.

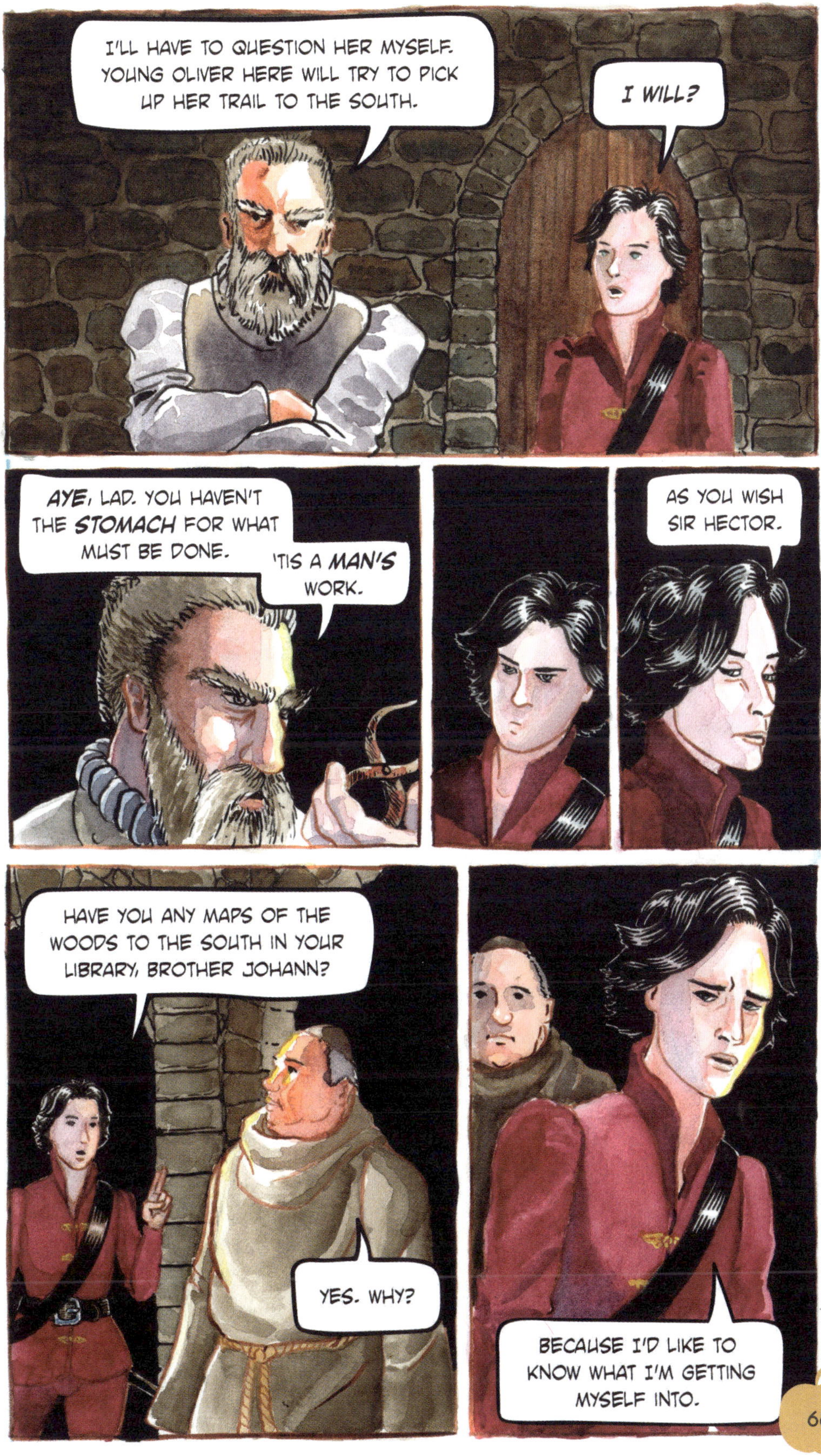
I'LL HAVE TO QUESTION HER MYSELF. YOUNG OLIVER HERE WILL TRY TO PICK UP HER TRAIL TO THE SOUTH.
I WILL?
AYE, LAD. YOU HAVEN'T THE STOMACH FOR WHAT MUST BE DONE.
'TIS A MAN'S WORK.
AS YOU WISH SIR HECTOR.
HAVE YOU ANY MAPS OF THE WOODS TO THE SOUTH IN YOUR LIBRARY, BROTHER JOHANN?
YES. WHY?
BECAUSE I'D LIKE TO KNOW WHAT I'M GETTING MYSELF INTO.

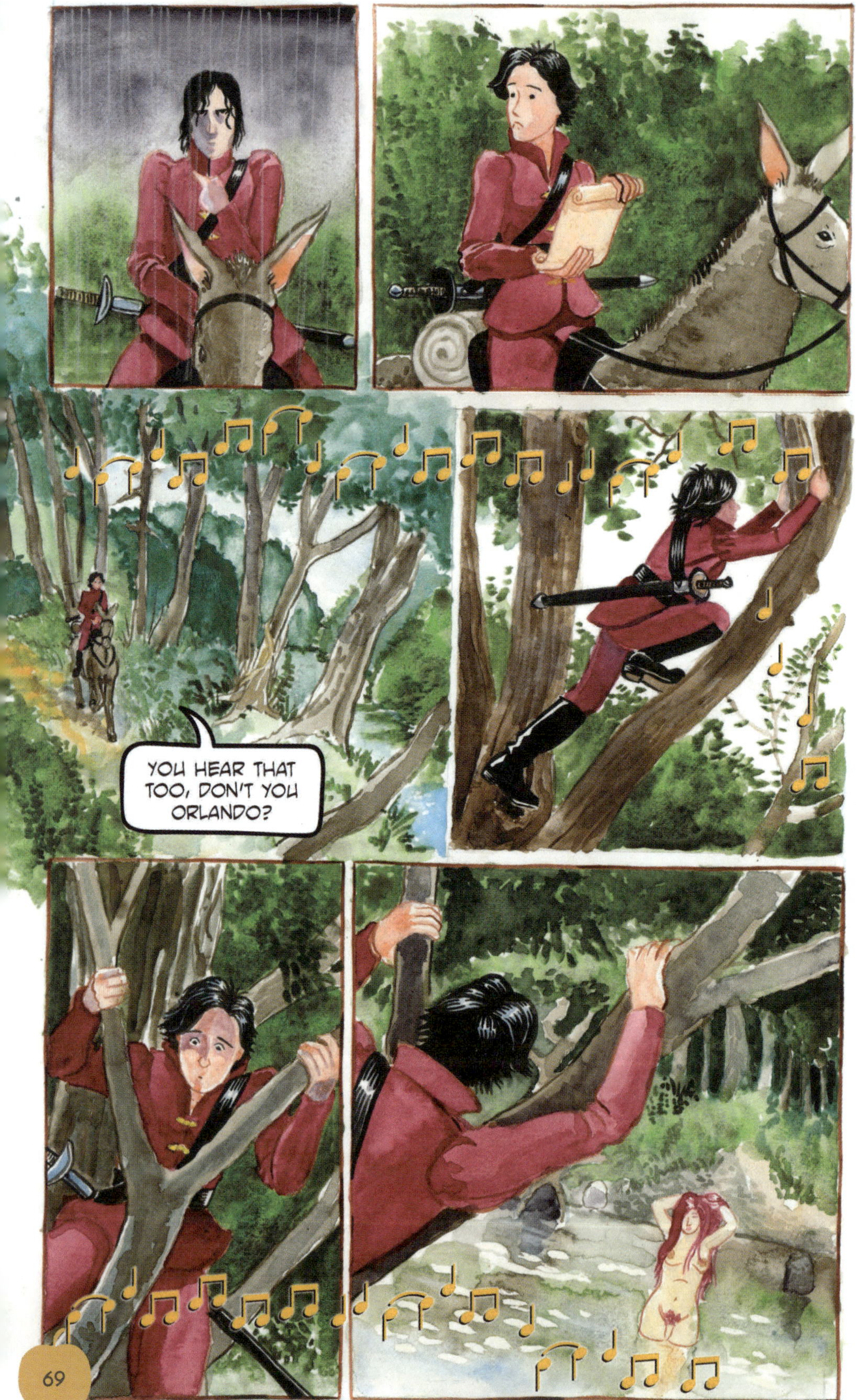
YOU HEAR THAT TOO, DON'T YOU ORLANDO?

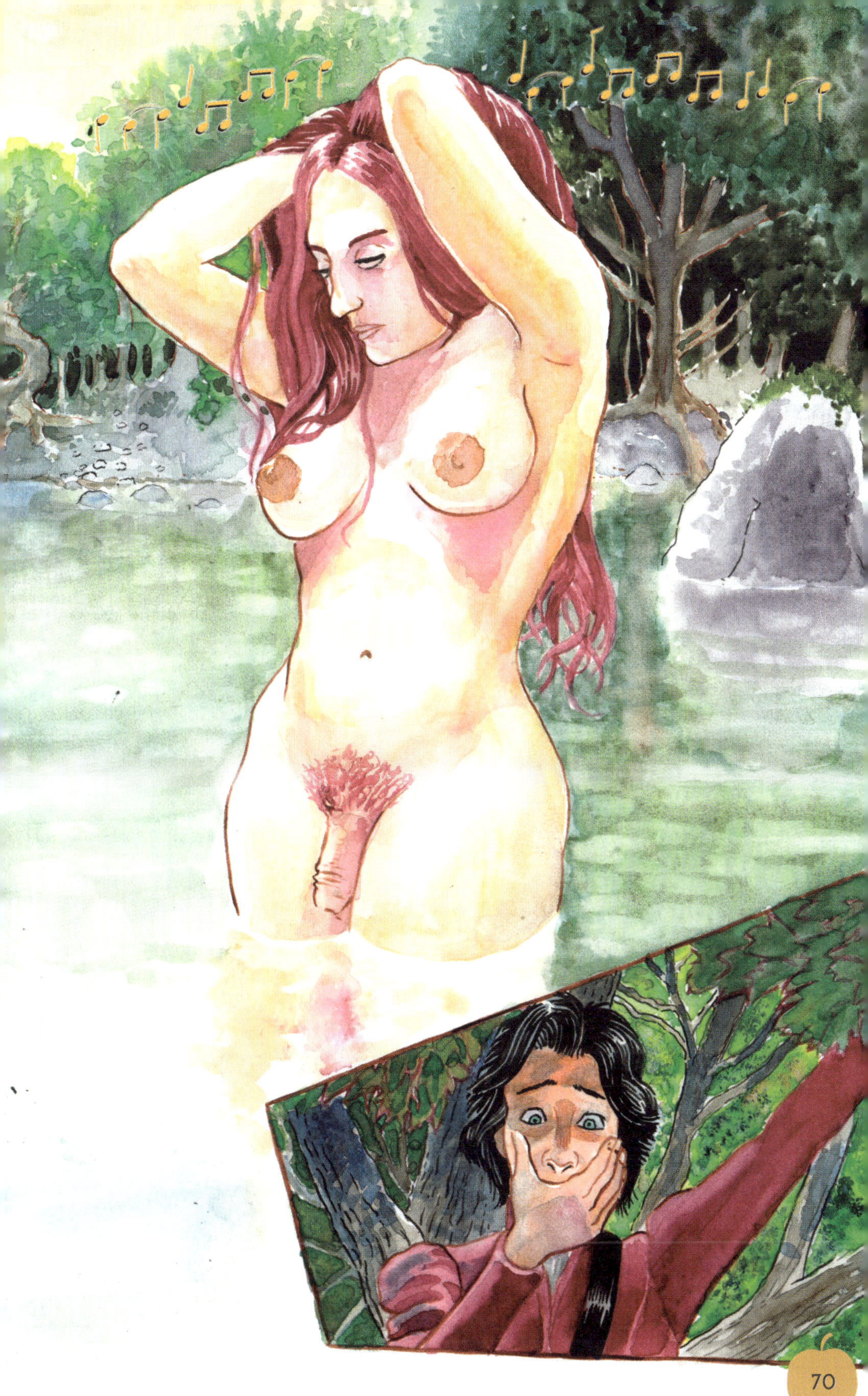

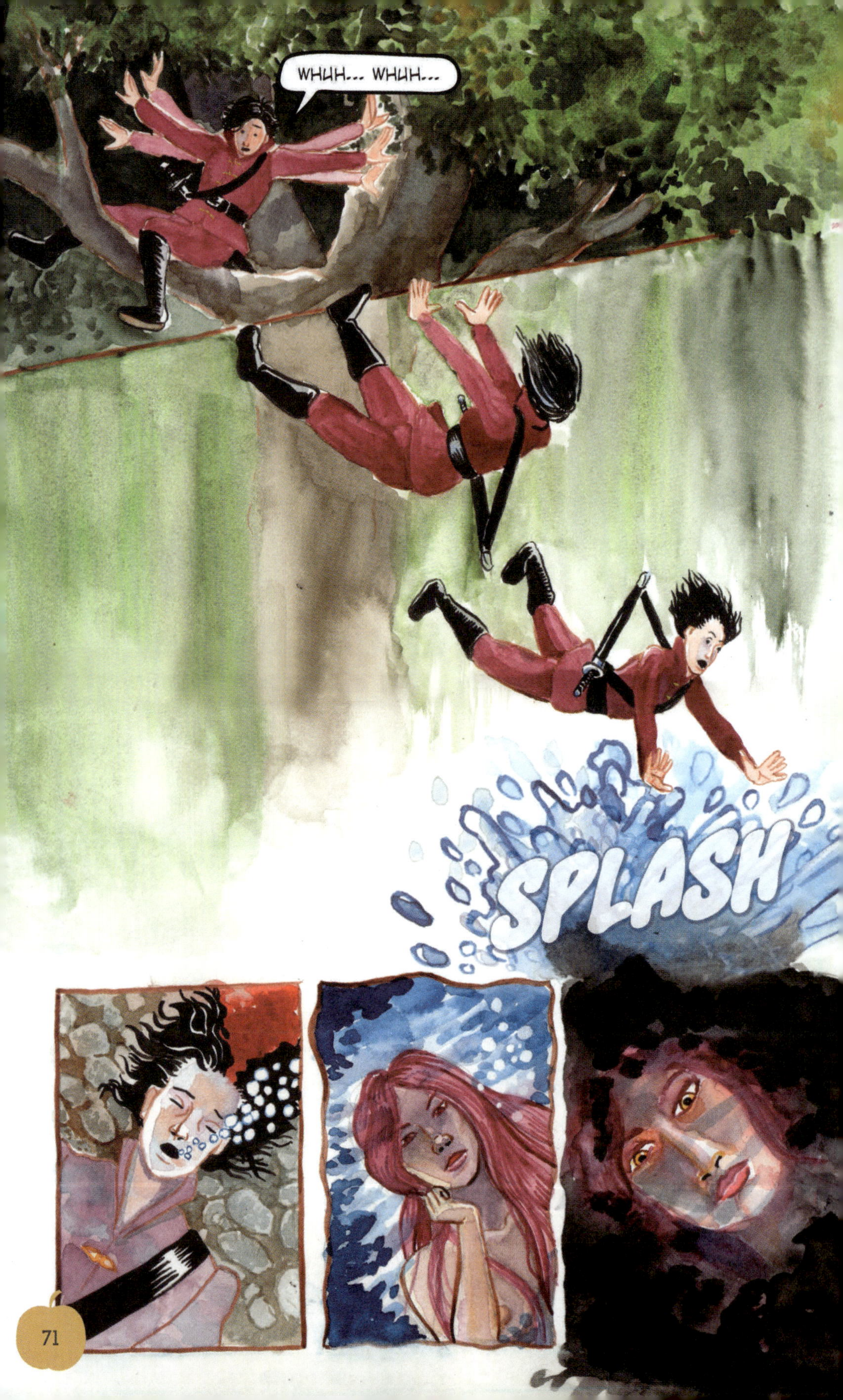
WHUH... WHUH...
SPLASH

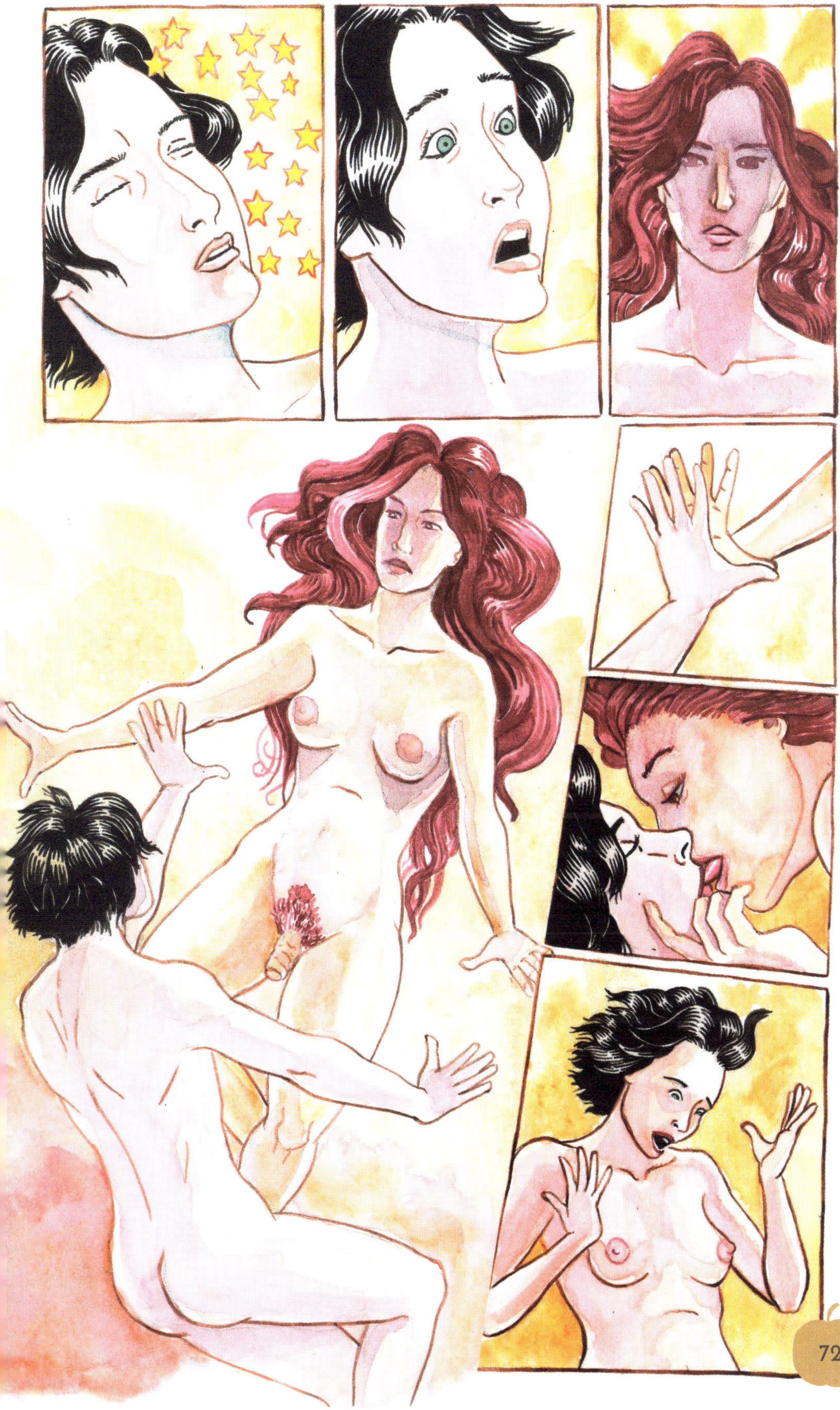

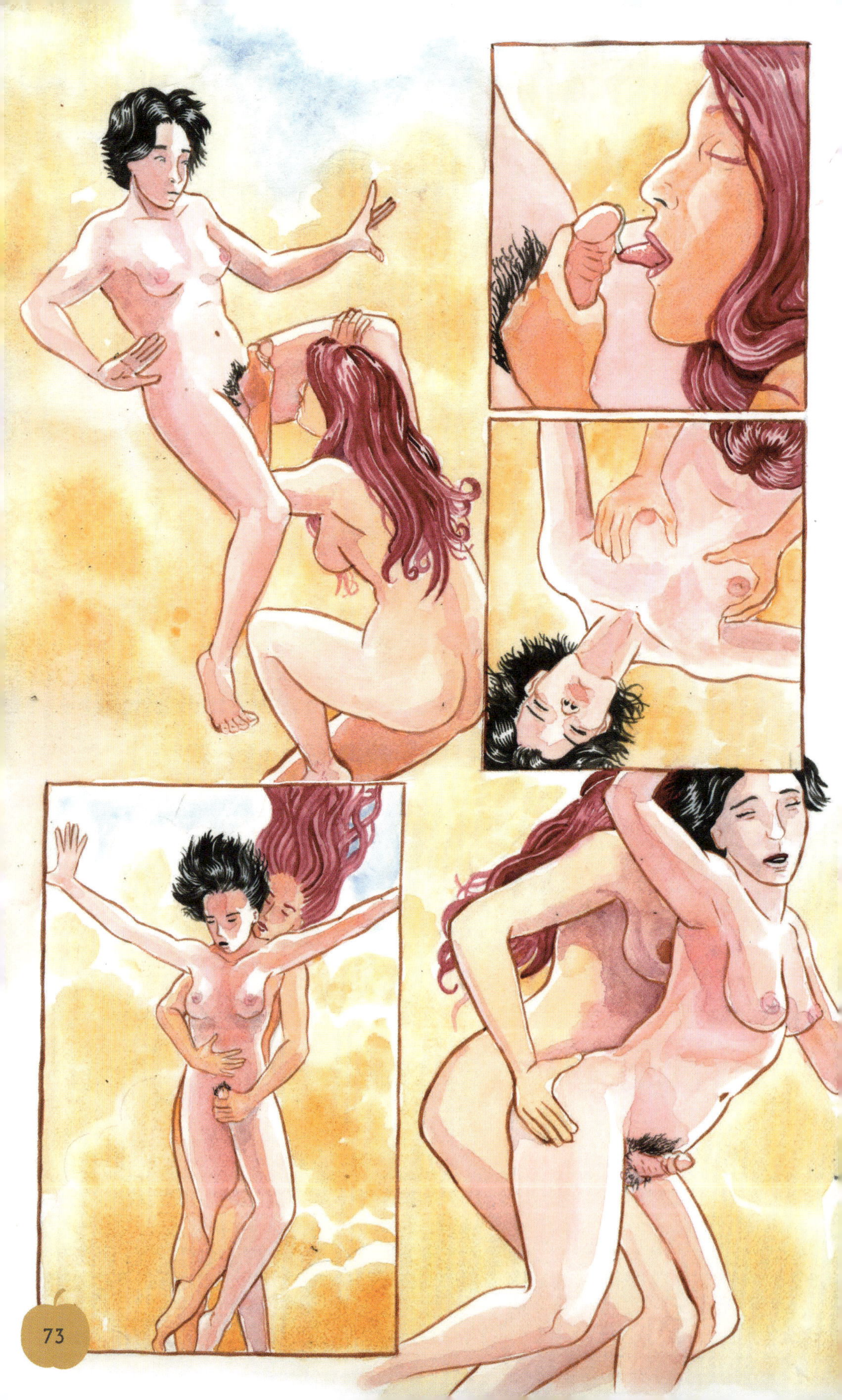

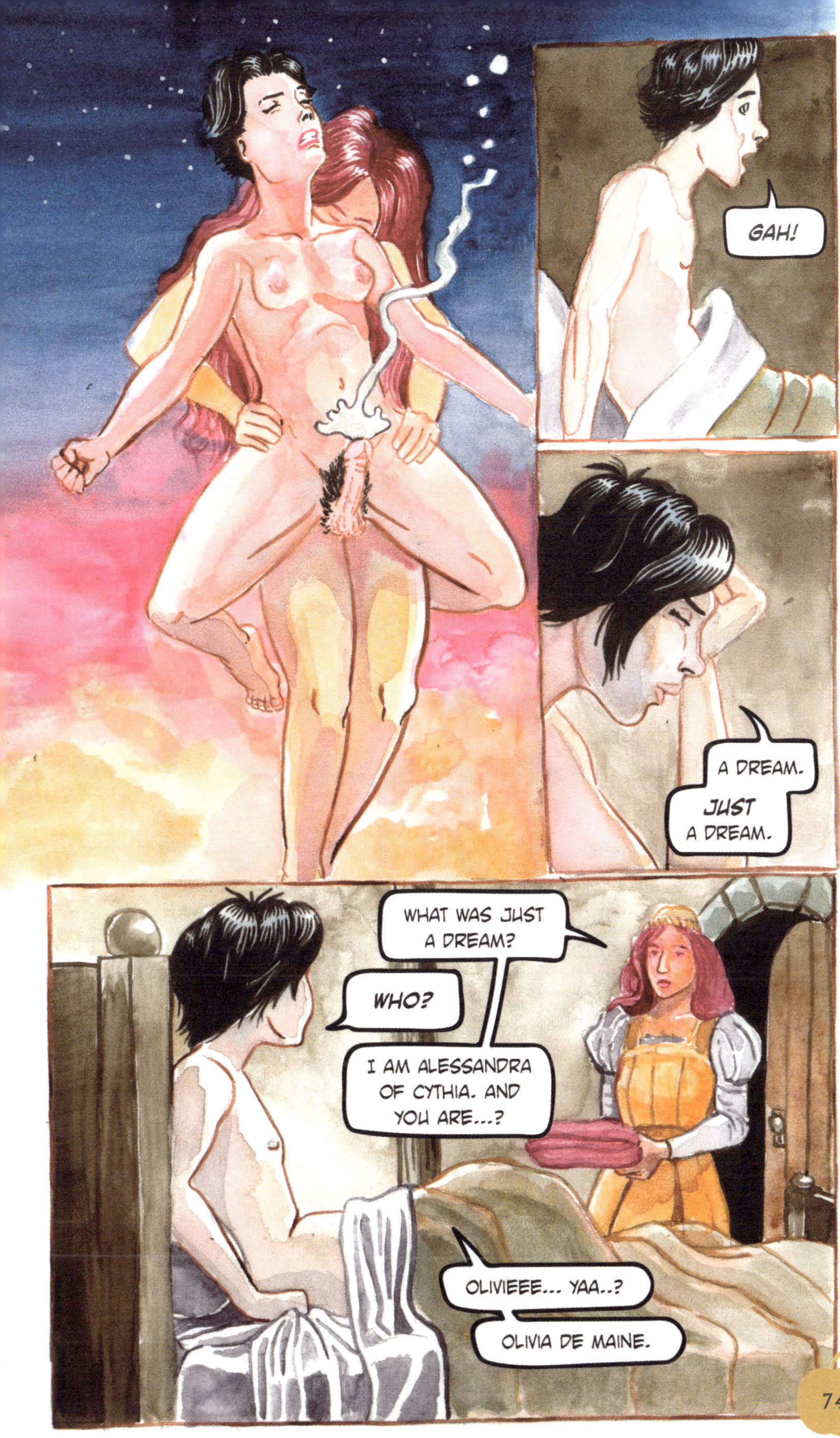

GAH!
A DREAM.
JUST A DREAM.
WHAT WAS JUST A DREAM?
WHO?
I AM ALESSANDRA OF CYTHIA. AND YOU ARE...?
OLIVIEEE... YAA..?
OLIVIA DE MAINE.

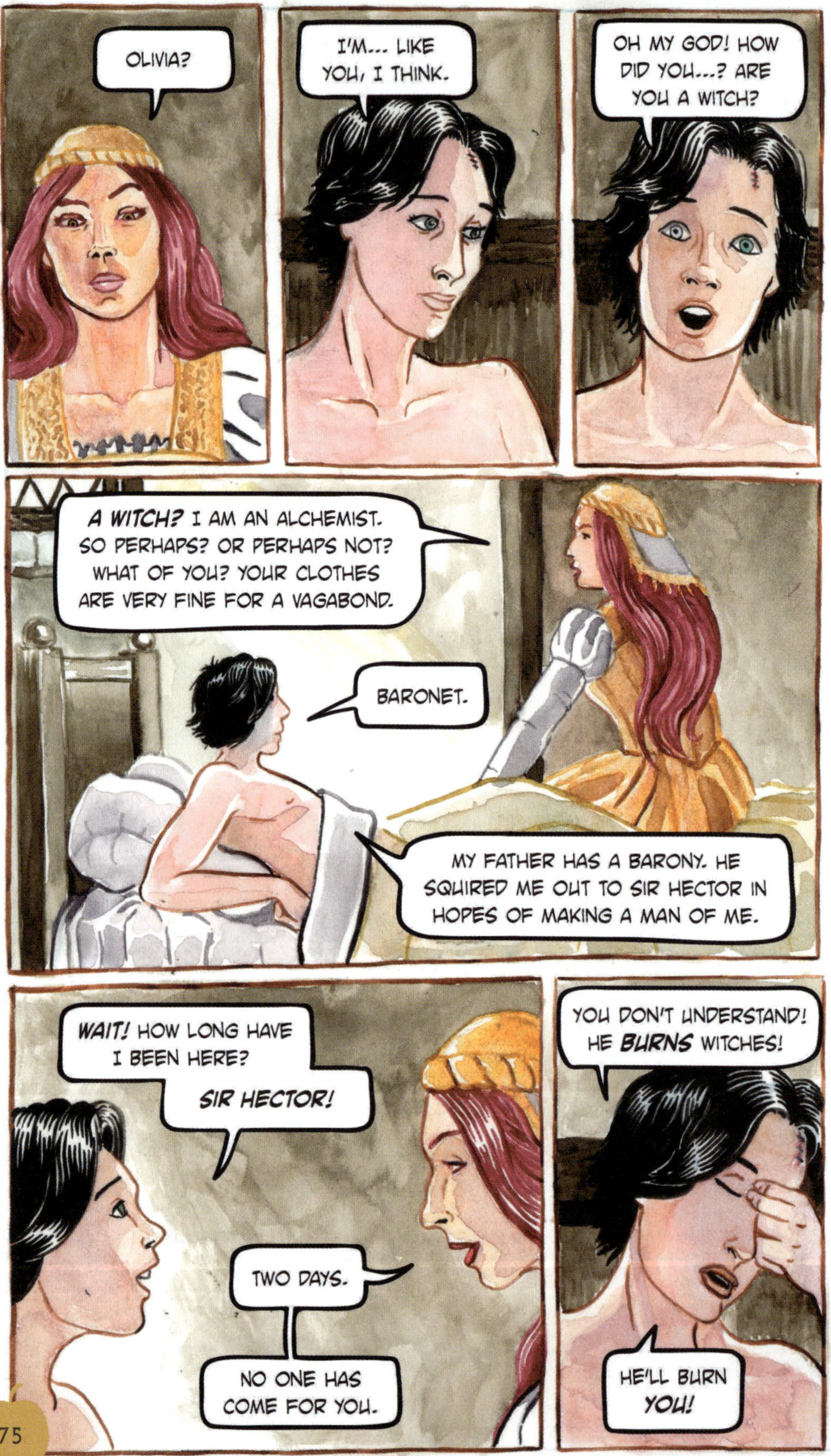
OLIVIA?
I'M... LIKE YOU, I THINK.
OH MY GOD! HOW DID YOU...? ARE YOU A WITCH?
A WITCH? I AM AN ALCHEMIST. SO PERHAPS? OR PERHAPS NOT? WHAT OF YOU? YOUR CLOTHES ARE VERY FINE FOR A VAGABOND.
BARONET.
MY FATHER HAS A BARONY. HE SQUIRED ME OUT TO SIR HECTOR IN HOPES OF MAKING A MAN OF ME.
WAIT! HOW LONG HAVE I BEEN HERE?
SIR HECTOR!
TWO DAYS.
NO ONE HAS COME FOR YOU.
YOU DON'T UNDERSTAND! HE BURNS WITCHES!
HE'LL BURN YOU!

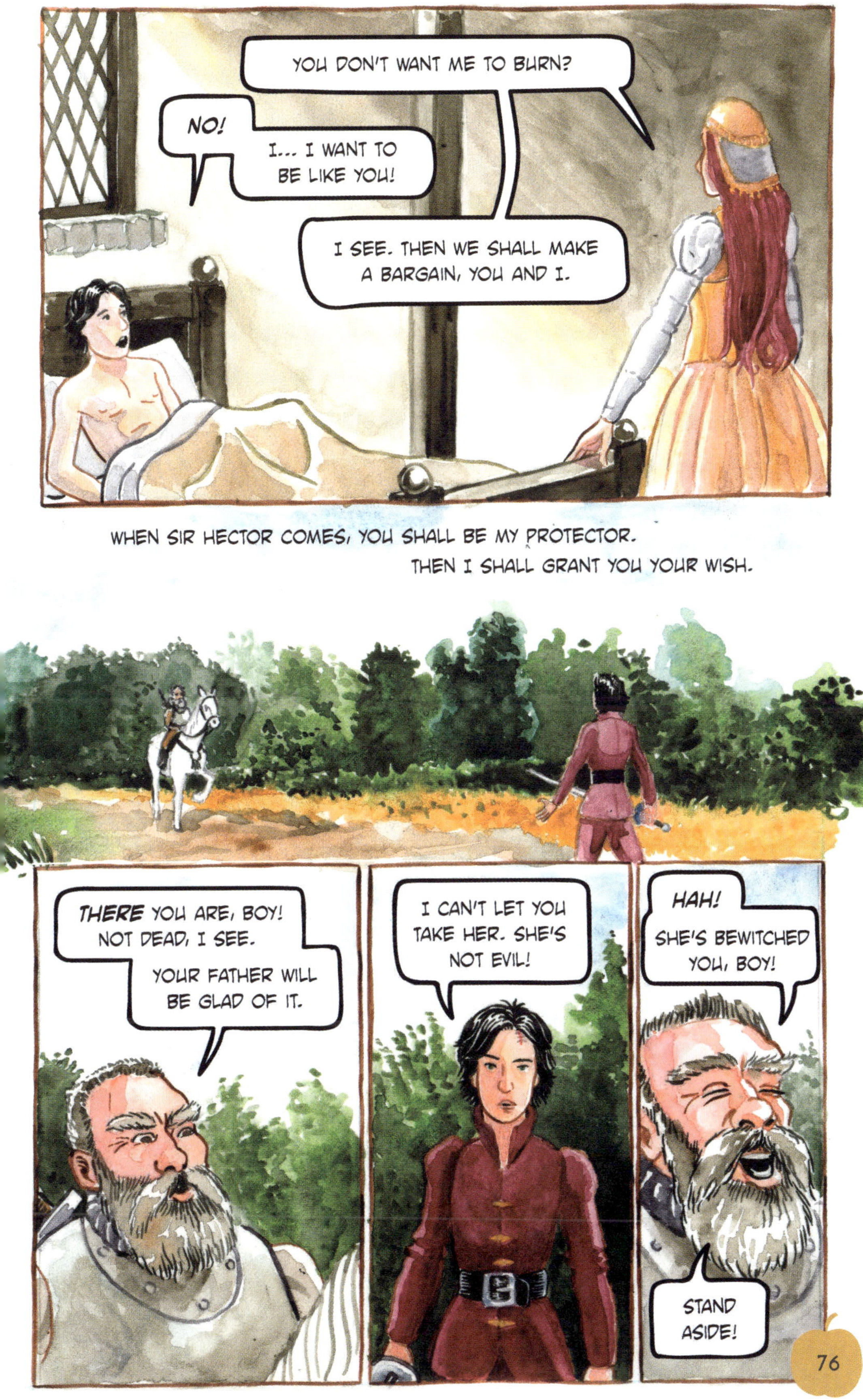
YOU DON'T WANT ME TO BURN?
NO!
I... I WANT TO BE LIKE YOU!
I SEE. THEN WE SHALL MAKE A BARGAIN, YOU AND I.
WHEN SIR HECTOR COMES, YOU SHALL BE MY PROTECTOR.
THEN I SHALL GRANT YOU YOUR WISH.
THERE YOU ARE, BOY! NOT DEAD, I SEE.
YOUR FATHER WILL BE GLAD OF IT.
I CAN'T LET YOU TAKE HER. SHE'S NOT EVIL!
HAH!
SHE'S BEWITCHED YOU, BOY!
STAND ASIDE!

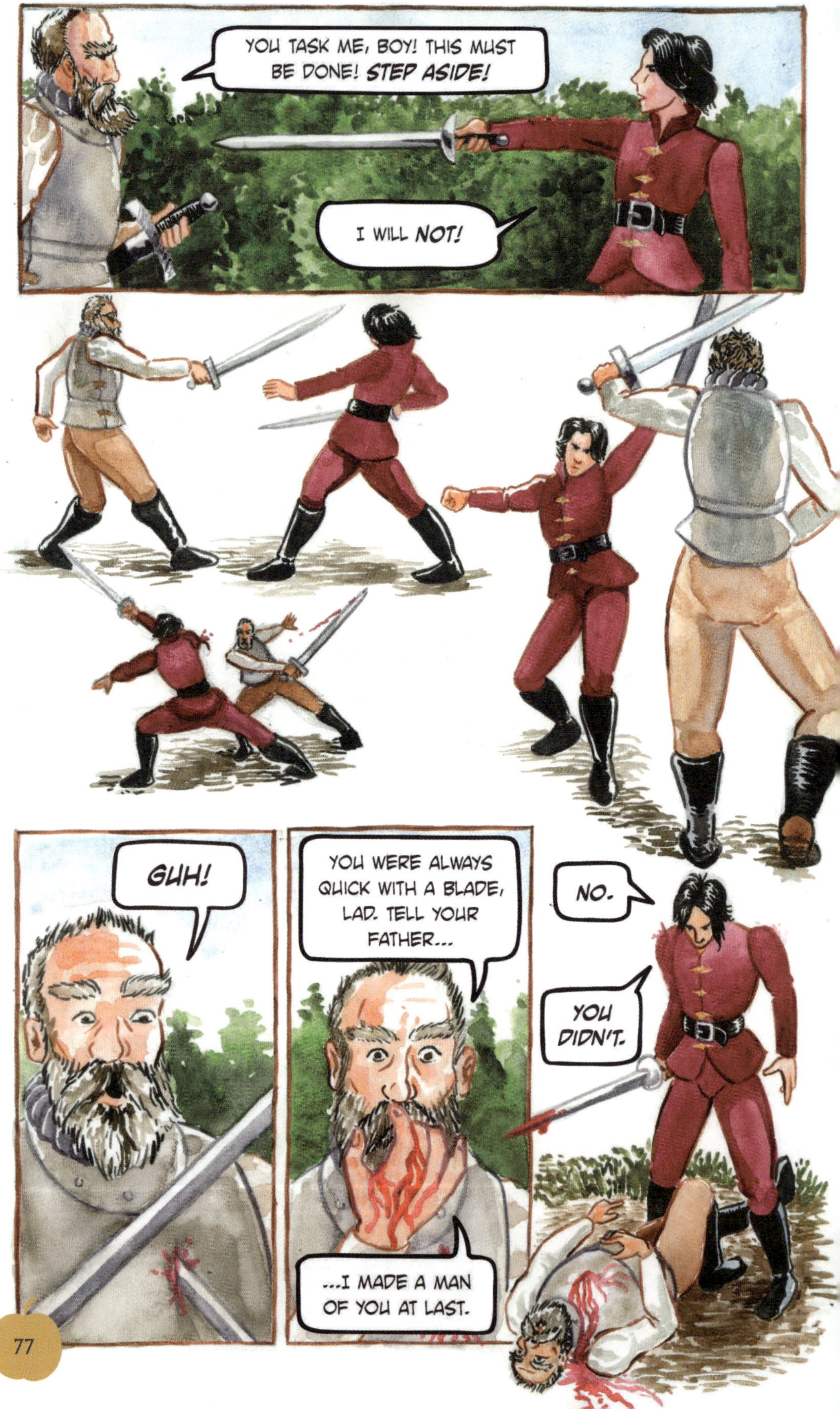

YOU TASK ME, BOY! THIS MUST BE DONE! STEP ASIDE!
I WILL NOT!
GUH!
YOU WERE ALWAYS QUICK WITH A BLADE, LAD. TELL YOUR FATHER...
...I MADE A MAN OF YOU AT LAST.
NO.
YOU DIDN'T.

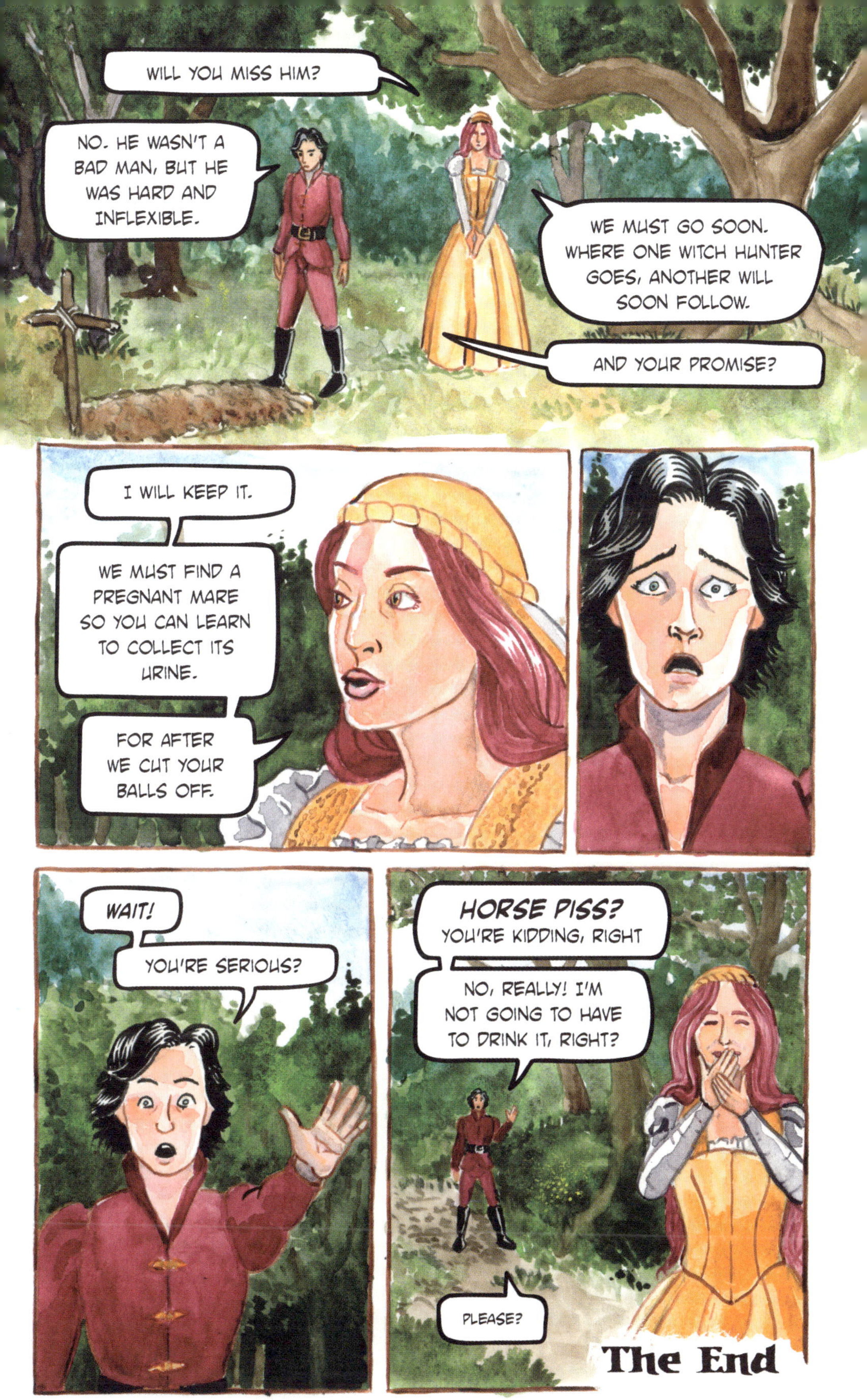
WILL YOU MISS HIM?
NO. HE WASN'T A BAD MAN, BUT HE WAS HARD AND INFLEXIBLE.
WE MUST GO SOON. WHERE ONE WITCH HUNTER GOES, ANOTHER WILL SOON FOLLOW.
AND YOUR PROMISE?
I WILL KEEP IT.
WE MUST FIND A PREGNANT MARE SO YOU CAN LEARN TO COLLECT ITS URINE.
FOR AFTER WE CUT YOUR BALLS OFF.
WAIT!
YOU'RE SERIOUS?
HORSE PISS? YOU'RE KIDDING, RIGHT
NO, REALLY! I'M NOT GOING TO HAVE TO DRINK IT, RIGHT?
PLEASE?
The End

Come Forth My Muse

Story by Michelle Parker - Art by Jey Pawlik

An artist summons a muse for a life drawing session, but some of the poses are much harder to hold than others...

Creators' Notes

" For this story we really wanted to focus on older characters being sexy, beautiful, and desirable. Our favourite part of any erotic comic is the build-up and foreplay, so we were excited to have the chance to focus exclusively on it for this anthology.

We were very glad to be involved in this anthology and showcase all of the different ways people can be trans. "

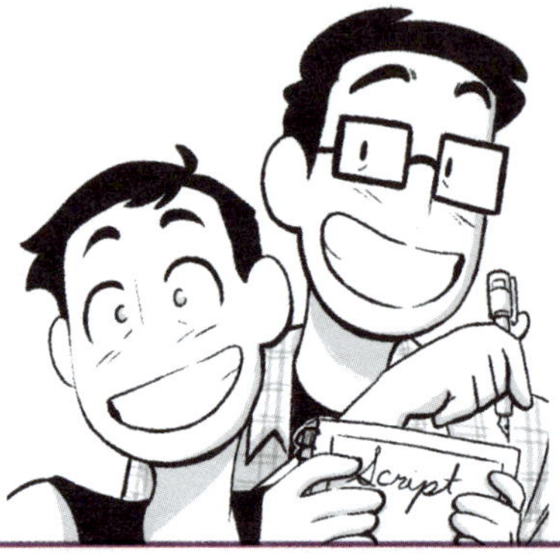

About the Creators

Michelle Parker (xey/xem) is a comic writer from Canada. Together with Jey Pawlik xey have written several comics, including the completed series "Dead City." Xeir work focuses on queer characters and relationships. If not forced to do something else, xey're probably reading.

TopazComics.com

Jey Pawlik (they/them) is a nonbinary freelance cartoonist from Canada. They have two completed webcomics under their belt, "Dead City" and "Gender Slices", with more queer stories on the way. They love sharks, tea and comics about people over 30

JPawlik.com

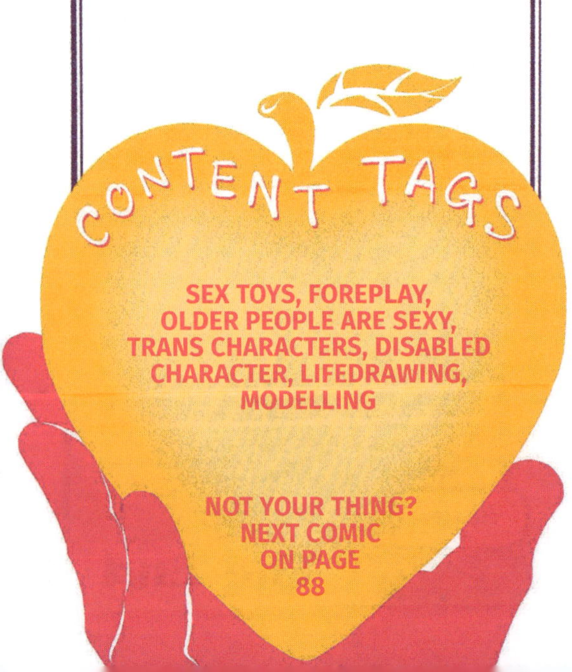

Come Forth My Muse

Michelle Parker & Jey Pawlik

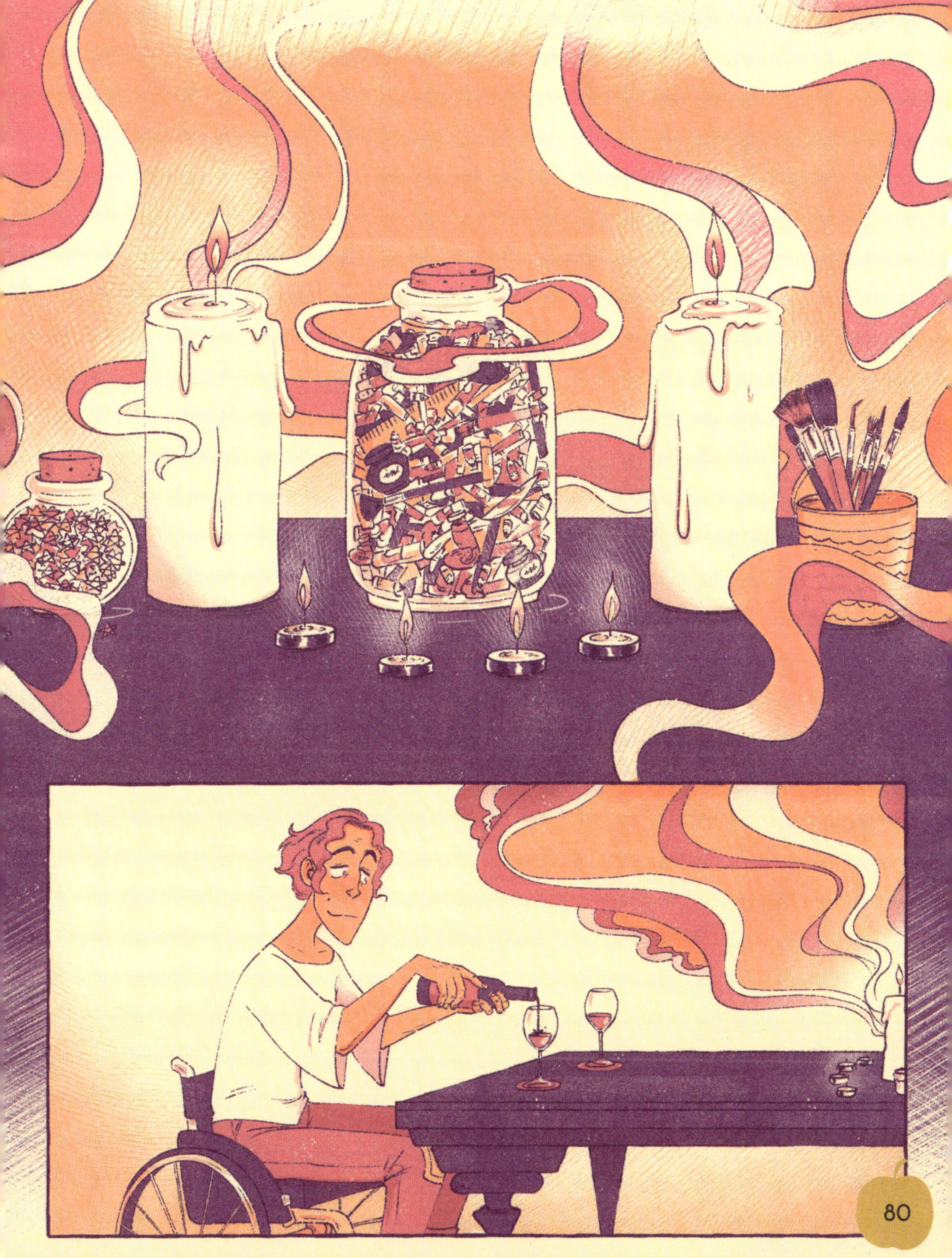

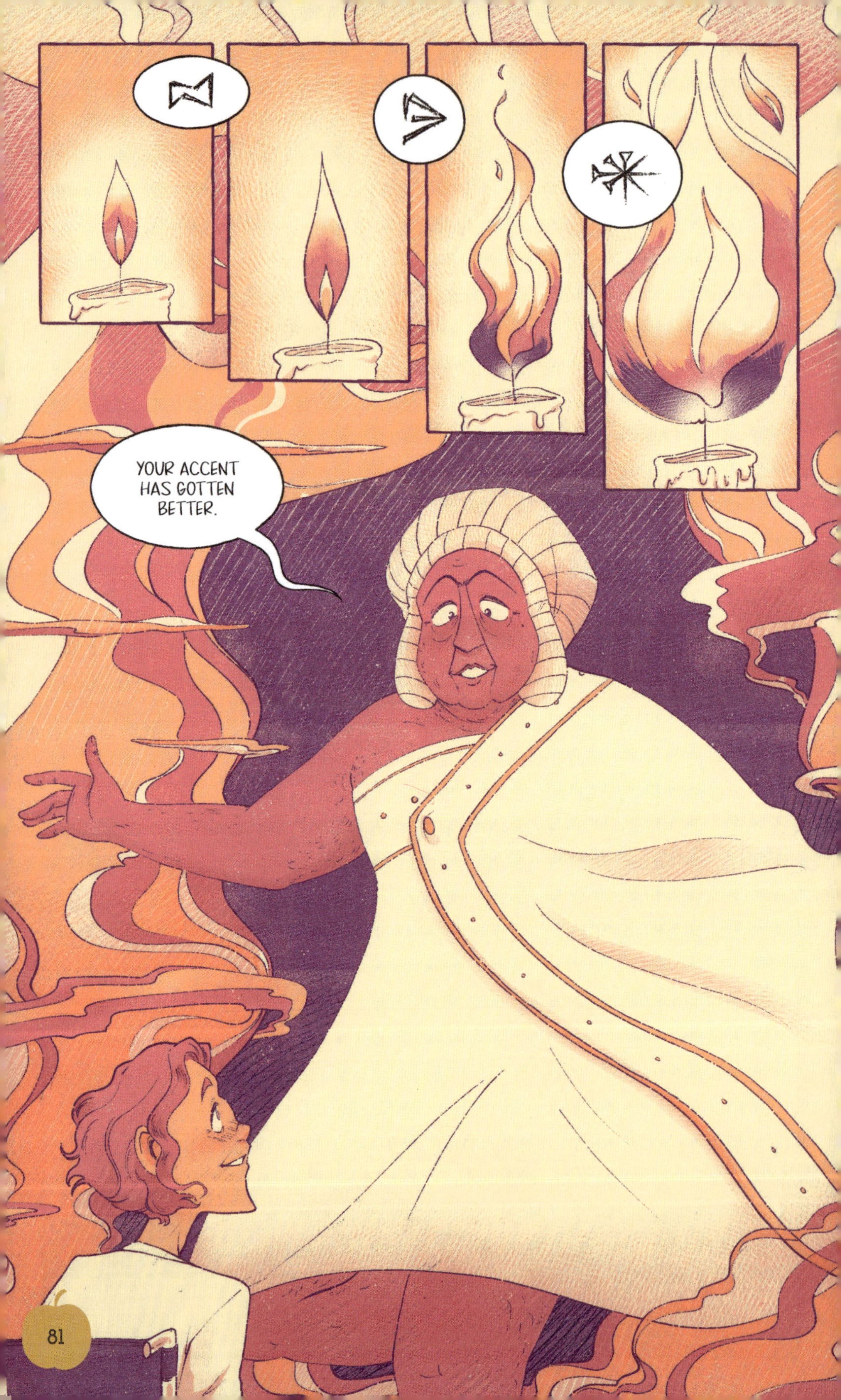
YOUR ACCENT HAS GOTTEN BETTER.

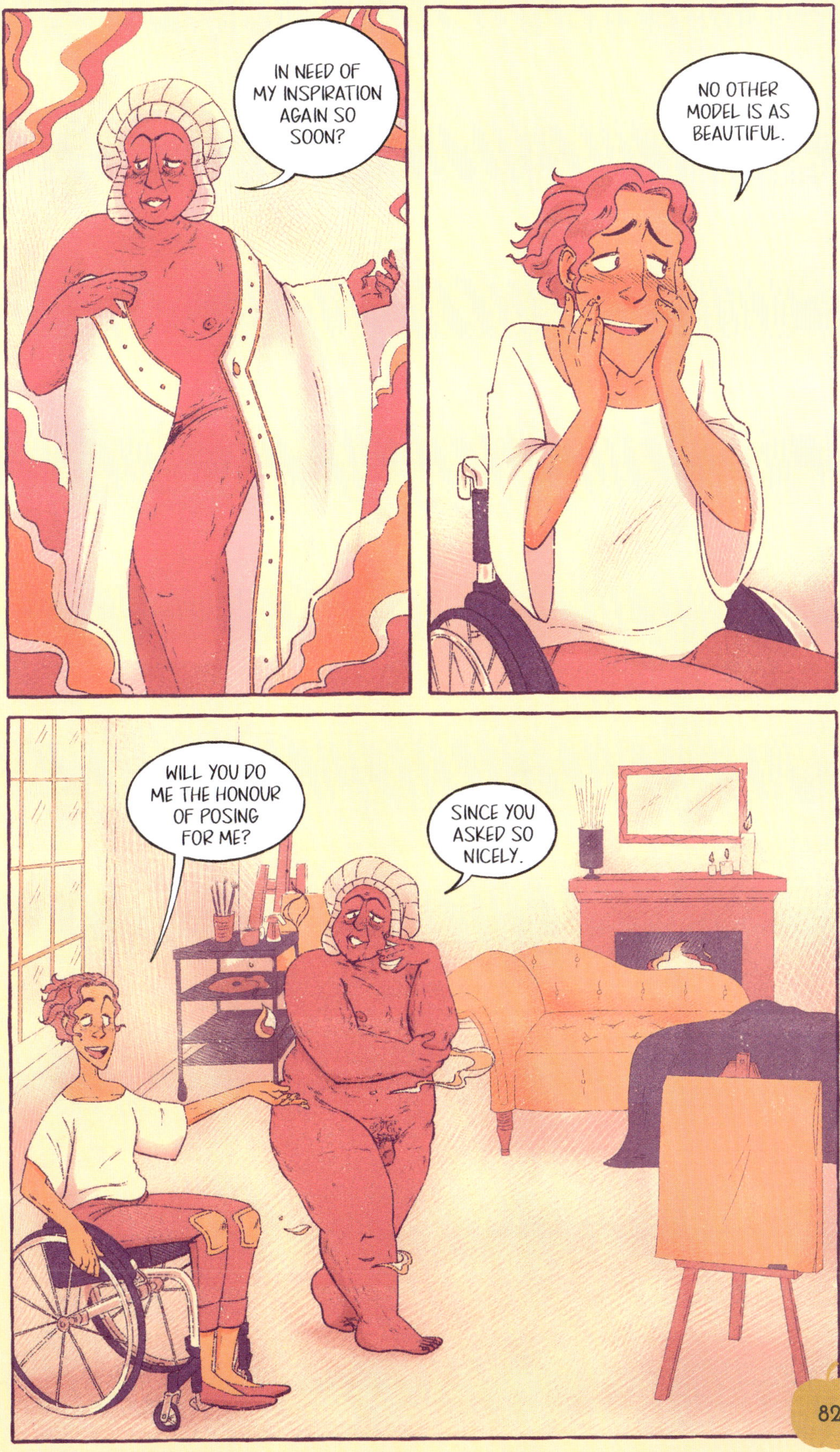
IN NEED OF MY INSPIRATION AGAIN SO SOON?
NO OTHER MODEL IS AS BEAUTIFUL.
WILL YOU DO ME THE HONOUR OF POSING FOR ME?
SINCE YOU ASKED SO NICELY.

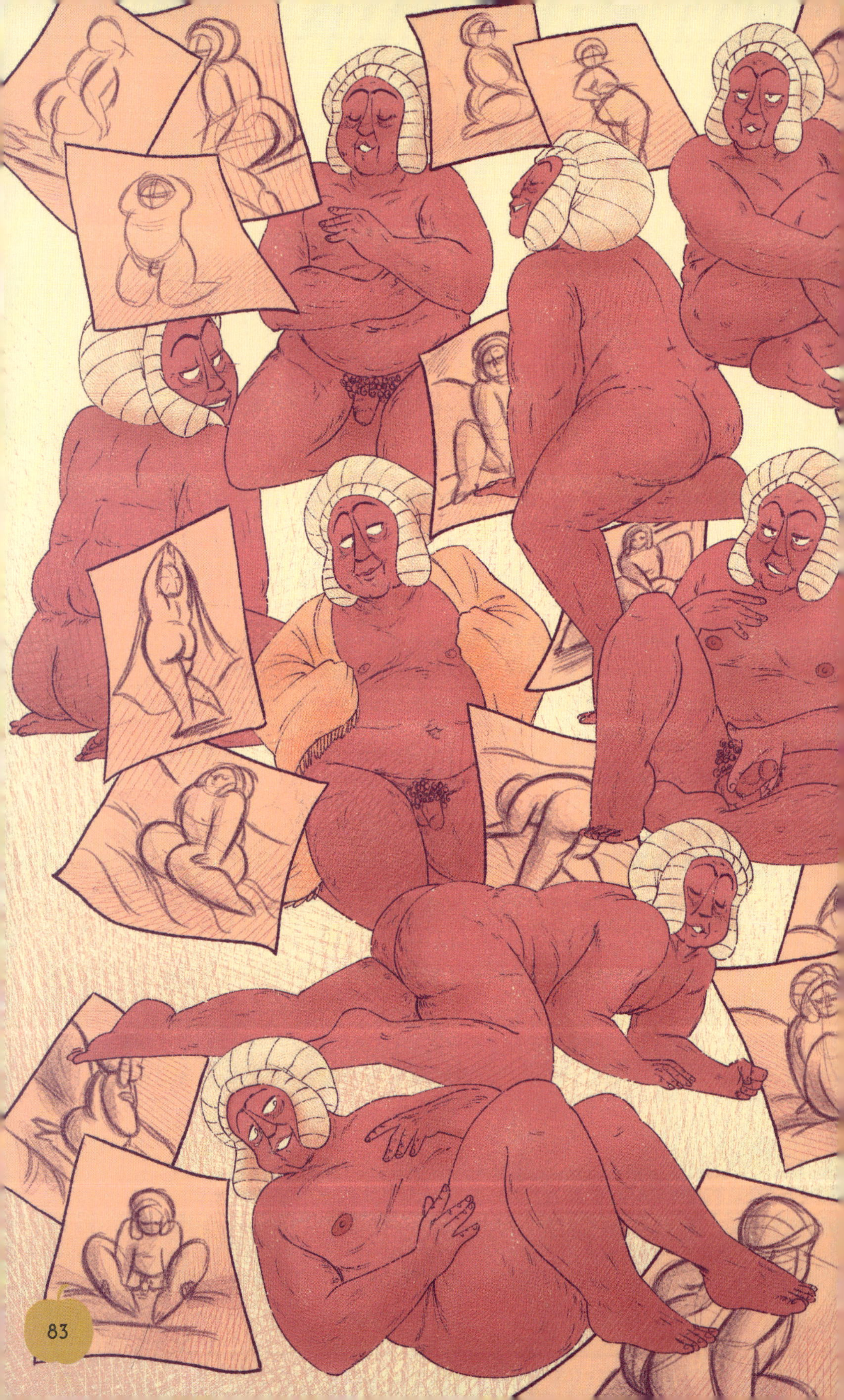

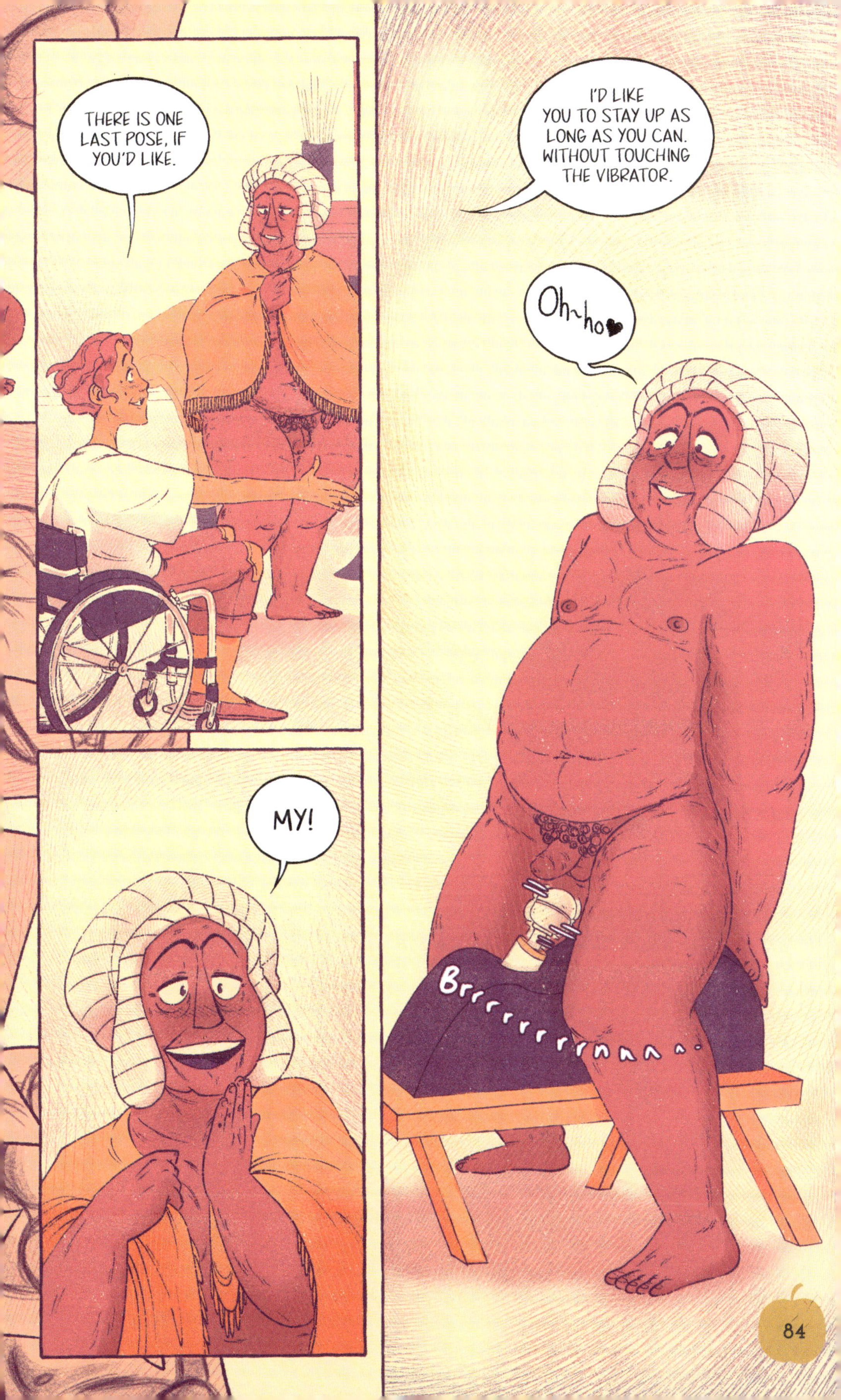
THERE IS ONE LAST POSE, IF YOU'D LIKE.
MY!
I'D LIKE YOU TO STAY UP AS LONG AS YOU CAN. WITHOUT TOUCHING THE VIBRATOR.
Oh~ho♥
Brrrrrrrrrnnnn..

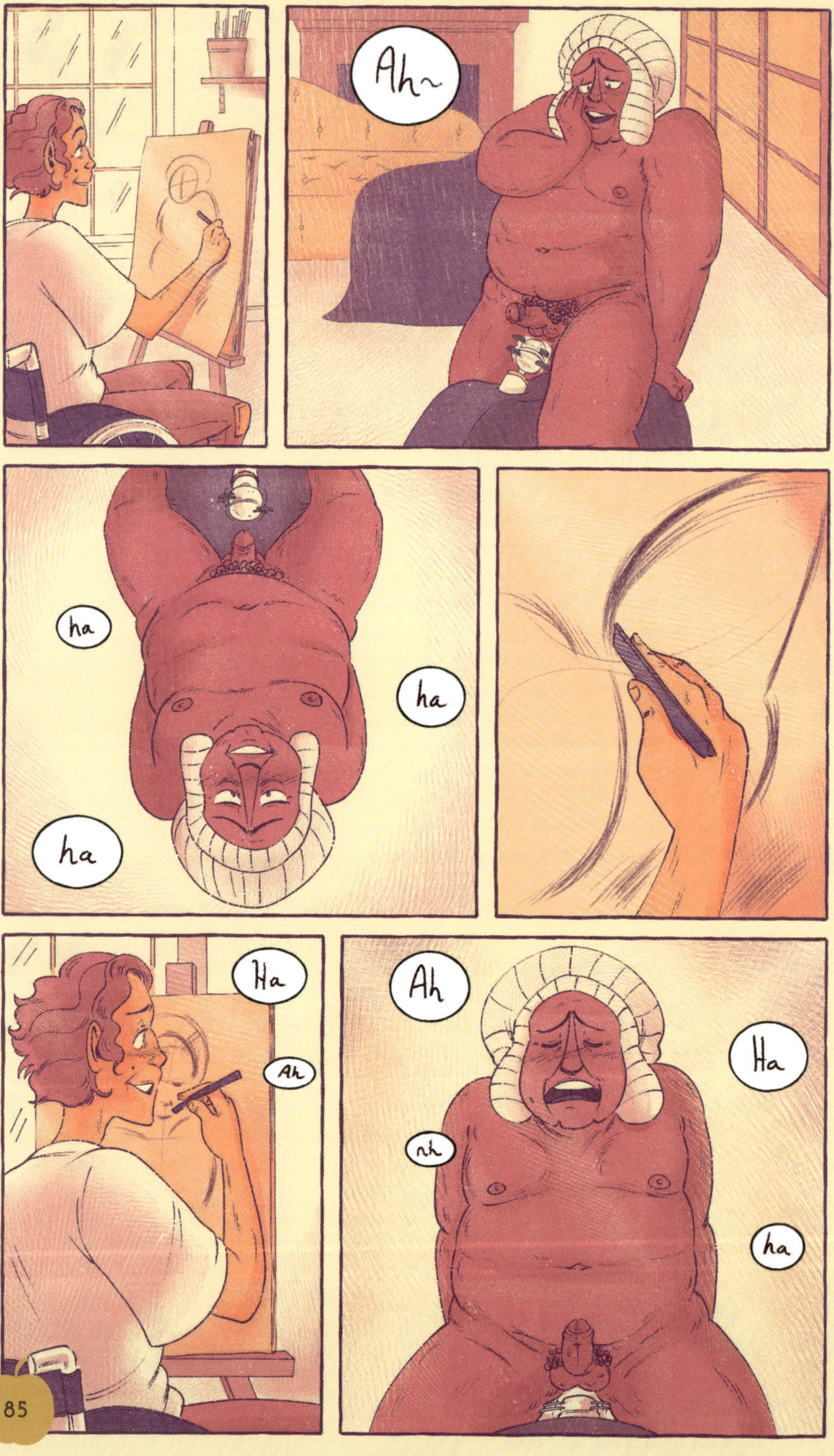
Ah~
ha
ha
ha
Ha
Ah
Ah
Ha
nh
ha

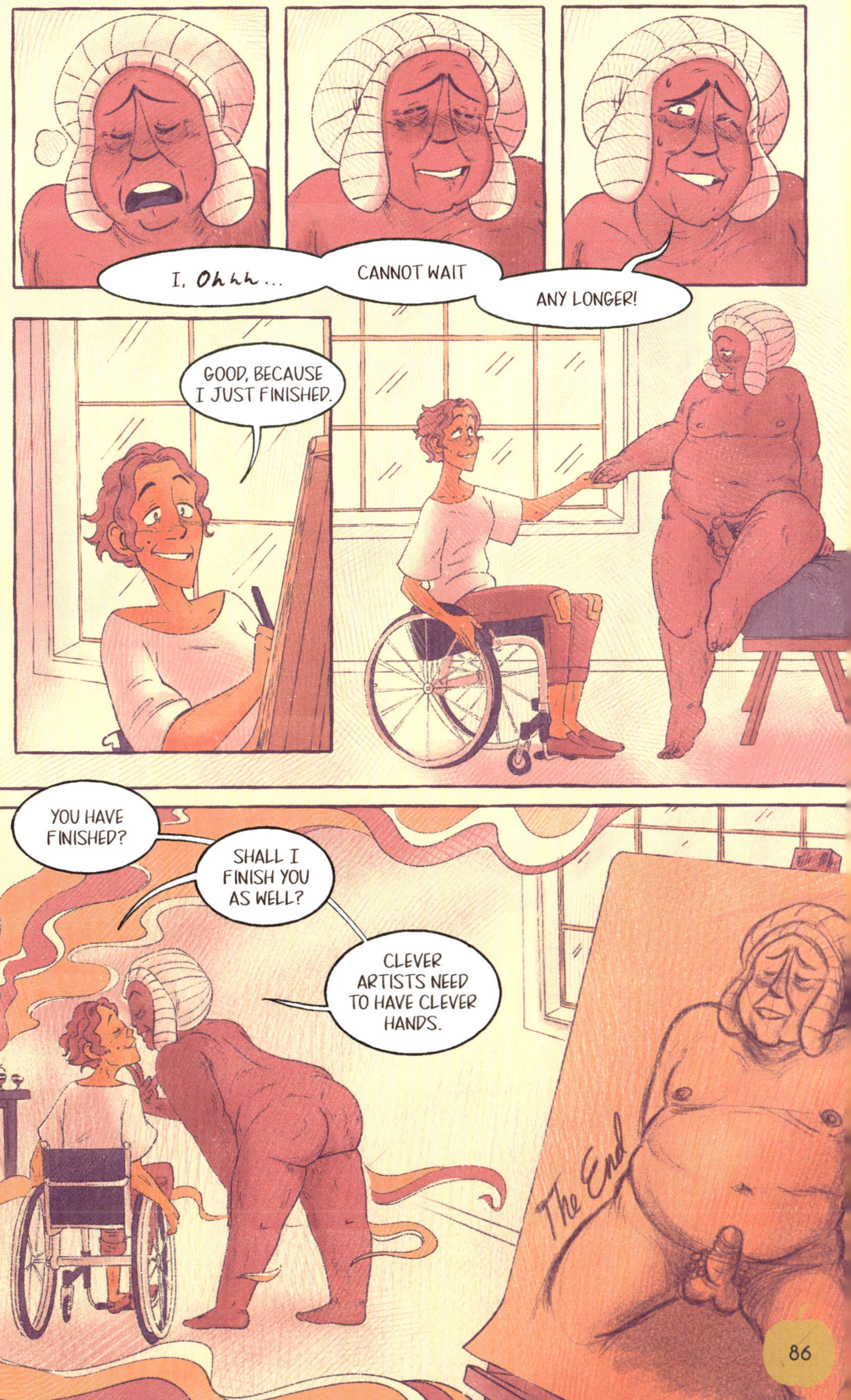
I, Ohhh...
CANNOT WAIT
ANY LONGER!
GOOD, BECAUSE I JUST FINISHED.
YOU HAVE FINISHED?
SHALL I FINISH YOU AS WELL?
CLEVER ARTISTS NEED TO HAVE CLEVER HANDS.
The End

A Little Friendly Competition

by NJ Barna

A pair of warriors compete in a series of trials, hoping to win favour and a night with a goddess. However the true test comes as they challenge the line between rival and romance.

Creator's Note

" I'm passionate about trans women in erotica!

I think our track record is pretty rough, and if you're a trans woman looking to see yourself in the things you get off to it can be a really rough time.

This story is a little love letter to the things I want in erotica- trans women allowed to be big and strong and still be cute and vulnerable, fat bodies being treated as hot on a mythic scale, and the closeness of rivals/ friends-to-lovers. I hope others enjoy it!! "

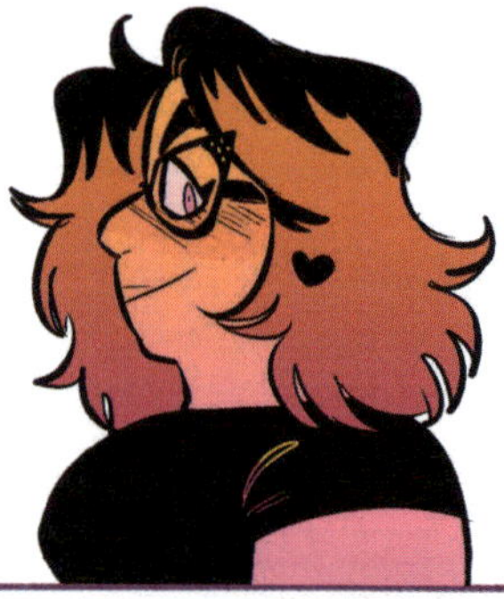

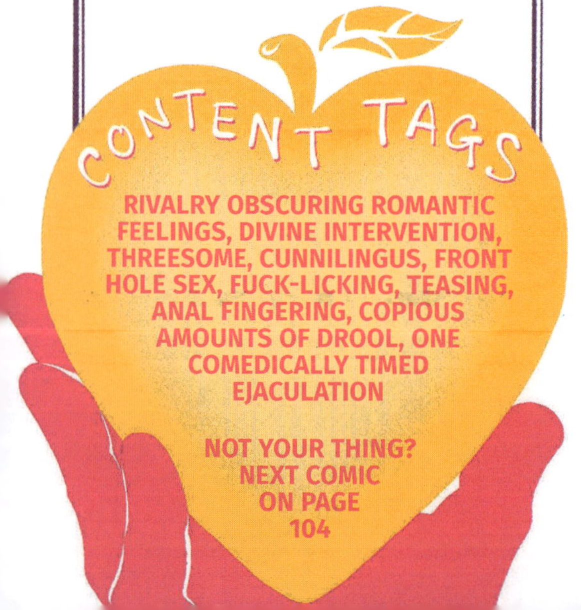

About the Creator

NJ "Nora Jawbones" Barna (she/her) is a transfemme comics powerhouse native to the American South.

She is fueled by her love of cool monsters, big women, and storytelling, and works full time making comics that feature these things.

If you thirst for more of her (less erotic) work, her webcomics include the superpowered action/rom-com Paradise and the underwater sci-fi/horror Anagenesis.

NeonJawbonePortfolio .tumblr.com

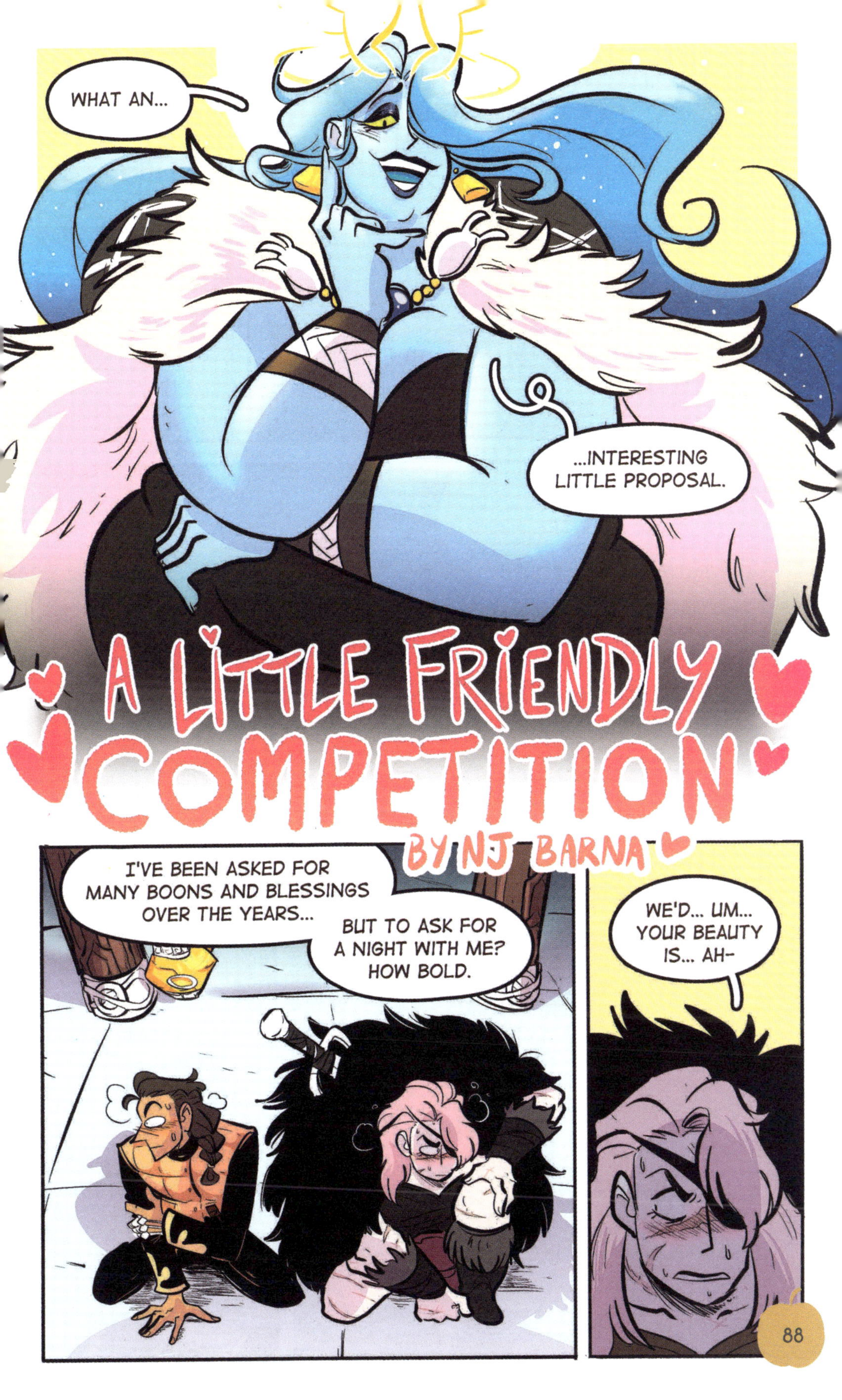

WHAT AN...
...INTERESTING LITTLE PROPOSAL.
A LITTLE FRIENDLY COMPETITION
BY NJ BARNA
I'VE BEEN ASKED FOR MANY BOONS AND BLESSINGS OVER THE YEARS...
BUT TO ASK FOR A NIGHT WITH ME? HOW BOLD.
WE'D... UM... YOUR BEAUTY IS... AH-

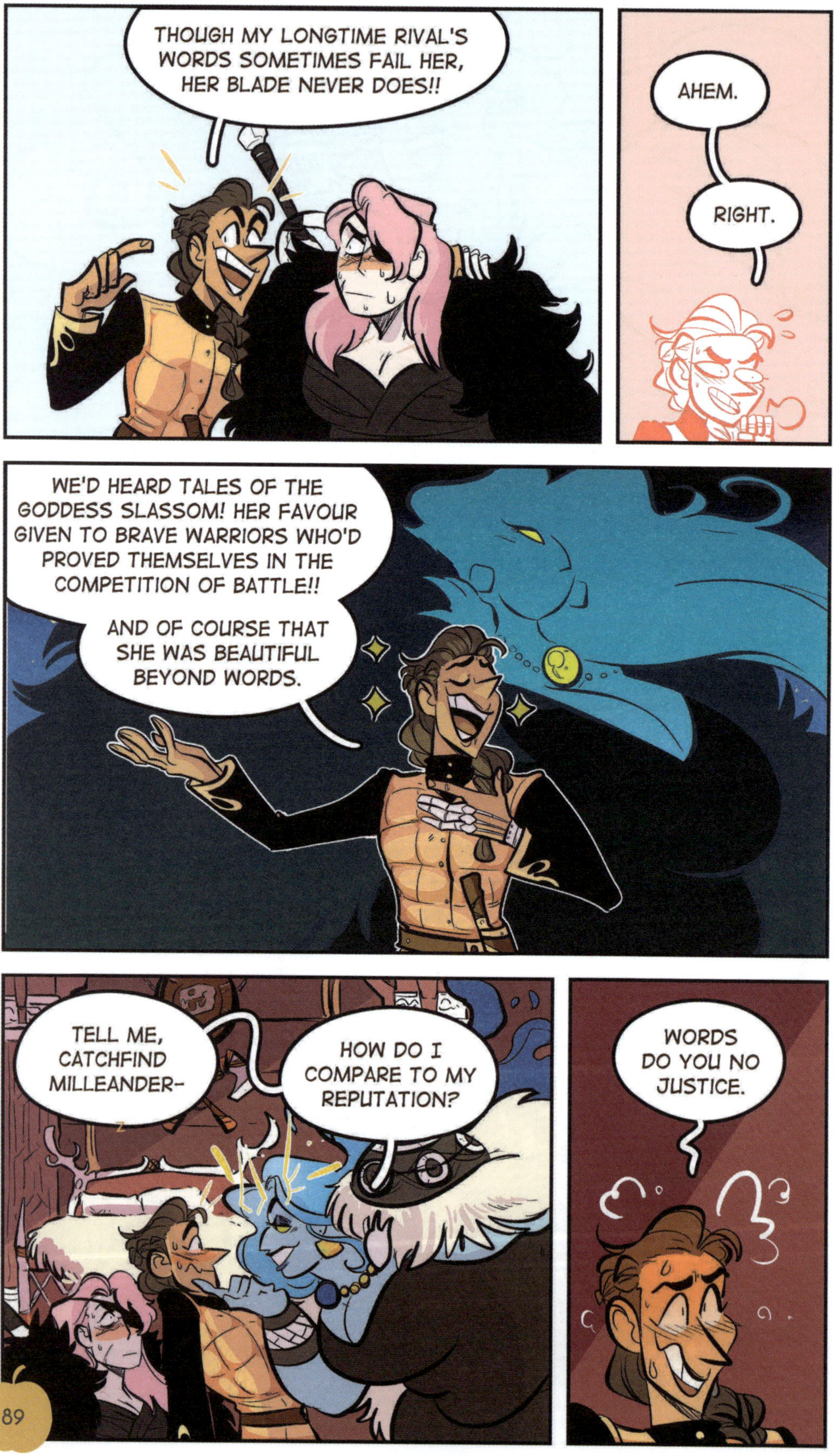
THOUGH MY LONGTIME RIVAL'S WORDS SOMETIMES FAIL HER, HER BLADE NEVER DOES!!
AHEM.
RIGHT.
WE'D HEARD TALES OF THE GODDESS SLASSOM! HER FAVOUR GIVEN TO BRAVE WARRIORS WHO'D PROVED THEMSELVES IN THE COMPETITION OF BATTLE!!
AND OF COURSE THAT SHE WAS BEAUTIFUL BEYOND WORDS.
TELL ME, CATCHFIND MILLEANDER-
HOW DO I COMPARE TO MY REPUTATION?
WORDS DO YOU NO JUSTICE.

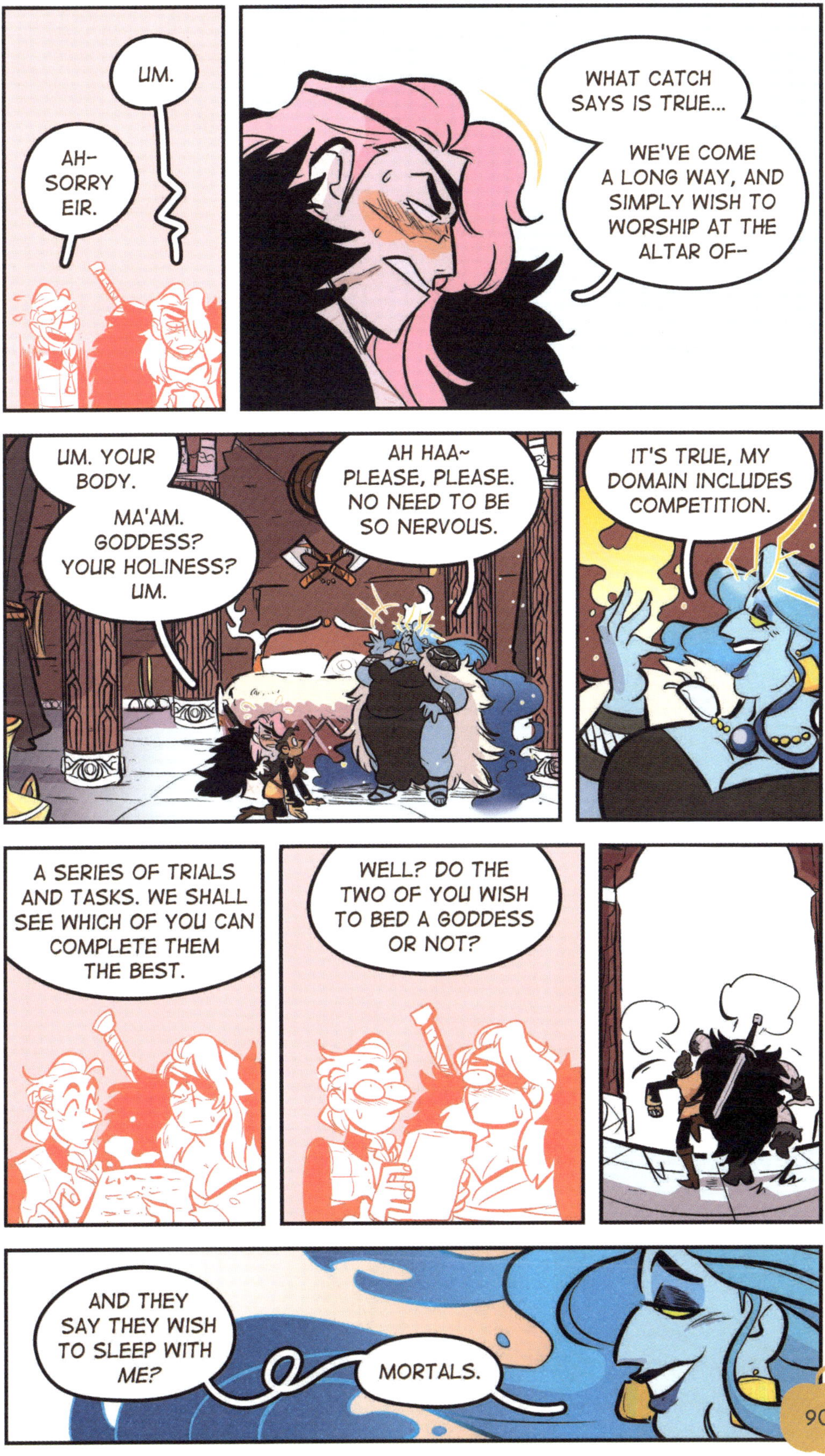
UM.
AH- SORRY EIR.
WHAT CATCH SAYS IS TRUE...
WE'VE COME A LONG WAY, AND SIMPLY WISH TO WORSHIP AT THE ALTAR OF-
UM. YOUR BODY.
MA'AM. GODDESS? YOUR HOLINESS? UM.
AH HAA~ PLEASE, PLEASE. NO NEED TO BE SO NERVOUS.
IT'S TRUE, MY DOMAIN INCLUDES COMPETITION.
A SERIES OF TRIALS AND TASKS. WE SHALL SEE WHICH OF YOU CAN COMPLETE THEM THE BEST.
WELL? DO THE TWO OF YOU WISH TO BED A GODDESS OR NOT?
AND THEY SAY THEY WISH TO SLEEP WITH ME?
MORTALS.

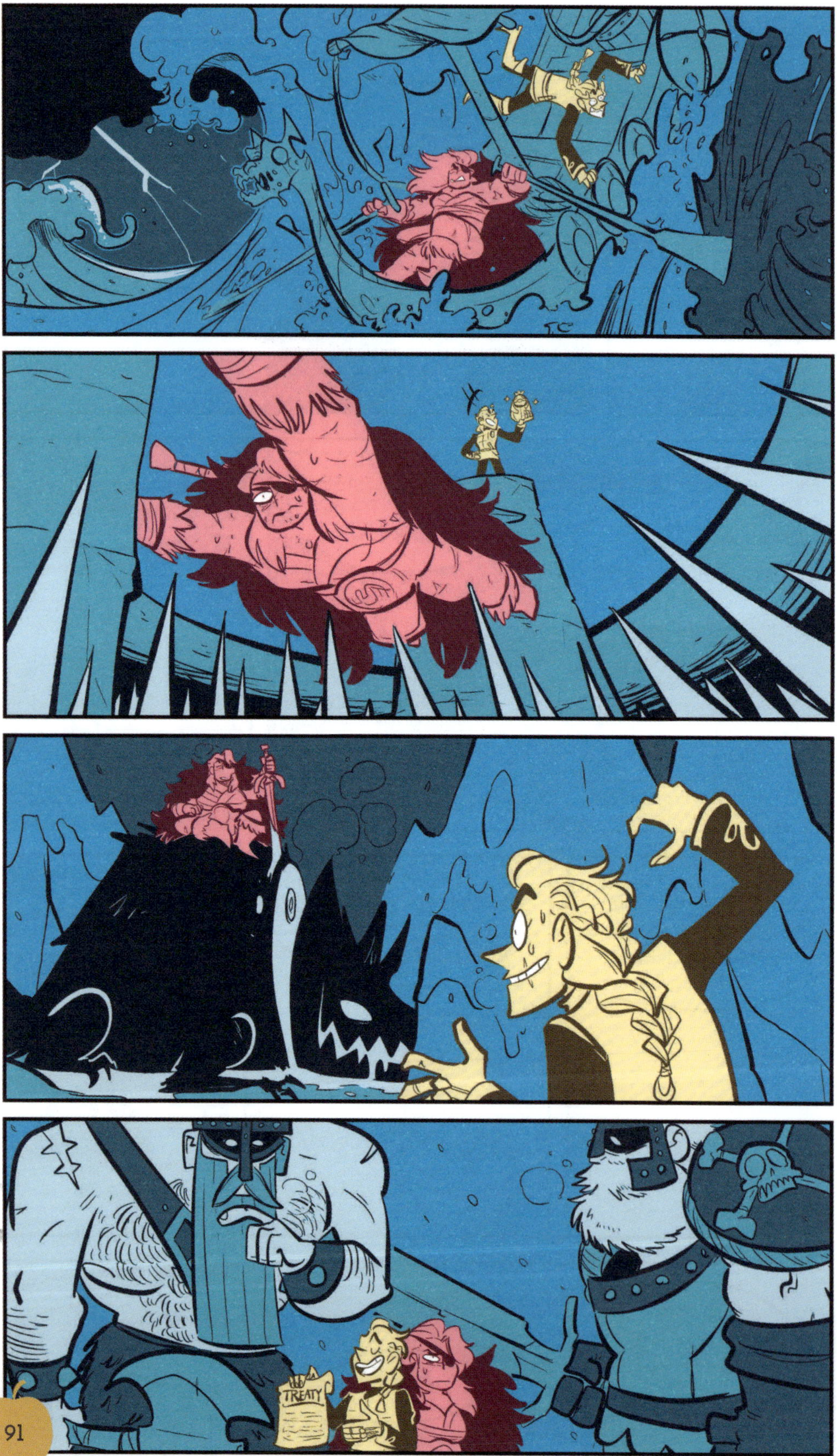
TREATY

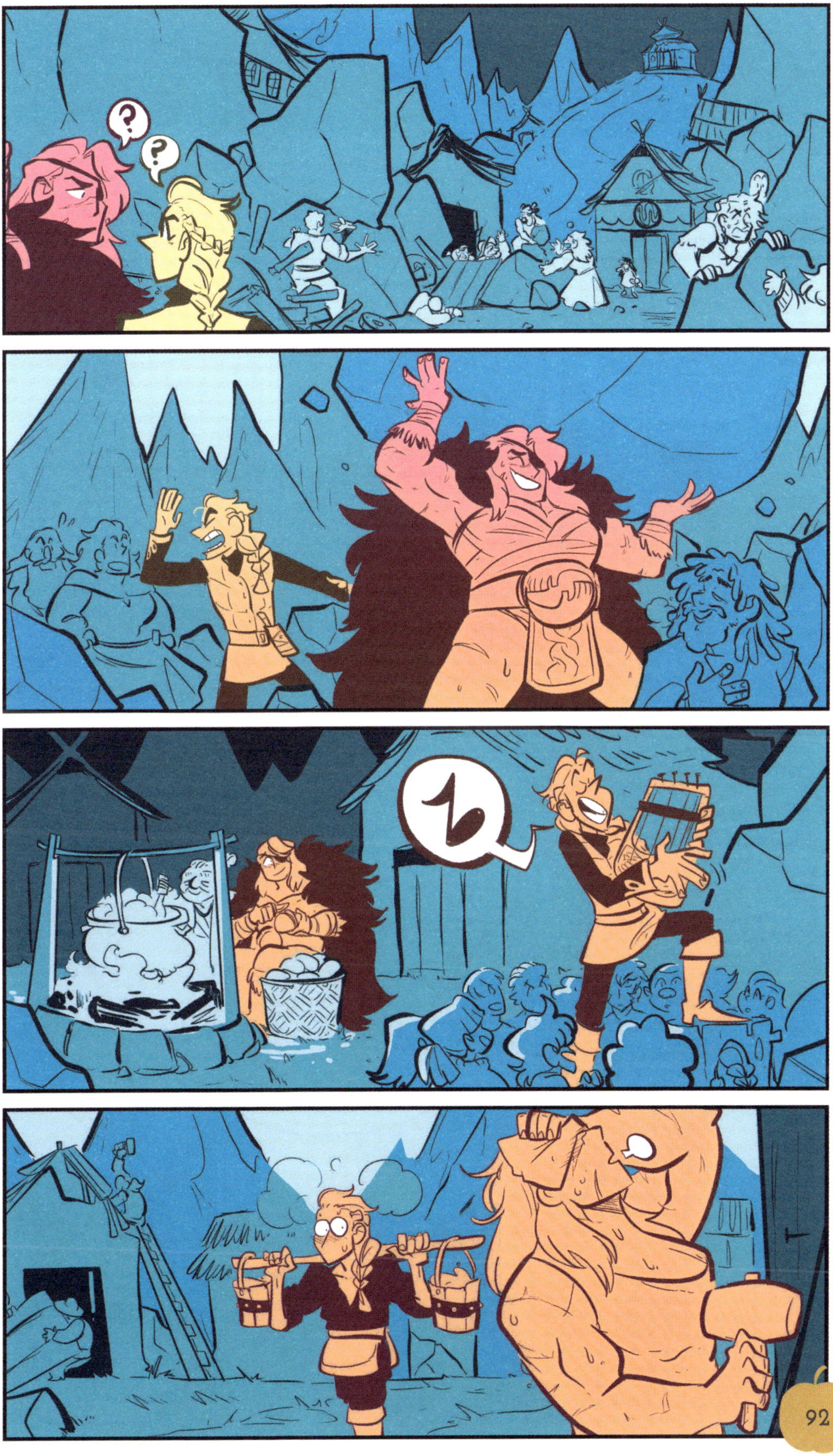

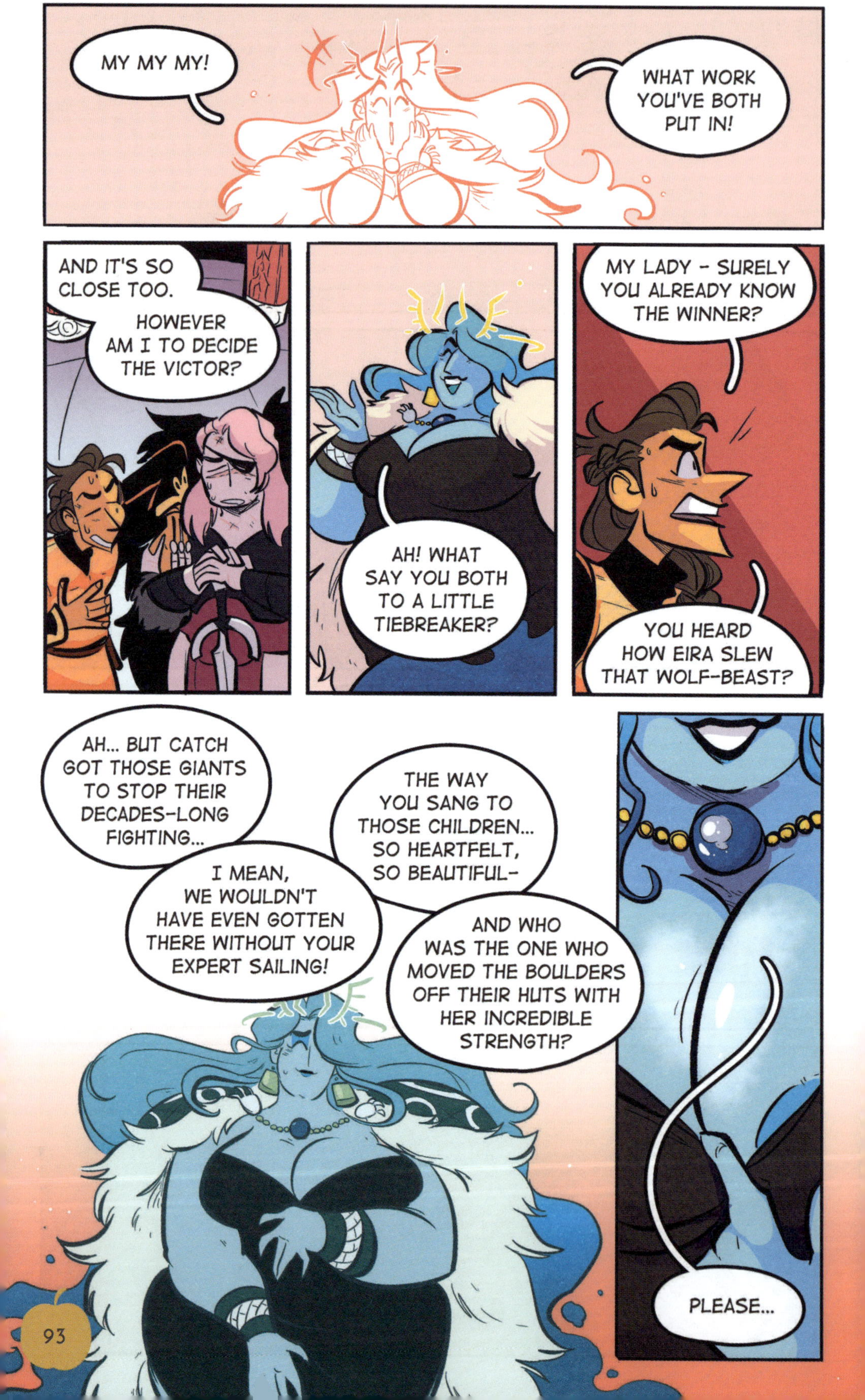
MY MY MY!
WHAT WORK YOU'VE BOTH PUT IN!
AND IT'S SO CLOSE TOO.
HOWEVER AM I TO DECIDE THE VICTOR?
AH! WHAT SAY YOU BOTH TO A LITTLE TIEBREAKER?
MY LADY - SURELY YOU ALREADY KNOW THE WINNER?
YOU HEARD HOW EIRA SLEW THAT WOLF-BEAST?
AH... BUT CATCH GOT THOSE GIANTS TO STOP THEIR DECADES-LONG FIGHTING...
THE WAY YOU SANG TO THOSE CHILDREN... SO HEARTFELT, SO BEAUTIFUL-
I MEAN, WE WOULDN'T HAVE EVEN GOTTEN THERE WITHOUT YOUR EXPERT SAILING!
AND WHO WAS THE ONE WHO MOVED THE BOULDERS OFF THEIR HUTS WITH HER INCREDIBLE STRENGTH?
PLEASE...

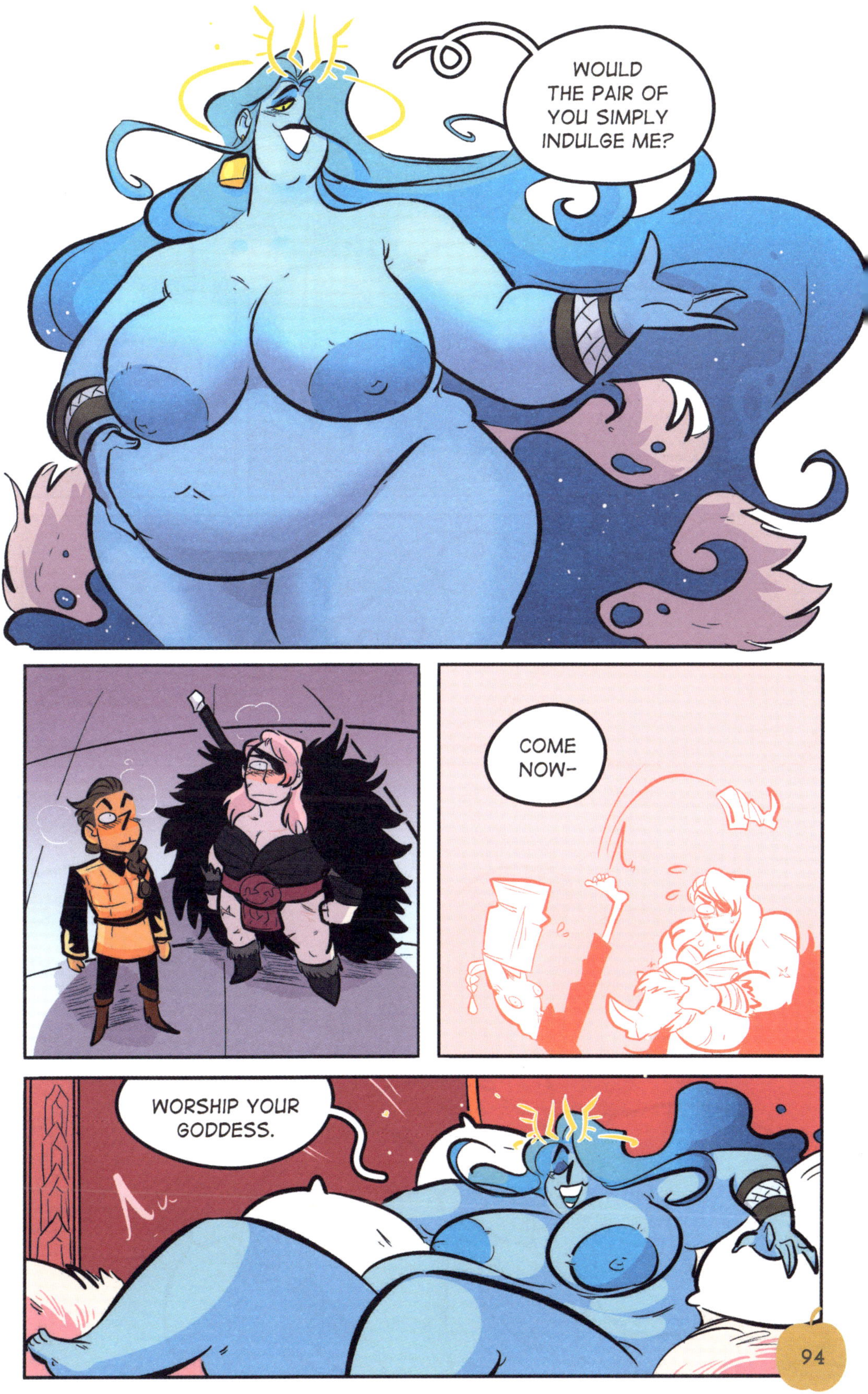
WOULD THE PAIR OF YOU SIMPLY INDULGE ME?
COME NOW-
WORSHIP YOUR GODDESS.

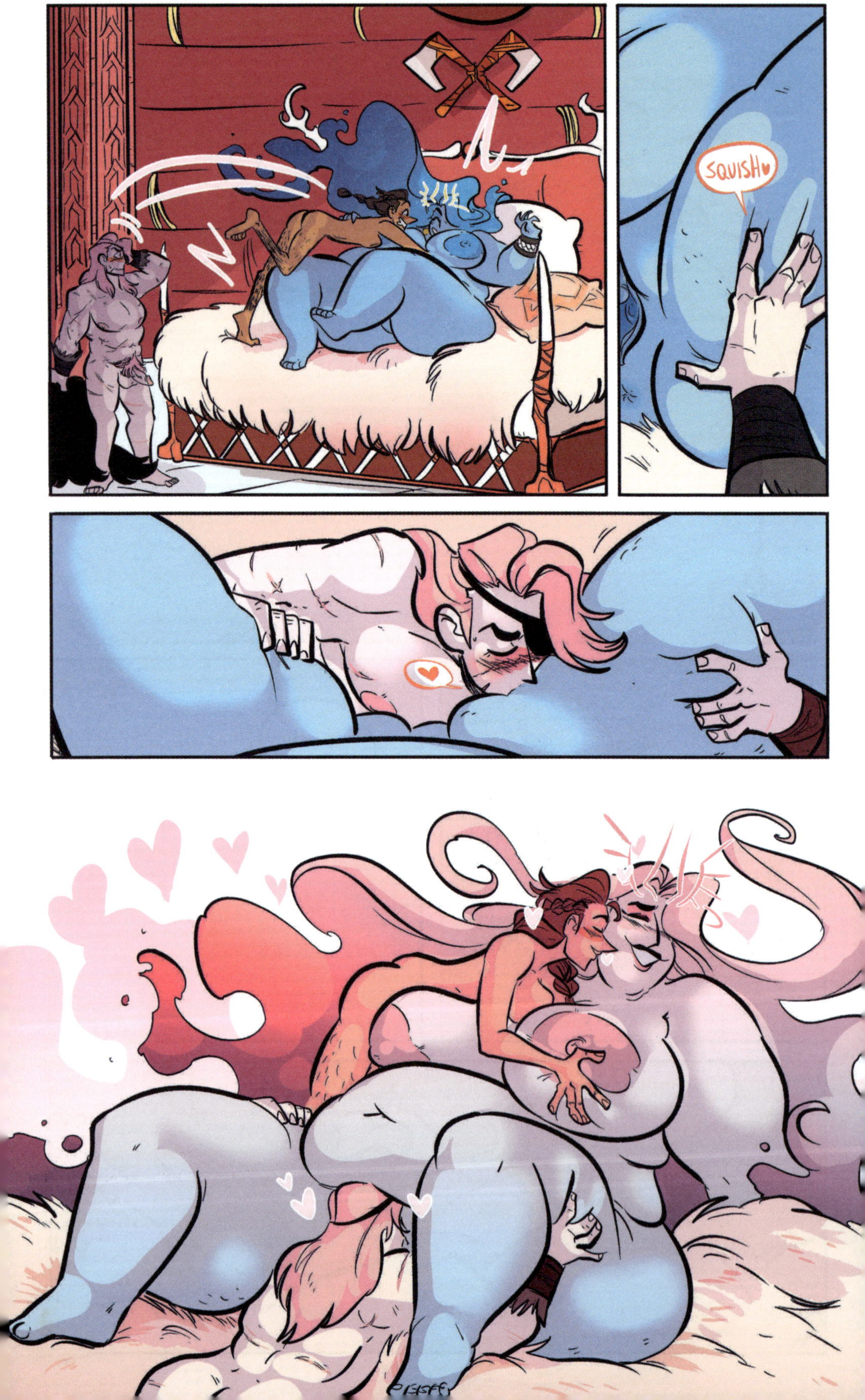
SQUISH♥

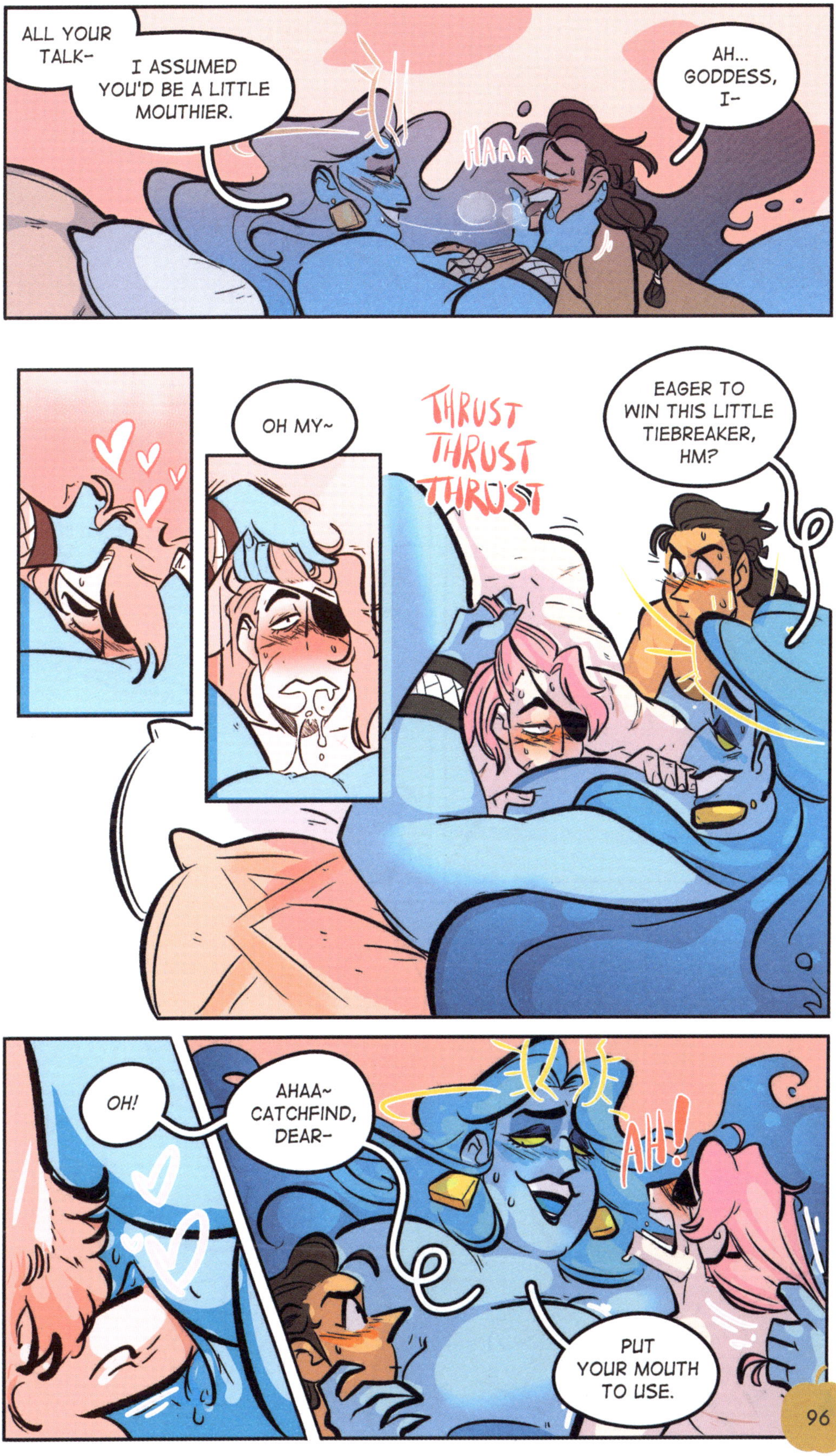
ALL YOUR TALK-
I ASSUMED YOU'D BE A LITTLE MOUTHIER.
HAAA
AH... GODDESS, I-
OH MY~
THRUST THRUST THRUST
EAGER TO WIN THIS LITTLE TIEBREAKER, HM?
OH!
AHAA~ CATCHFIND, DEAR-
AH!
PUT YOUR MOUTH TO USE.

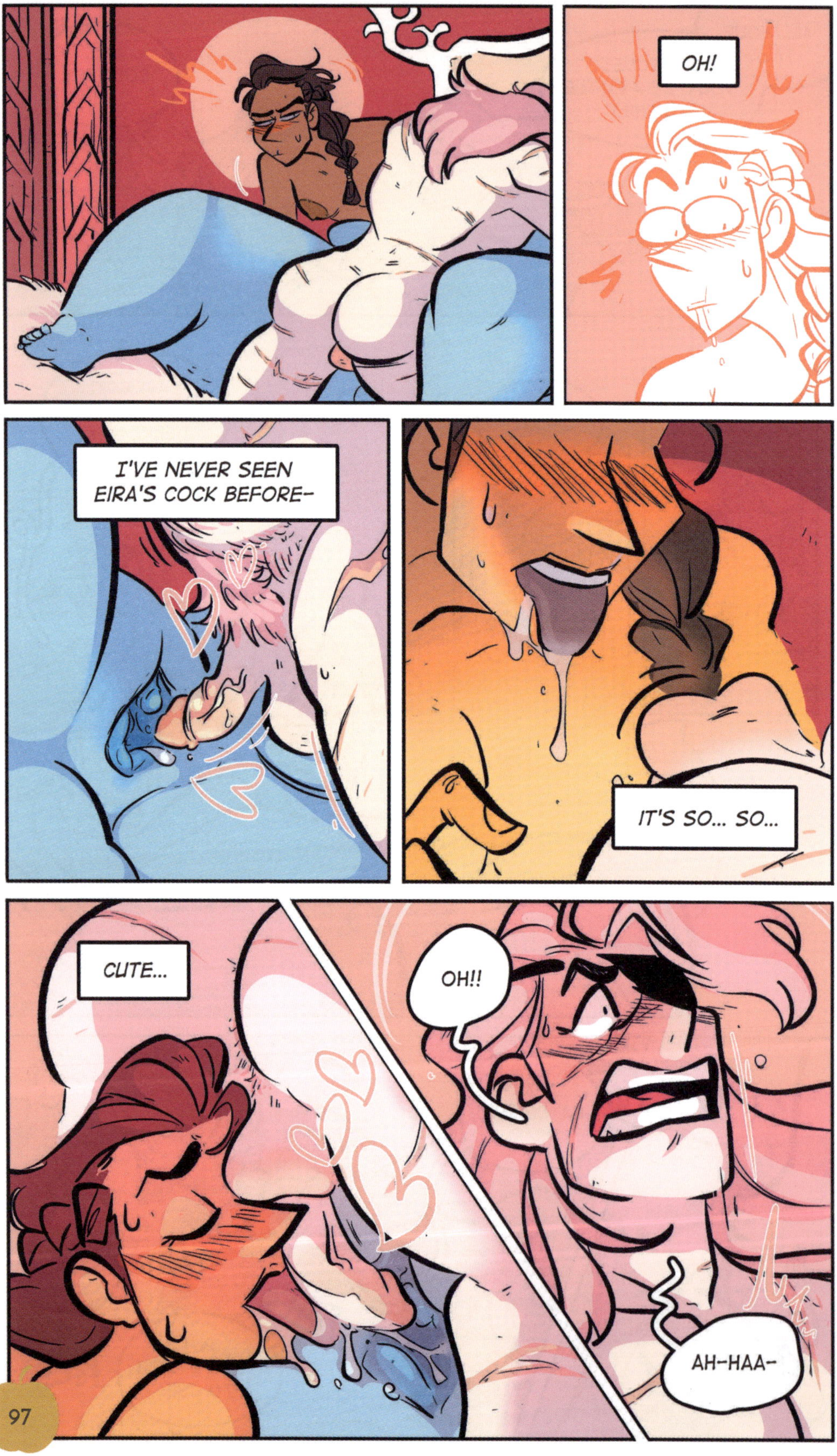
OH!
I'VE NEVER SEEN EIRA'S COCK BEFORE-
IT'S SO... SO...
CUTE...
OH!!
AH-HAA-

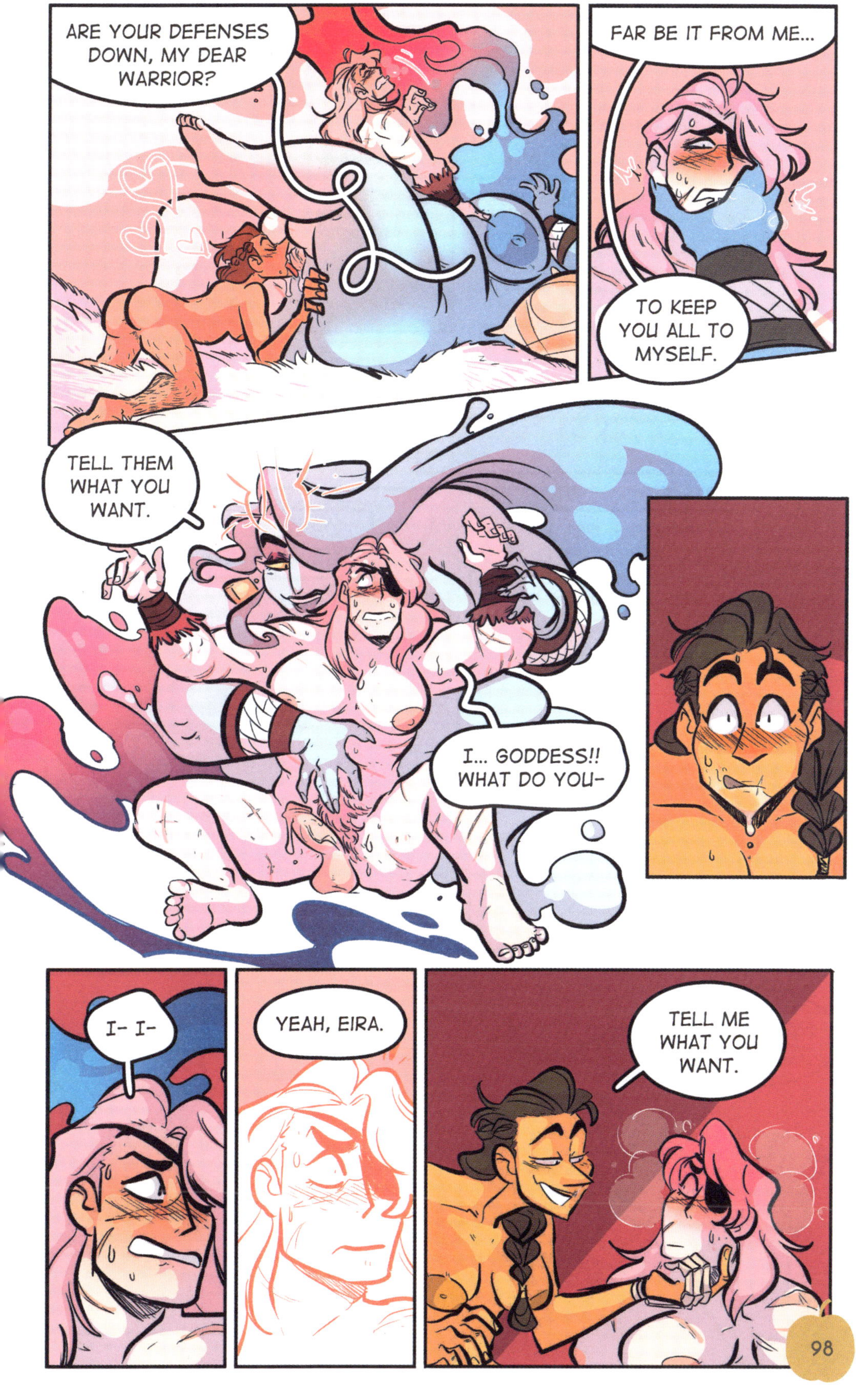
ARE YOUR DEFENSES DOWN, MY DEAR WARRIOR?
FAR BE IT FROM ME...
TO KEEP YOU ALL TO MYSELF.
TELL THEM WHAT YOU WANT.
I... GODDESS!! WHAT DO YOU-
I- I-
YEAH, EIRA.
TELL ME WHAT YOU WANT.

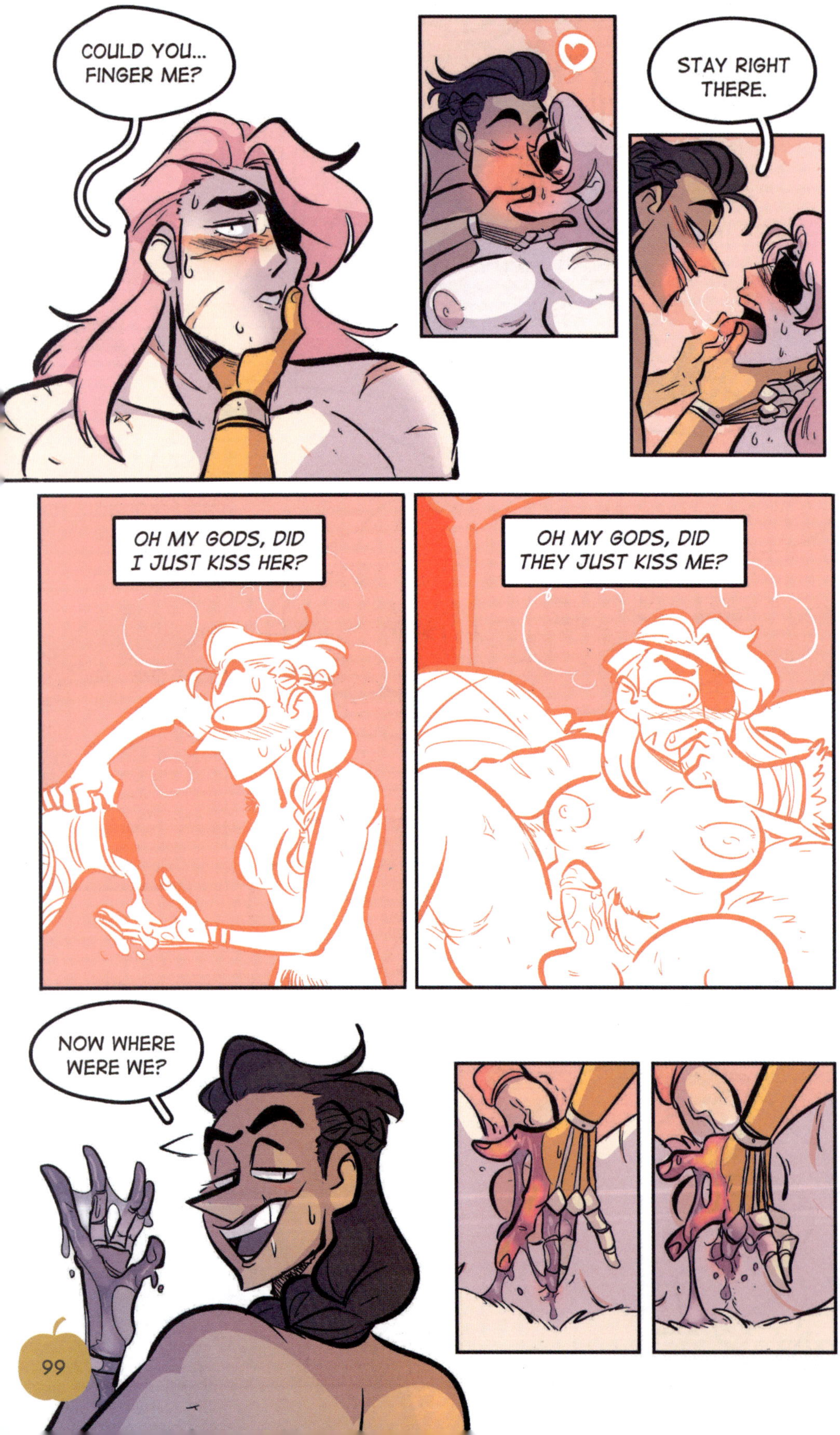
COULD YOU... FINGER ME?
STAY RIGHT THERE.
OH MY GODS, DID I JUST KISS HER?
OH MY GODS, DID THEY JUST KISS ME?
NOW WHERE WERE WE?

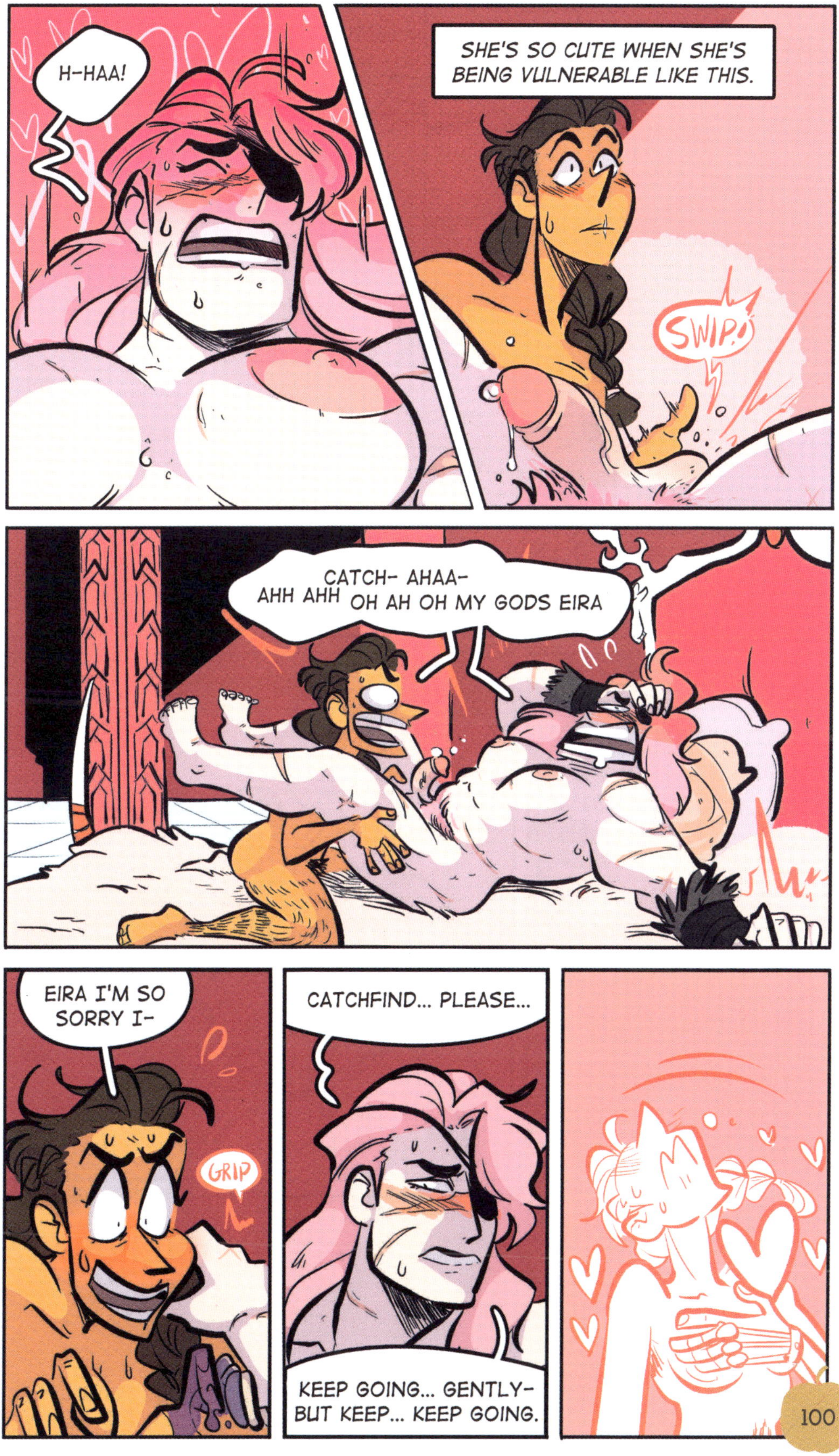
H-HAA!
SHE'S SO CUTE WHEN SHE'S BEING VULNERABLE LIKE THIS.
SWIP!
CATCH- AHAA- AHH AHH OH AH OH MY GODS EIRA
EIRA I'M SO SORRY I-
GRIP
CATCHFIND... PLEASE...
KEEP GOING... GENTLY- BUT KEEP... KEEP GOING.

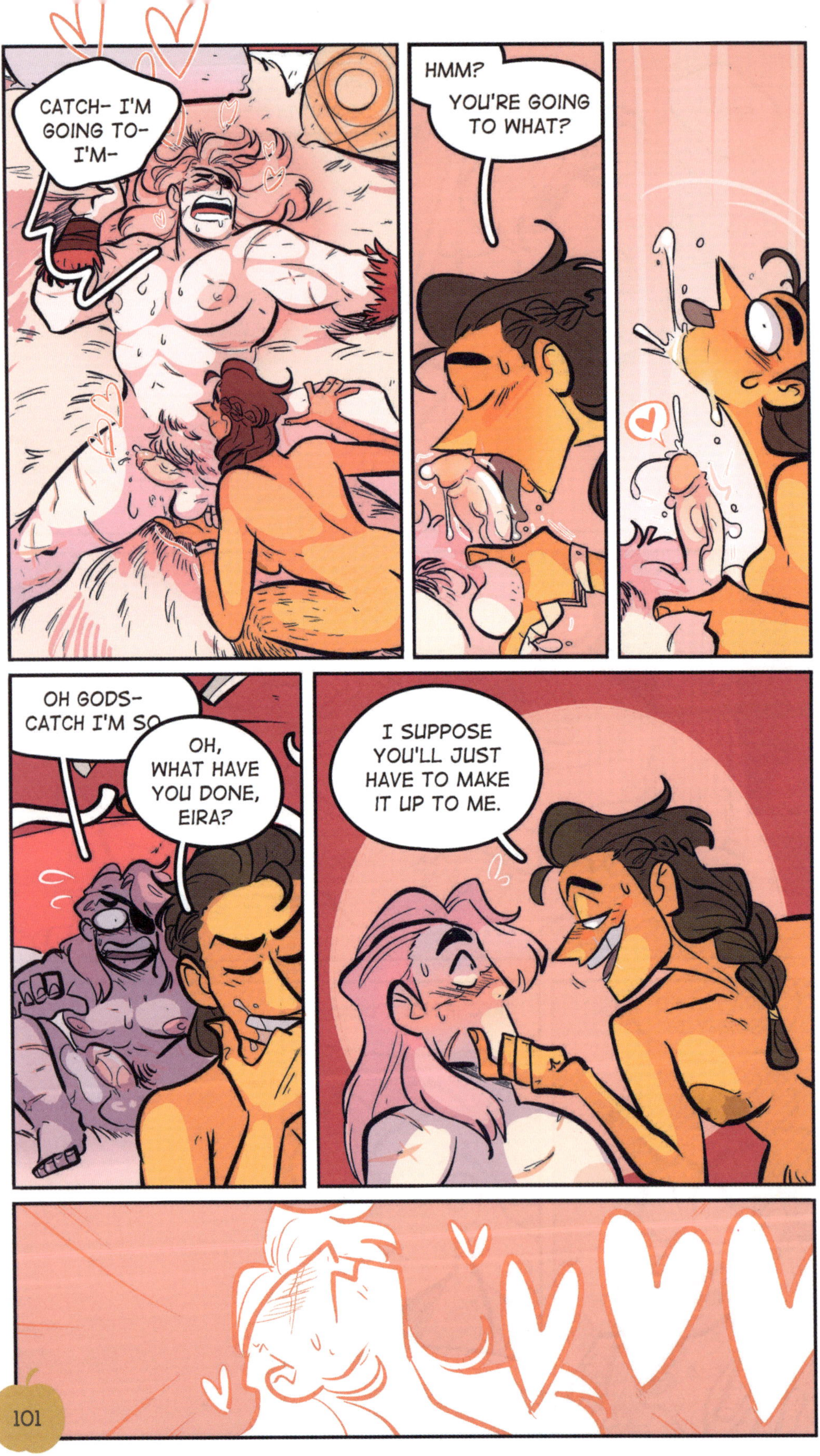
CATCH- I'M GOING TO- I'M-
HMM?
YOU'RE GOING TO WHAT?
OH GODS- CATCH I'M SO
OH, WHAT HAVE YOU DONE, EIRA?
I SUPPOSE YOU'LL JUST HAVE TO MAKE IT UP TO ME.

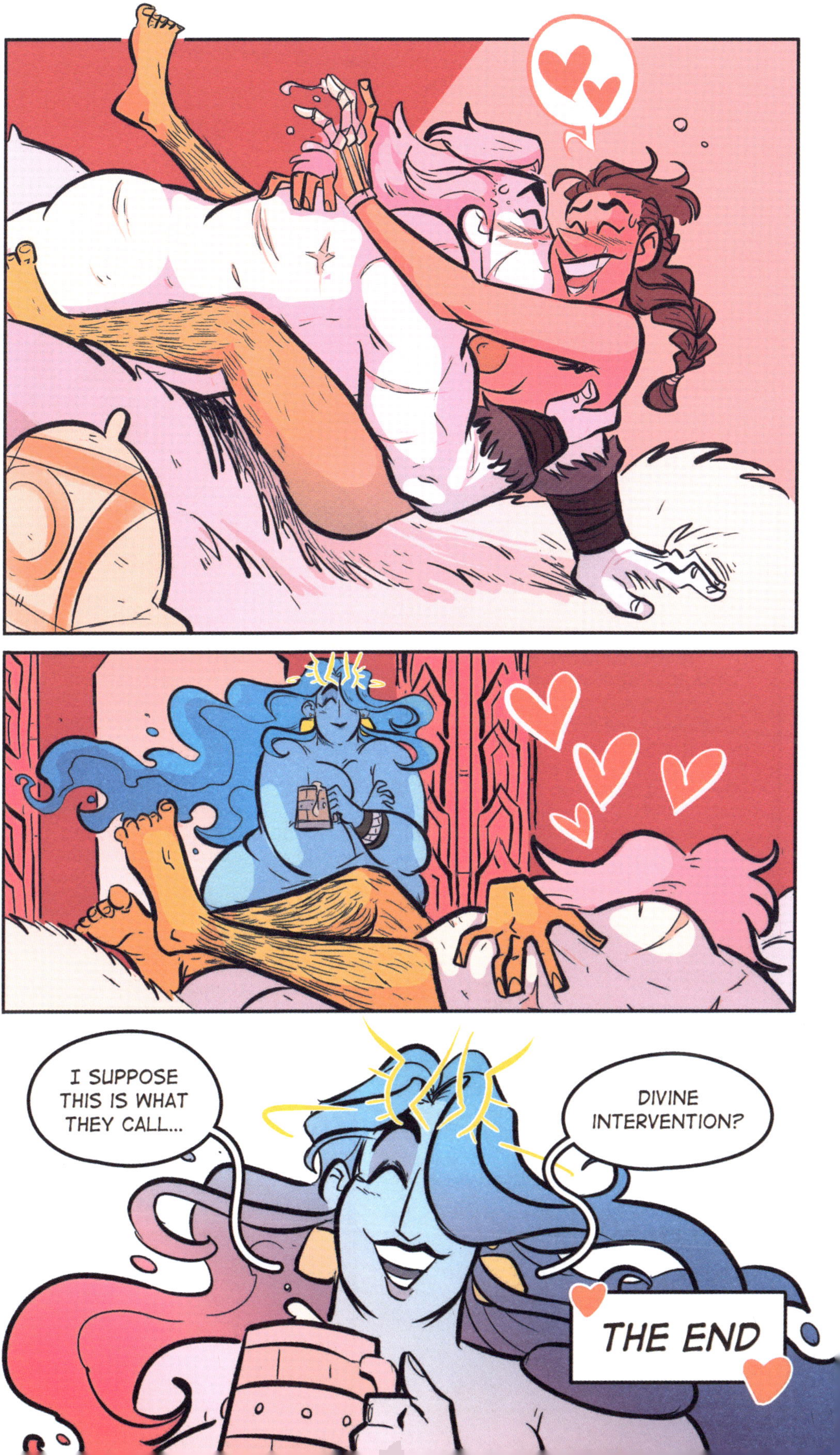
I SUPPOSE THIS IS WHAT THEY CALL...
DIVINE INTERVENTION?
THE END

Divine

Story by Jaylee Warren - Art by Kori Michele Handwerker

Distracted by intrusive thoughts, Queen Poseidon descends into the sea where she is embraced by and is submissive to her lover, a sea witch.

Writer's Note

" With Divine I wanted to acknowledge the way our humanity feels up for debate and scrutiny in public spaces, and show how trust and intimacy in our private lives can be a balm for these burdens.

I decided to use submission to a loving partner to illustrate the freedom we feel when we're given space to be our authentic selves.

When you spend your days being hyper-vigilant against bigotry, feeling comfortable enough to let your guard down can be euphoric and empowering. "

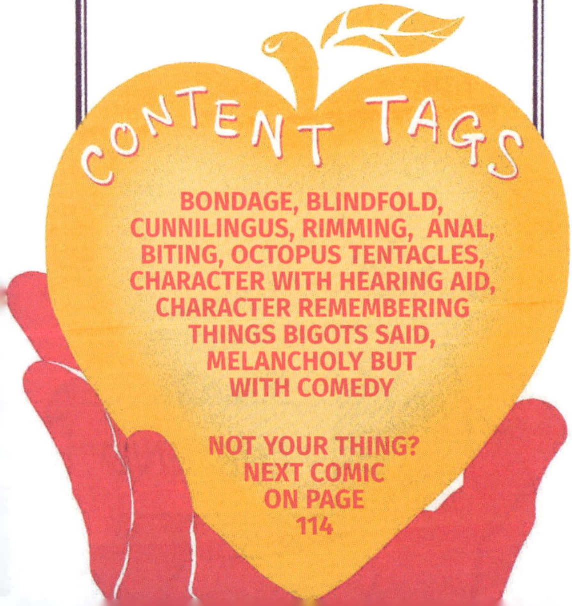

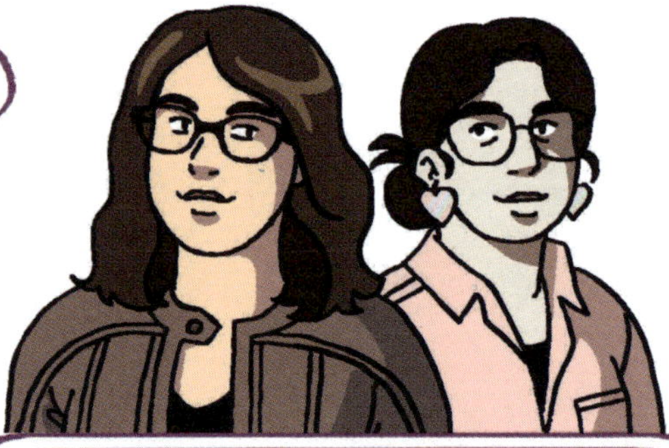

About the Creators

Jaylee Warren (she/her) is a queer trans writer from the Pacific Northwest. Her debut comic, "Growth," was featured in the second volume of the Beyond Anthology.

When she isn't writing comics about queer resilience and joy, she passes the time painting miniatures and overthinking video games.

Twitter.com/JustJaylee

Kori Michele Handwerker (they/them) draws comics and makes zines out of the northeastern United States.

By day they teach about comics publishing and by night they draw stories about identity, transness, romance, and monsters.

KoriMichele.com

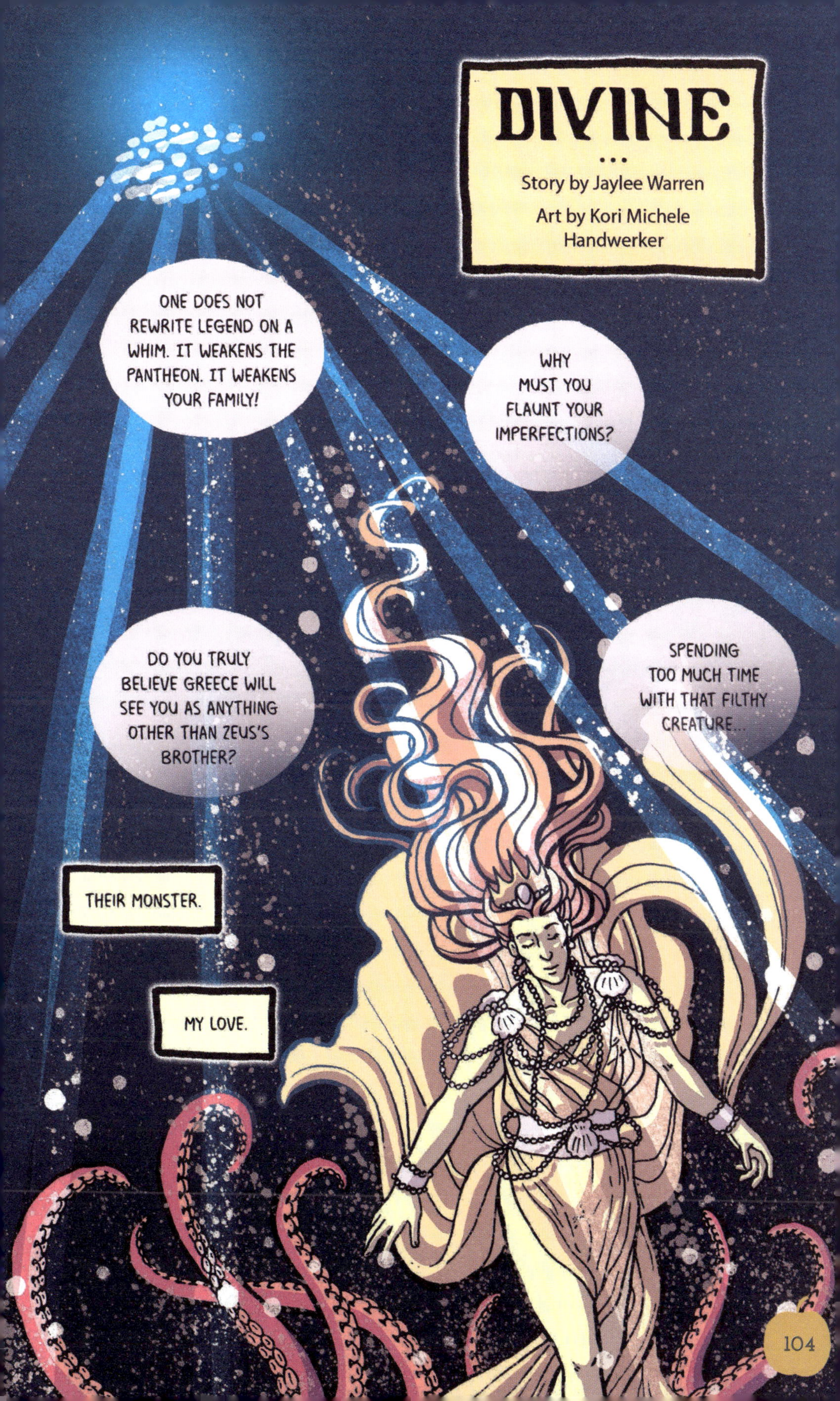
DIVINE
Story by Jaylee Warren
Art by Kori Michele Handwerker
ONE DOES NOT REWRITE LEGEND ON A WHIM. IT WEAKENS THE PANTHEON. IT WEAKENS YOUR FAMILY!
WHY MUST YOU FLAUNT YOUR IMPERFECTIONS?
DO YOU TRULY BELIEVE GREECE WILL SEE YOU AS ANYTHING OTHER THAN ZEUS'S BROTHER?
SPENDING TOO MUCH TIME WITH THAT FILTHY CREATURE...
THEIR MONSTER.
MY LOVE.

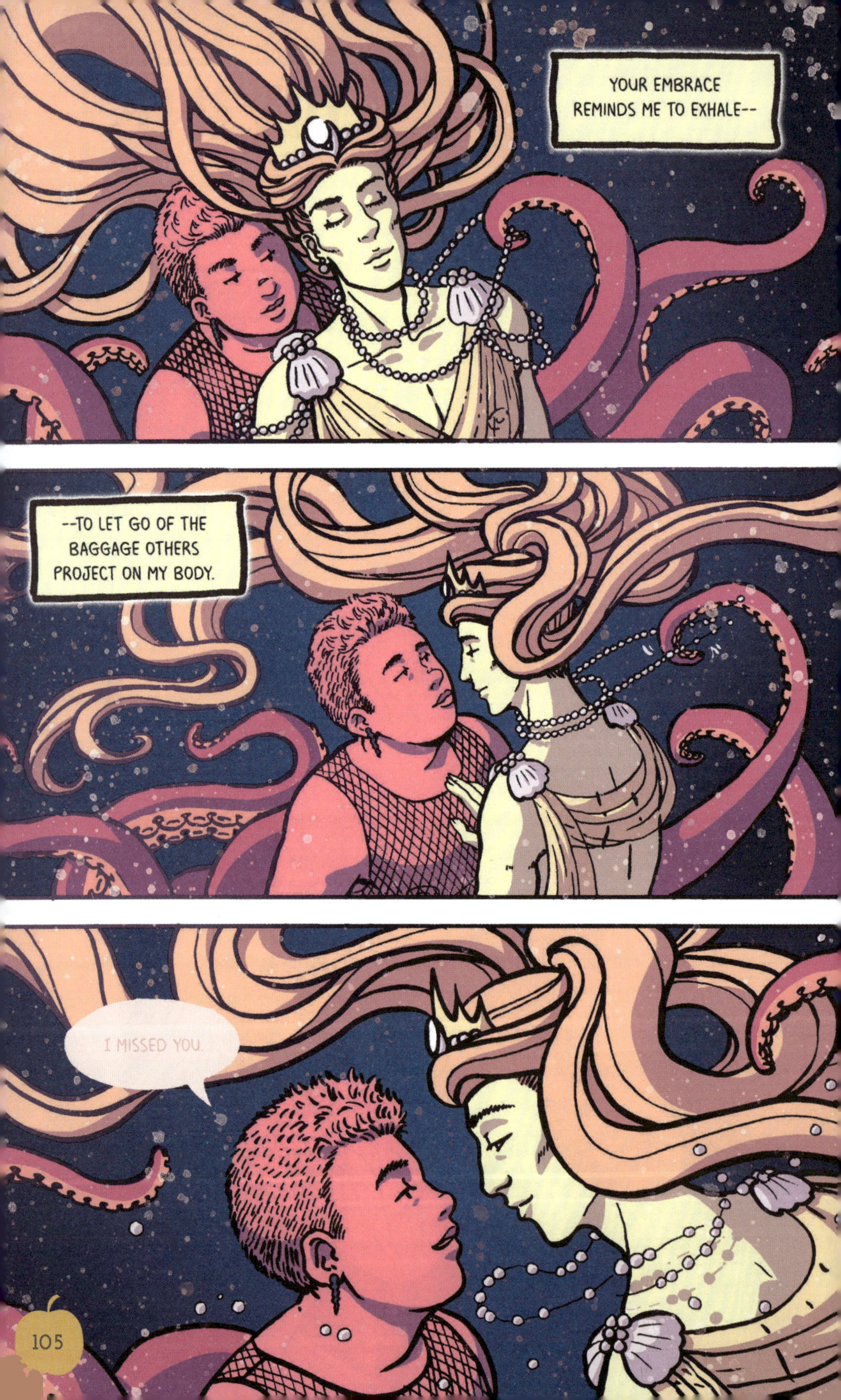
YOUR EMBRACE REMINDS ME TO EXHALE--
--TO LET GO OF THE BAGGAGE OTHERS PROJECT ON MY BODY.
I MISSED YOU.

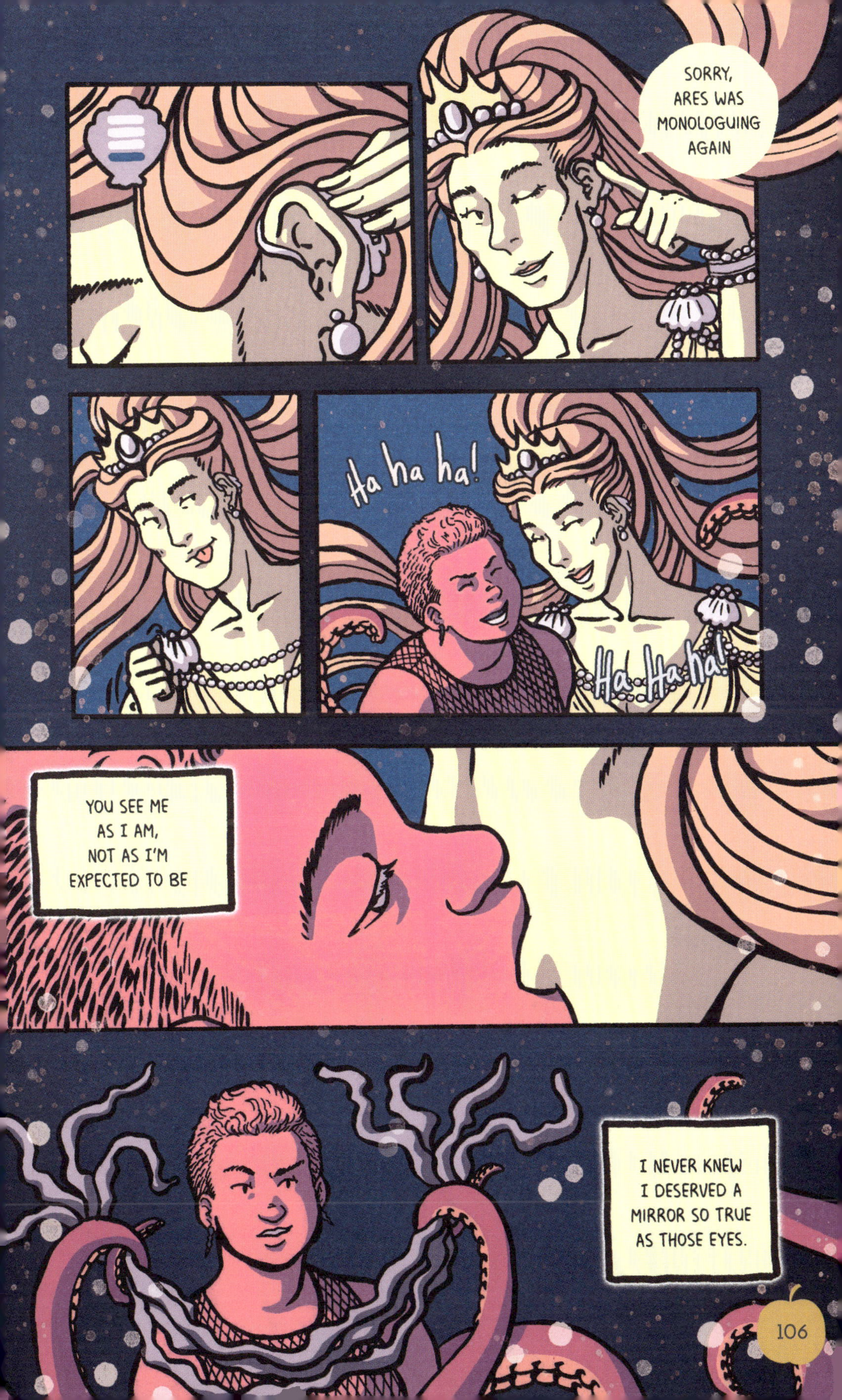
SORRY, ARES WAS MONOLOGUING AGAIN
Ha ha ha!
Ha Ha ha!
YOU SEE ME AS I AM, NOT AS I'M EXPECTED TO BE
I NEVER KNEW I DESERVED A MIRROR SO TRUE AS THOSE EYES.

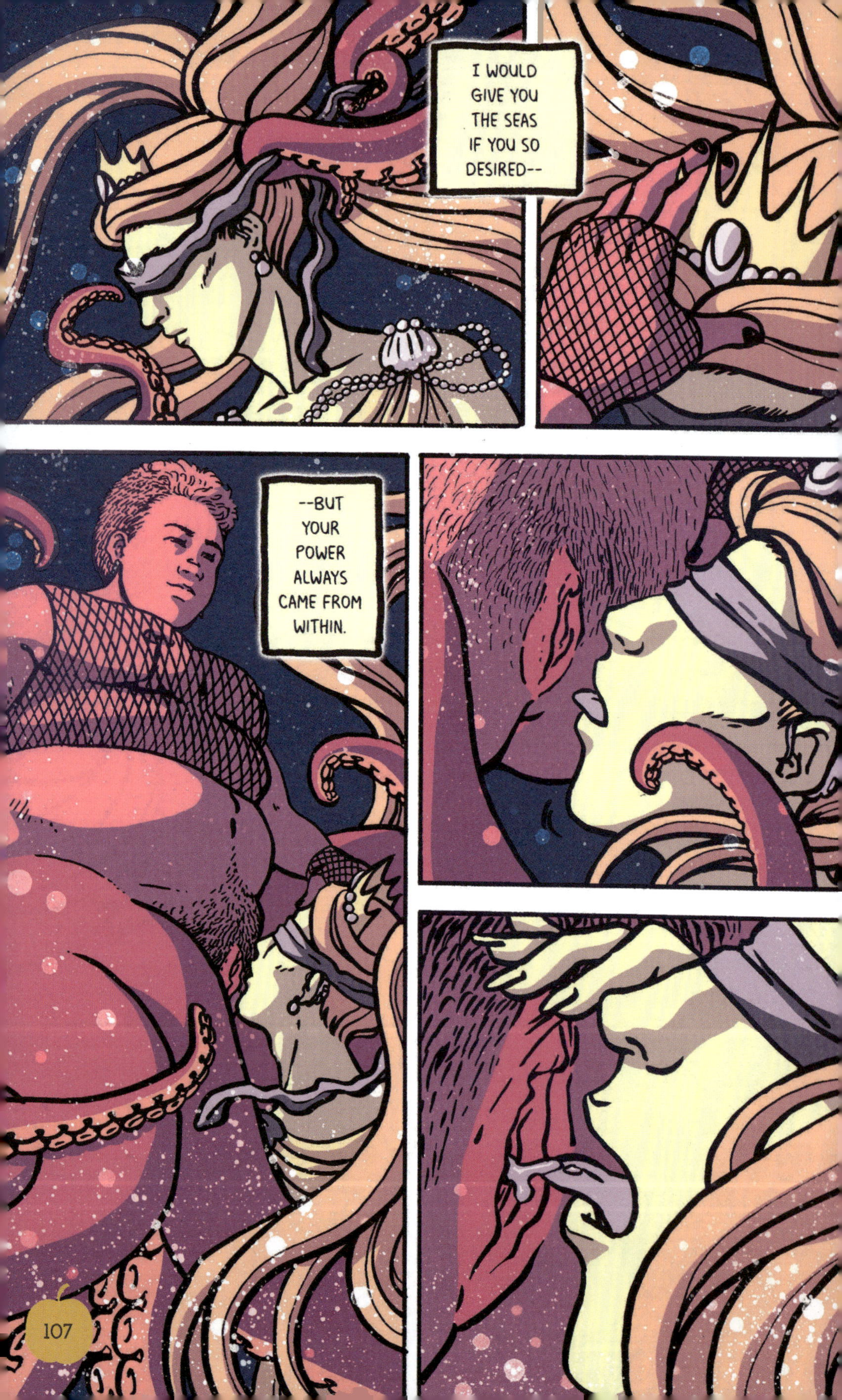
I WOULD GIVE YOU THE SEAS IF YOU SO DESIRED--
--BUT YOUR POWER ALWAYS CAME FROM WITHIN.

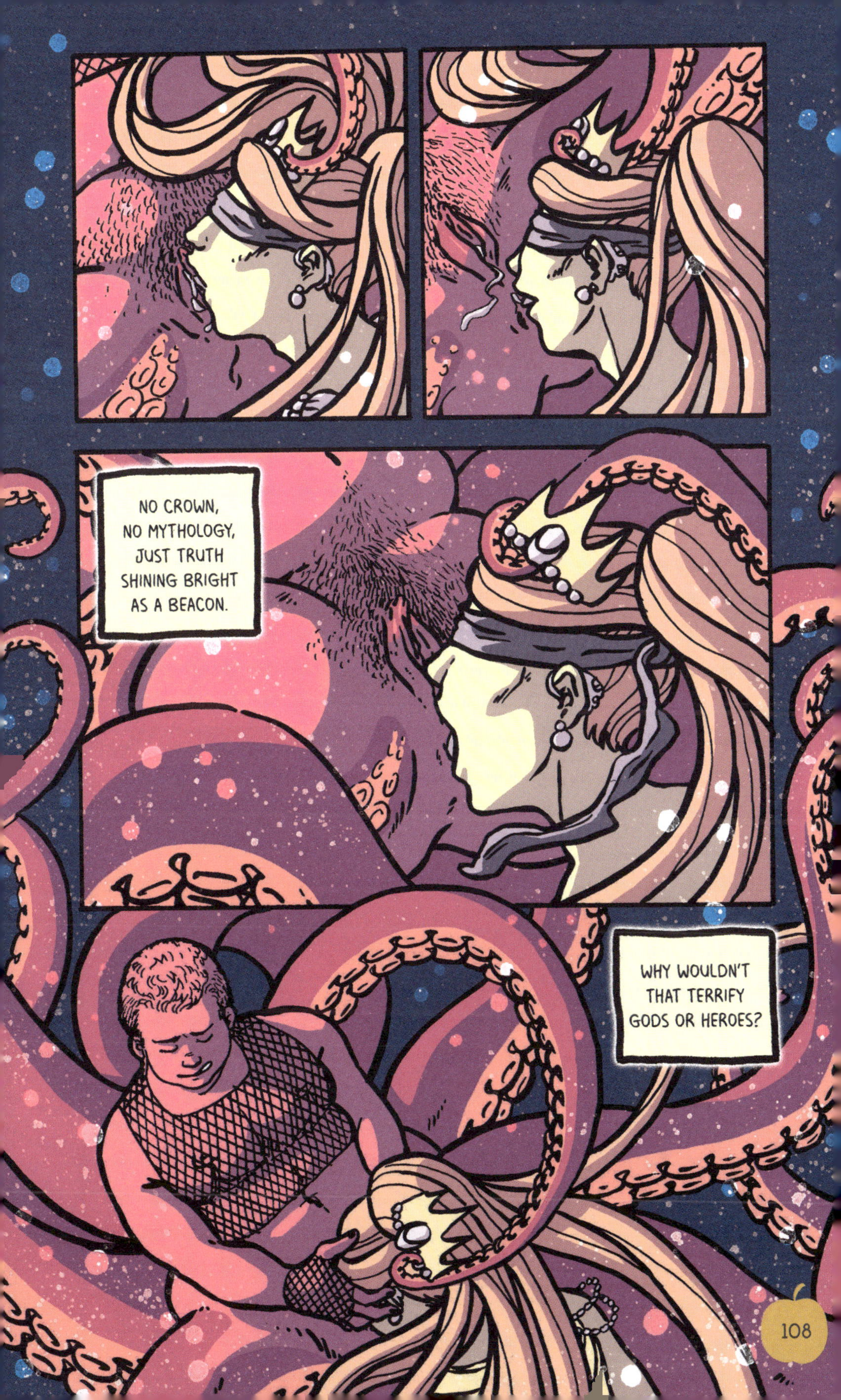
NO CROWN, NO MYTHOLOGY, JUST TRUTH SHINING BRIGHT AS A BEACON.
WHY WOULDN'T THAT TERRIFY GODS OR HEROES?

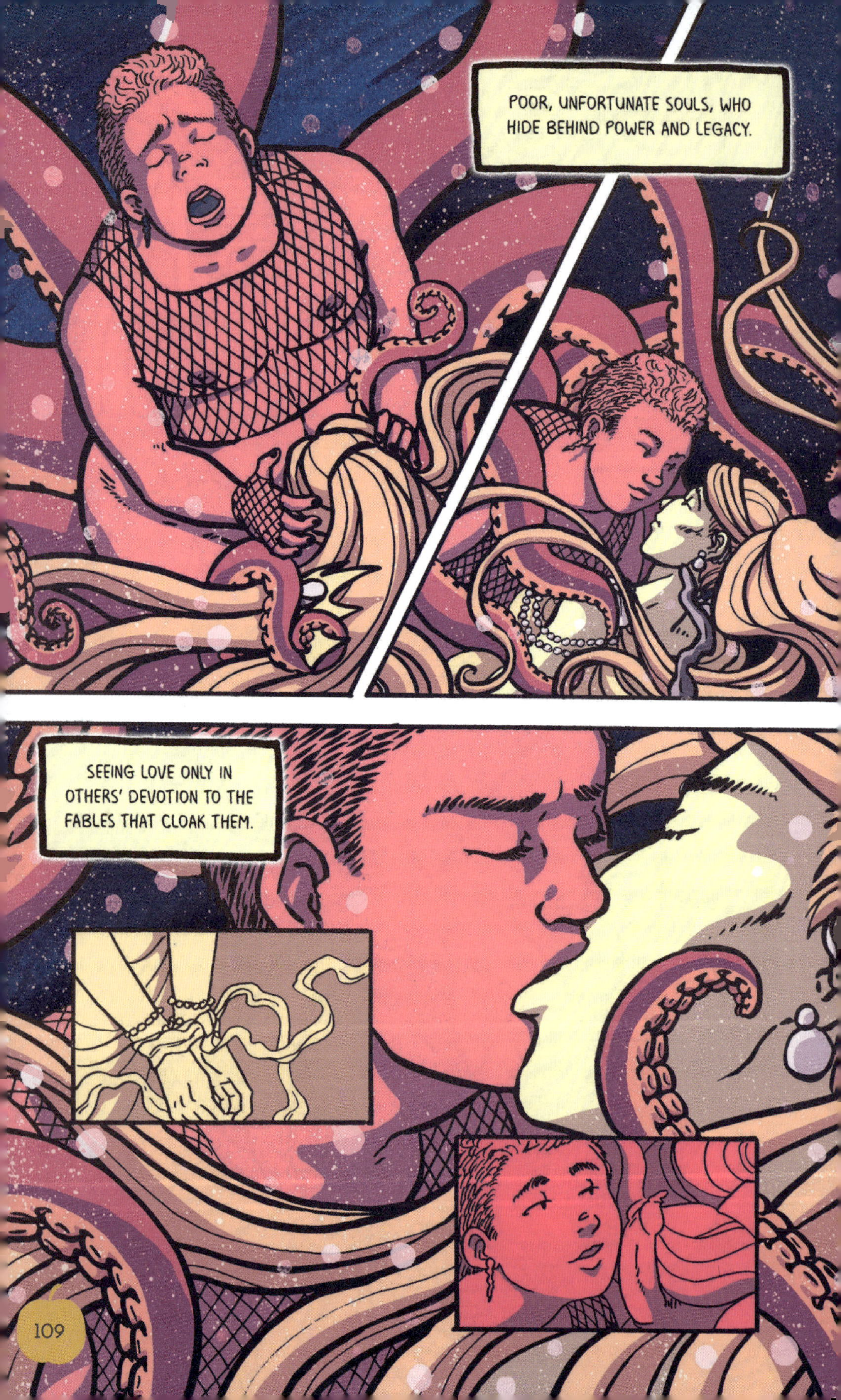
POOR, UNFORTUNATE SOULS, WHO HIDE BEHIND POWER AND LEGACY.
SEEING LOVE ONLY IN OTHERS' DEVOTION TO THE FABLES THAT CLOAK THEM.

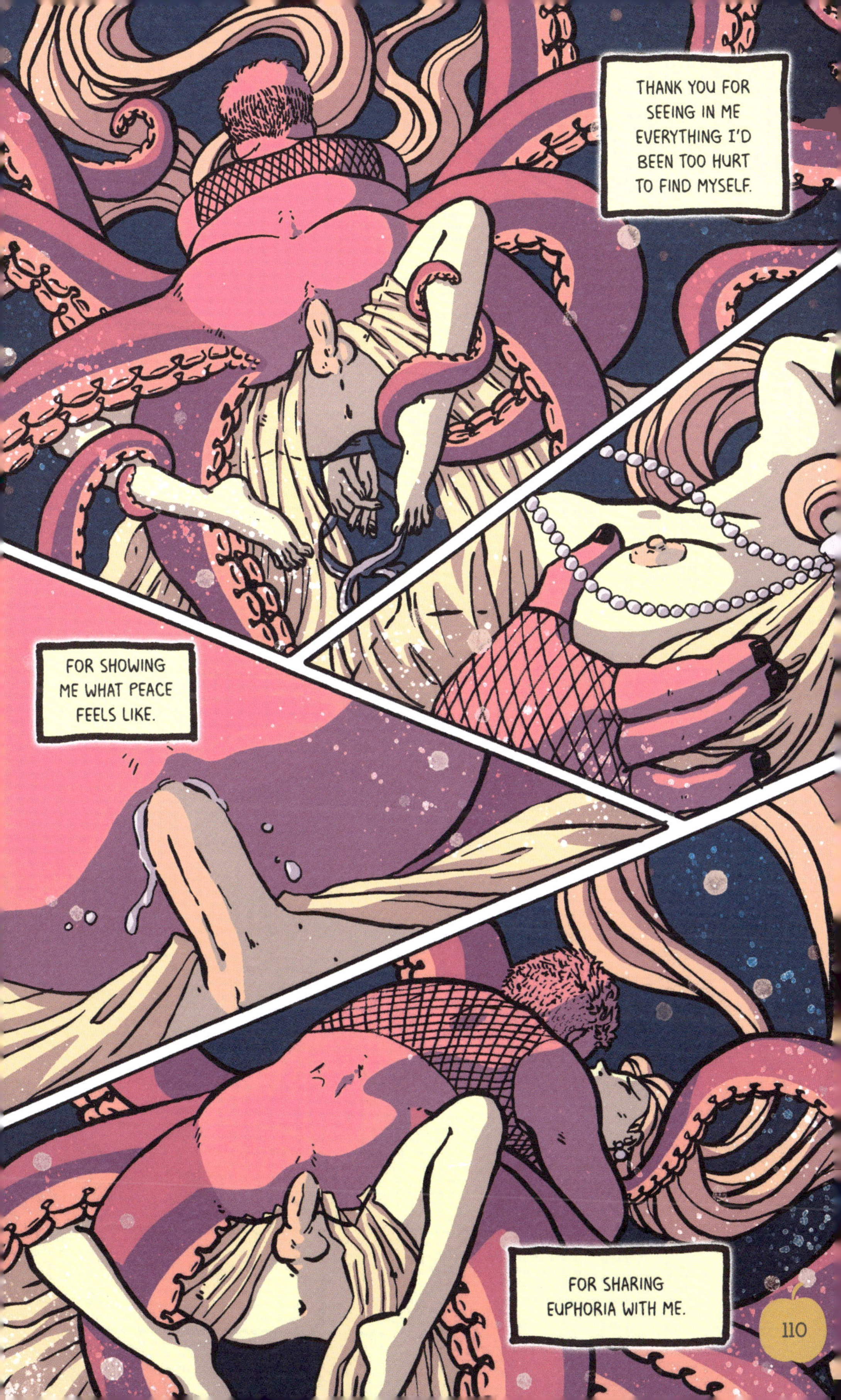
THANK YOU FOR SEEING IN ME EVERYTHING I'D BEEN TOO HURT TO FIND MYSELF.
FOR SHOWING ME WHAT PEACE FEELS LIKE.
FOR SHARING EUPHORIA WITH ME.

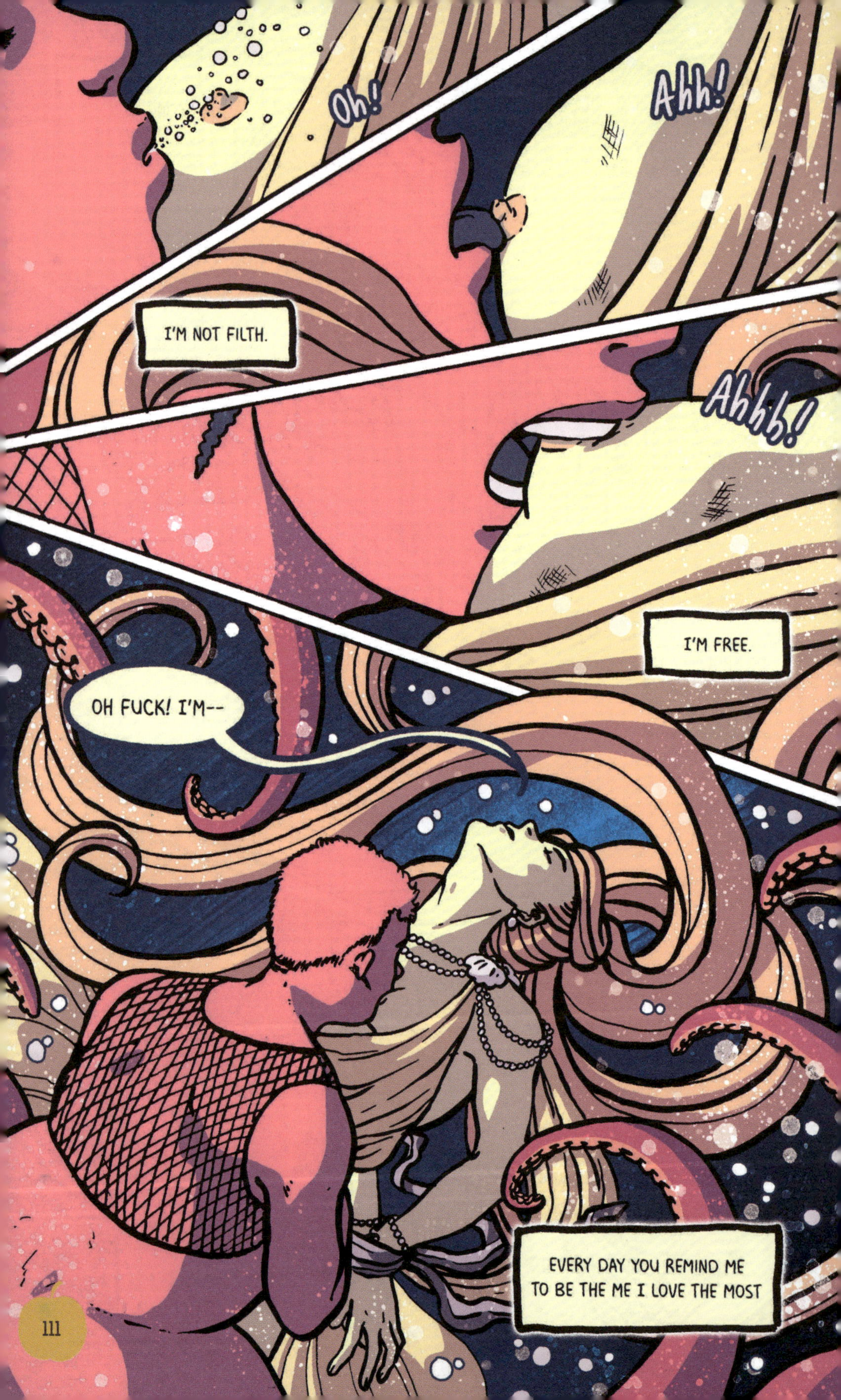
Oh!
Ahh!
I'M NOT FILTH.
Ahhh!
I'M FREE.
OH FUCK! I'M--
EVERY DAY YOU REMIND ME
TO BE THE ME I LOVE THE MOST

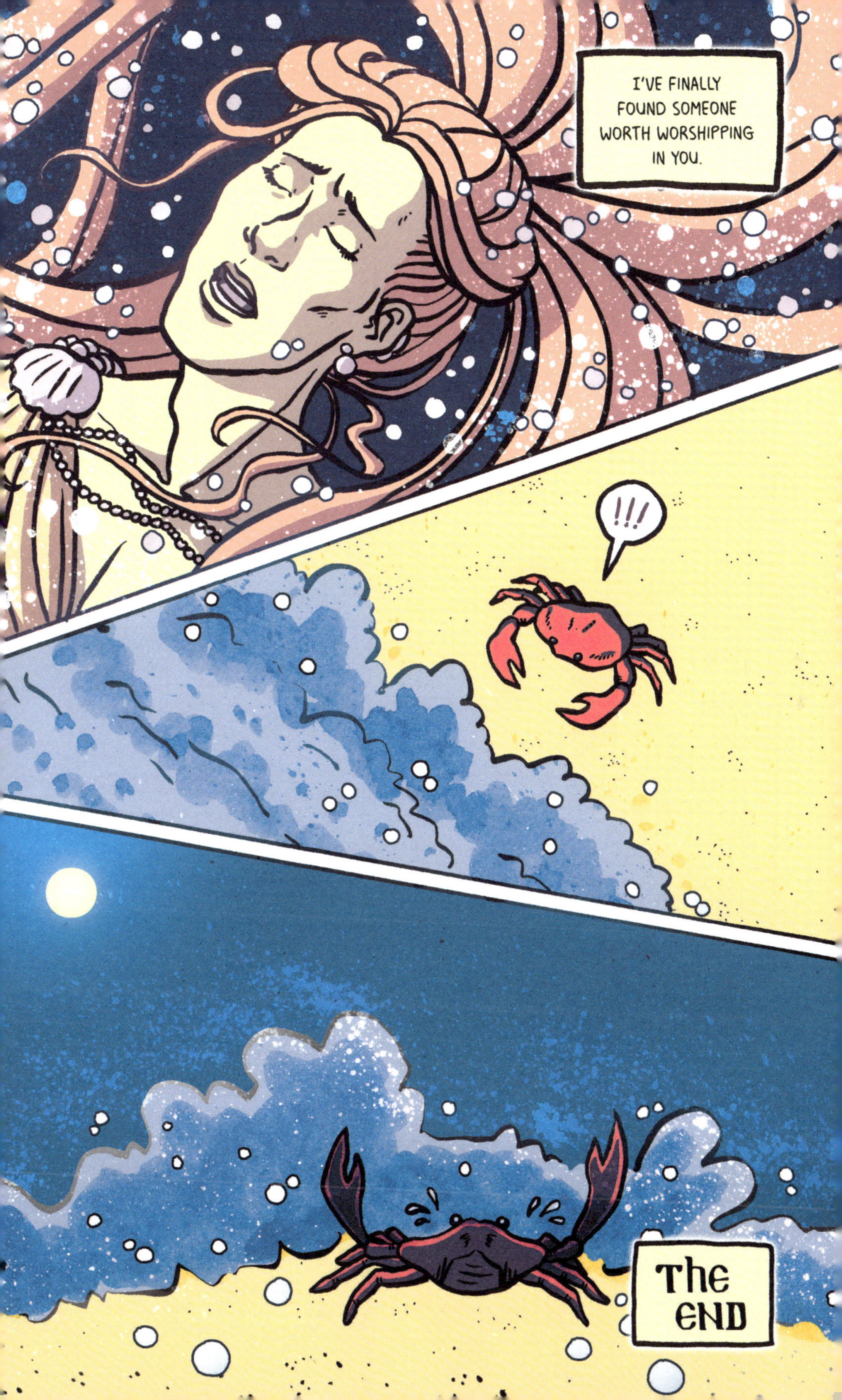
I'VE FINALLY FOUND SOMEONE WORTH WORSHIPPING IN YOU.
!!!
THE END

Princex Tegan and the Demon of Love

Story by Jonathan W. Thurston-Torres
Art by G Romero-Johnson

Princex Tegan is followed by the shadow of their curse, a deer monster known as Tox. The nectar of the anemone flower keeps them safe, but will a passing Prince be able to look beyond what the townspeople say about them?

Writer's Note

" People like me, people with HIV, don't get happy endings. That's what I was taught in grade school.

This anthology gave me a chance to change and challenge that. People with HIV are worthy of love. They're worthy of sex. Hell, they're worthy of bareback sex.

This story envisions a world where people, at least some of them, can be educated on how sex and HIV actually work. And it's the kind of story I wish I had been exposed to earlier on. "

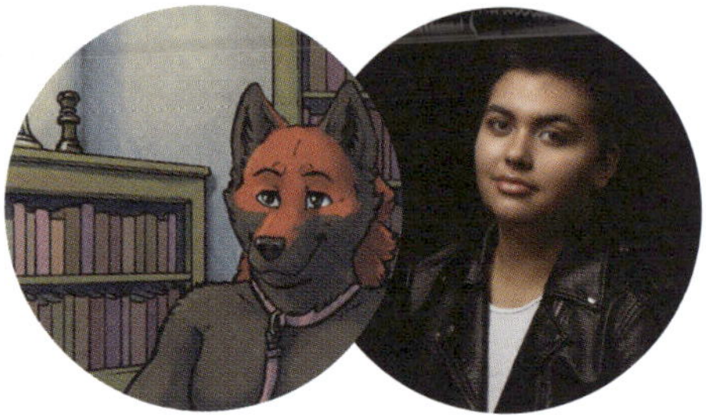

About the Creators

Jonathan Thurston-Torres (they/them) is a writer in Lansing, Michigan. They are an HIV-positive activist there and teach English classes at Michigan State University.

Their book Blood Criminals talks about HIV in 21st century America, as does their TEDx Talk, "Being Positive." They are also an editor. Their comic, "Princex Tegan," is all about dealing with HIV stigma in a fairy tale setting!

Twitter.com/JThurstonMSU

G Romero-Johnson (she/her) is a Minneapolis based queer latinx cartoonist. She enjoys horror romance and is passionate about 80s slashers and Kate Bush. G's currently working on SFSX volume 2, that will be out later this year.

GromeroJohnson.com

Editors note: Due to scheduling conflicts, rendering on page six onwards as well as inks and colours on page nine onwards were completed by Tab Kimpton.

Content Tags

HIV, AIDS, UNDETECTABLE, GAY, BIGENDER, TRANS, THREESOME, BAREBACK, CHASTITY, RIMMING, DOUBLE ANAL, CREAMPIE, FURRY, DEER PERSON, ANGRY BIGOT VILLAGERS, NO ONE DIES

NOT YOUR THING? NEXT COMIC ON PAGE 128

PRINCEX TEGAN AND THE DEMON OF LOVE

Jonathan W. Thurston-Torres
G Romero-Johnson

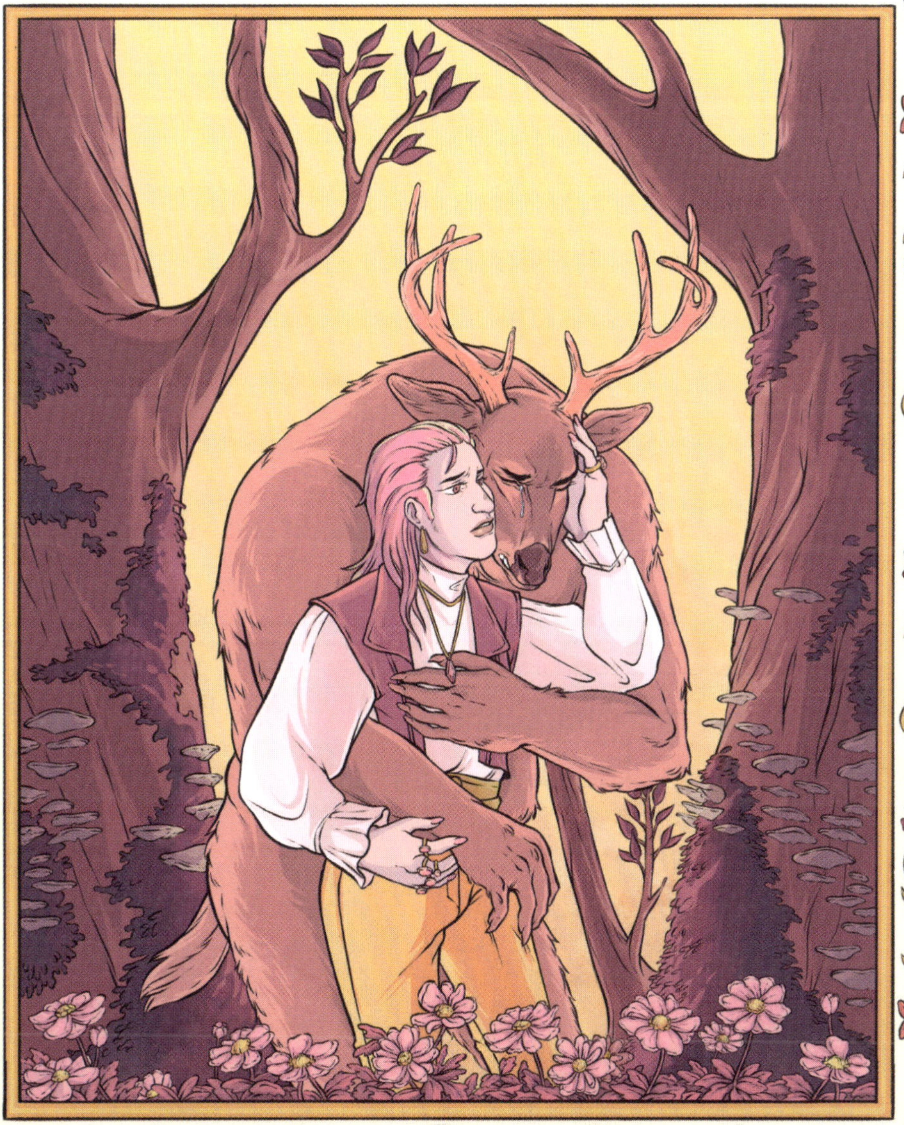

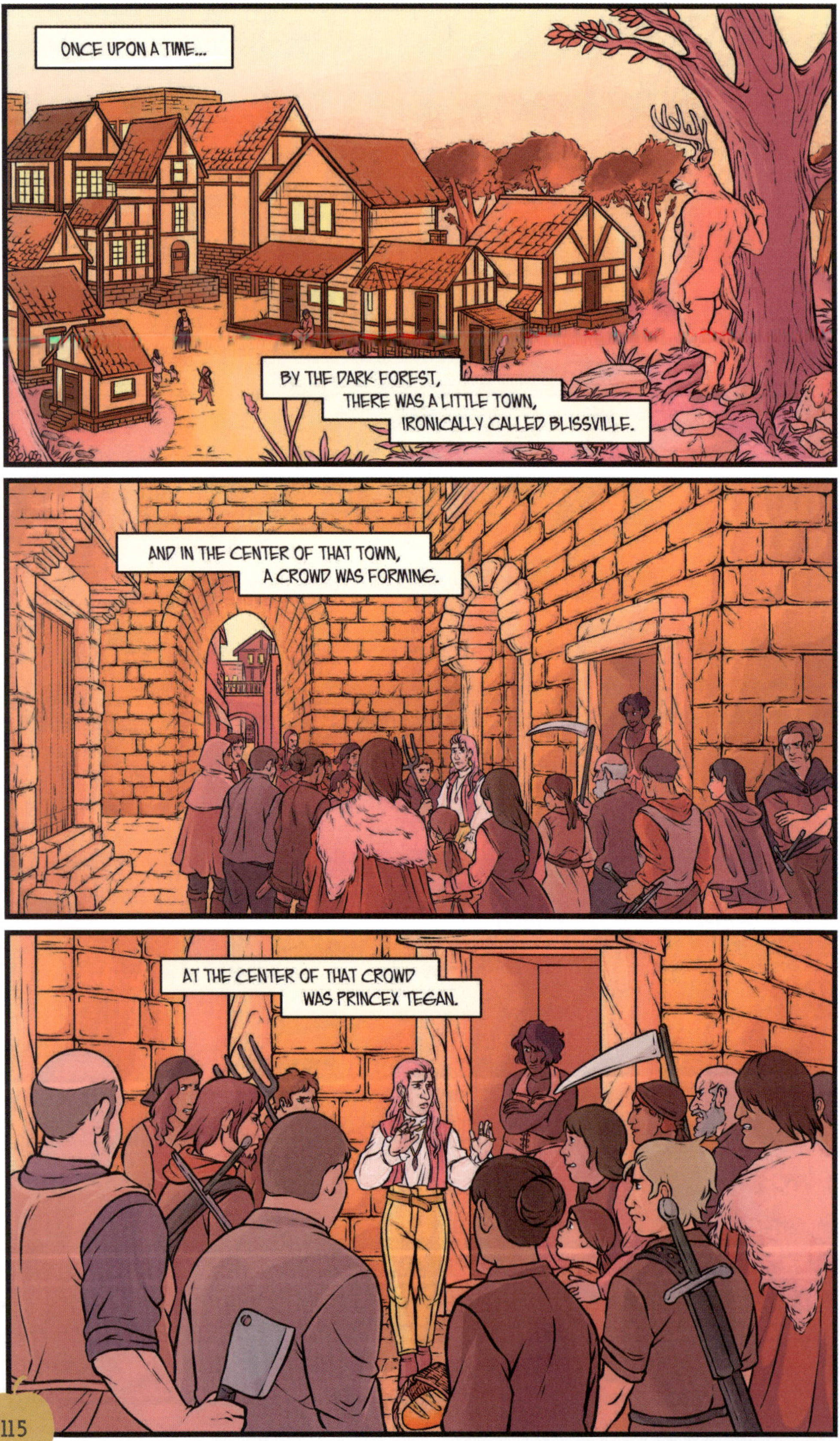
ONCE UPON A TIME...
BY THE DARK FOREST,
THERE WAS A LITTLE TOWN,
IRONICALLY CALLED BLISSVILLE.
AND IN THE CENTER OF THAT TOWN,
A CROWD WAS FORMING.
AT THE CENTER OF THAT CROWD
WAS PRINCEX TEGAN.

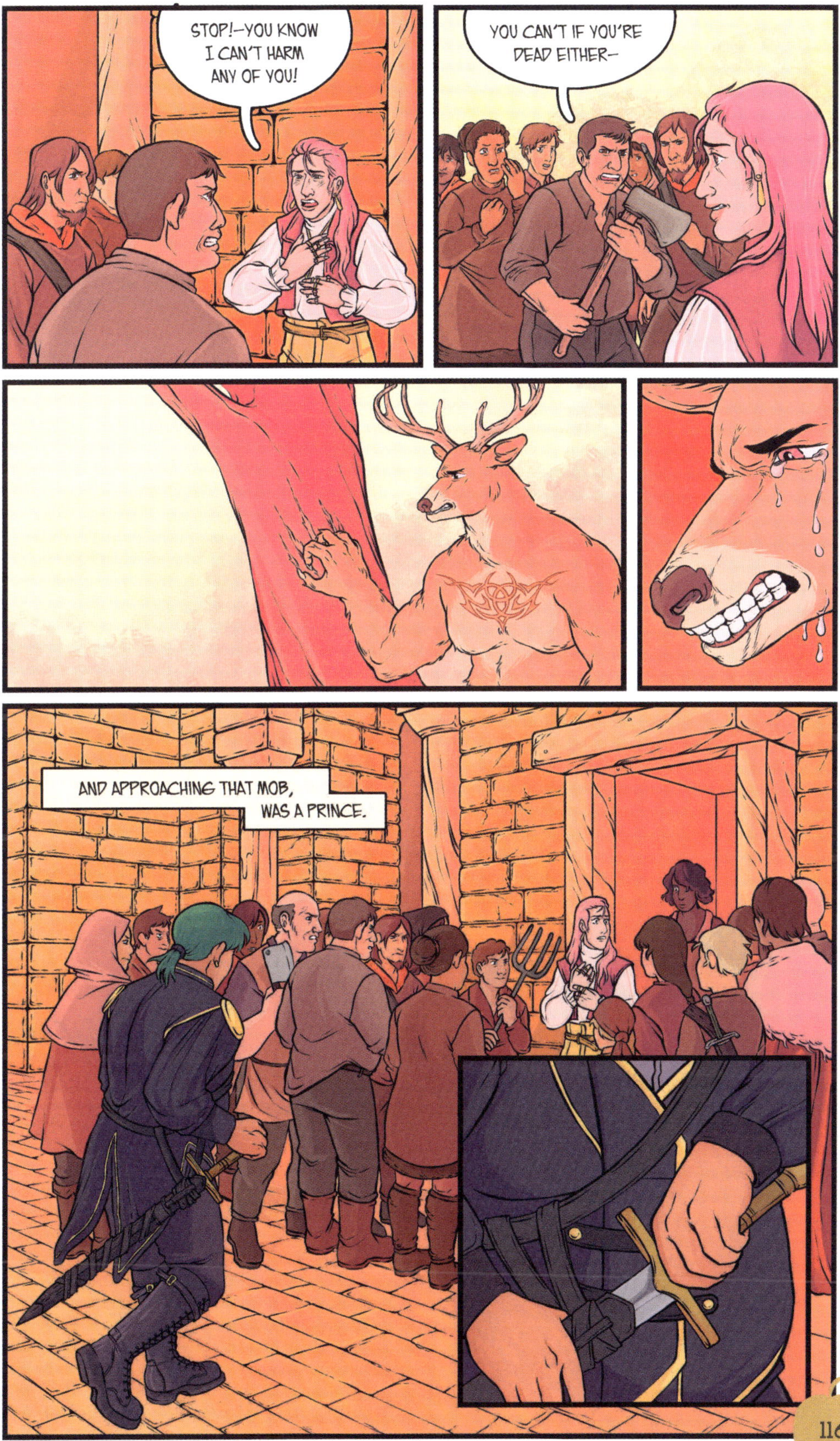
STOP!—YOU KNOW I CAN'T HARM ANY OF YOU!
YOU CAN'T IF YOU'RE DEAD EITHER—
AND APPROACHING THAT MOB, WAS A PRINCE.

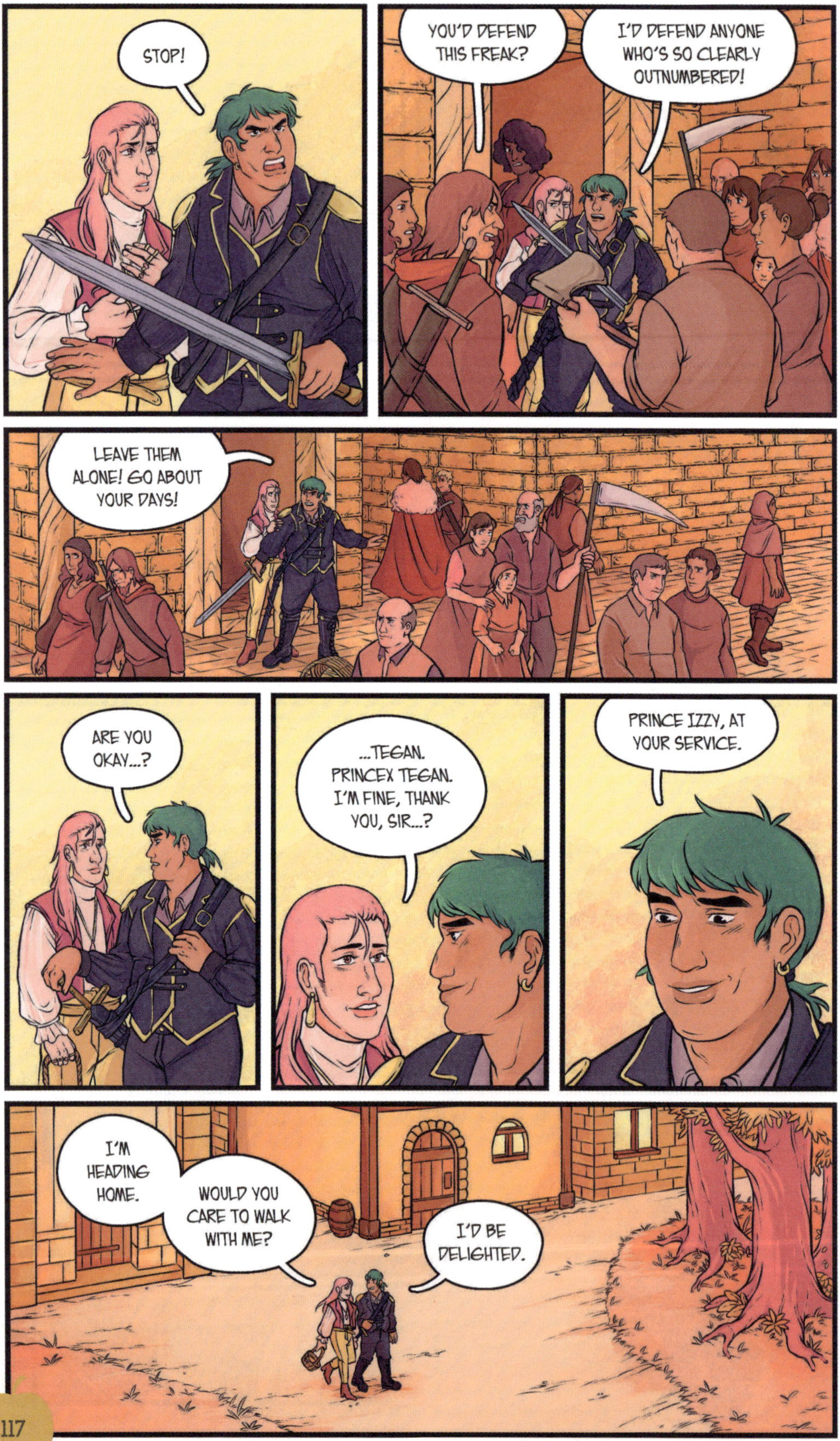
STOP!
YOU'D DEFEND THIS FREAK?
I'D DEFEND ANYONE WHO'S SO CLEARLY OUTNUMBERED!
LEAVE THEM ALONE! GO ABOUT YOUR DAYS!
ARE YOU OKAY...?
...TEGAN. PRINCEX TEGAN. I'M FINE, THANK YOU, SIR...?
PRINCE IZZY, AT YOUR SERVICE.
I'M HEADING HOME.
WOULD YOU CARE TO WALK WITH ME?
I'D BE DELIGHTED.

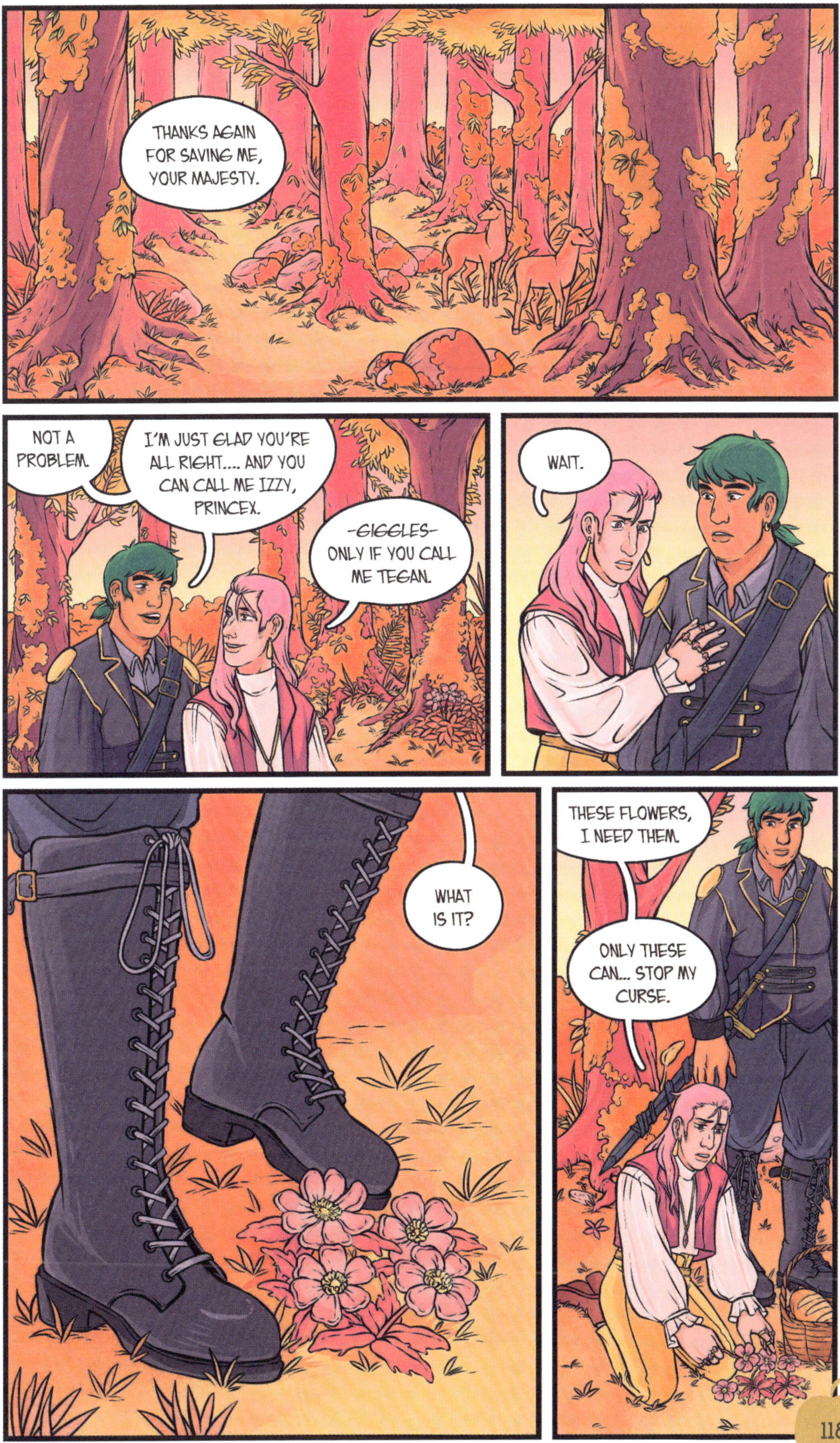
THANKS AGAIN FOR SAVING ME, YOUR MAJESTY.
NOT A PROBLEM.
I'M JUST GLAD YOU'RE ALL RIGHT.... AND YOU CAN CALL ME IZZY, PRINCEX.
-GIGGLES-
ONLY IF YOU CALL ME TEGAN.
WAIT.
WHAT IS IT?
THESE FLOWERS, I NEED THEM.
ONLY THESE CAN... STOP MY CURSE.

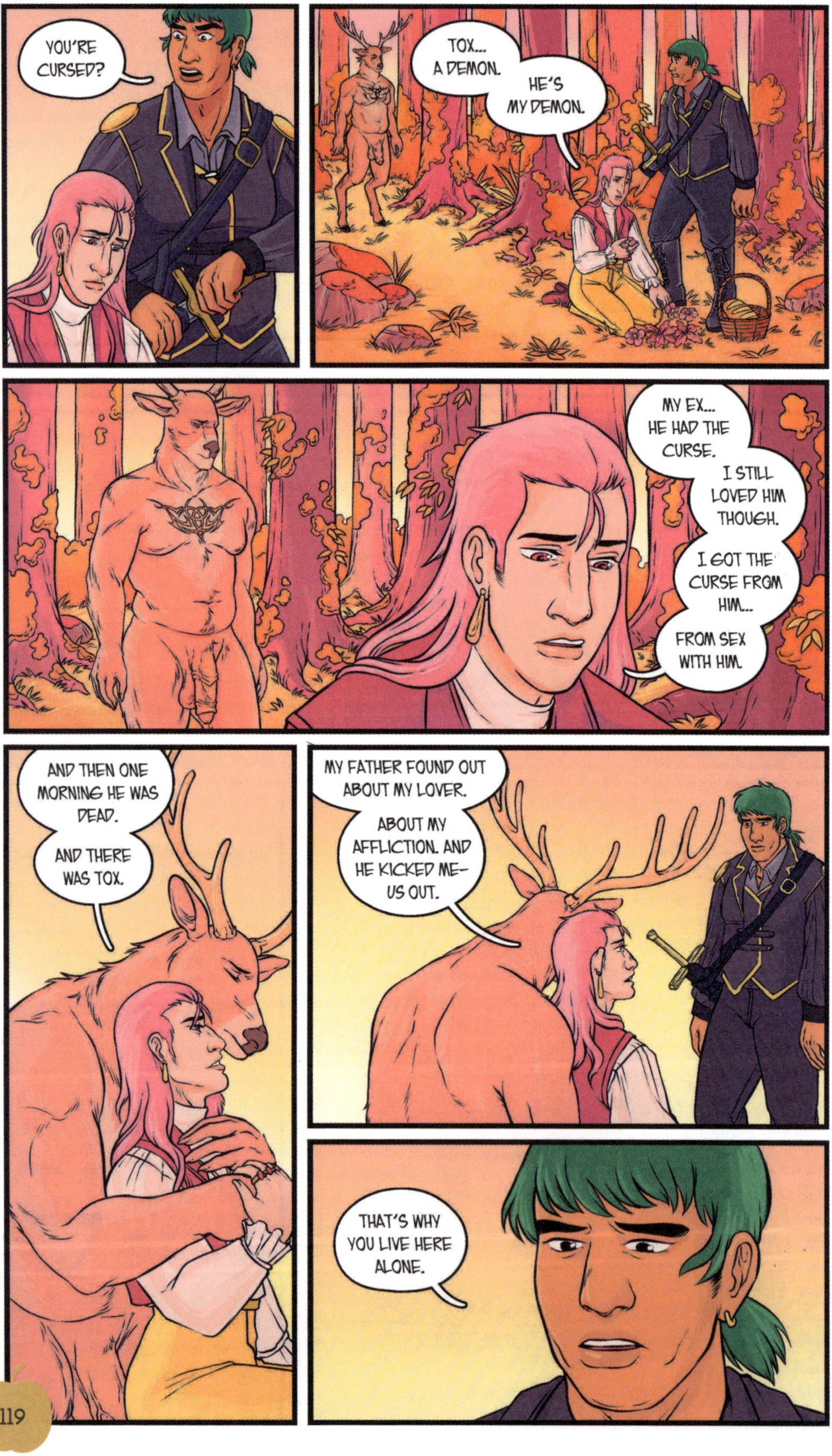
YOU'RE CURSED?
TOX... A DEMON.
HE'S MY DEMON.
MY EX... HE HAD THE CURSE.
I STILL LOVED HIM THOUGH.
I GOT THE CURSE FROM HIM...
FROM SEX WITH HIM.
AND THEN ONE MORNING HE WAS DEAD.
AND THERE WAS TOX.
MY FATHER FOUND OUT ABOUT MY LOVER.
ABOUT MY AFFLICTION. AND HE KICKED ME- US OUT.
THAT'S WHY YOU LIVE HERE ALONE.

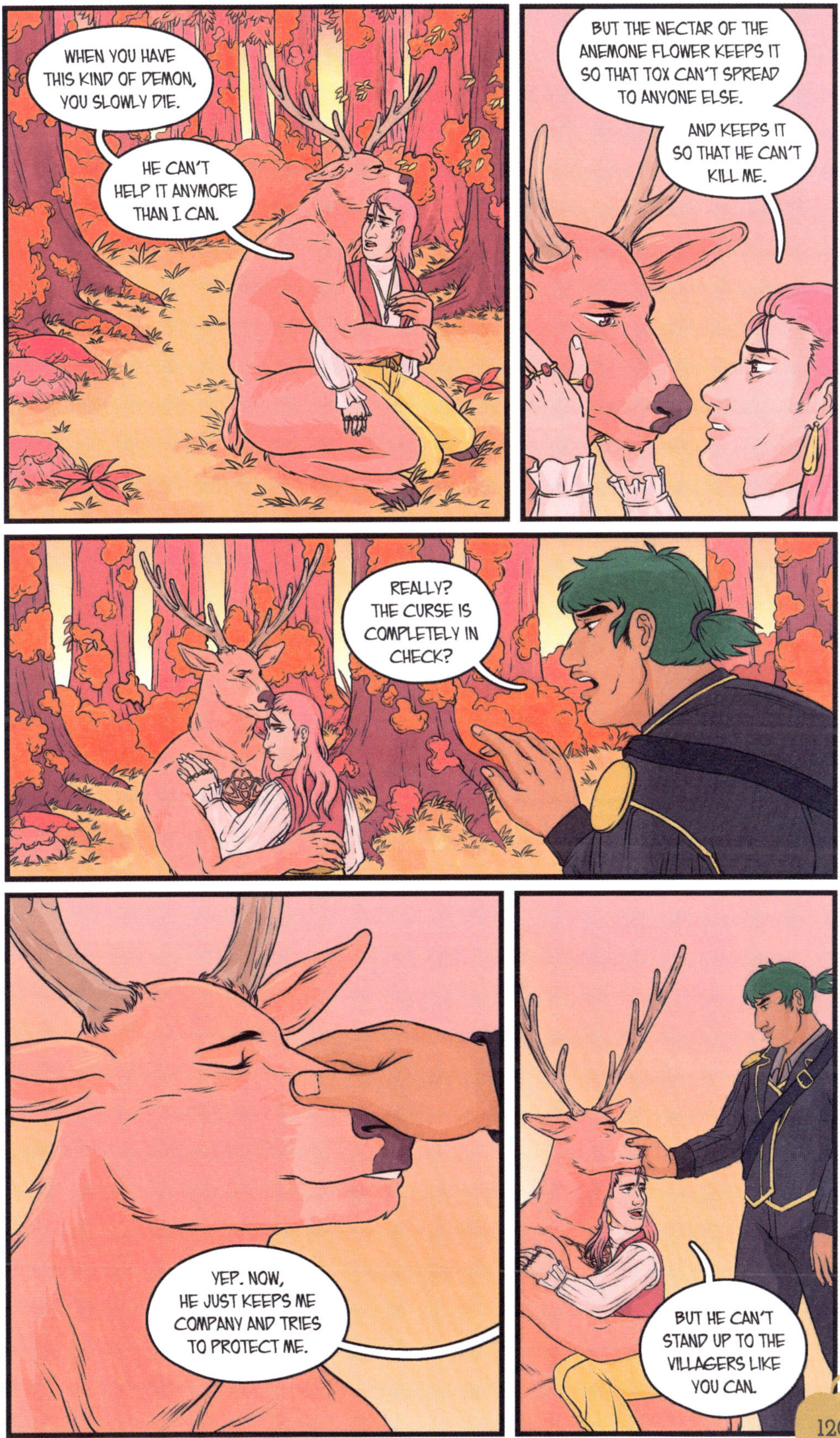
WHEN YOU HAVE THIS KIND OF DEMON, YOU SLOWLY DIE.
HE CAN'T HELP IT ANYMORE THAN I CAN.
BUT THE NECTAR OF THE ANEMONE FLOWER KEEPS IT SO THAT TOX CAN'T SPREAD TO ANYONE ELSE.
AND KEEPS IT SO THAT HE CAN'T KILL ME.
REALLY? THE CURSE IS COMPLETELY IN CHECK?
YEP. NOW, HE JUST KEEPS ME COMPANY AND TRIES TO PROTECT ME.
BUT HE CAN'T STAND UP TO THE VILLAGERS LIKE YOU CAN.

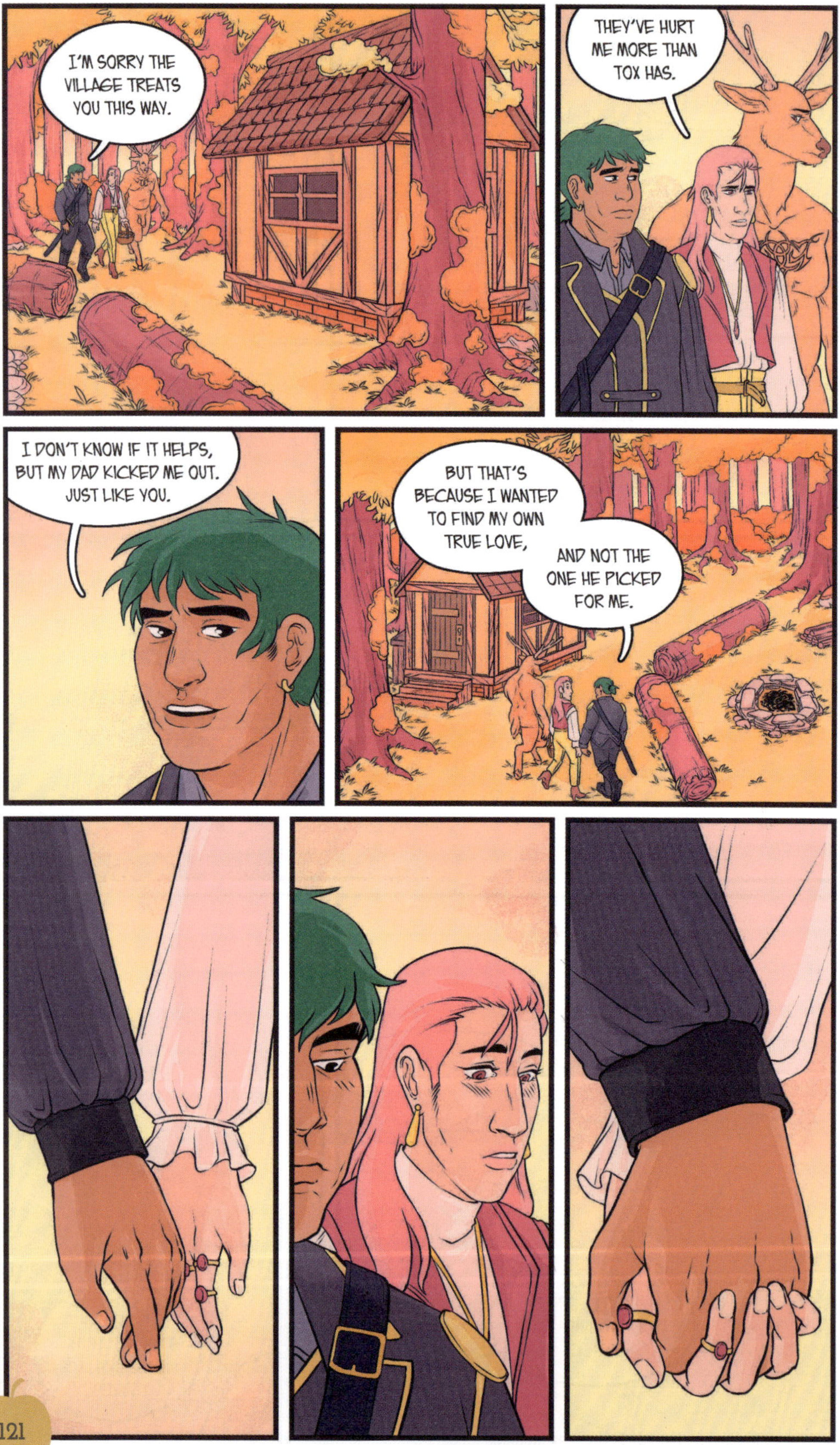
I'M SORRY THE VILLAGE TREATS YOU THIS WAY.
THEY'VE HURT ME MORE THAN TOX HAS.
I DON'T KNOW IF IT HELPS, BUT MY DAD KICKED ME OUT. JUST LIKE YOU.
BUT THAT'S BECAUSE I WANTED TO FIND MY OWN TRUE LOVE,
AND NOT THE ONE HE PICKED FOR ME.

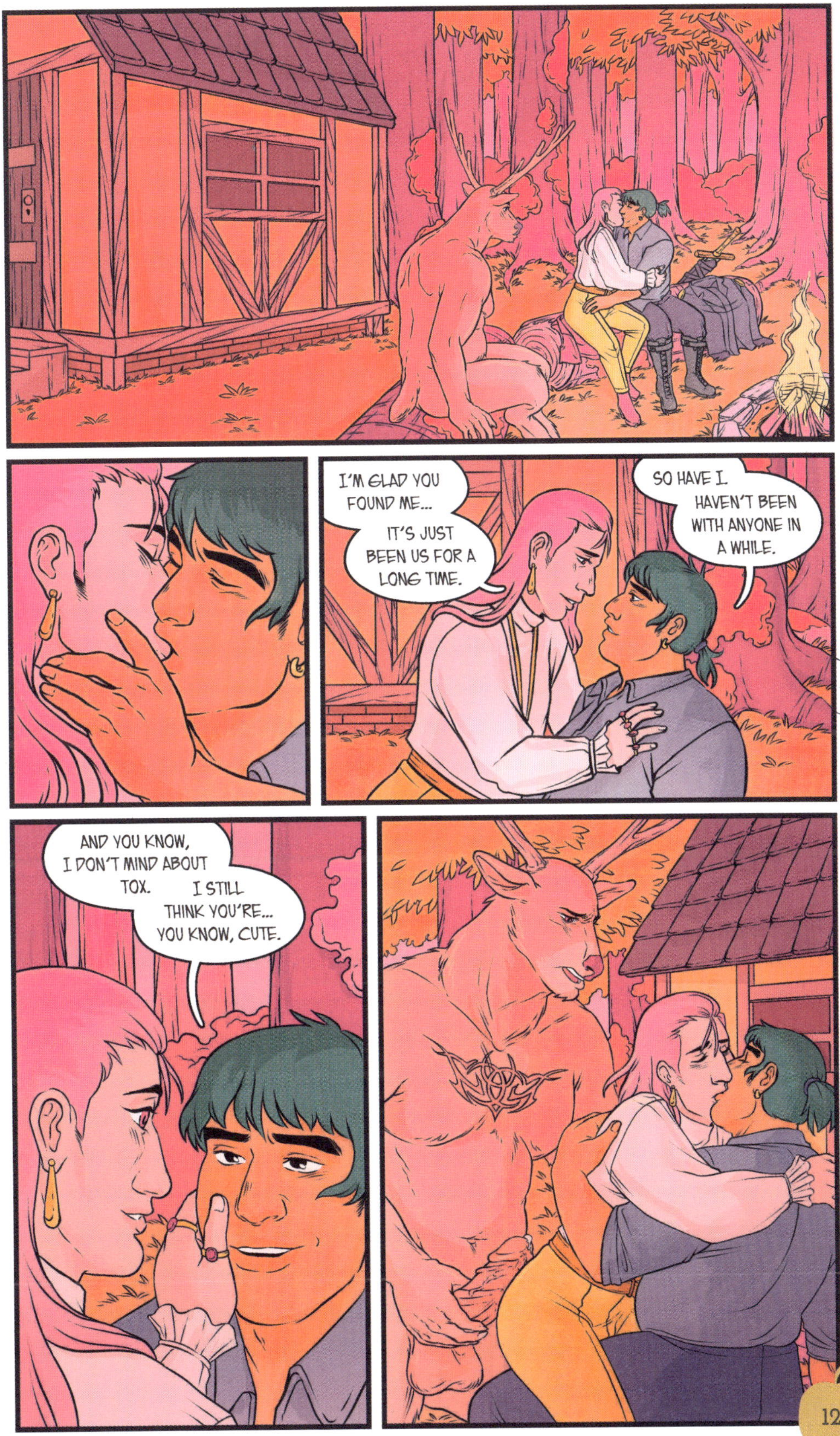
I'M GLAD YOU FOUND ME...
IT'S JUST BEEN US FOR A LONG TIME.
SO HAVE I. HAVEN'T BEEN WITH ANYONE IN A WHILE.
AND YOU KNOW, I DON'T MIND ABOUT TOX.
I STILL THINK YOU'RE... YOU KNOW, CUTE.

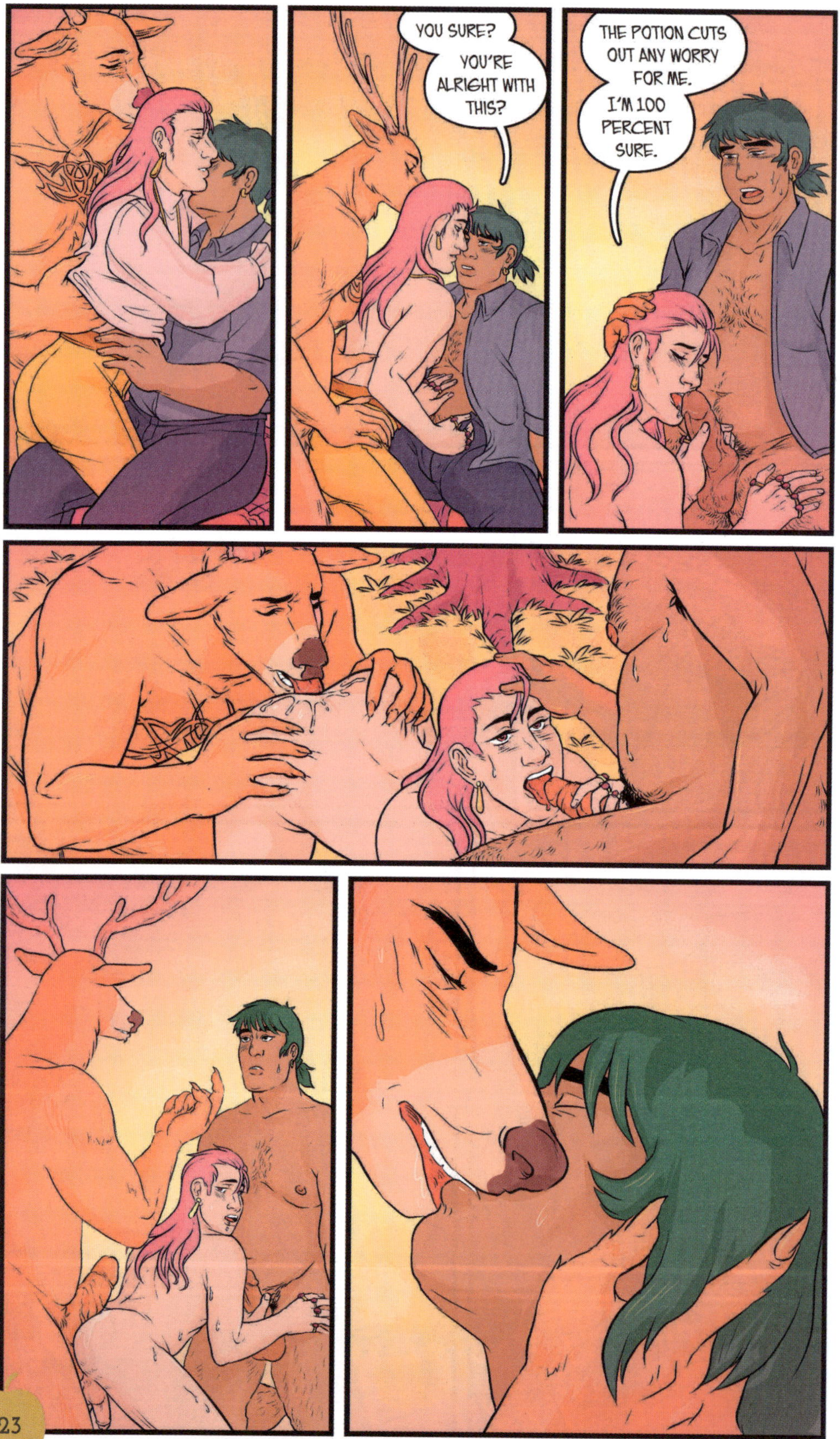
YOU SURE?
YOU'RE ALRIGHT WITH THIS?
THE POTION CUTS OUT ANY WORRY FOR ME.
I'M 100 PERCENT SURE.

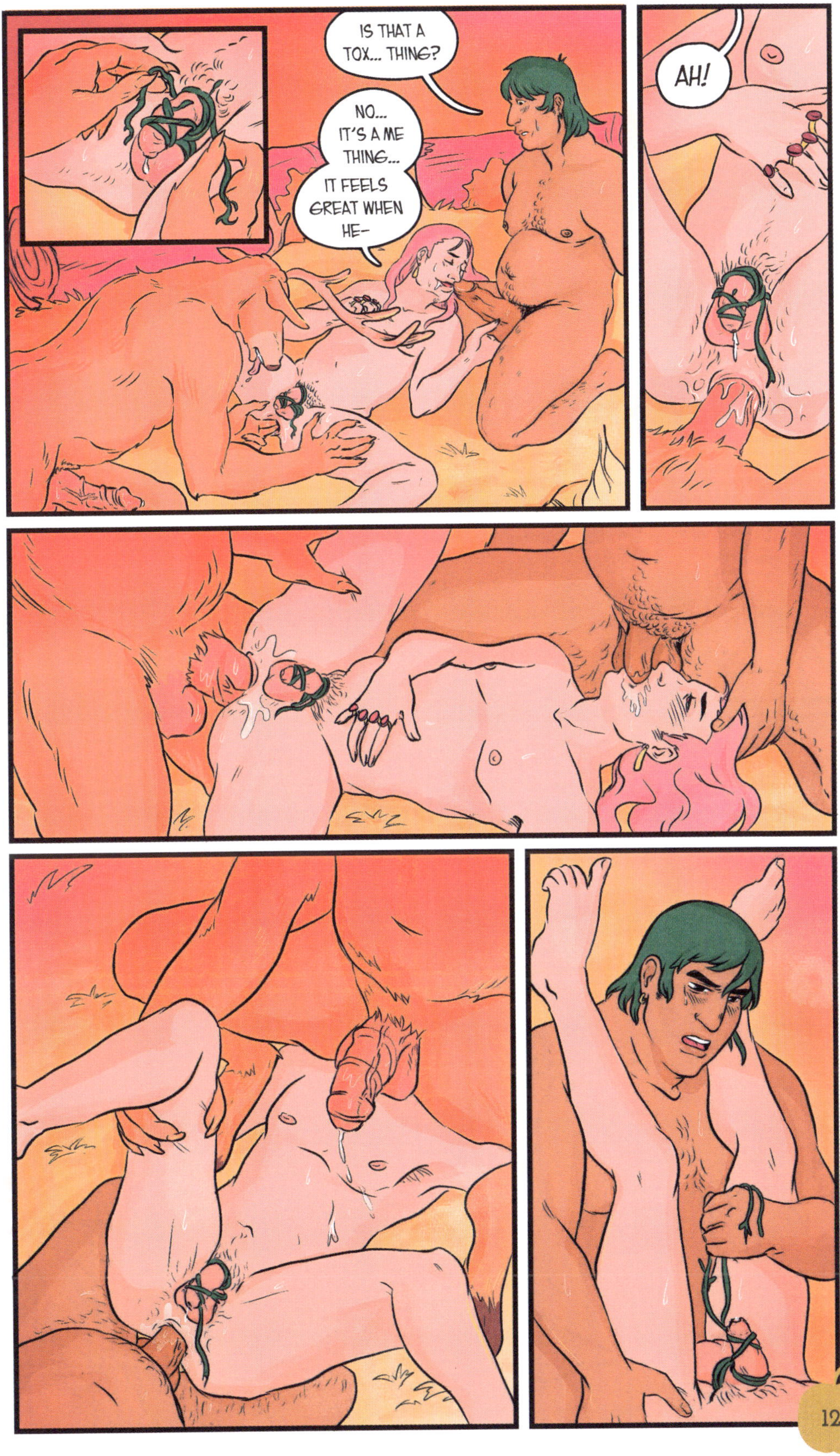
IS THAT A TOX... THING?
NO... IT'S A ME THING...
IT FEELS GREAT WHEN HE-
AH!

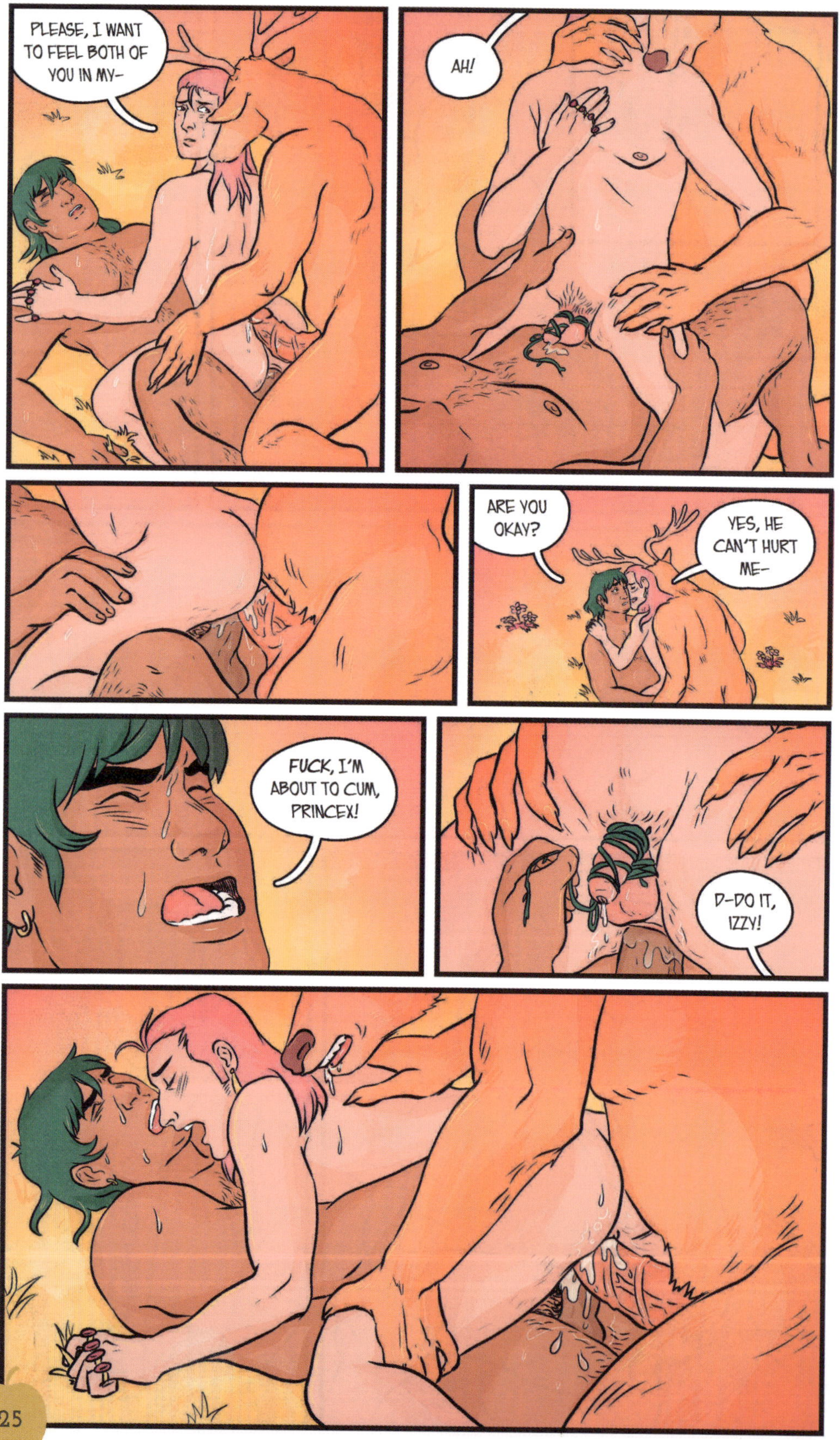
PLEASE, I WANT TO FEEL BOTH OF YOU IN MY-
AH!
ARE YOU OKAY?
YES, HE CAN'T HURT ME-
FUCK, I'M ABOUT TO CUM, PRINCEX!
D-DO IT, IZZY!

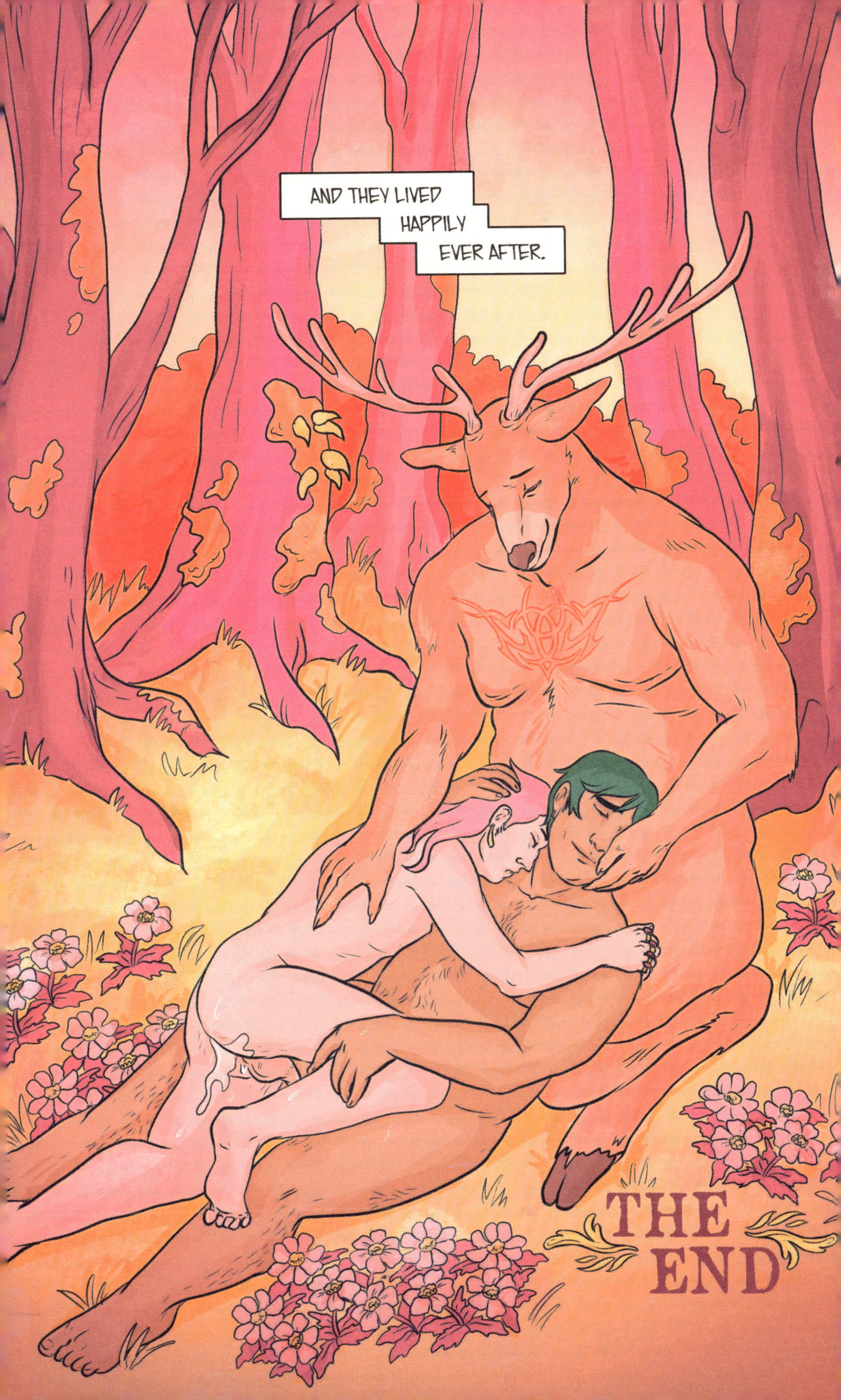
AND THEY LIVED HAPPILY EVER AFTER.
THE END

Adam & Eve

by G.C. Houle

A monk who struggles to fit in with their brothers has an ecstatic vision, in which an angel bestows unto them an important mission, and the great depth of God's love.

Creator's Note

" I'm a bit obsessed with Teresa of Ávila's supposed ecstatic encounter with an angel. It's always struck me as rather erotic - in her own words: 'I saw in his hand a long spear of gold, (...). He appeared to me to be thrusting it at times into my heart, and to pierce my very entrails; when he drew it out, he seemed to draw them out also, and to leave me all on fire with a great love of God.'

With this story I was interested in bridging the gap between physical ecstasy and spiritual ecstasy. The monk in our story becomes one with God in both senses, via an angel intermediary.

Though the comic itself is steeped in Christianity, ecstatic experiences have been reported in many different cultures and religions. It's a mysterious phenomenon! "

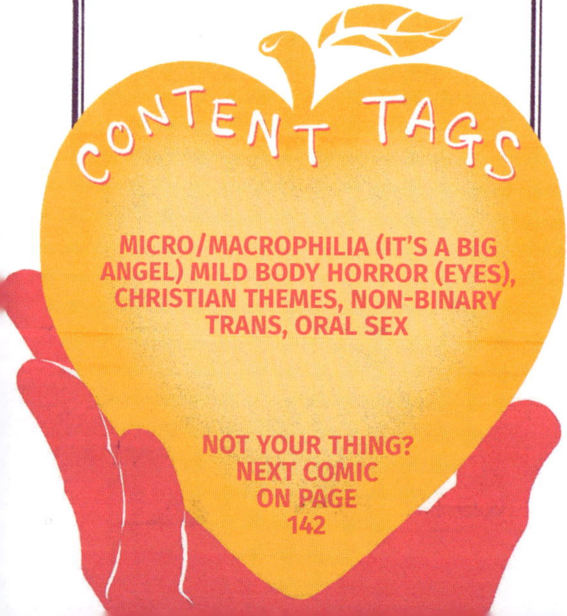

MICRO/MACROPHILIA (IT'S A BIG ANGEL) MILD BODY HORROR (EYES), CHRISTIAN THEMES, NON-BINARY TRANS, ORAL SEX

NOT YOUR THING? NEXT COMIC ON PAGE 142

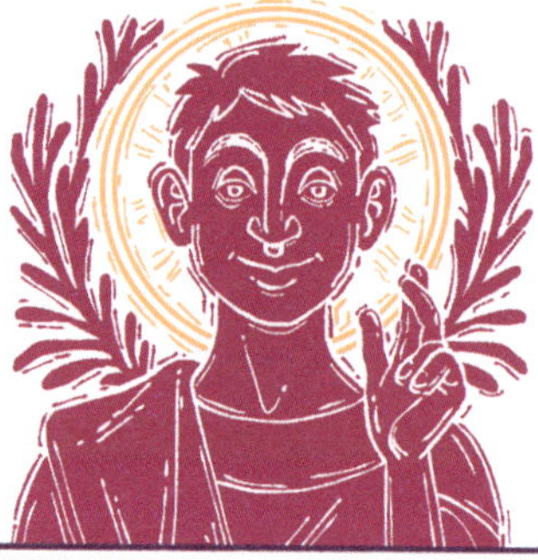

About the Creator

G.C. Houle is a French-Canadian comic artist and graphic designer from the Maritime provinces.

They were raised Catholic, which is echoed in much of their work - they are interested in queering the aesthetics of the Church and themes of the Bible.

GCHoule.com

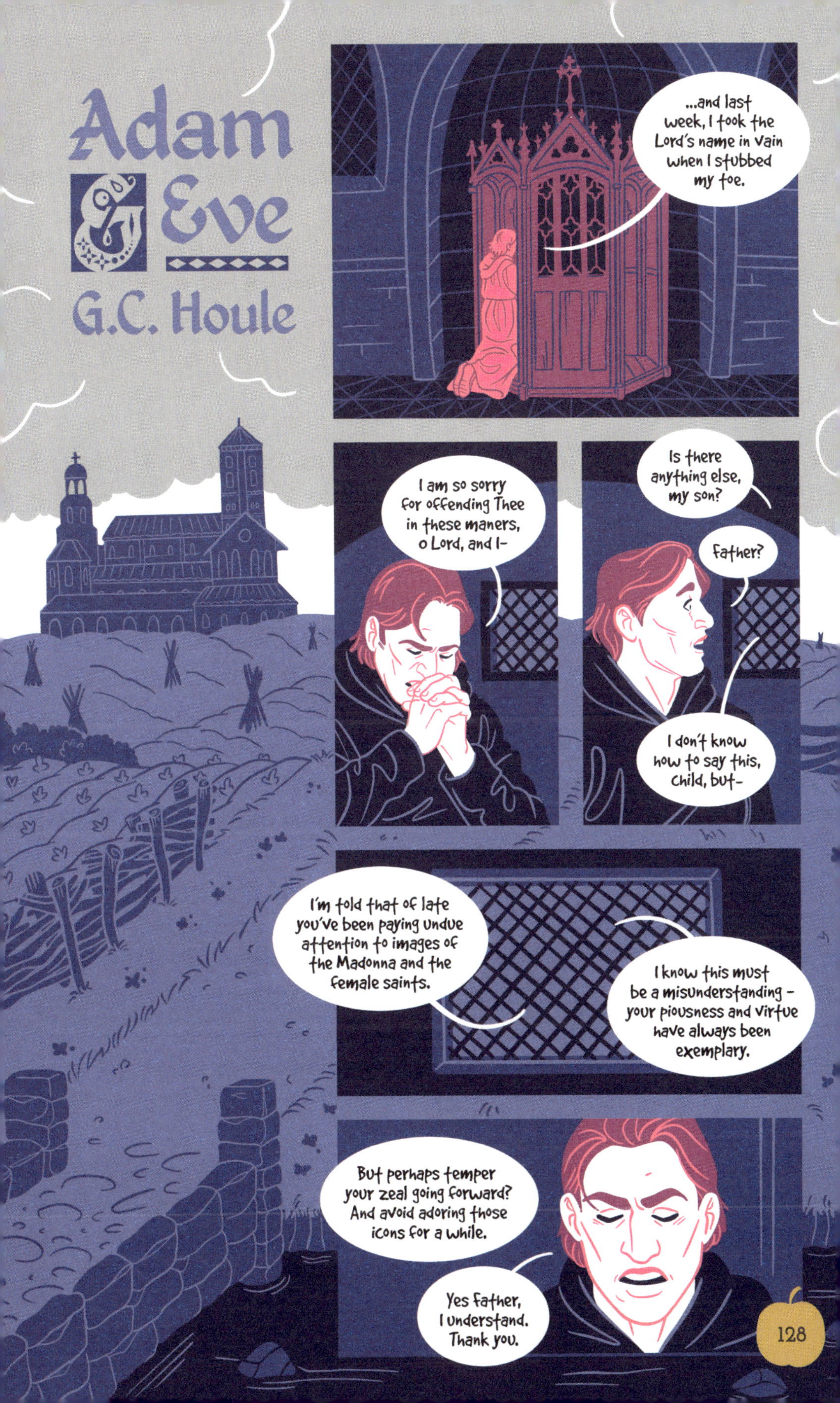

Adam & Eve
G.C. Houle
...and last week, I took the Lord's name in vain when I stubbed my toe.
I am so sorry for offending Thee in these maners, o Lord, and I-
Is there anything else, my son?
Father?
I don't know how to say this, child, but-
I'm told that of late you've been paying undue attention to images of the Madonna and the female saints.
I know this must be a misunderstanding - your piousness and virtue have always been exemplary.
But perhaps temper your zeal going forward? And avoid adoring those icons for a while.
Yes Father, I understand. Thank you.

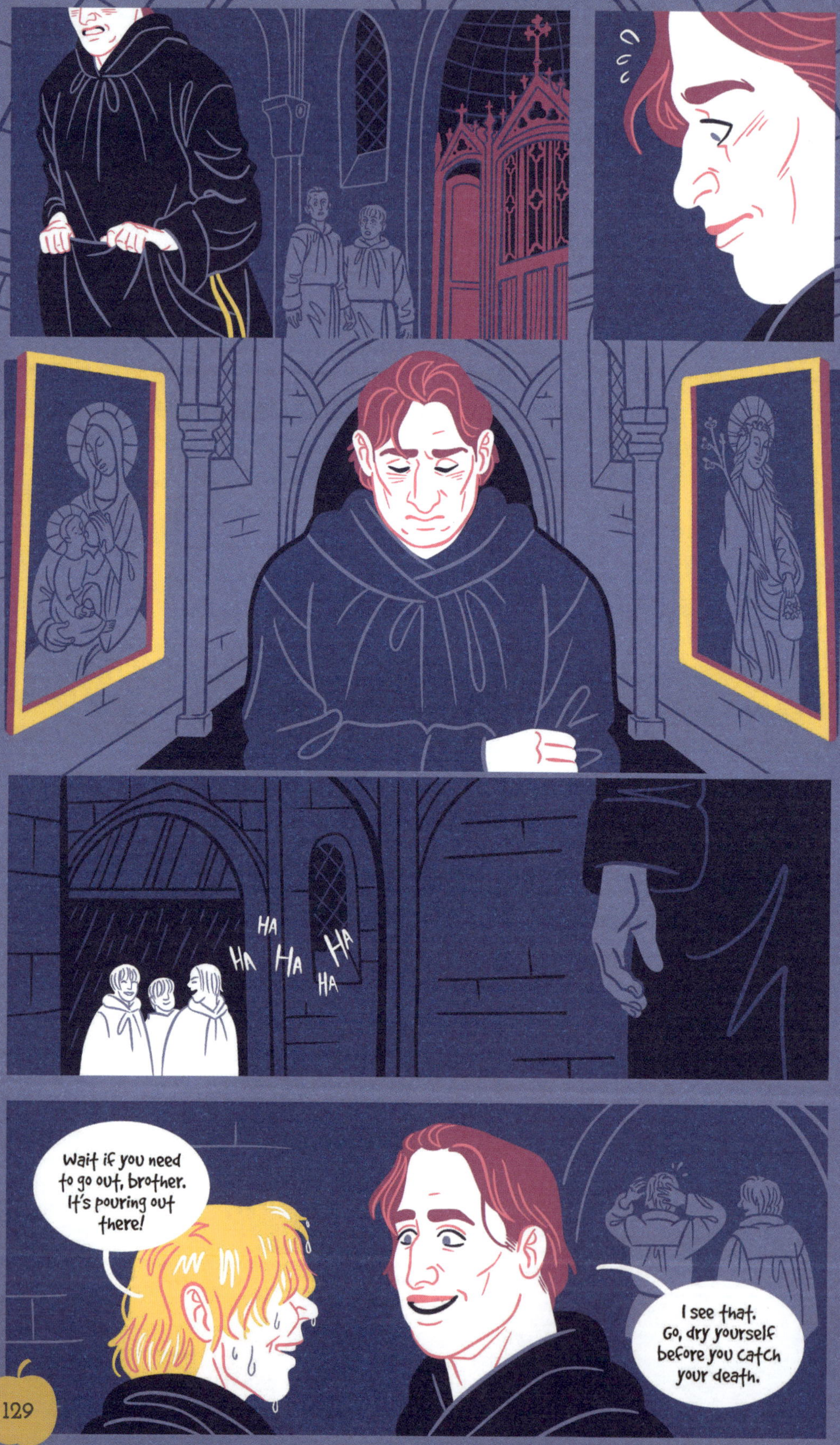
HA
HA
HA
HA
HA
HA
Wait if you need to go out, brother. It's pouring out there!
I see that. Go, dry yourself before you catch your death.

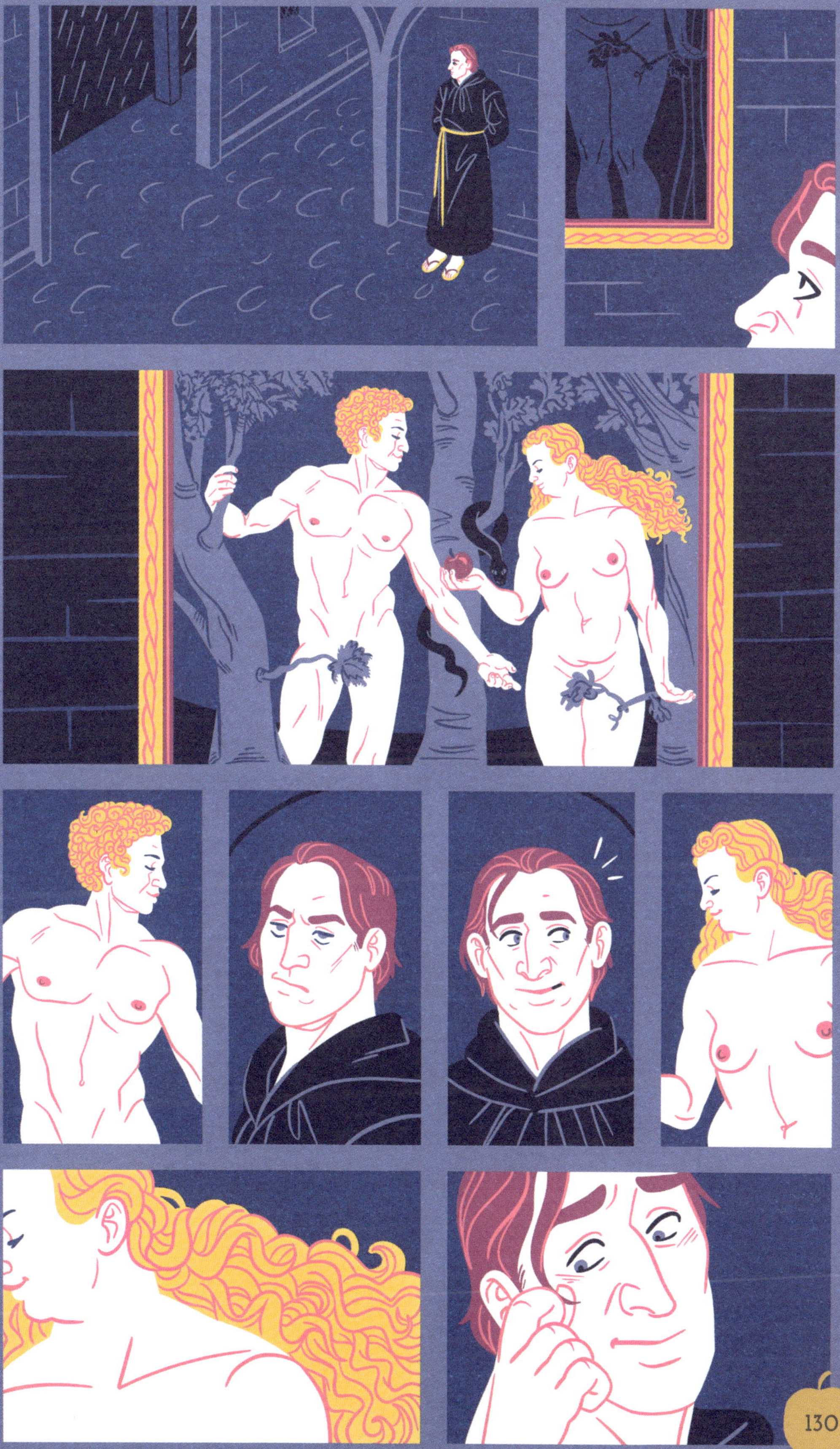

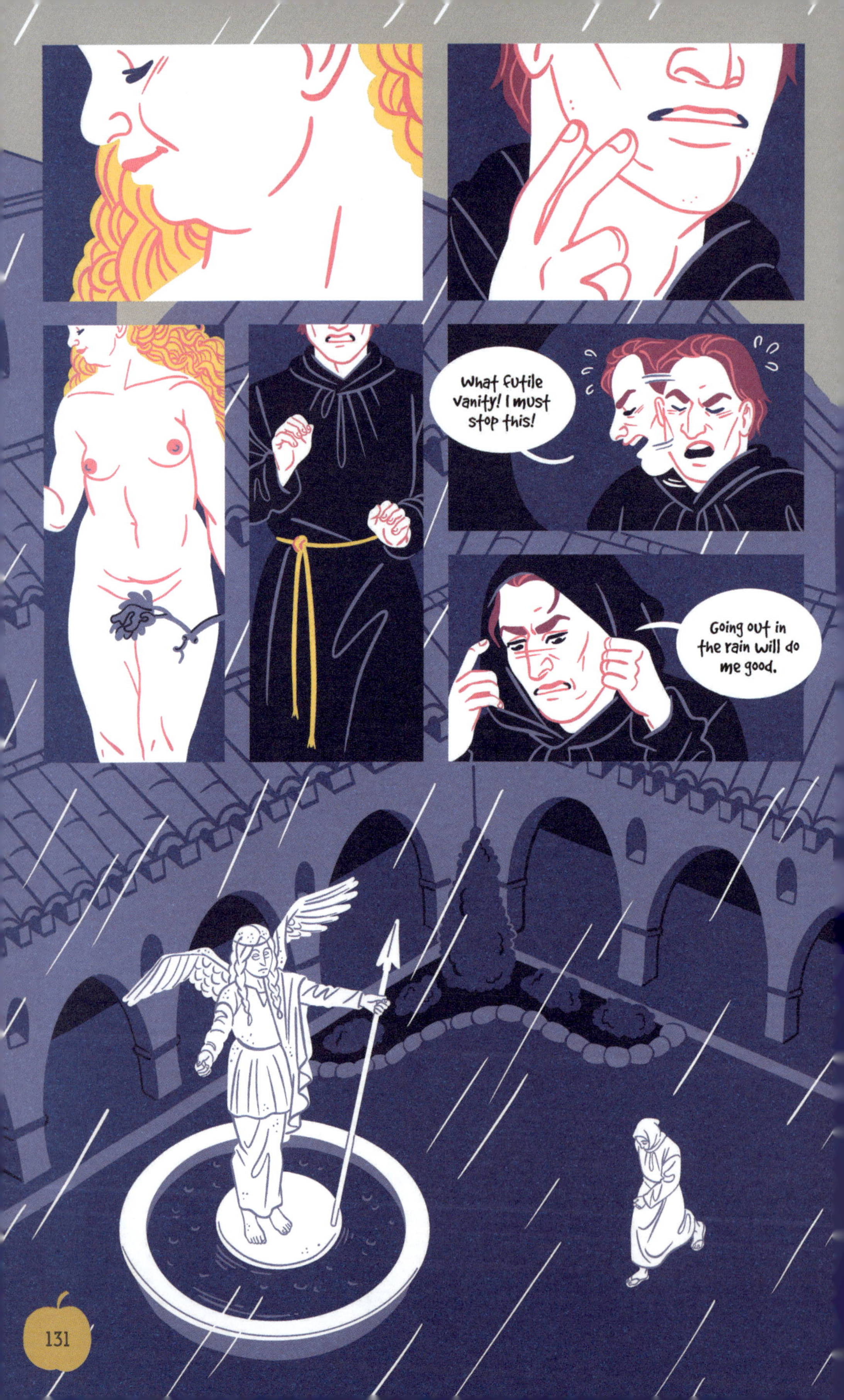
What futile vanity! I must stop this!
Going out in the rain will do me good.

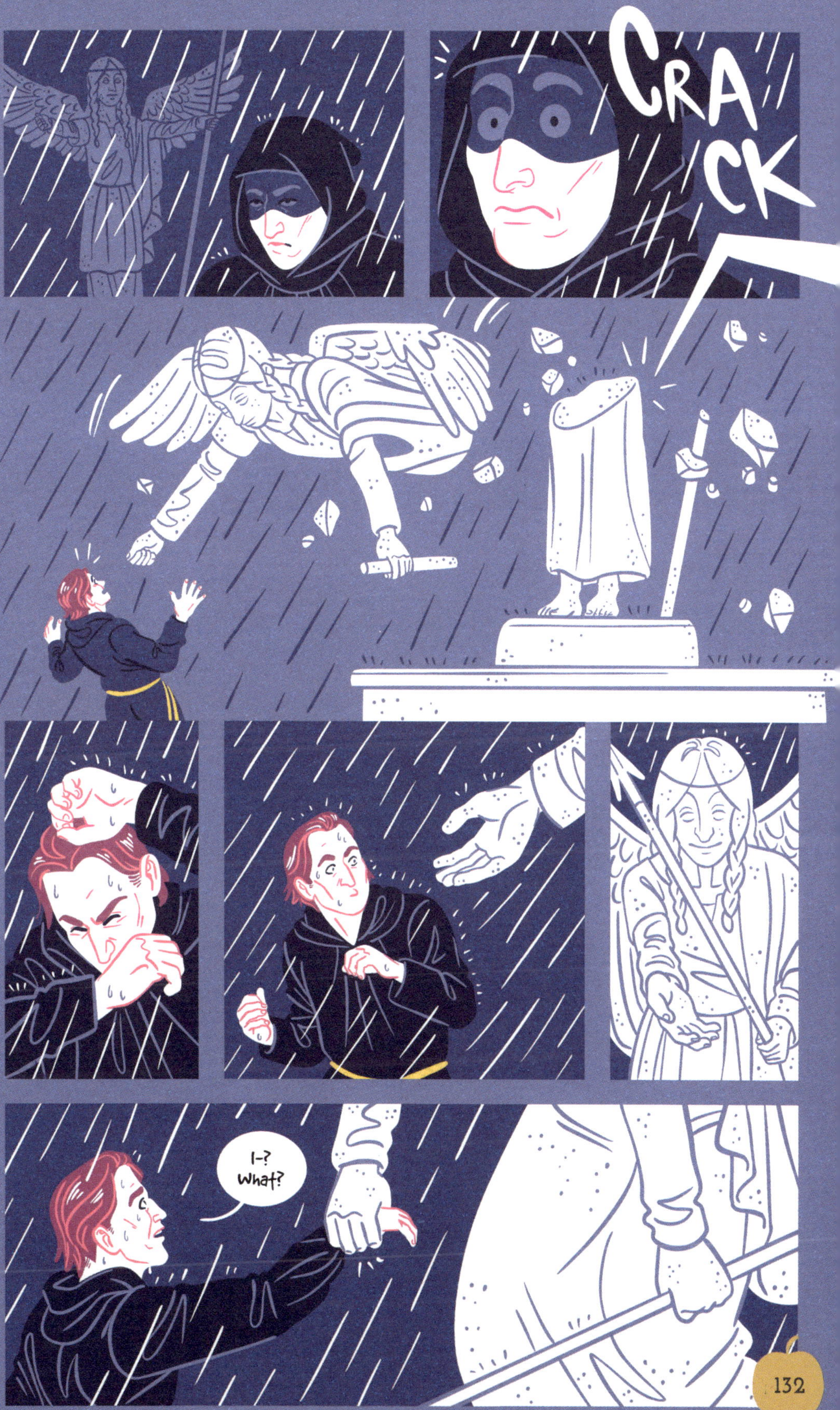
CRACK
I-? what?

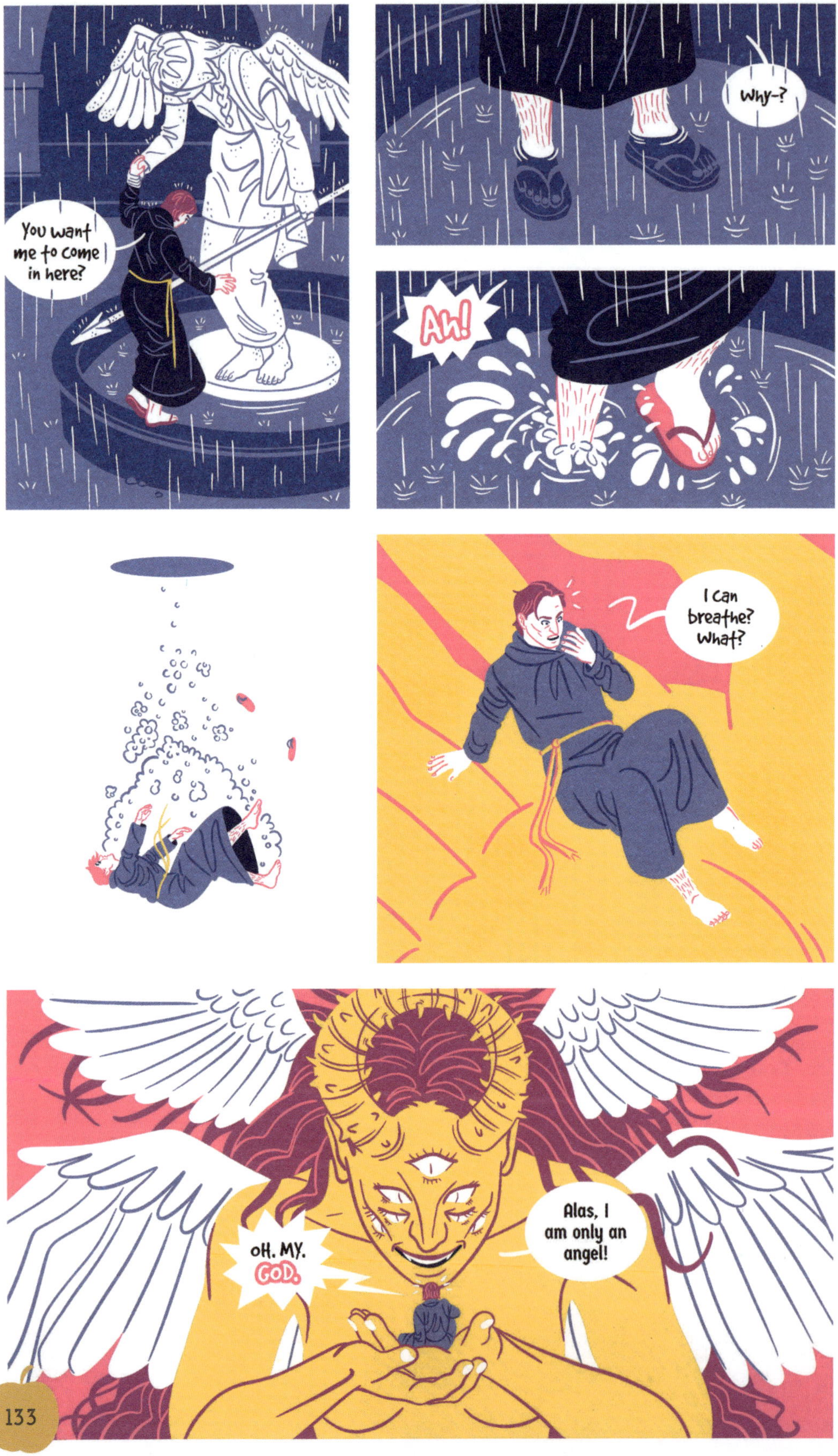
You want me to come in here?
Why-?
Ah!
I can breathe? What?
OH. MY. GOD.
Alas, I am only an angel!

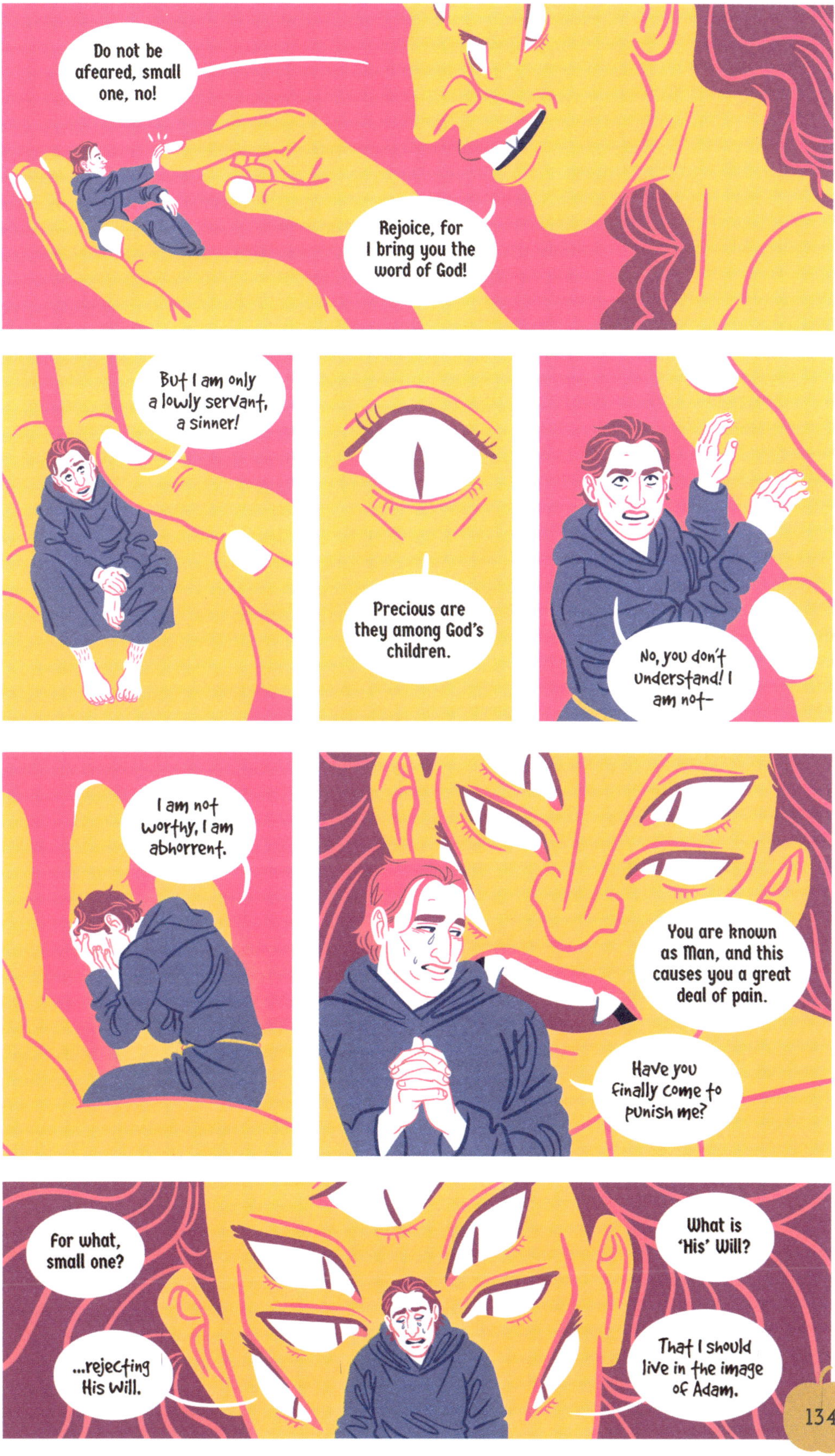

Do not be afeared, small one, no!
Rejoice, for I bring you the word of God!
But I am only a lowly servant, a sinner!
Precious are they among God's children.
No, you don't understand! I am not–
I am not worthy, I am abhorrent.
You are known as Man, and this causes you a great deal of pain.
Have you finally come to punish me?
For what, small one?
What is 'His' Will?
...rejecting His Will.
That I should live in the image of Adam.

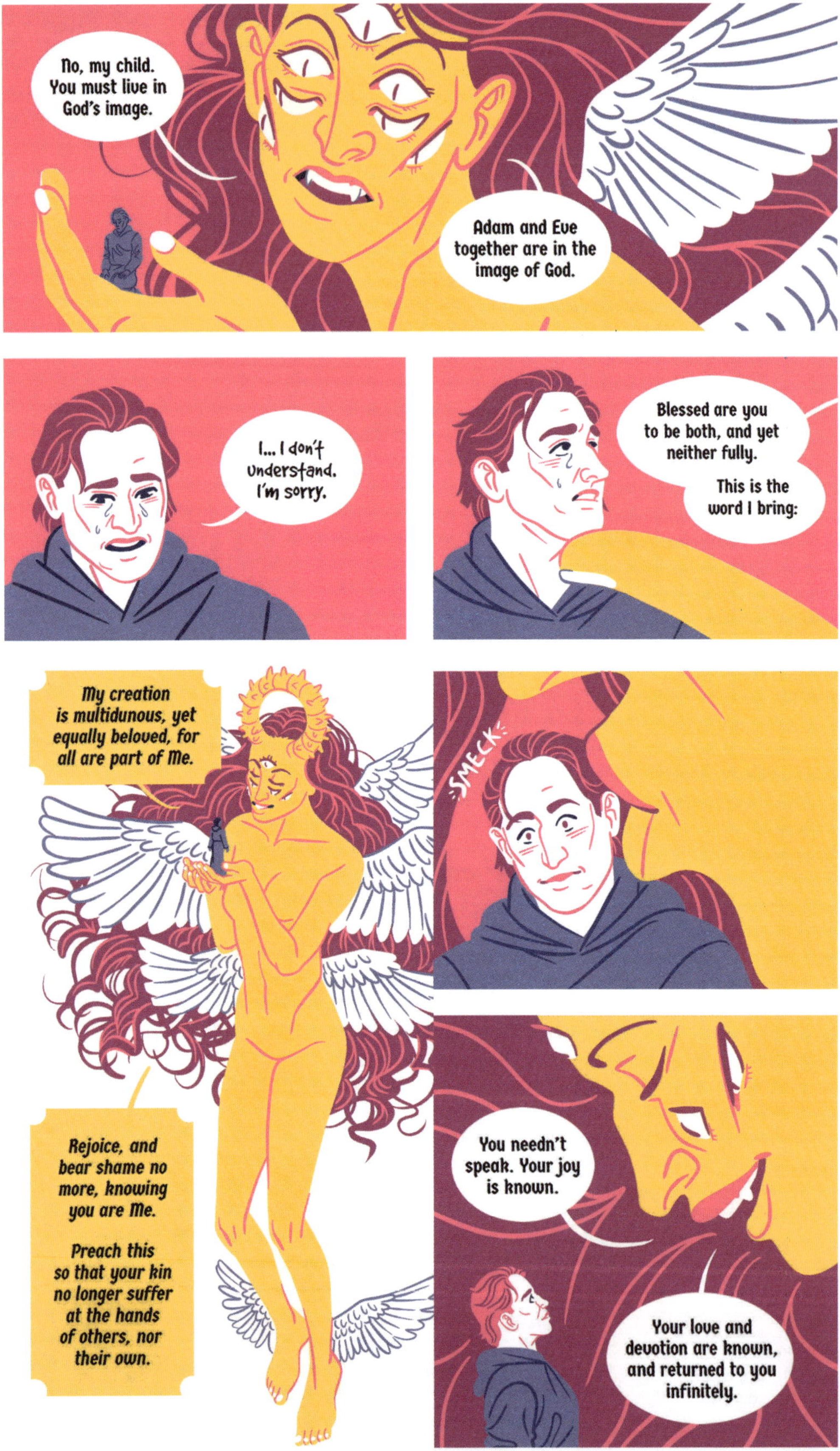
No, my child. You must live in God's image.
Adam and Eve together are in the image of God.
I... I don't understand. I'm sorry.
Blessed are you to be both, and yet neither fully.
This is the word I bring:
My creation is multidunous, yet equally beloved, for all are part of Me.
Rejoice, and bear shame no more, knowing you are Me.
Preach this so that your kin no longer suffer at the hands of others, nor their own.
SMECK
You needn't speak. Your joy is known.
Your love and devotion are known, and returned to you infinitely.

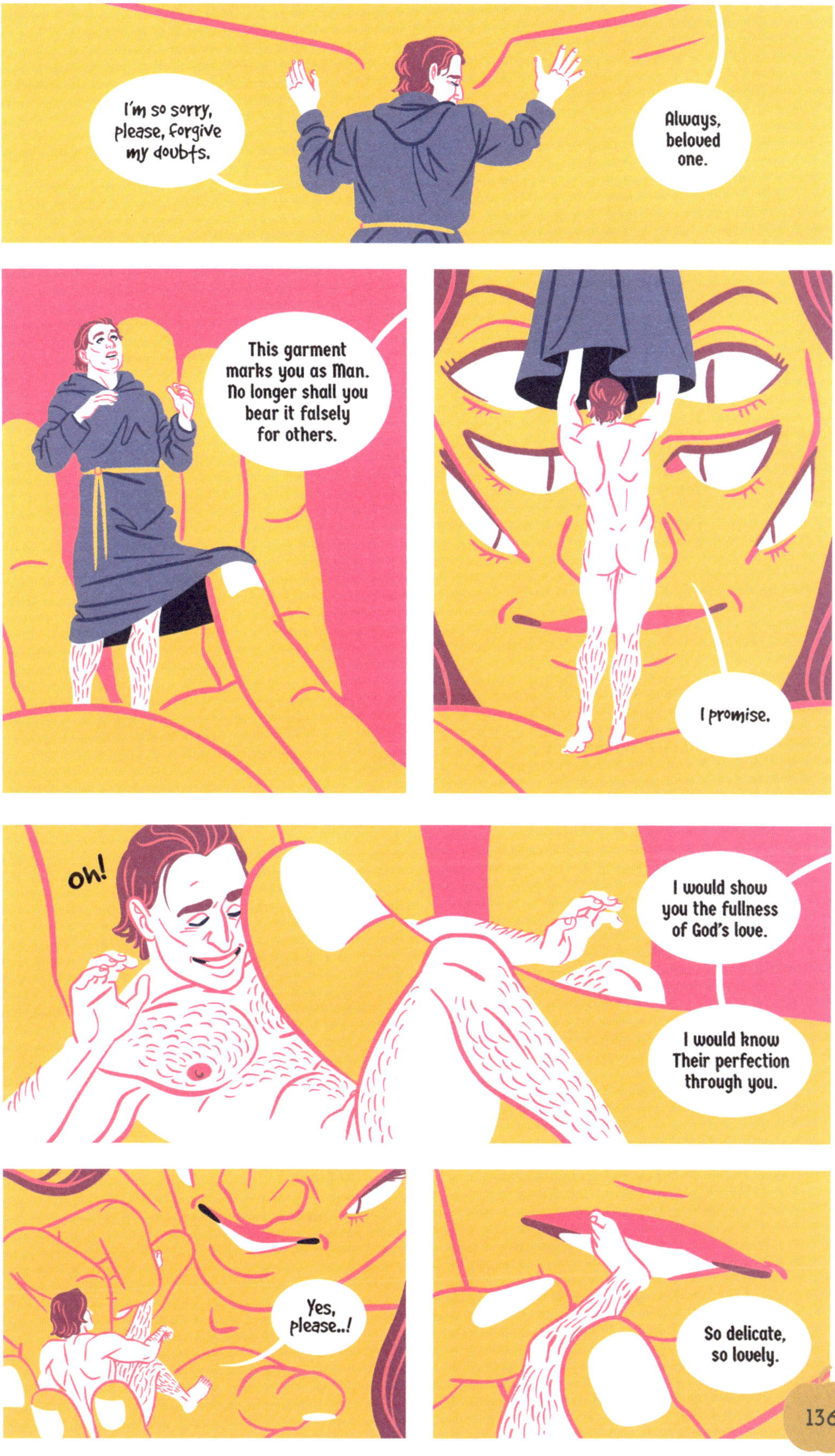

I'm so sorry, please, forgive my doubts.
Always, beloved one.
This garment marks you as Man. No longer shall you bear it falsely for others.
I promise.
oh!
I would show you the fullness of God's love.
I would know Their perfection through you.
Yes, please...!
So delicate, so lovely.

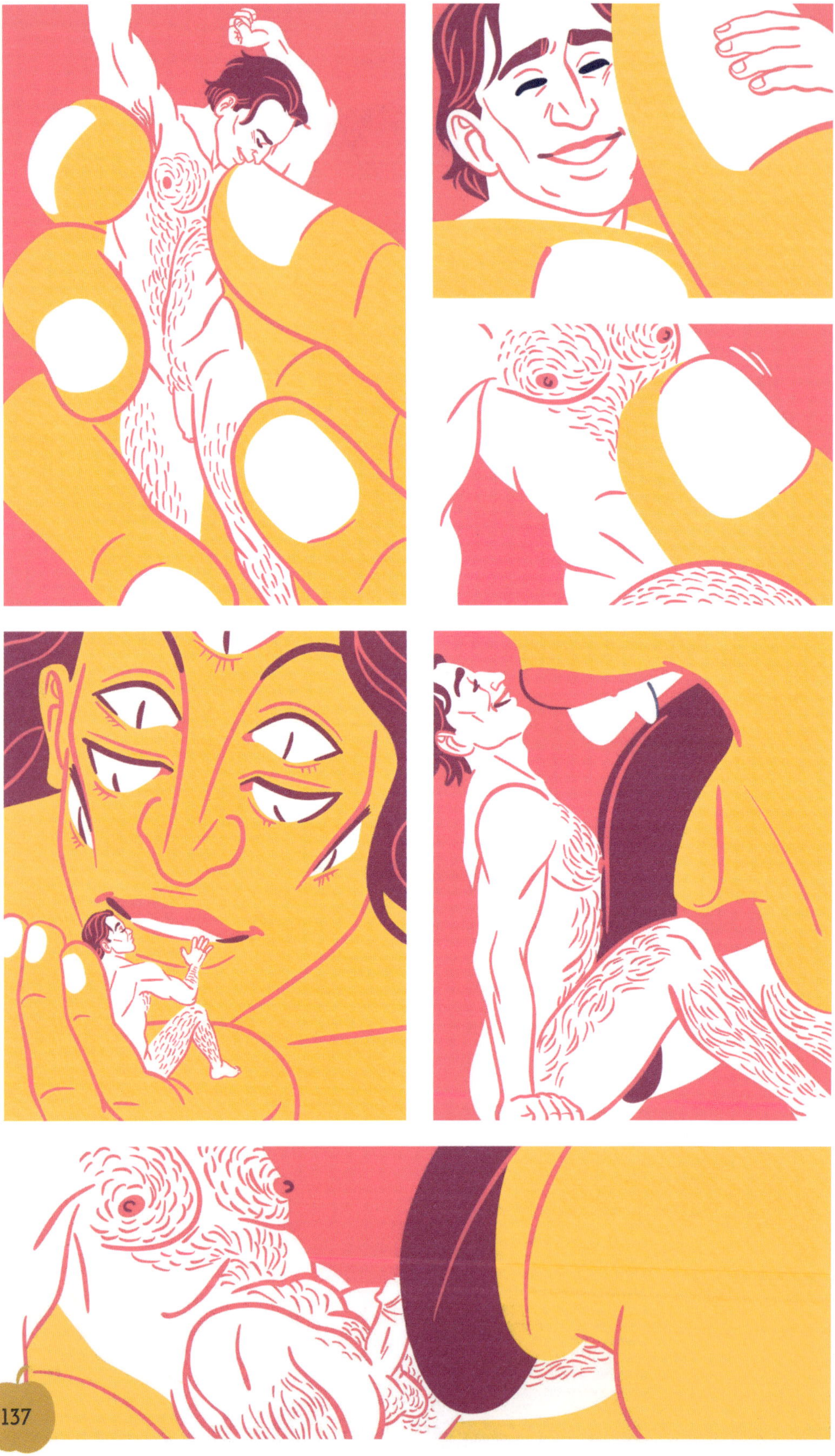

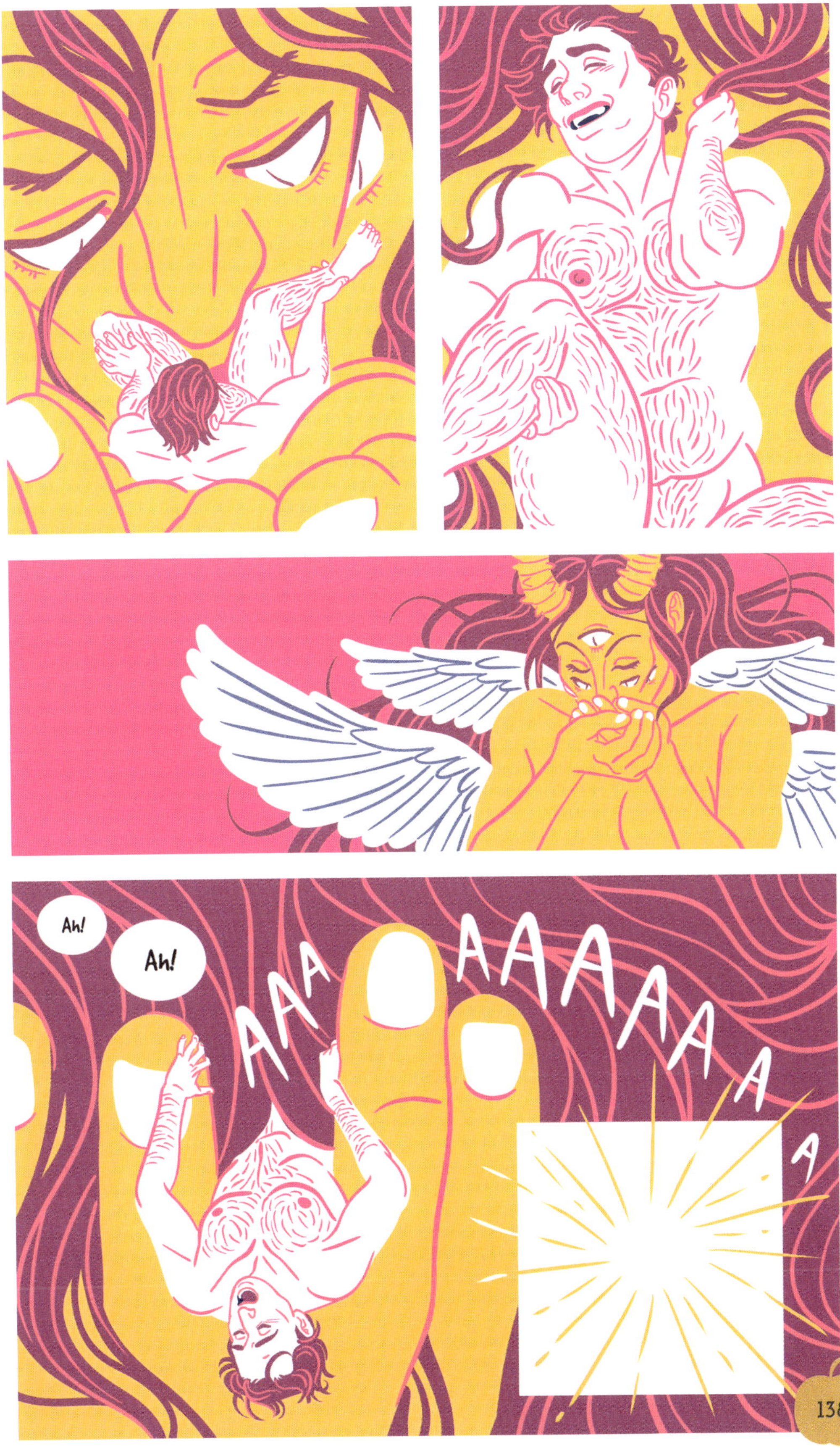

Ah!
Ah!
AAAAAAAAAA

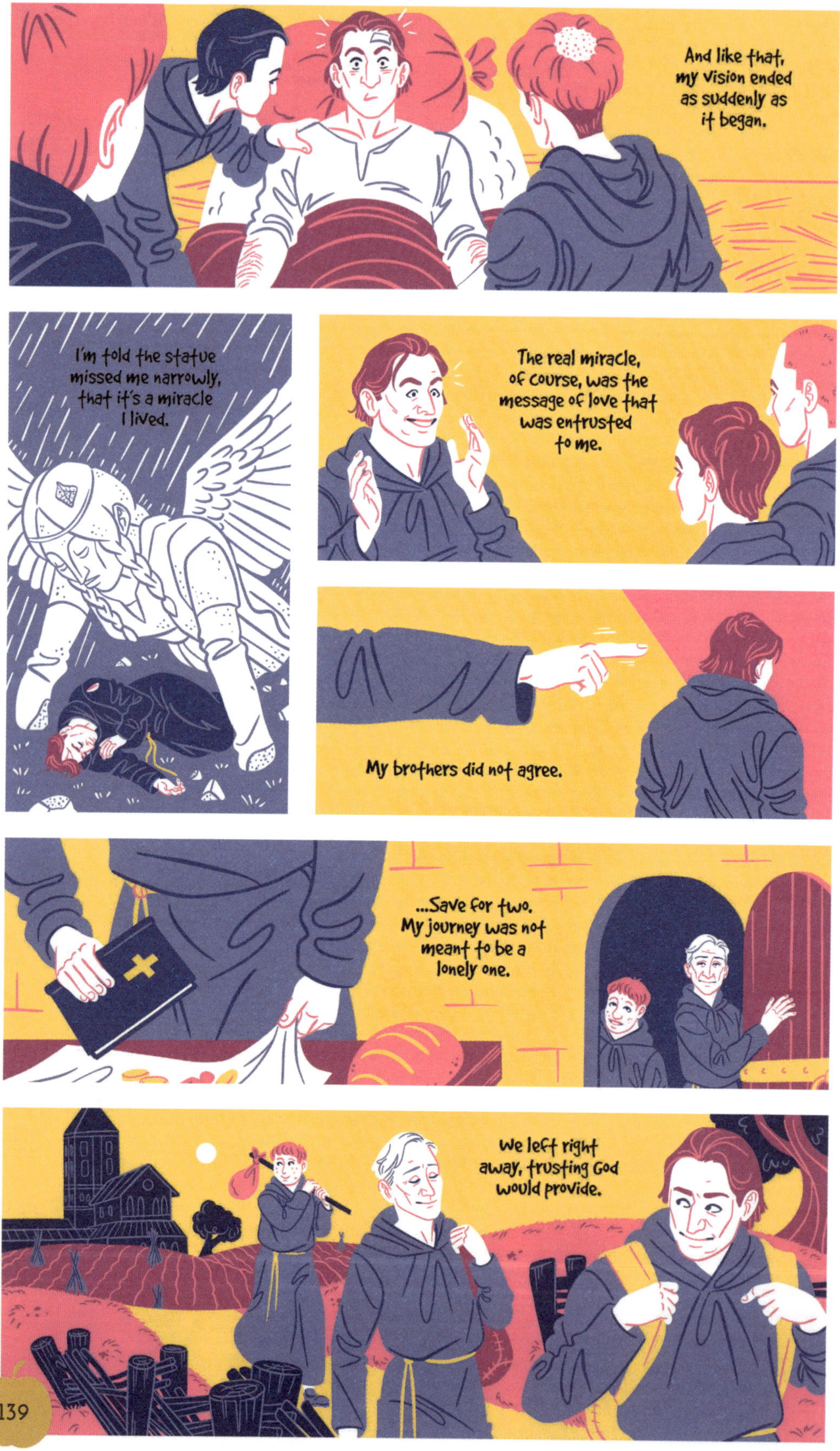
And like that, my vision ended as suddenly as it began.
I'm told the statue missed me narrowly, that it's a miracle I lived.
The real miracle, of course, was the message of love that was entrusted to me.
My brothers did not agree.
...Save for two. My journey was not meant to be a lonely one.
We left right away, trusting God would provide.

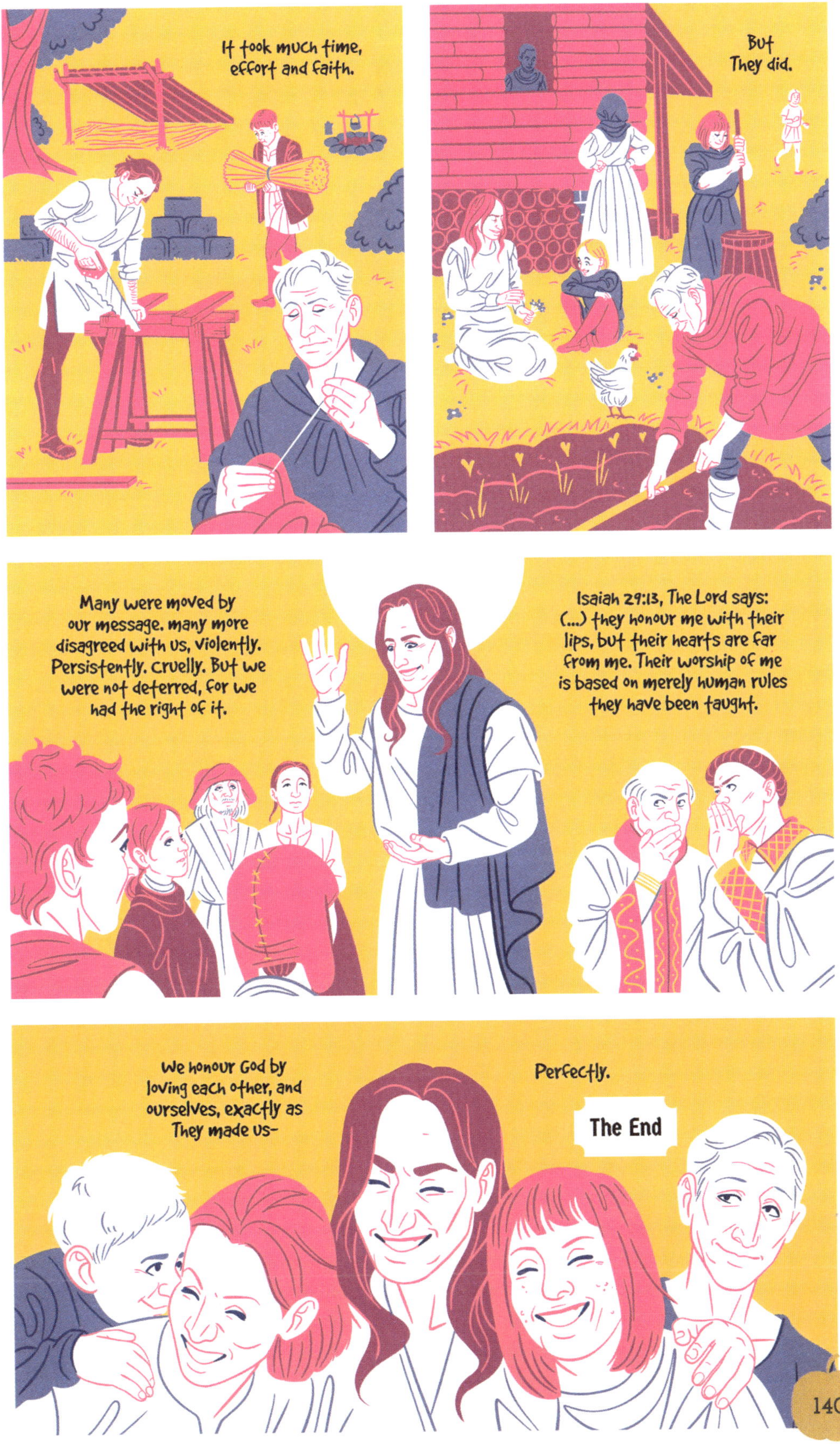
It took much time, effort and faith.
But They did.
Many were moved by our message. many more disagreed with us, violently. Persistently. cruelly. But we were not deterred, for we had the right of it.
Isaiah 29:13, The Lord says: (...) they honour me with their lips, but their hearts are far from me. Their worship of me is based on merely human rules they have been taught.
We honour God by loving each other, and ourselves, exactly as They made us-
Perfectly.
The End

Against the Tide

Story by Asahina Nakama - Art by Tab Kimpton

Yui has been unable to find a hajitiya willing to provide the hand tattoos that signify her coming-of-age from child to adult woman. In despair she prays to the sea, not expecting the spirit to answer back...

Writer's Note

" To be Okinawan is to be largely forgotten thanks to the impact of two colonizing empires over the past 150 years. Our many languages and our culture have languished in that time, now at risk of extinction. I wanted to do more than showcase my people with this story, though. In the same spirit of envisioning pleasurable trans-centered sexuality, I saw a chance to bring pre-colonized Okinawa to life. In doing so, I hope to show not just who we were as a people, but that indigenous ways of being can accommodate queerness as well or better than the Western models imposed on us.

I was excited to work with Tab on this; he is an excellent collaborator, and I hope the parts of him interwoven through this story delight you as much as they do me. "

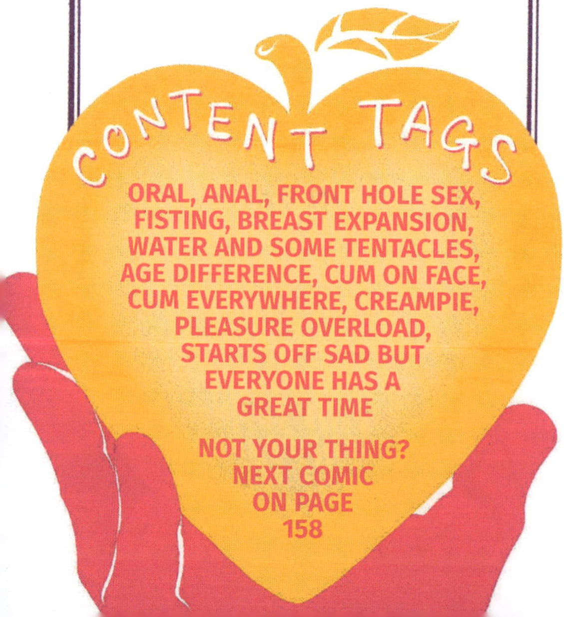

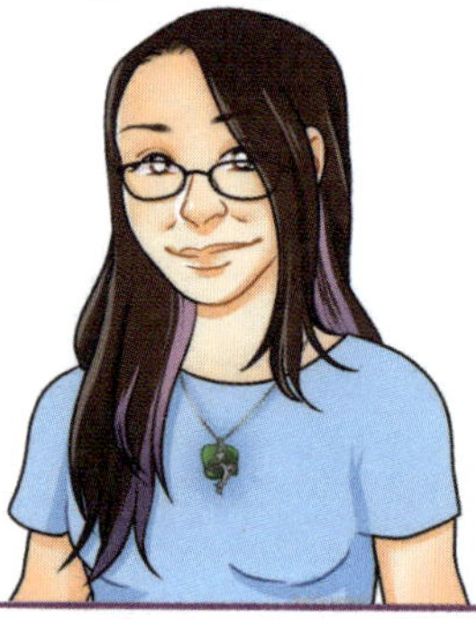

About the Creators

Asahina Nakama (she/her) is an Okinawan-American enby femme second-gen immigrant and first-gen university graduate with work in games, fiction, and now comics.

She currently lives in Rhode Island (in the US) and spends a lot of time dreaming up better, kinder futures. She does her best to find time to put those dreams into practice--or at least tell stories of them--in between all the labor that comes from surviving the world as a queer person. Caring people doing their best is her biggest turn-on.

Twitter.com/arnakama

Tab Kimpton (he/him) is a Manchester (UK) based comic artist and the co-editor of the anthology!

His works include Minority Monsters, Sir Butler & Boy, and our previous anthologies Come Together & Ambrosia

DiscordComics.com

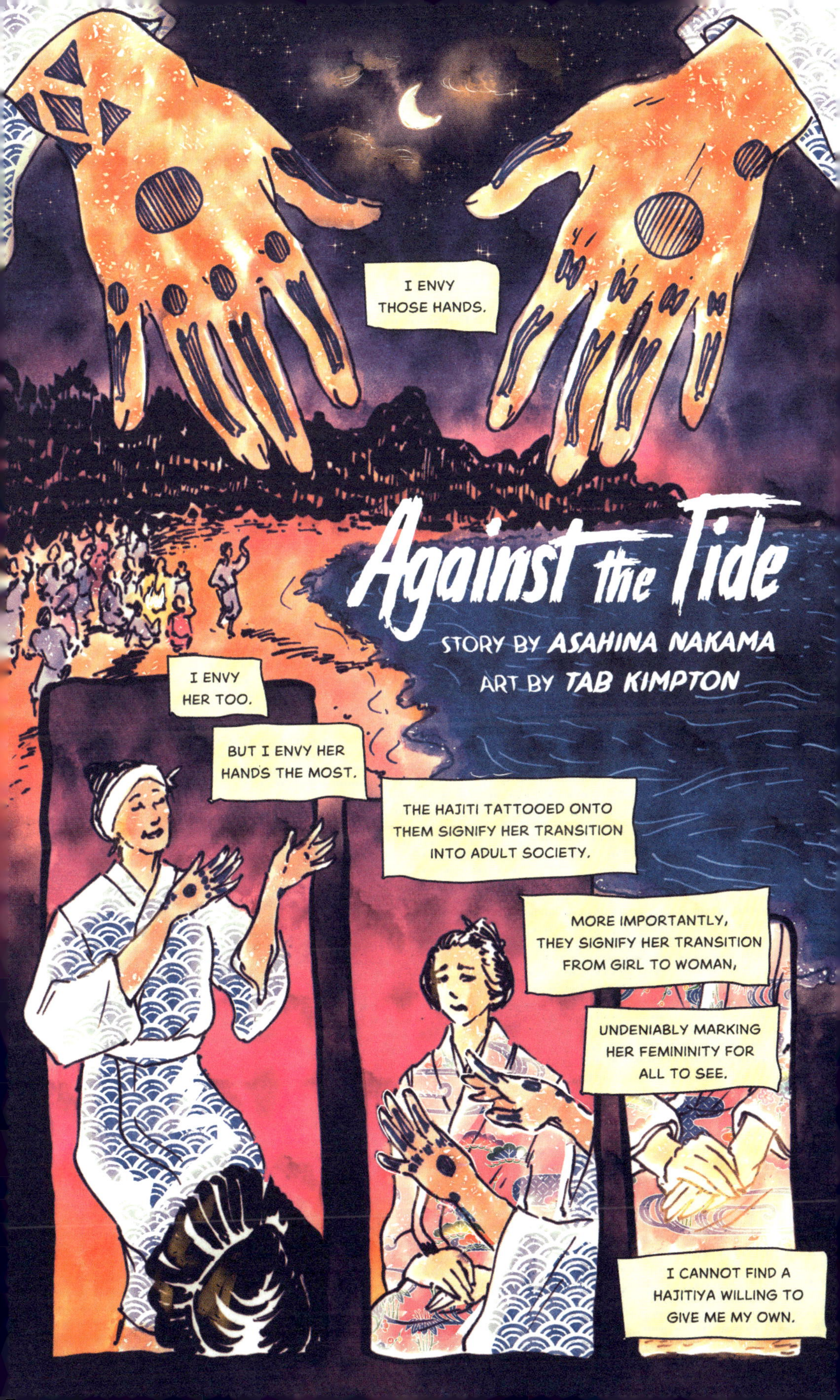
I ENVY THOSE HANDS.
Against the Tide
STORY BY ASAHINA NAKAMA
ART BY TAB KIMPTON
I ENVY HER TOO.
BUT I ENVY HER HANDS THE MOST.
THE HAJITI TATTOOED ONTO THEM SIGNIFY HER TRANSITION INTO ADULT SOCIETY.
MORE IMPORTANTLY, THEY SIGNIFY HER TRANSITION FROM GIRL TO WOMAN,
UNDENIABLY MARKING HER FEMININITY FOR ALL TO SEE.
I CANNOT FIND A HAJITIYA WILLING TO GIVE ME MY OWN.

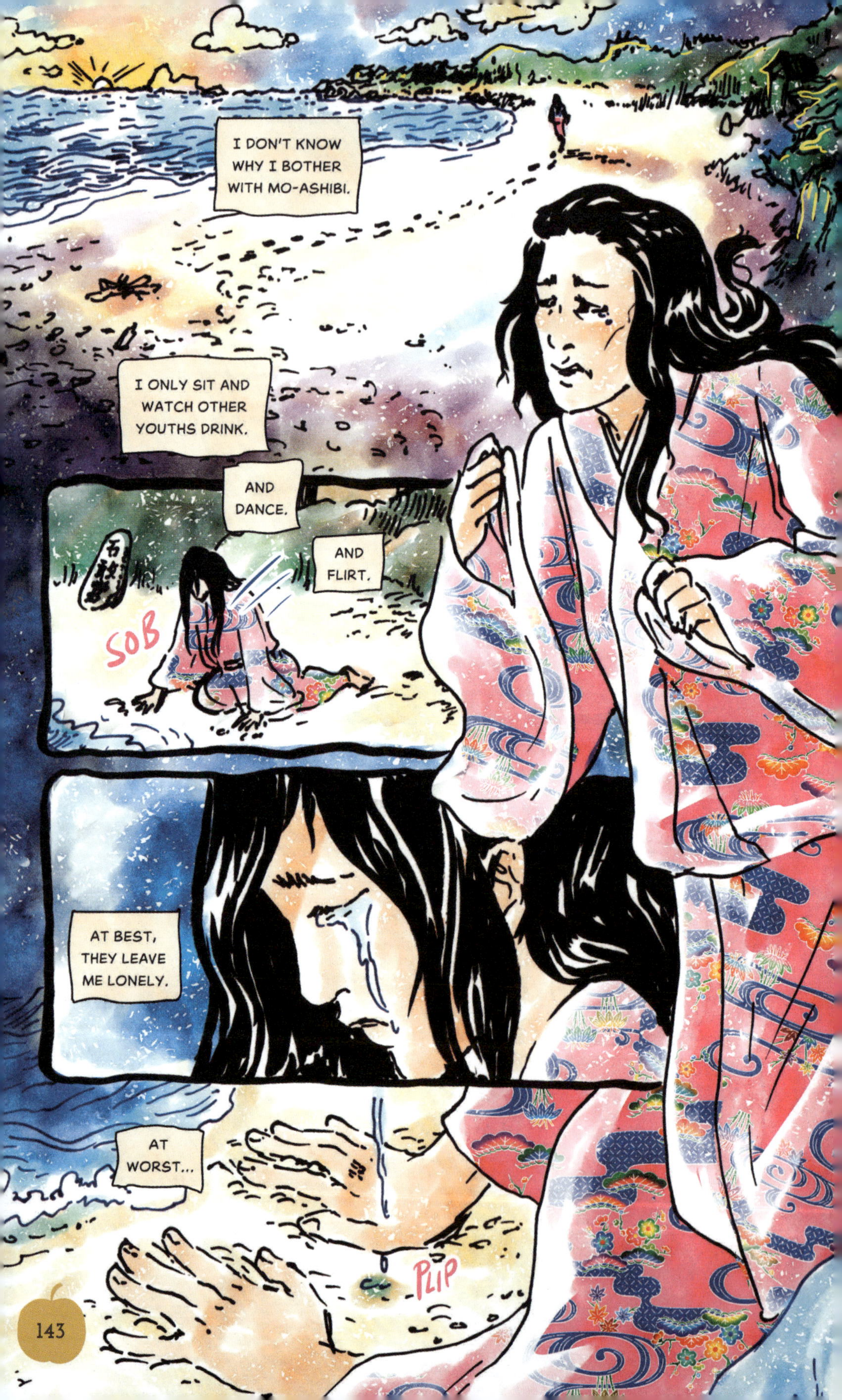
I DON'T KNOW WHY I BOTHER WITH MO-ASHIBI.
I ONLY SIT AND WATCH OTHER YOUTHS DRINK.
AND DANCE.
AND FLIRT.
SOB
AT BEST, THEY LEAVE ME LONELY.
AT WORST...
PLIP

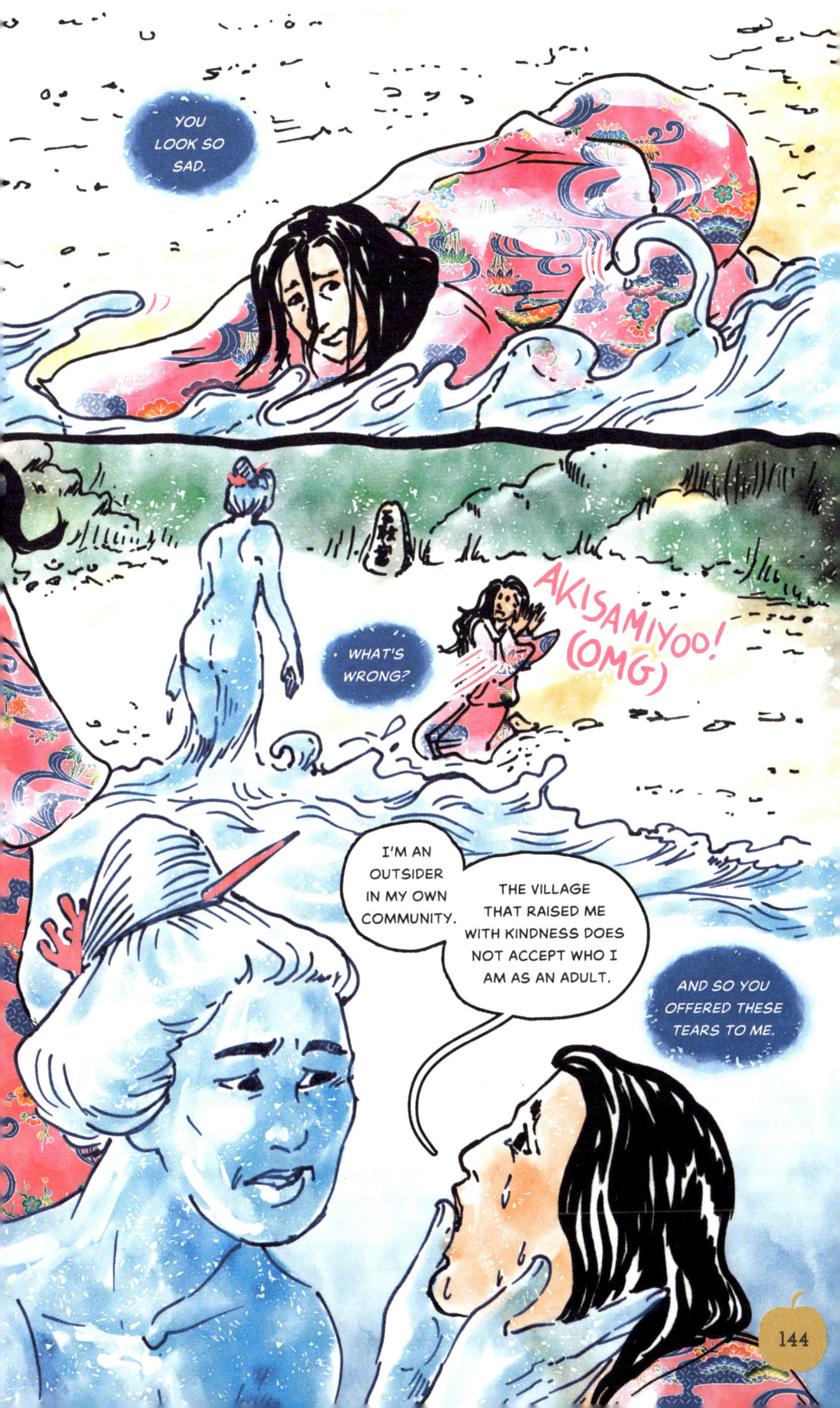
YOU LOOK SO SAD.
AKISAMIYOO! (OMG)
WHAT'S WRONG?
I'M AN OUTSIDER IN MY OWN COMMUNITY.
THE VILLAGE THAT RAISED ME WITH KINDNESS DOES NOT ACCEPT WHO I AM AS AN ADULT.
AND SO YOU OFFERED THESE TEARS TO ME.

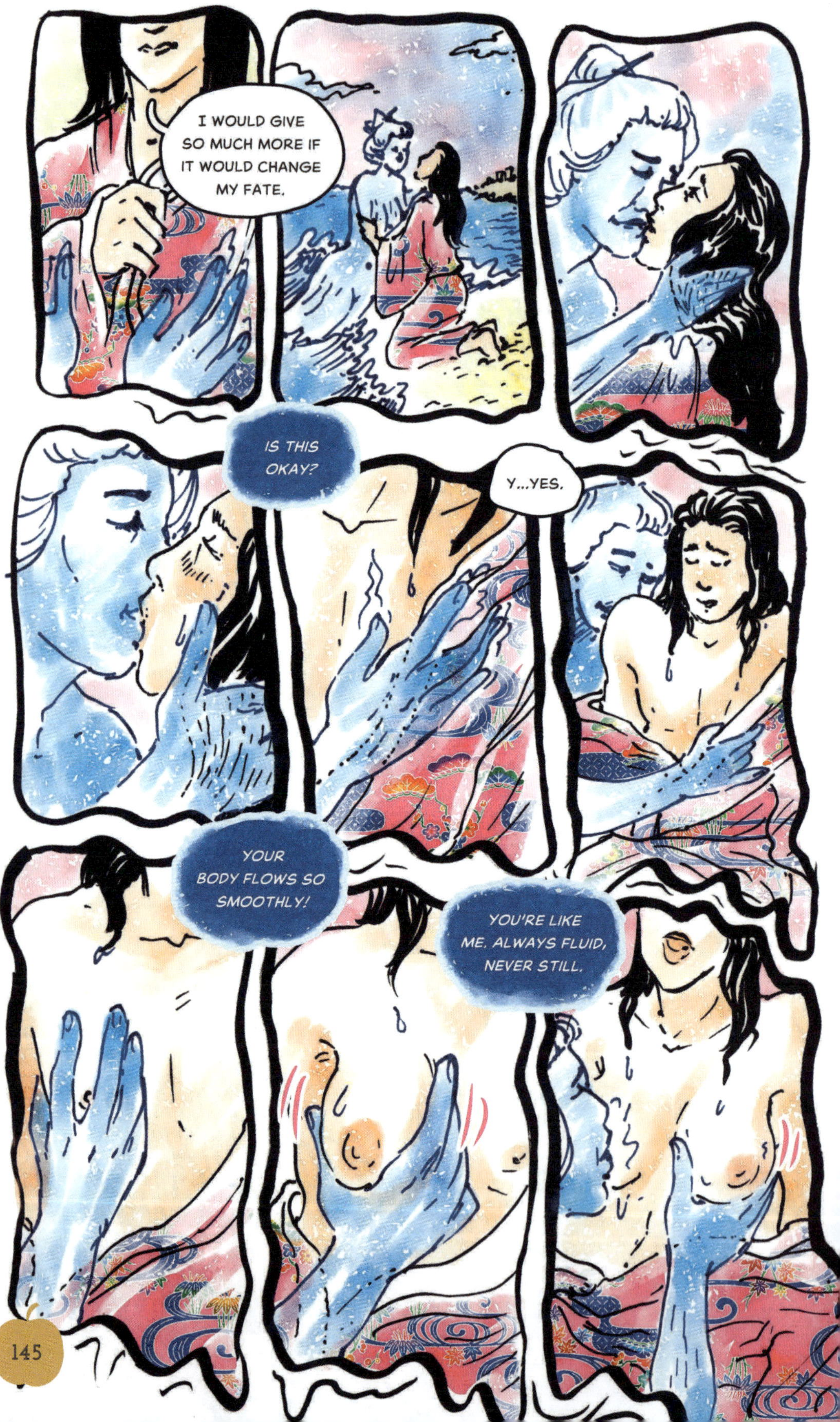
I WOULD GIVE SO MUCH MORE IF IT WOULD CHANGE MY FATE.
IS THIS OKAY?
Y...YES.
YOUR BODY FLOWS SO SMOOTHLY!
YOU'RE LIKE ME. ALWAYS FLUID, NEVER STILL.

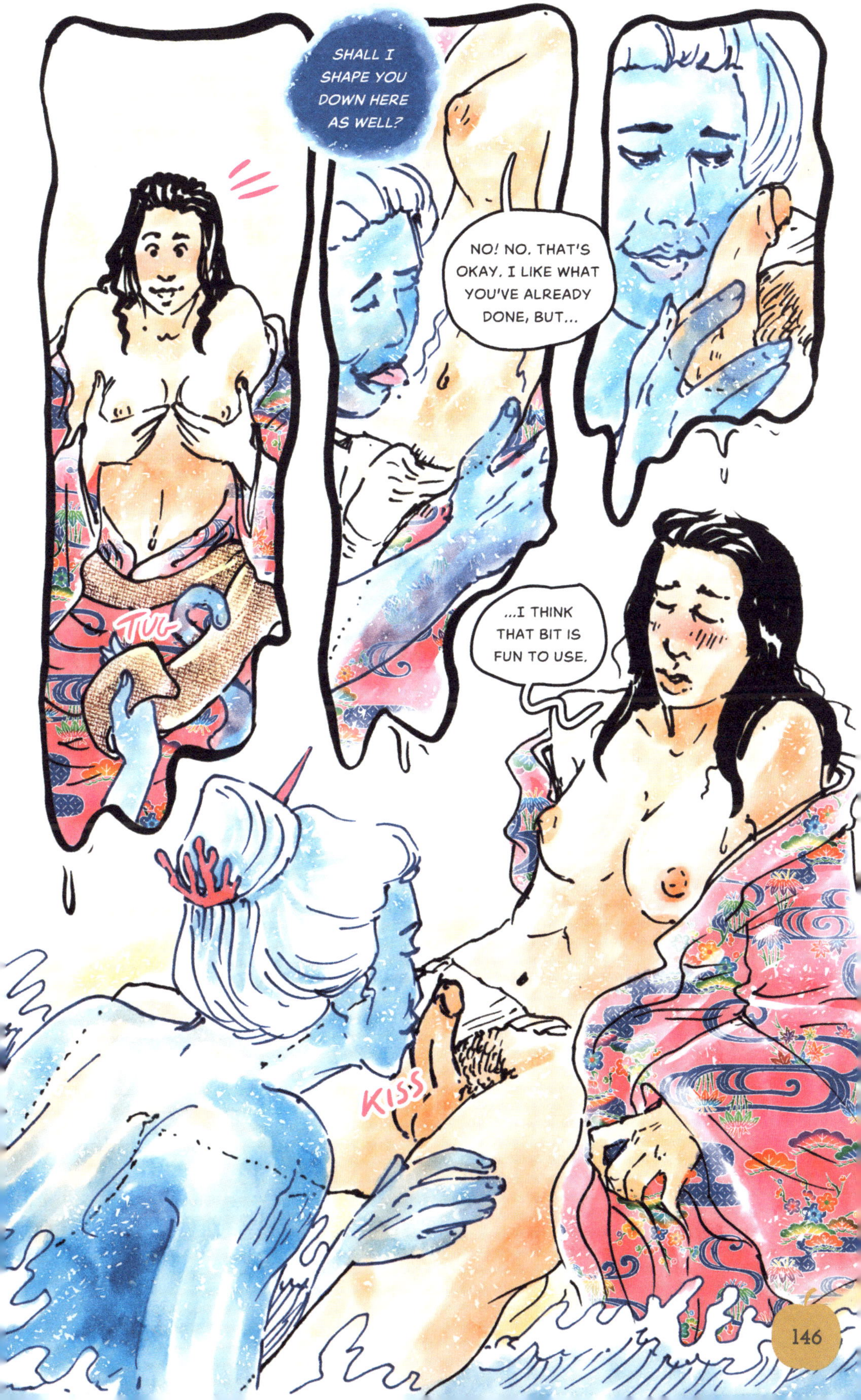

SHALL I SHAPE YOU DOWN HERE AS WELL?
TW
NO! NO. THAT'S OKAY. I LIKE WHAT YOU'VE ALREADY DONE, BUT...
...I THINK THAT BIT IS FUN TO USE.
KISS

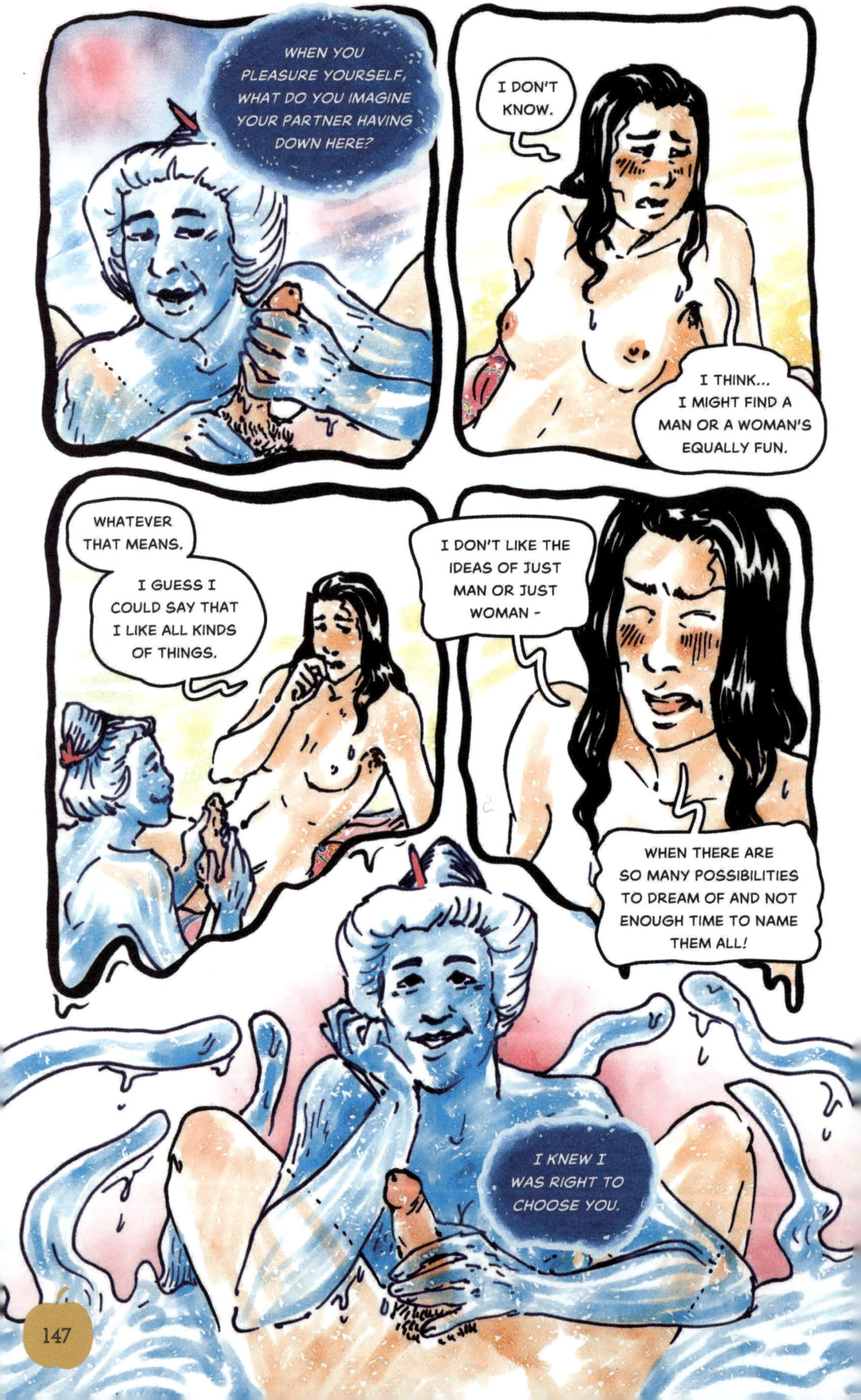
WHEN YOU PLEASURE YOURSELF, WHAT DO YOU IMAGINE YOUR PARTNER HAVING DOWN HERE?
I DON'T KNOW.
I THINK... I MIGHT FIND A MAN OR A WOMAN'S EQUALLY FUN.
WHATEVER THAT MEANS.
I GUESS I COULD SAY THAT I LIKE ALL KINDS OF THINGS.
I DON'T LIKE THE IDEAS OF JUST MAN OR JUST WOMAN -
WHEN THERE ARE SO MANY POSSIBILITIES TO DREAM OF AND NOT ENOUGH TIME TO NAME THEM ALL!
I KNEW I WAS RIGHT TO CHOOSE YOU.

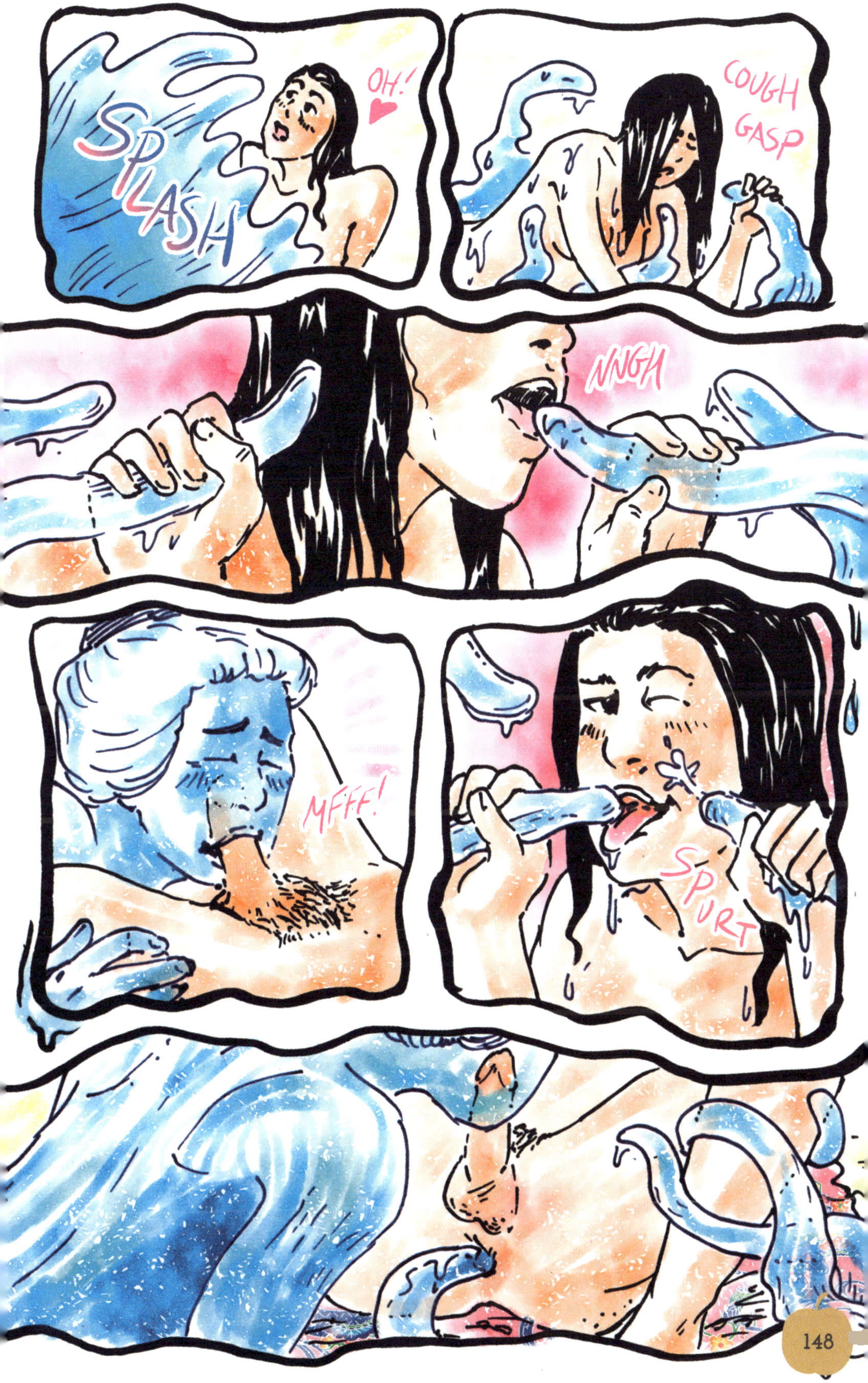
SPLASH
OH!
COUGH
GASP
NNGH
MFFF!
SPURT

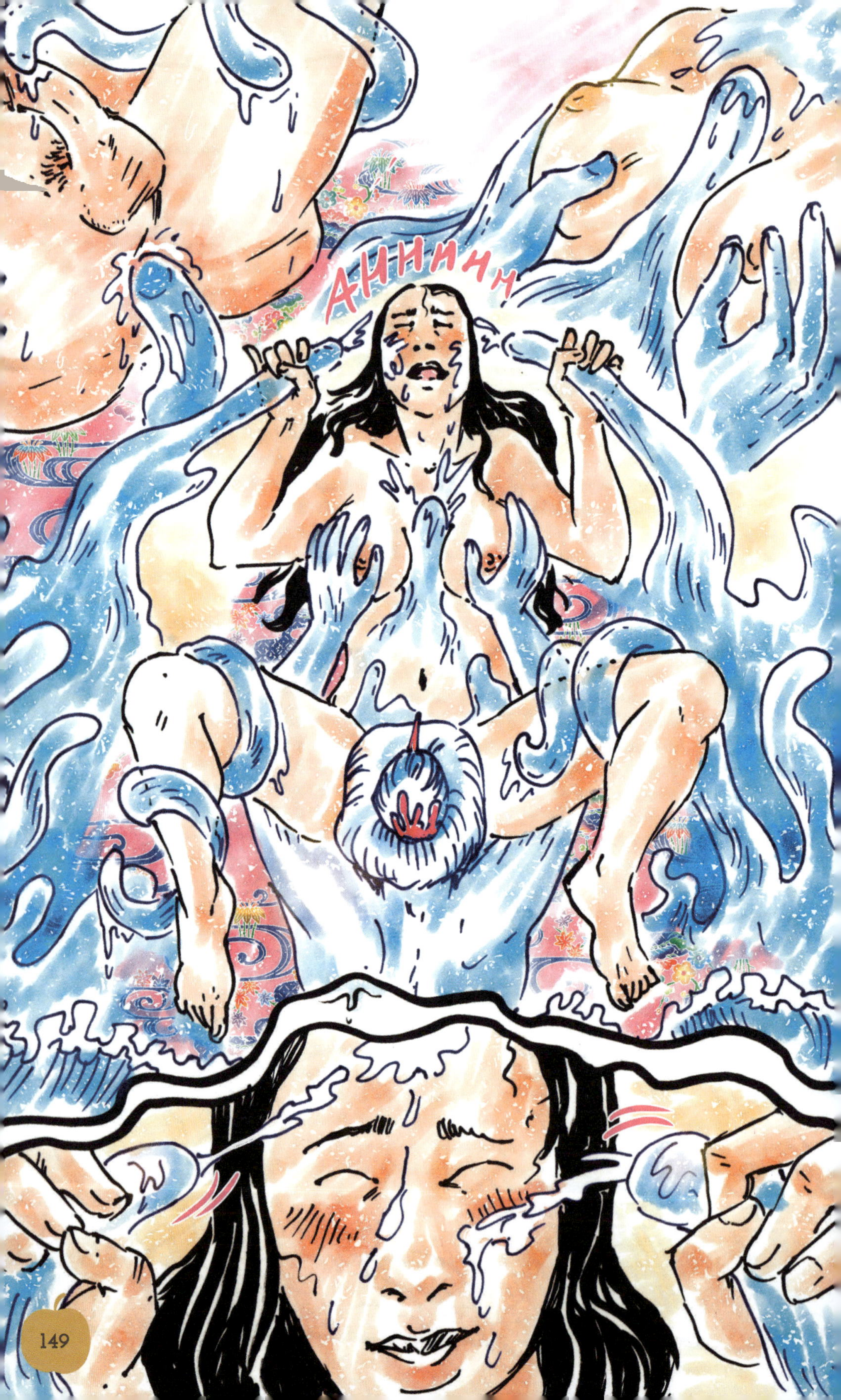
AHHHHHH

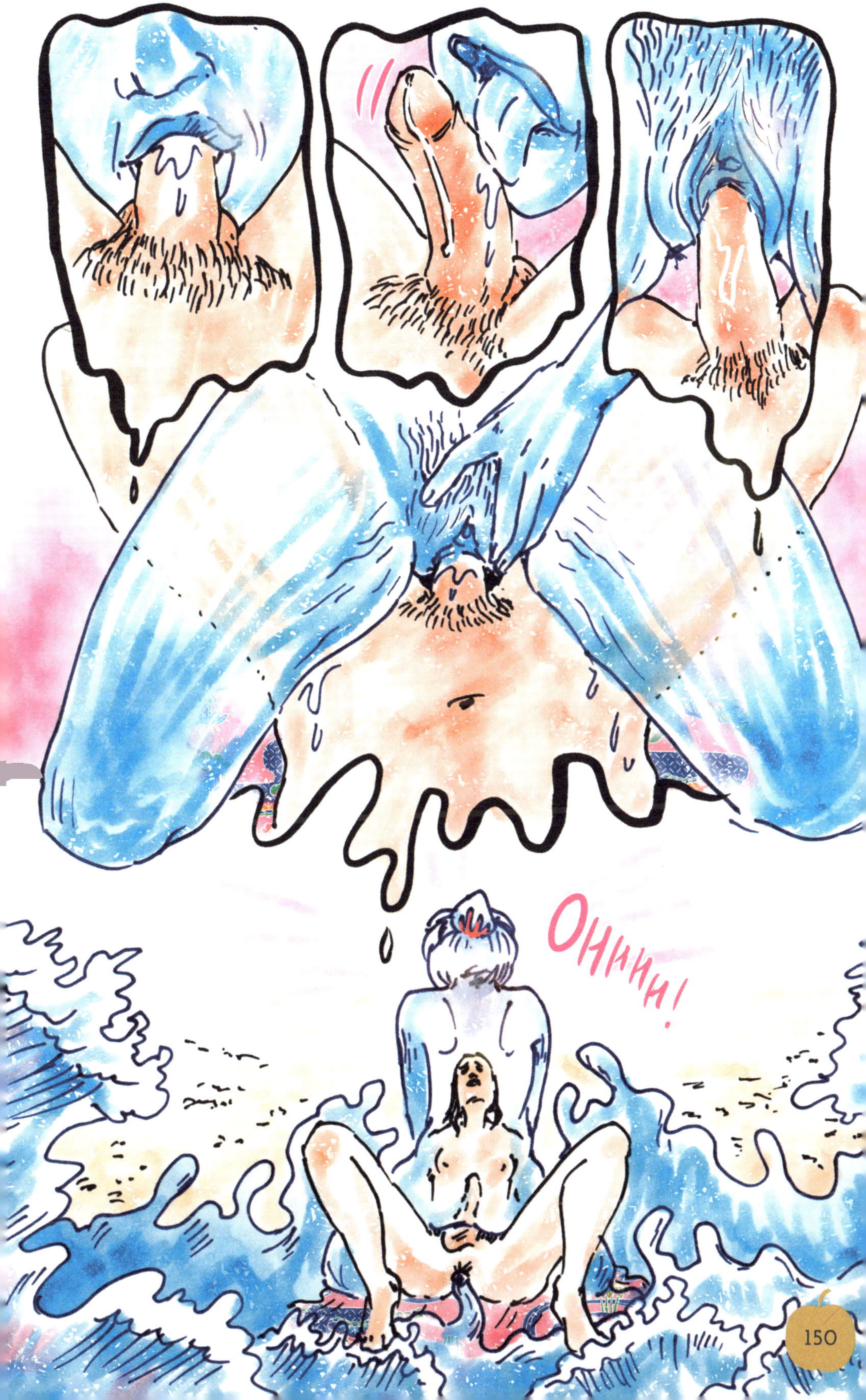
Ohhhh!

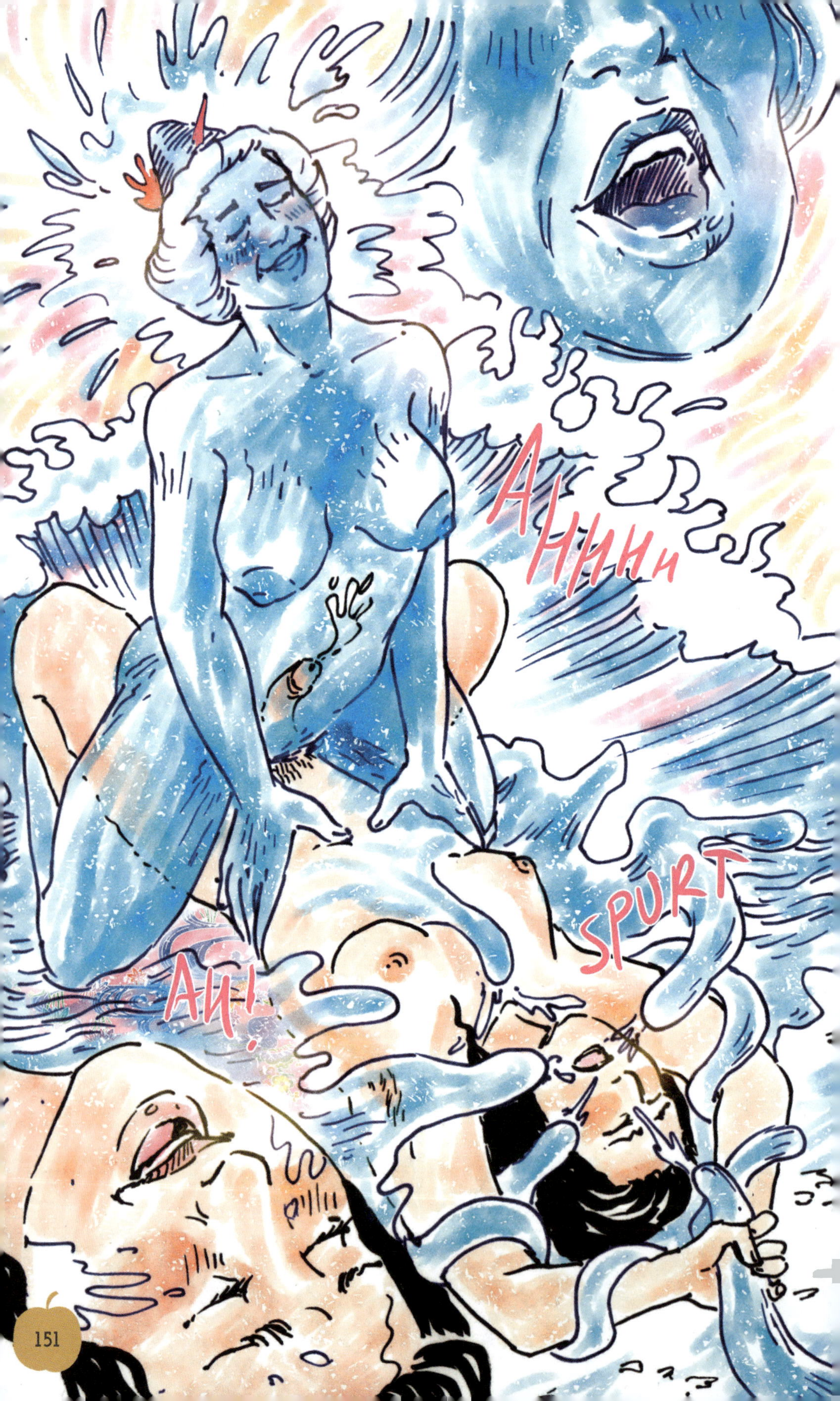
AHHHHH
SPURT
AH!

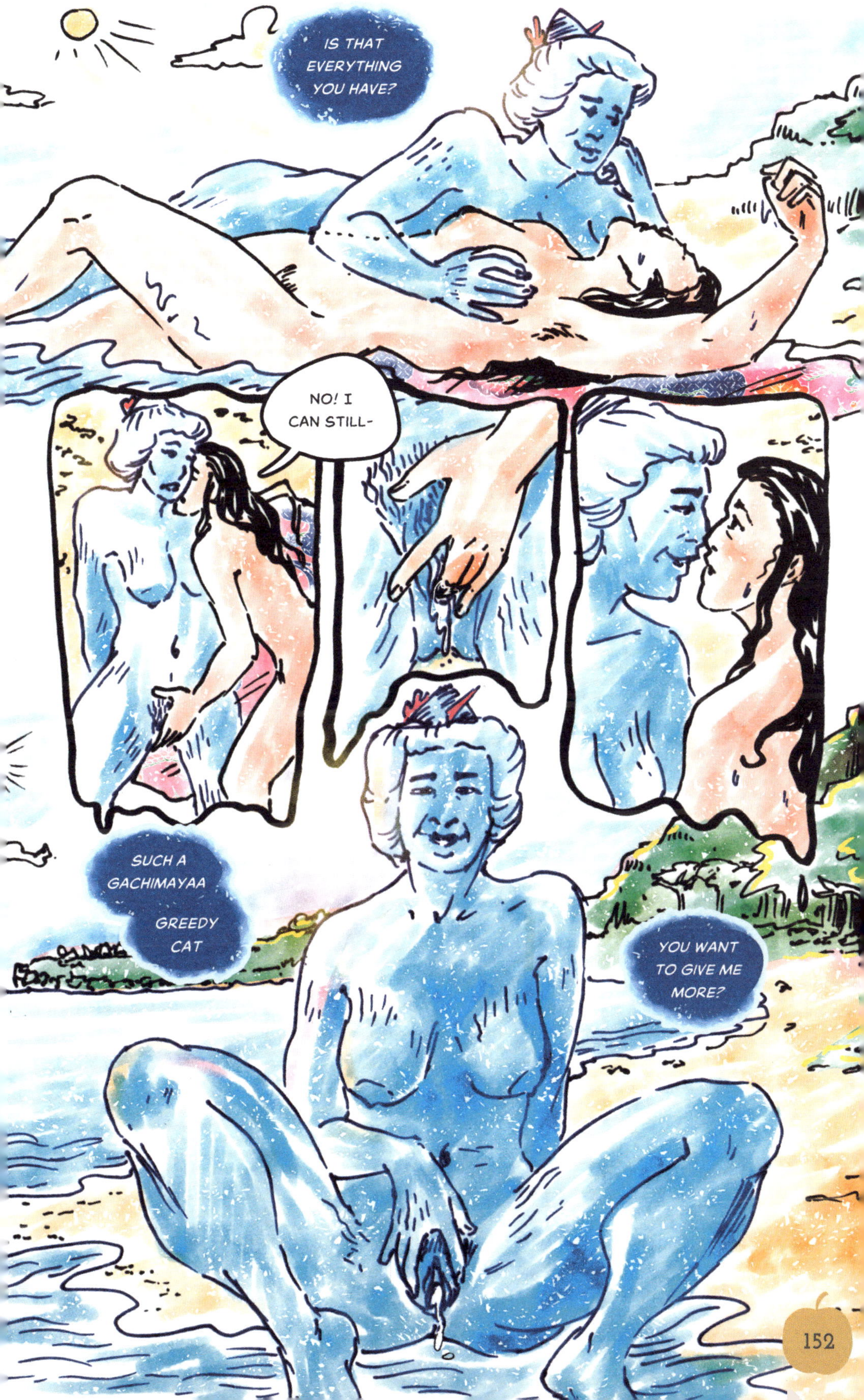
IS THAT EVERYTHING YOU HAVE?
NO! I CAN STILL-
SUCH A GACHIMAYAA
GREEDY CAT
YOU WANT TO GIVE ME MORE?

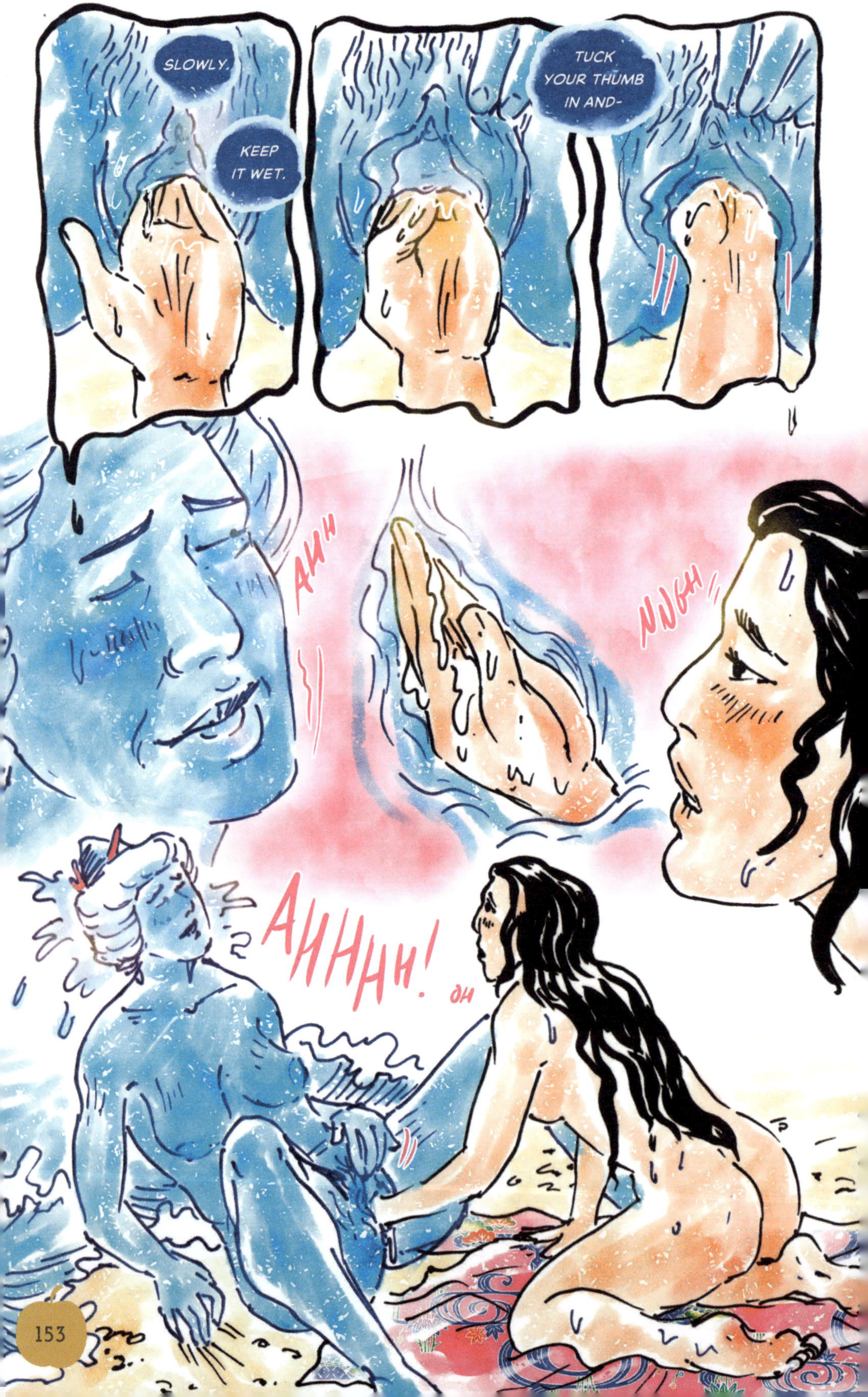
SLOWLY.
KEEP IT WET.
TUCK YOUR THUMB IN AND-
AHH
NNGH
AHHHH!
OH

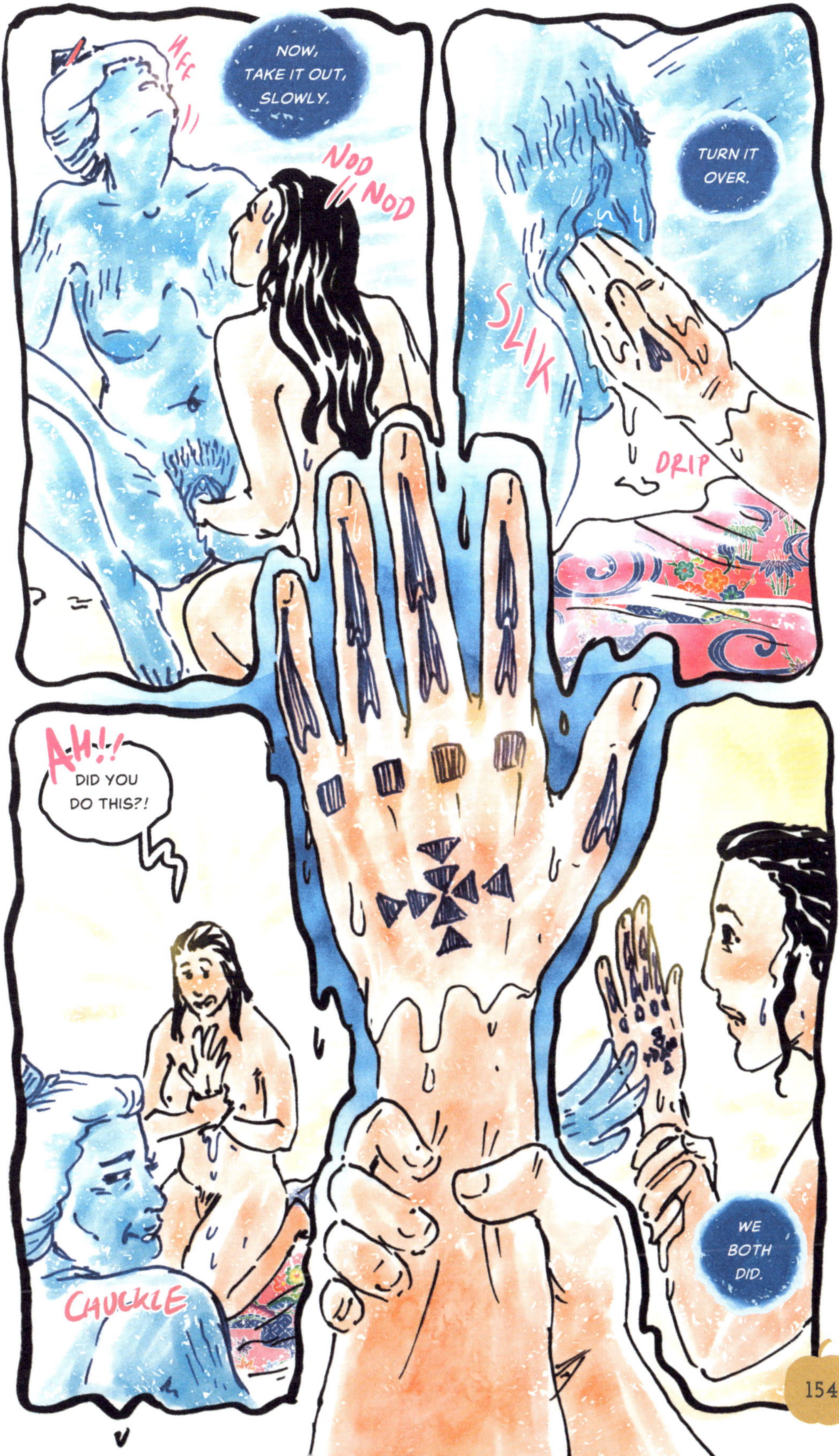
HFF
NOW, TAKE IT OUT, SLOWLY.
NOD NOD
TURN IT OVER.
SLIK
DRIP
AH!!
DID YOU DO THIS?!
CHUCKLE
WE BOTH DID.

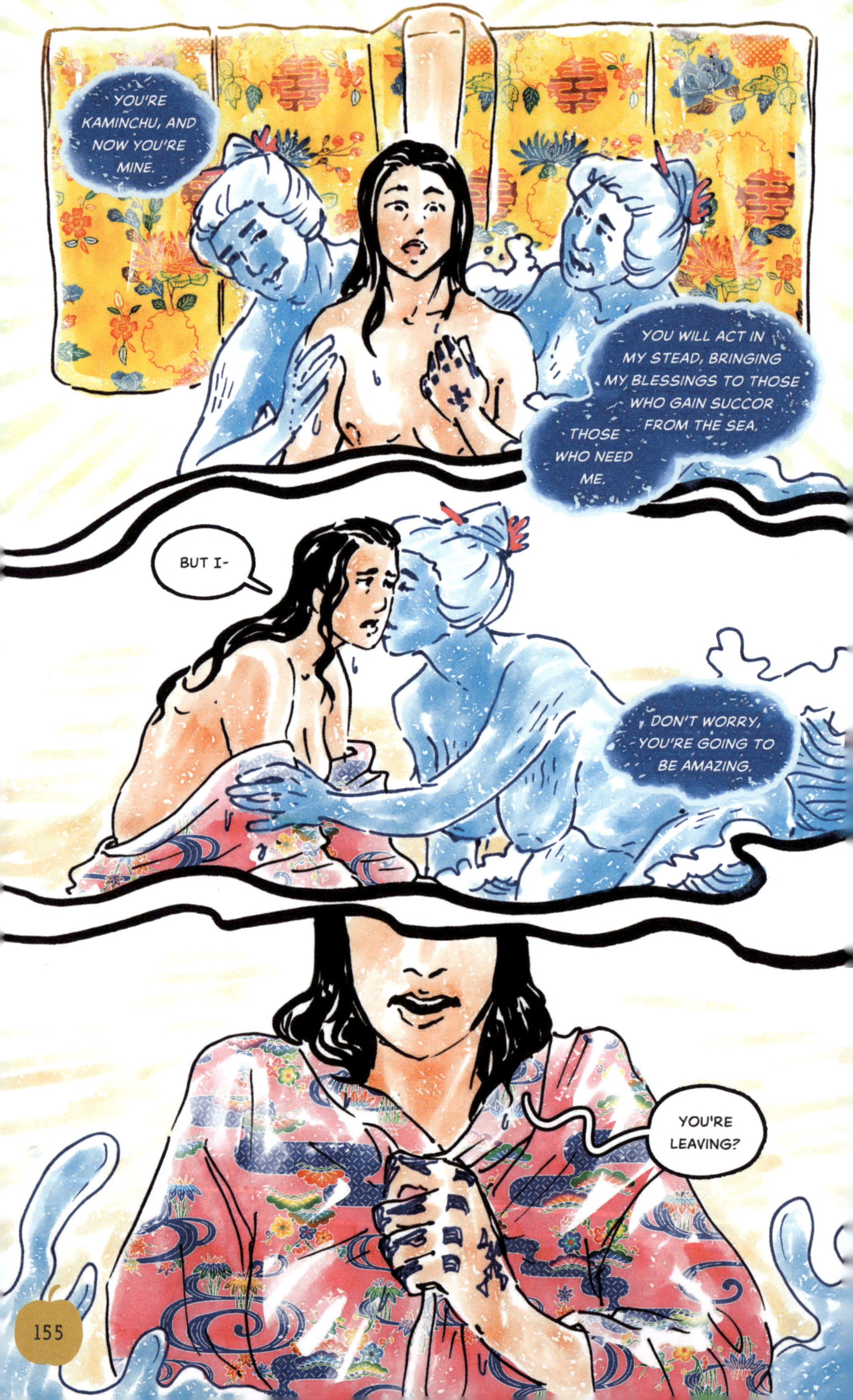
YOU'RE KAMINCHU, AND NOW YOU'RE MINE.
YOU WILL ACT IN MY STEAD, BRINGING MY BLESSINGS TO THOSE WHO GAIN SUCCOR FROM THE SEA.
THOSE WHO NEED ME.
BUT I-
DON'T WORRY, YOU'RE GOING TO BE AMAZING.
YOU'RE LEAVING?

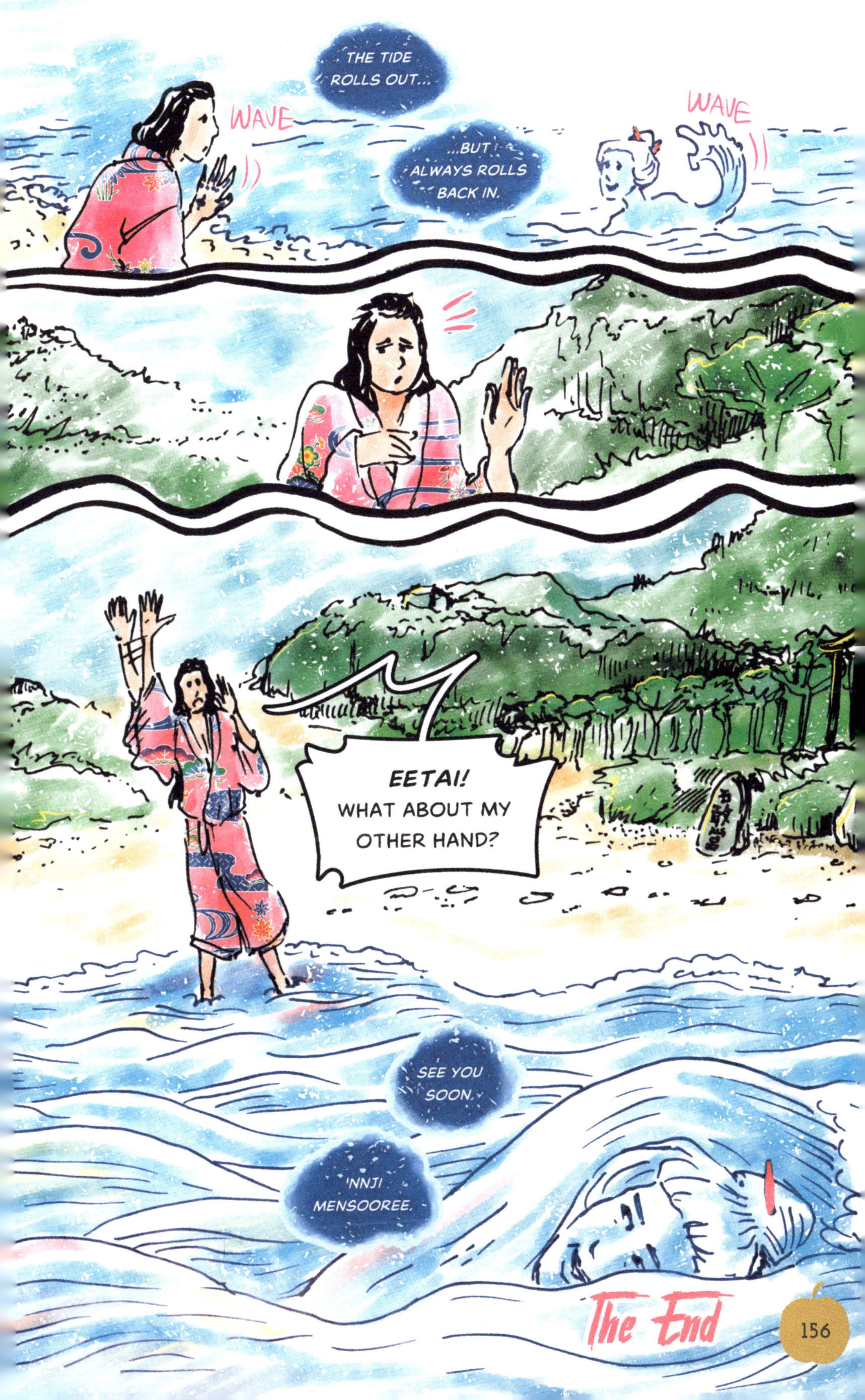
THE TIDE ROLLS OUT...
WAVE
...BUT ALWAYS ROLLS BACK IN.
WAVE
EETAI! WHAT ABOUT MY OTHER HAND?
SEE YOU SOON.
'NNJI MENSOOREE.
The End

Cuntsmith

Story by Harry-Anne Bentley - Art by Phineas Klier

Sculptor Galatea has been tasked to craft her girlfriend, Narcissa, the perfect vagina. Can their other girlfriend, Medusa, help with her nerves?

Writer's Note

" Ancient Myths change, update and reincorperate into cultures as they move into new eras and areas. Where once Medusa was 'punished' with snake hair by Athena, for being assaulted in her temple (WTF?), later she was 'blessed' with protection from men who would hurt her.

This story came from re-assessing Greek Figures from a queer & feminist angle. What if Galatea didn't like the 'Beautiful' body Pygmalion made for her to sit down and be quiet in? Or Maybe Medusa actually liked her unconventional appearance, and repelled men because she was hella gay. "

Content Tags

MONSTER SEX, SNAKES, A LITTLE DYSPHORIA, A LOT OF EUPHORIA, QUEERING OF GREEK MYTH, SELF DOUBT, THREESOME, POLYAMOURY, BUTT STUFF, WALL OF CLAYBIA (CLAY-LABIA), GENITAL RE-ASSIGNMENT, GORGON SEMPAI NOTICING YOU, TURNED TO STONE BUT WE FIXED IT.

NOT YOUR THING? NEXT COMIC ON PAGE 172

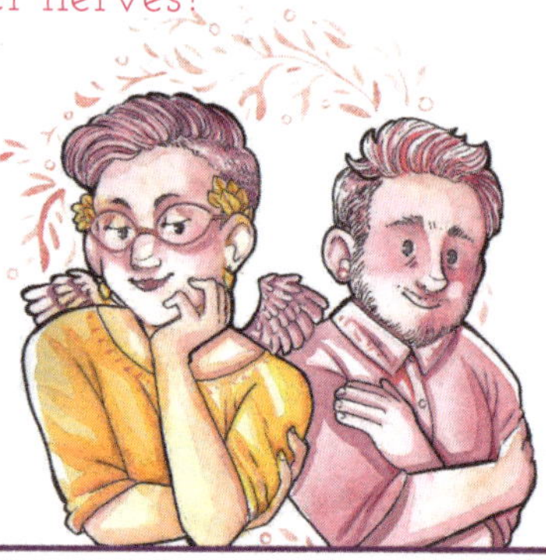

About the Creators

Harry-Anne (she/they) is an indie publisher, comic artist, podcaster, streamer and workaholic.

She believes in the power of representation in fiction, writing their own narratives from a tiny loft-conversion office in Leeds, UK.

Instagram.com/GenderQuest

Phineas (he/they) is a comic-artist, illustrator and student from Germany, who has dedicated their art towards exploring subjects of queer identity and relationships on their own and together with other authors.

PhineasKlier.wordpress.com

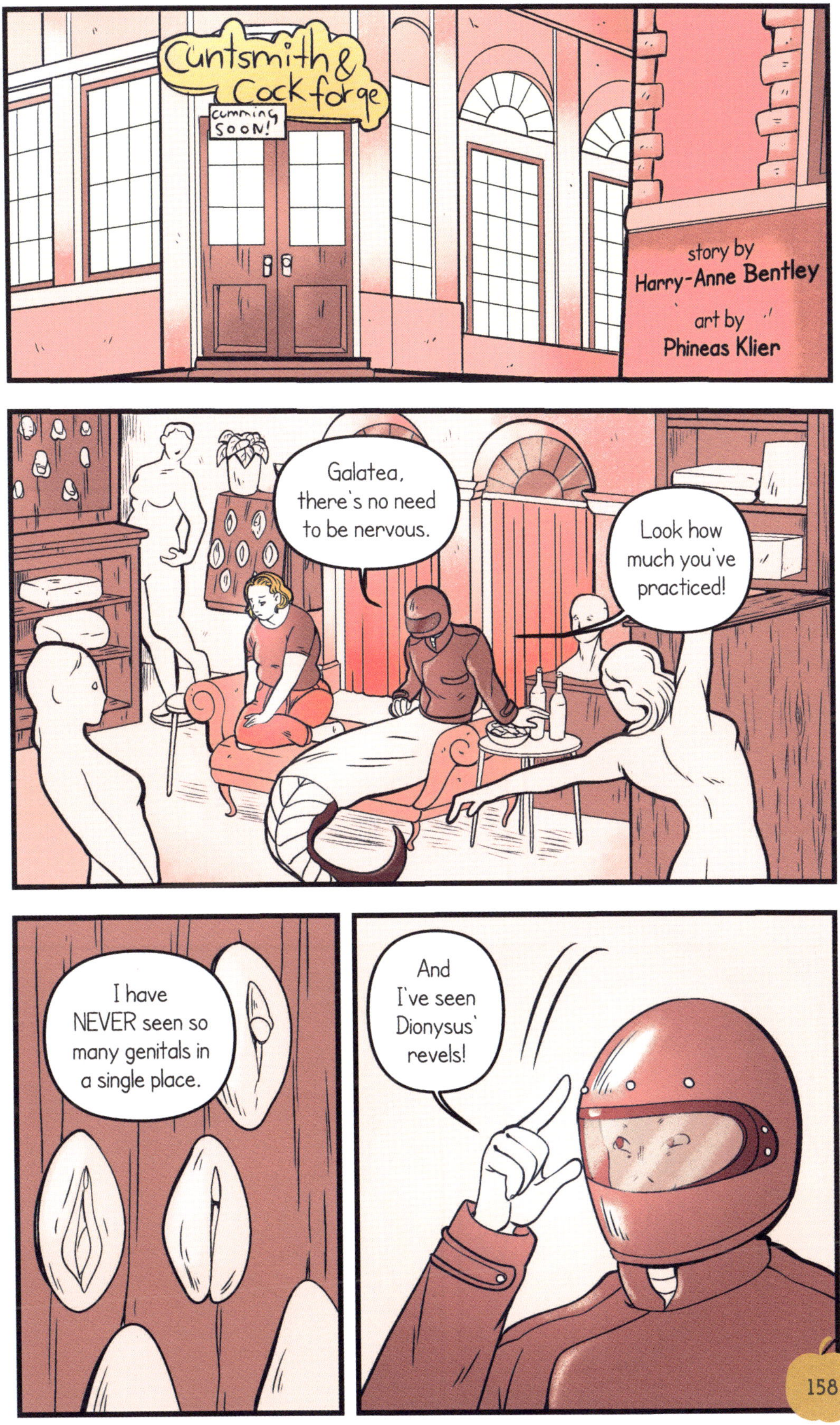
Cuntsmith & Cockforge
cumming SOON!
story by
Harry-Anne Bentley
art by
Phineas Klier
Galatea, there's no need to be nervous.
Look how much you've practiced!
I have NEVER seen so many genitals in a single place.
And I've seen Dionysus' revels!

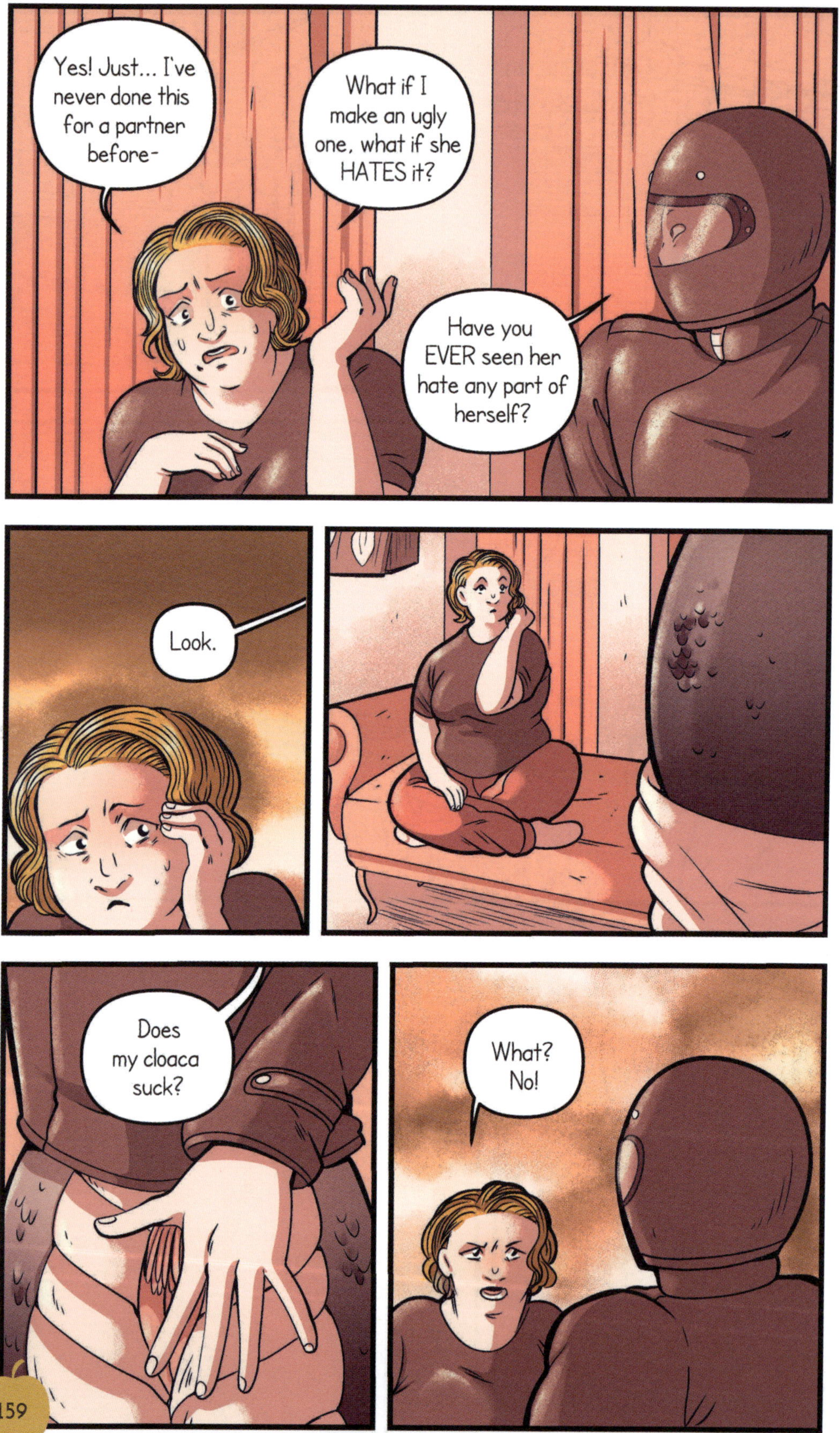
Yes! Just... I've never done this for a partner before-
What if I make an ugly one, what if she HATES it?
Have you EVER seen her hate any part of herself?
Look.
Does my cloaca suck?
What? No!

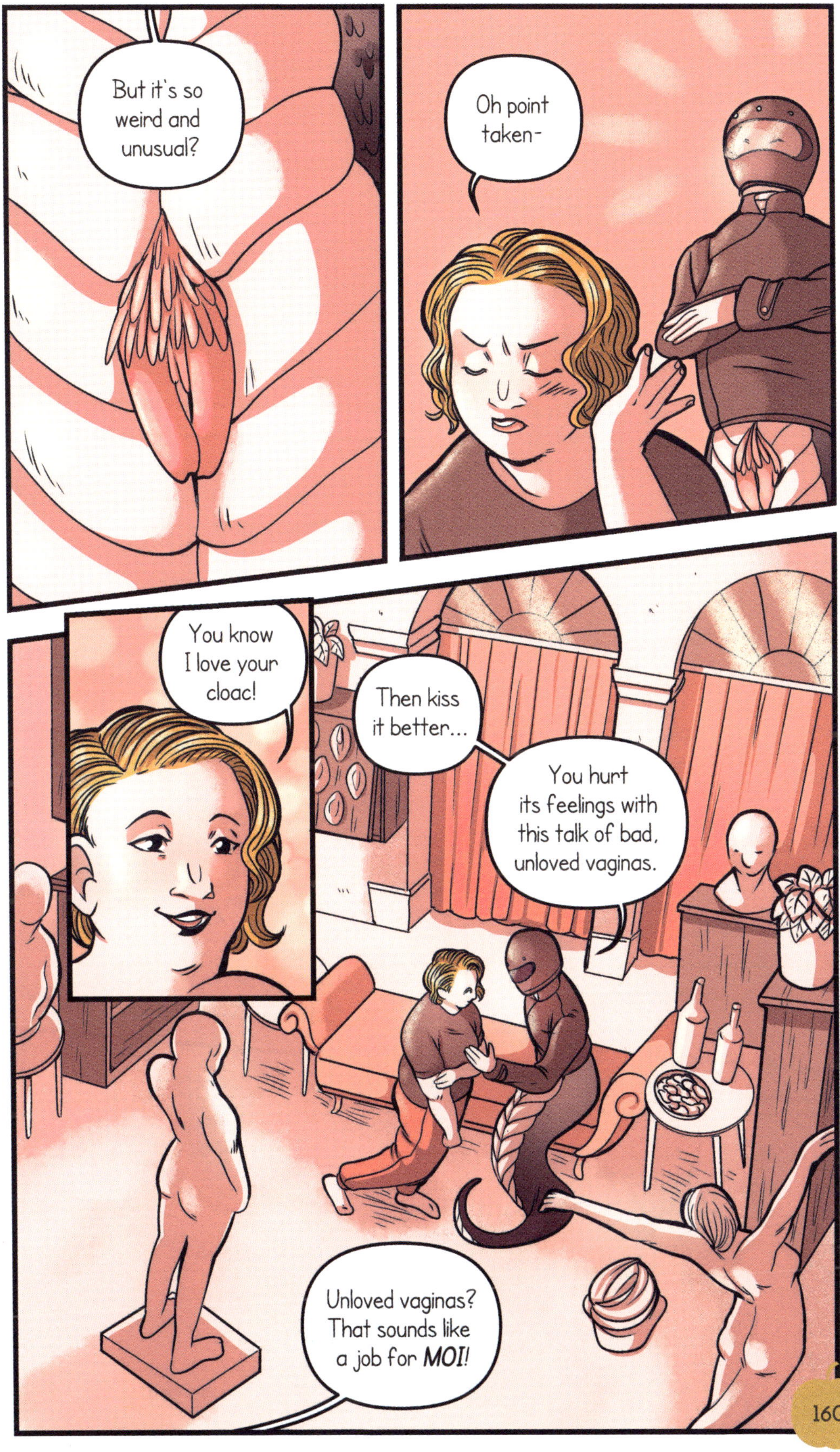
But it's so weird and unusual?
Oh point taken-
You know I love your cloac!
Then kiss it better...
You hurt its feelings with this talk of bad, unloved vaginas.
Unloved vaginas? That sounds like a job for MOI!

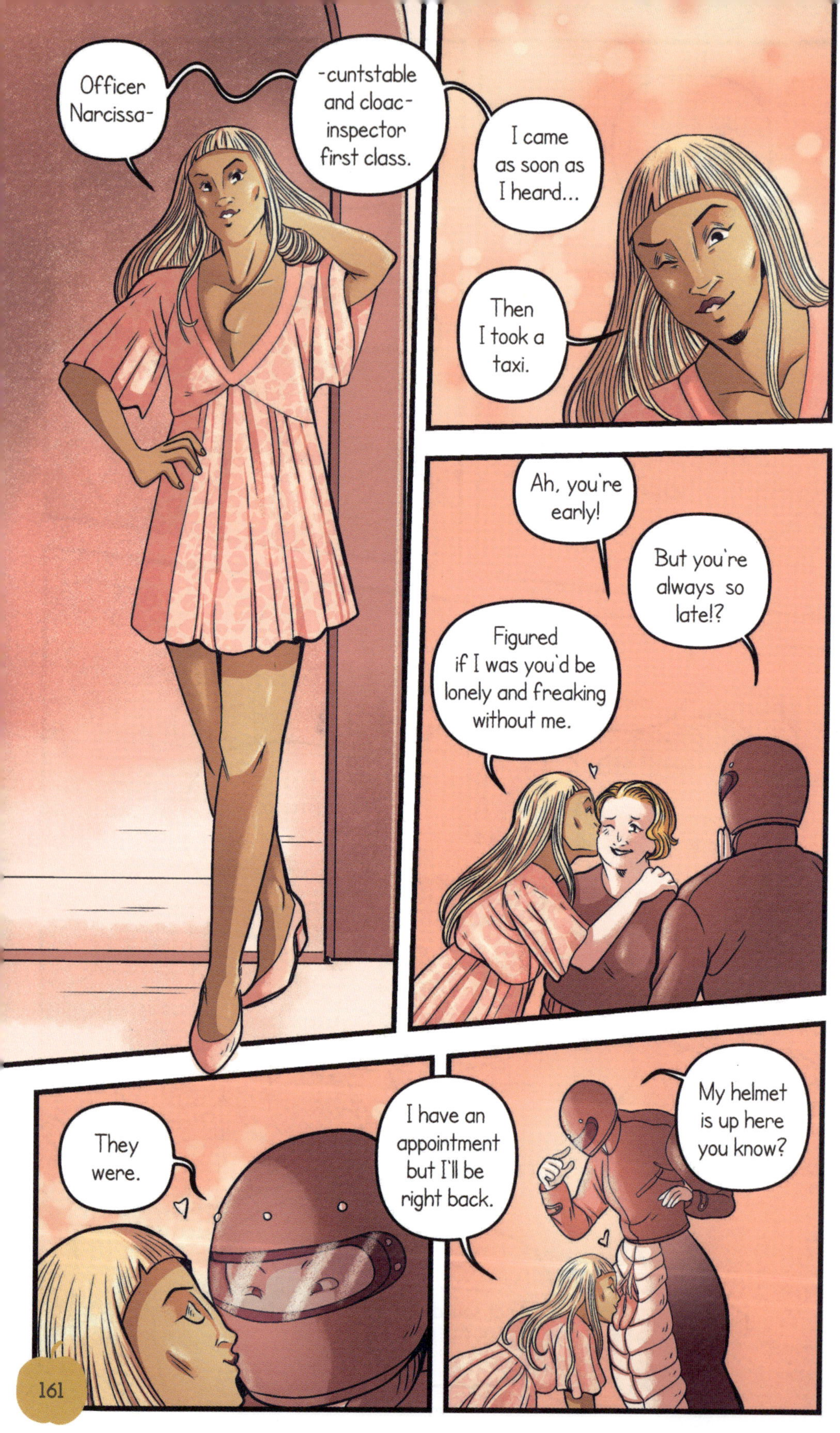
Officer Narcissa-
-cuntstable and cloac-inspector first class.
I came as soon as I heard...
Then I took a taxi.
Ah, you're early!
But you're always so late!?
Figured if I was you'd be lonely and freaking without me.
They were.
I have an appointment but I'll be right back.
My helmet is up here you know?

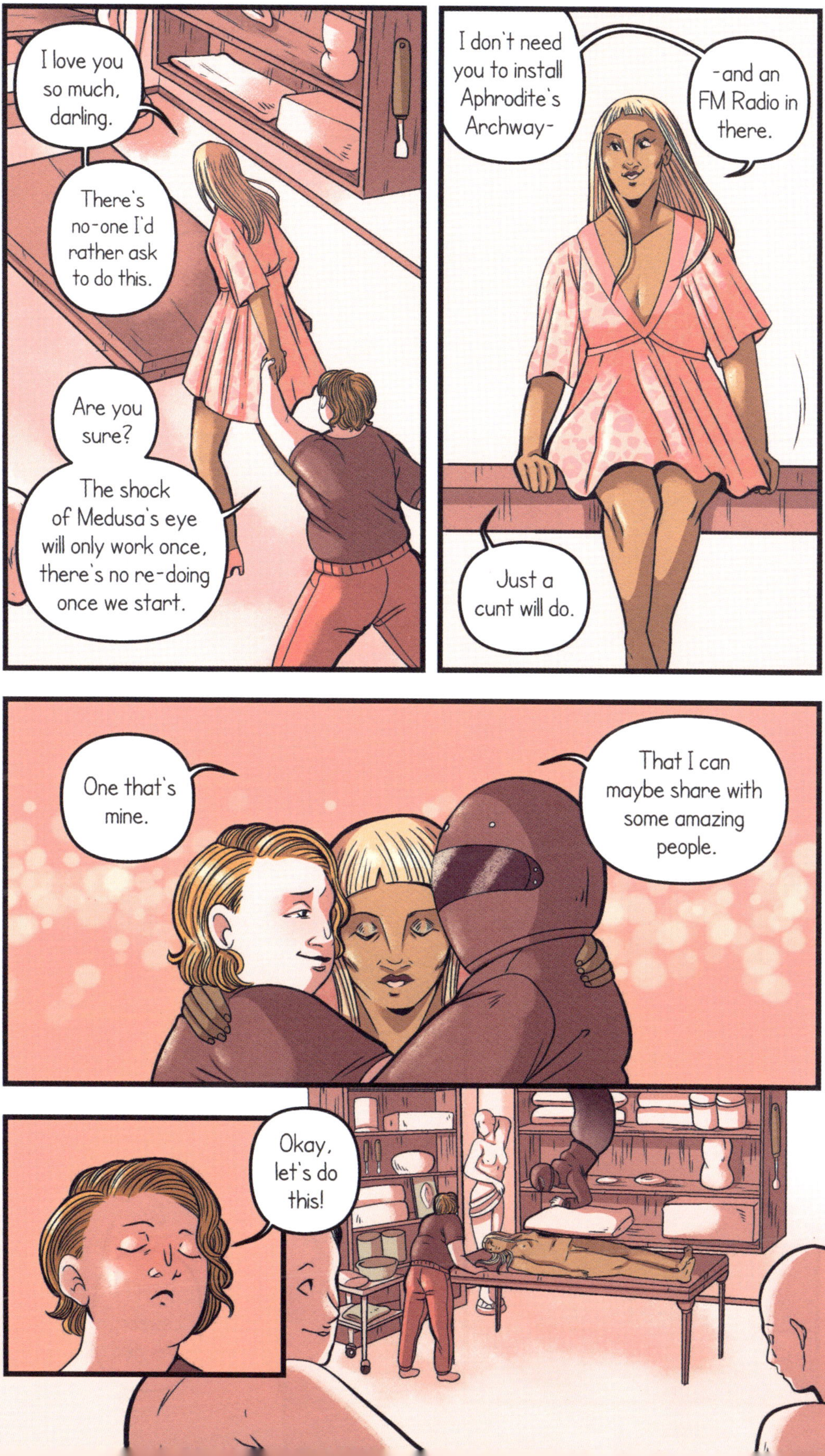
I love you so much, darling.
There's no-one I'd rather ask to do this.
Are you sure?
The shock of Medusa's eye will only work once, there's no re-doing once we start.
I don't need you to install Aphrodite's Archway-
-and an FM Radio in there.
Just a cunt will do.
One that's mine.
That I can maybe share with some amazing people.
Okay, let's do this!

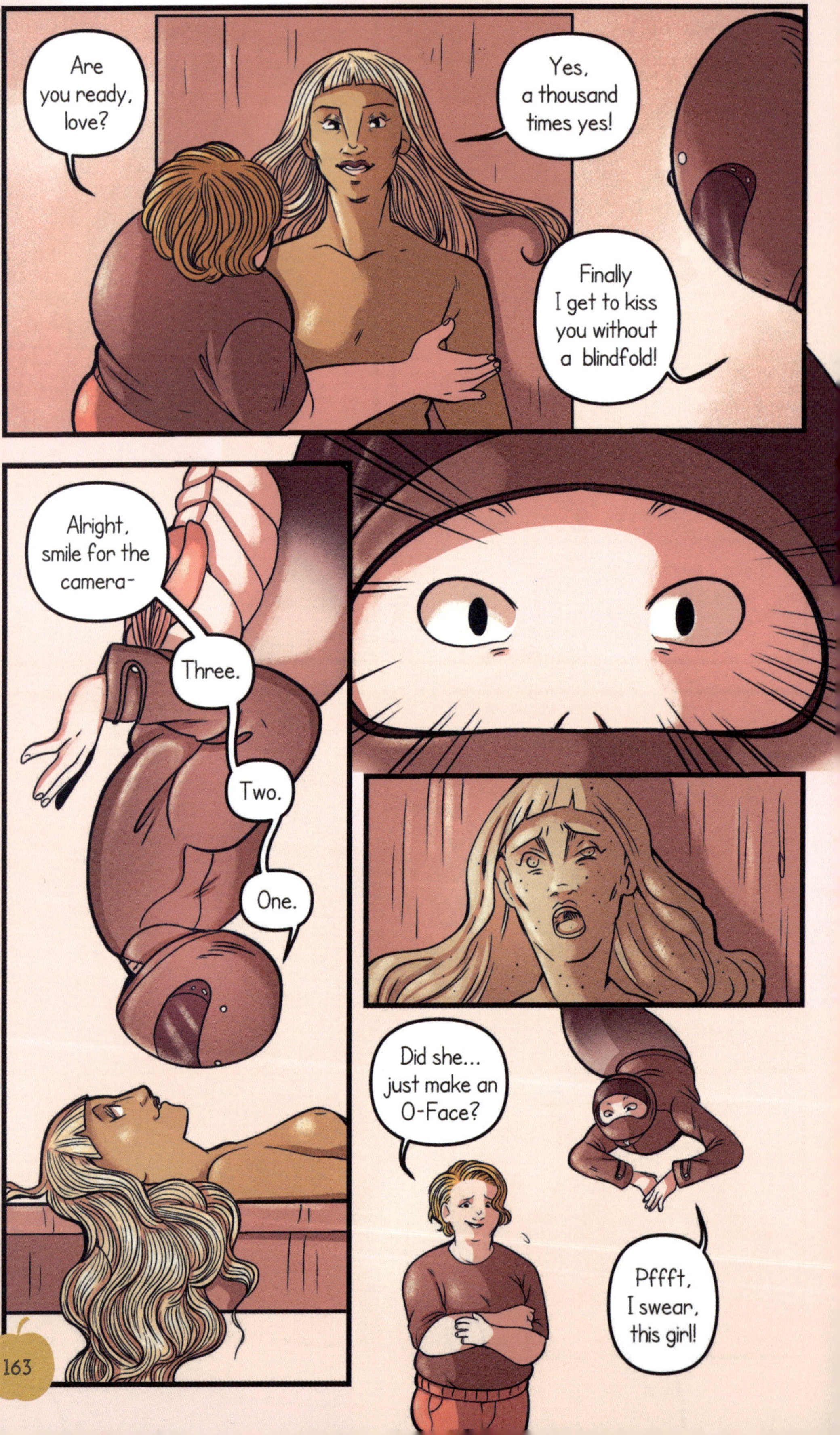
Are you ready, love?
Yes, a thousand times yes!
Finally I get to kiss you without a blindfold!
Alright, smile for the camera-
Three.
Two.
One.
Did she... just make an O-Face?
Pffft, I swear, this girl!

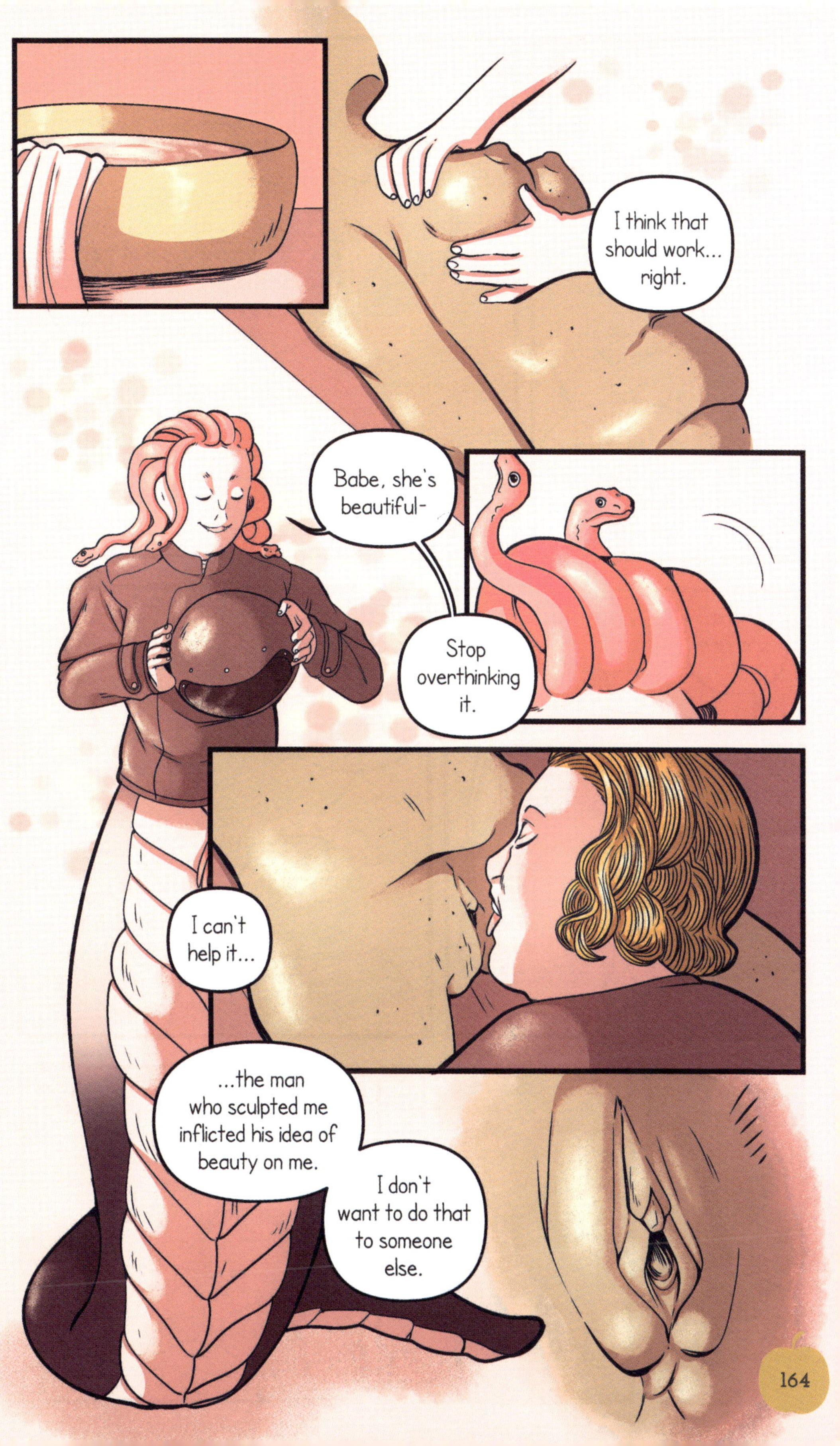
I think that should work... right.
Babe, she's beautiful-
Stop overthinking it.
I can't help it...
...the man who sculpted me inflicted his idea of beauty on me.
I don't want to do that to someone else.

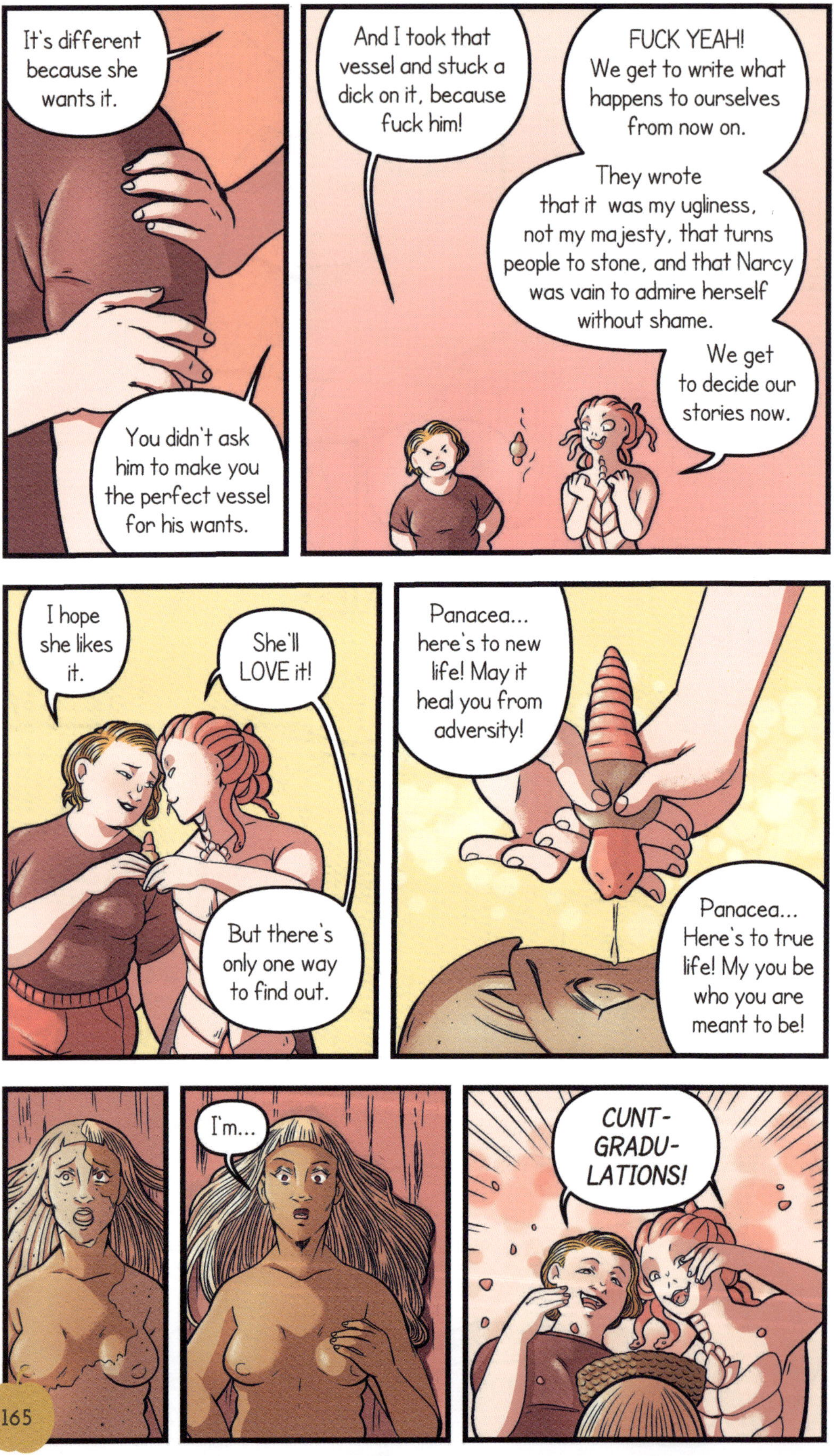
It's different because she wants it.
You didn't ask him to make you the perfect vessel for his wants.
And I took that vessel and stuck a dick on it, because fuck him!
FUCK YEAH! We get to write what happens to ourselves from now on.
They wrote that it was my ugliness, not my majesty, that turns people to stone, and that Narcy was vain to admire herself without shame.
We get to decide our stories now.
I hope she likes it.
She'll LOVE it!
But there's only one way to find out.
Panacea... here's to new life! May it heal you from adversity!
Panacea... Here's to true life! My you be who you are meant to be!
I'm...
CUNT-GRADU-LATIONS!

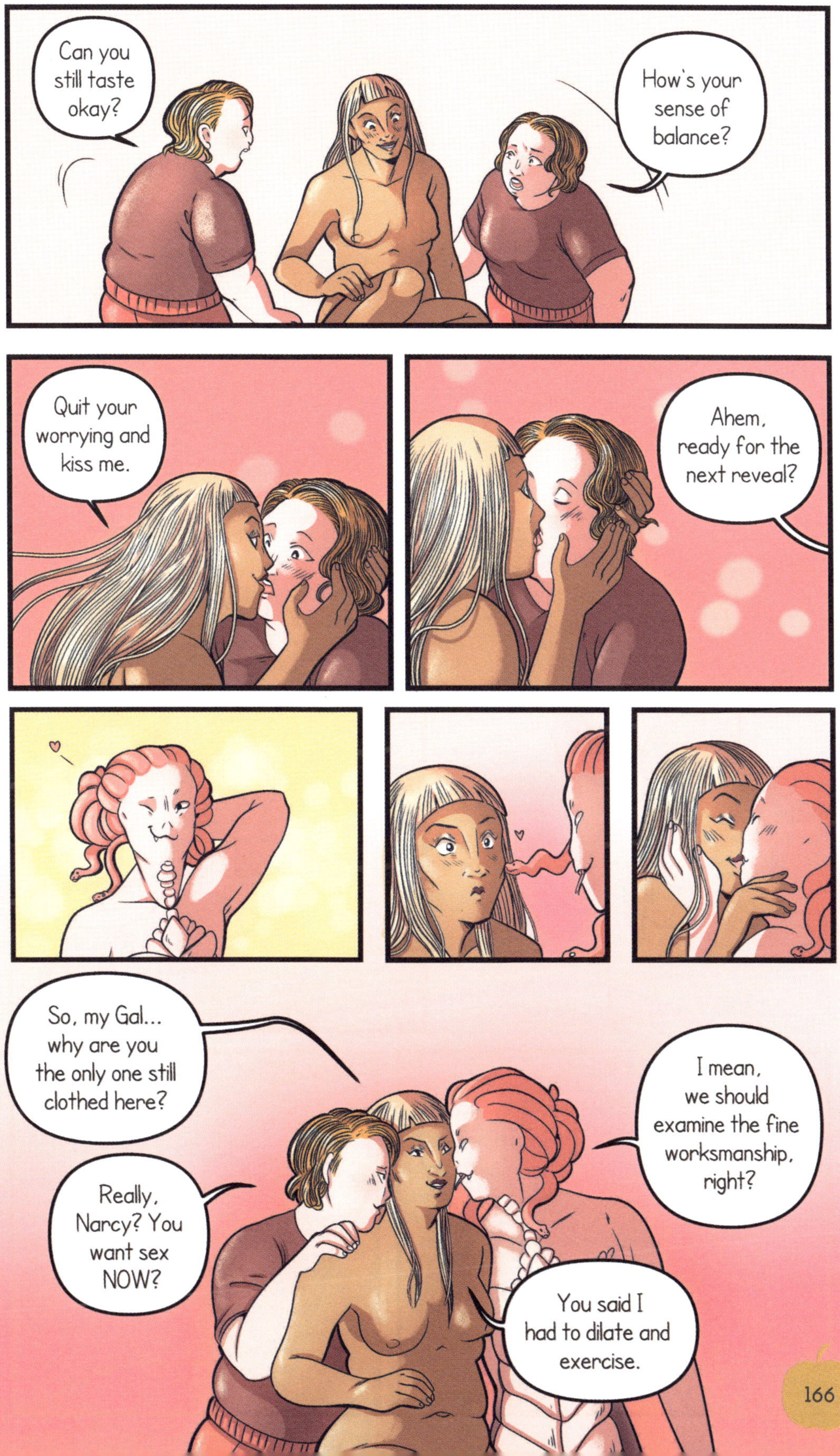
Can you still taste okay?
How's your sense of balance?
Quit your worrying and kiss me.
Ahem, ready for the next reveal?
So, my Gal... why are you the only one still clothed here?
I mean, we should examine the fine workmanship, right?
Really, Narcy? You want sex NOW?
You said I had to dilate and exercise.

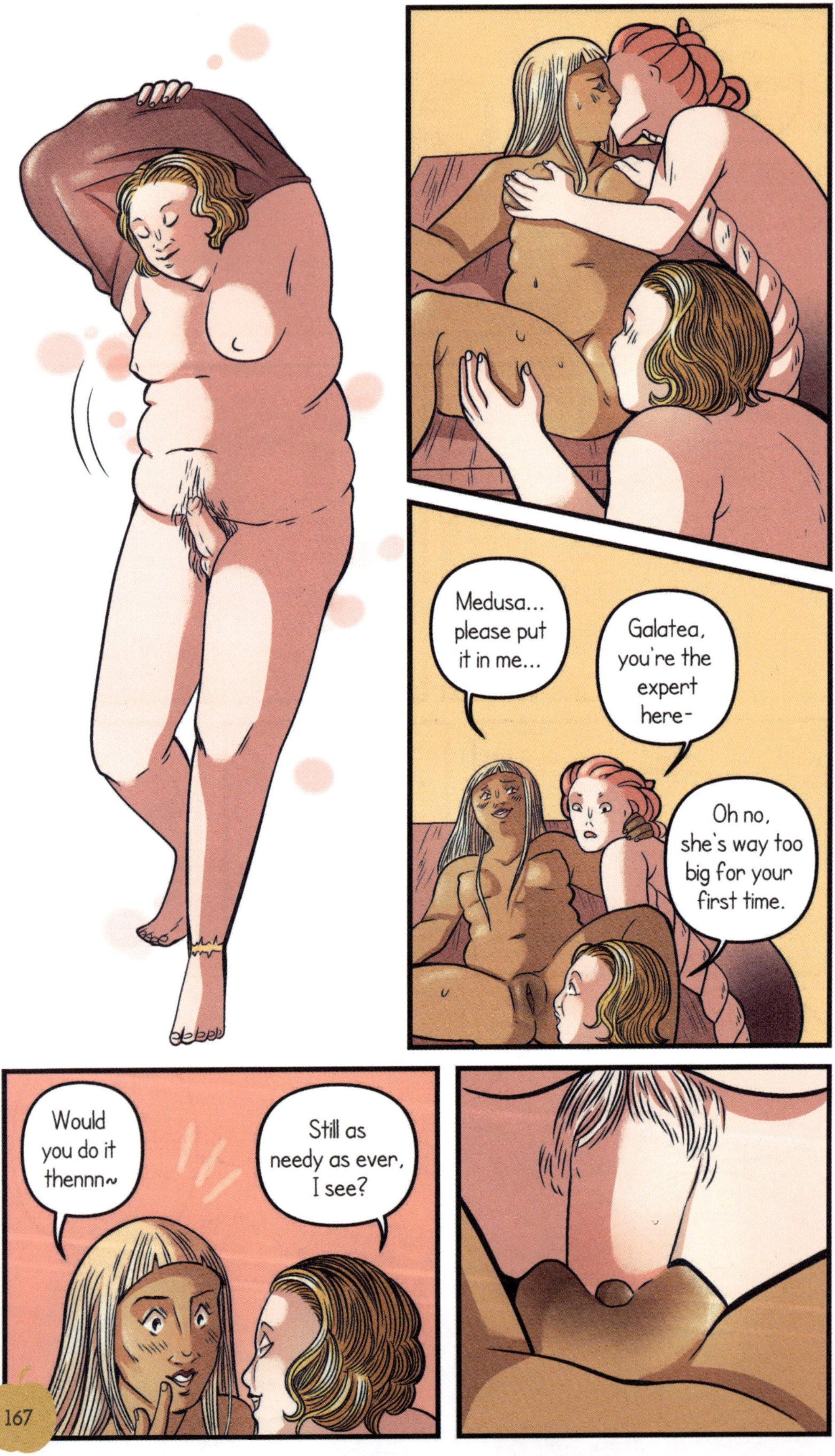
Medusa... please put it in me...
Galatea, you're the expert here-
Oh no, she's way too big for your first time.
Would you do it thennn~
Still as needy as ever, I see?

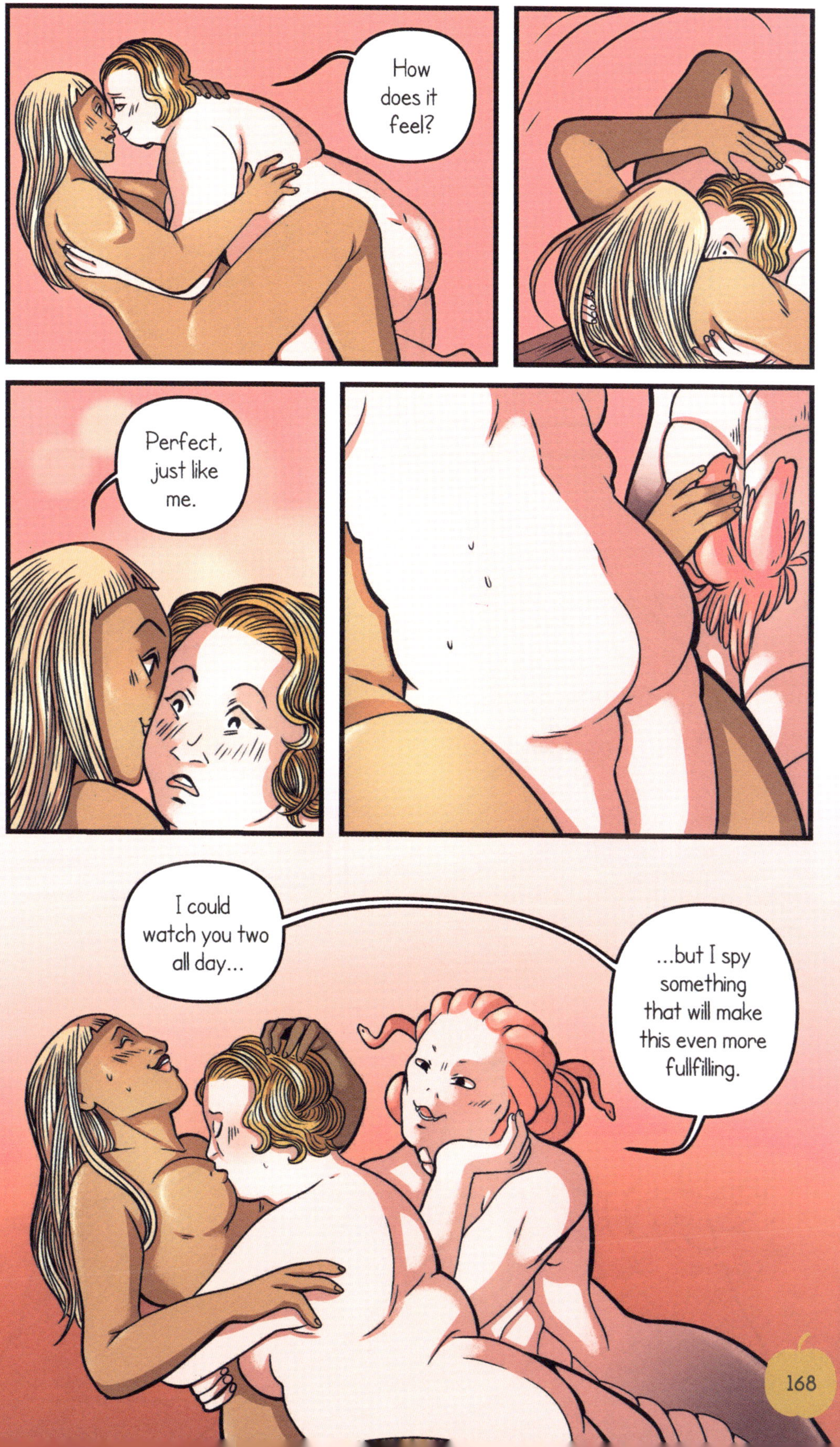
How does it feel?
Perfect, just like me.
I could watch you two all day...
...but I spy something that will make this even more fullfilling.

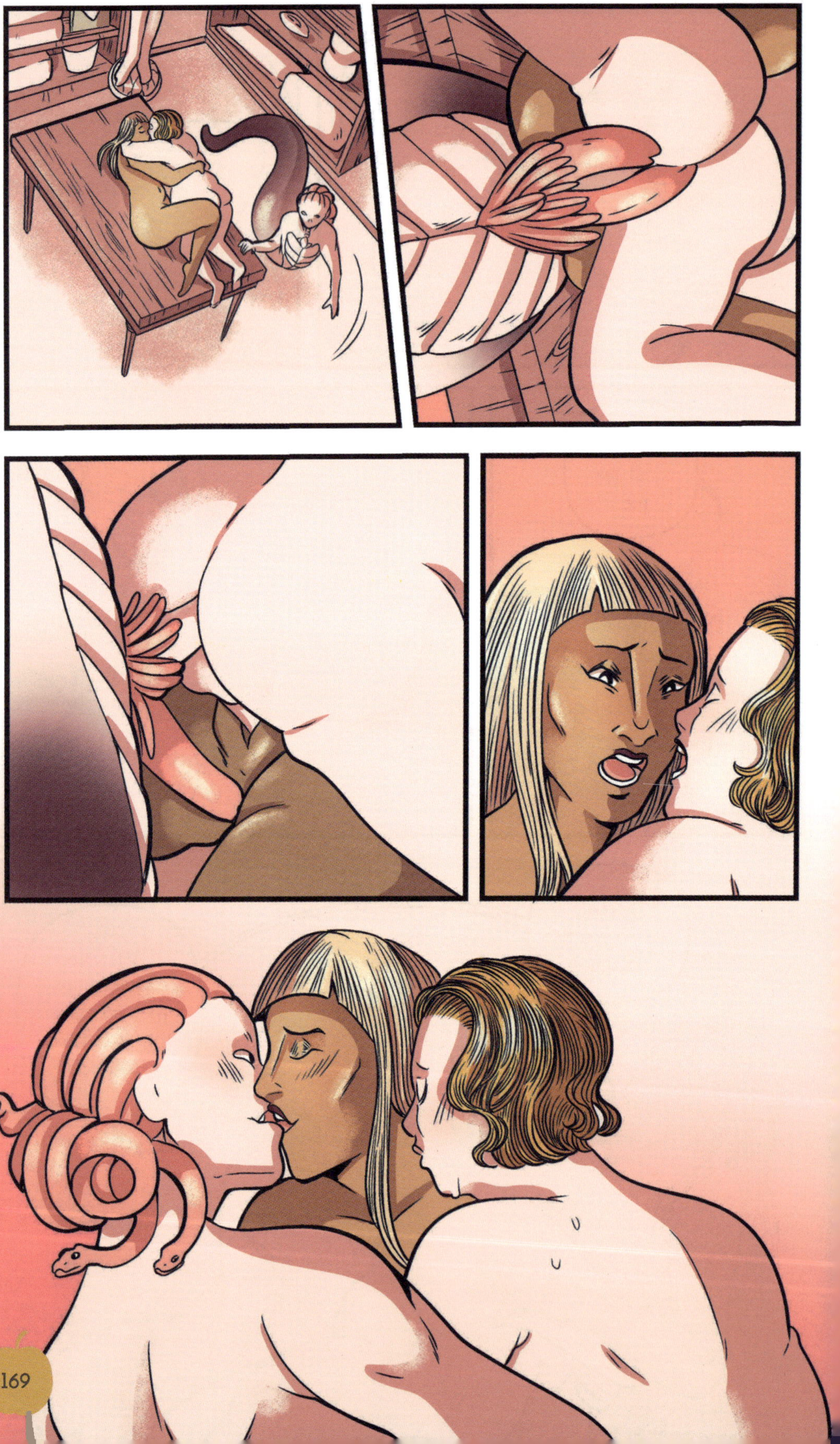

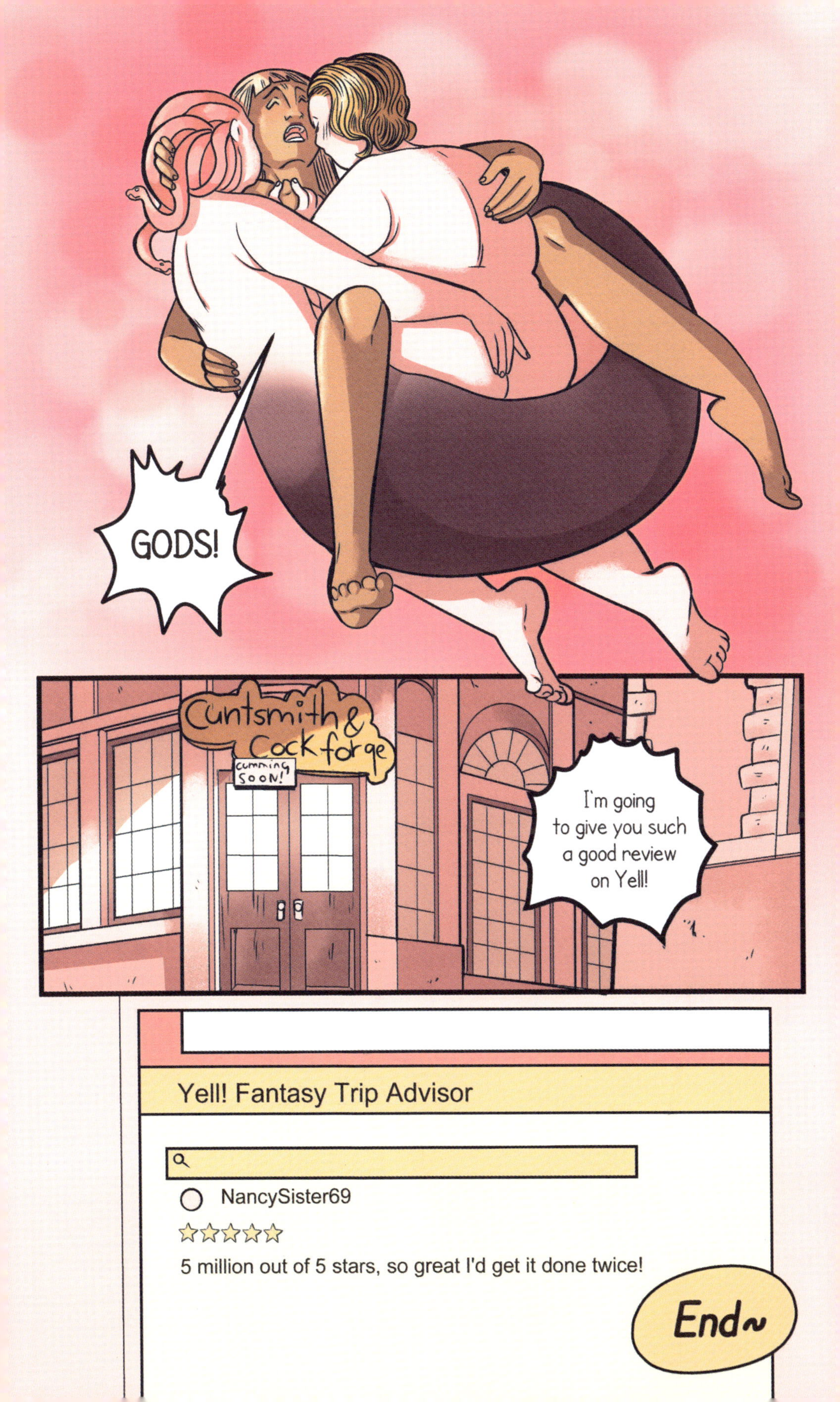
GODS!
Cuntsmith & Cockforge
cumming soon!
I'm going to give you such a good review on Yell!
Yell! Fantasy Trip Advisor
NancySister69
5 million out of 5 stars, so great I'd get it done twice!
End~

Four Seasons

Story by Mx Andromeda Star - Art by Alina Wahab

The Four Seasons bar is special, serving cocktails that show a taste of your future, if you're brave enough to take a sip.

Writer's Note

" Four Seasons is a very personal story for me. It is a story of change. Of letting go of the fears that hold us in place. Of allowing ourselves to be happy.

In our imperfect world, transitioning is a very hard and taxing thing for many trans people to do. As a transgender person who is part way through her own transition journey, I oftentimes find myself looking back at how far I've come, and at all the things I've experienced. And while I have had to work through hardships and dark times, what shines out the most when I look back is the love, acceptance and kindness I have been gifted. That is what inspired this story: the beacons of love and kindness that guided me out of darkness.

I hope it brightens your day. "

About the Creators

Andromeda Star (she/her/they/them) is a non-binary trans-femme asexual writer and producer from Lincoln, UK. She enjoys making emotionally fueled stories that explore the amazing breadth and depth of humanity - particularly the parts that conventional media too often ignore or misrepresent.

Most of her time is spent working on other people's projects, but more recently she has started developing her own original content (like the story in this fantastic book you are holding!).

Twitter.com/MxAndromeda

Alina Wahab (they/them) is a bi comic artist and illustrator from India. Their work is very inspired by pinup aesthetics, vintage anime, and high fashion. They got their start in comics through online fanzines, and are currently working on making more original comics. They love to draw fancy outfits and hot people kissing, as well as exploring tenderness and yearning in their art.

Twitter.com/CowGirlOnGirl

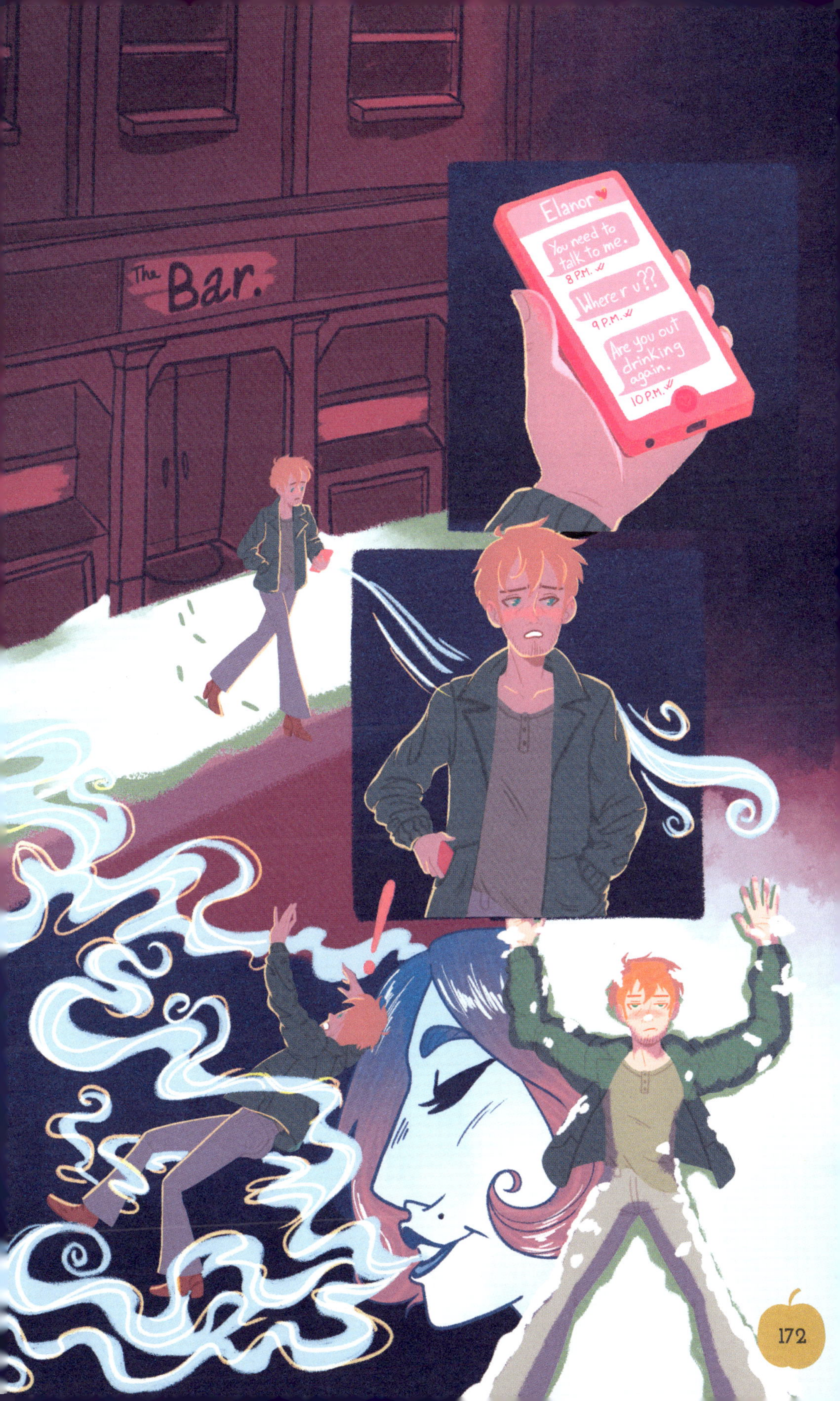
The Bar.
Elanor
You need to talk to me.
8 P.M.
Where r u??
9 P.M.
Are you out drinking again.
10 P.M.
!

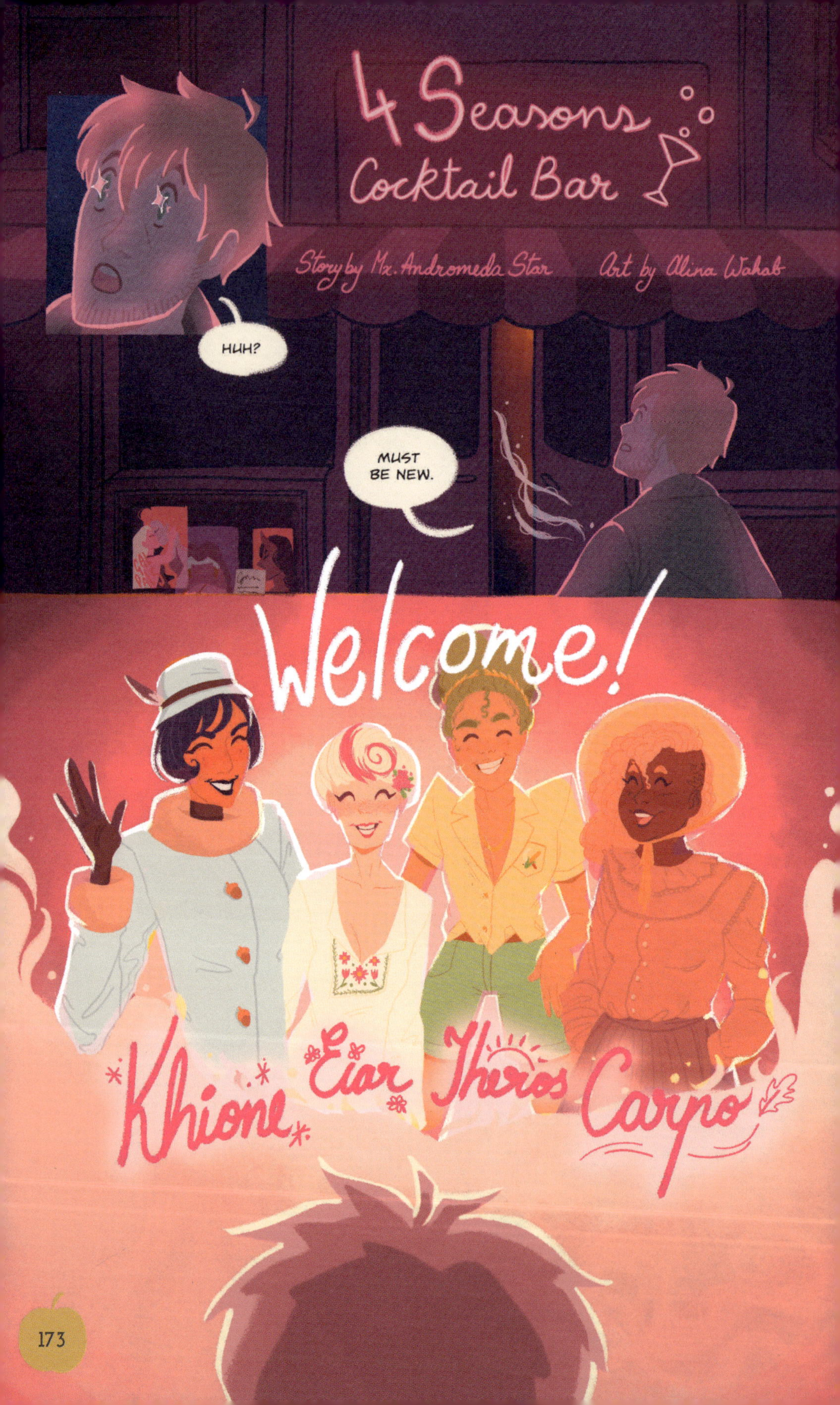
4 Seasons
Cocktail Bar
Story by Mx. Andromeda Star
Art by Alina Wahab
HUH?
MUST BE NEW.
Welcome!
Khione
Eiar
Theros
Carpo

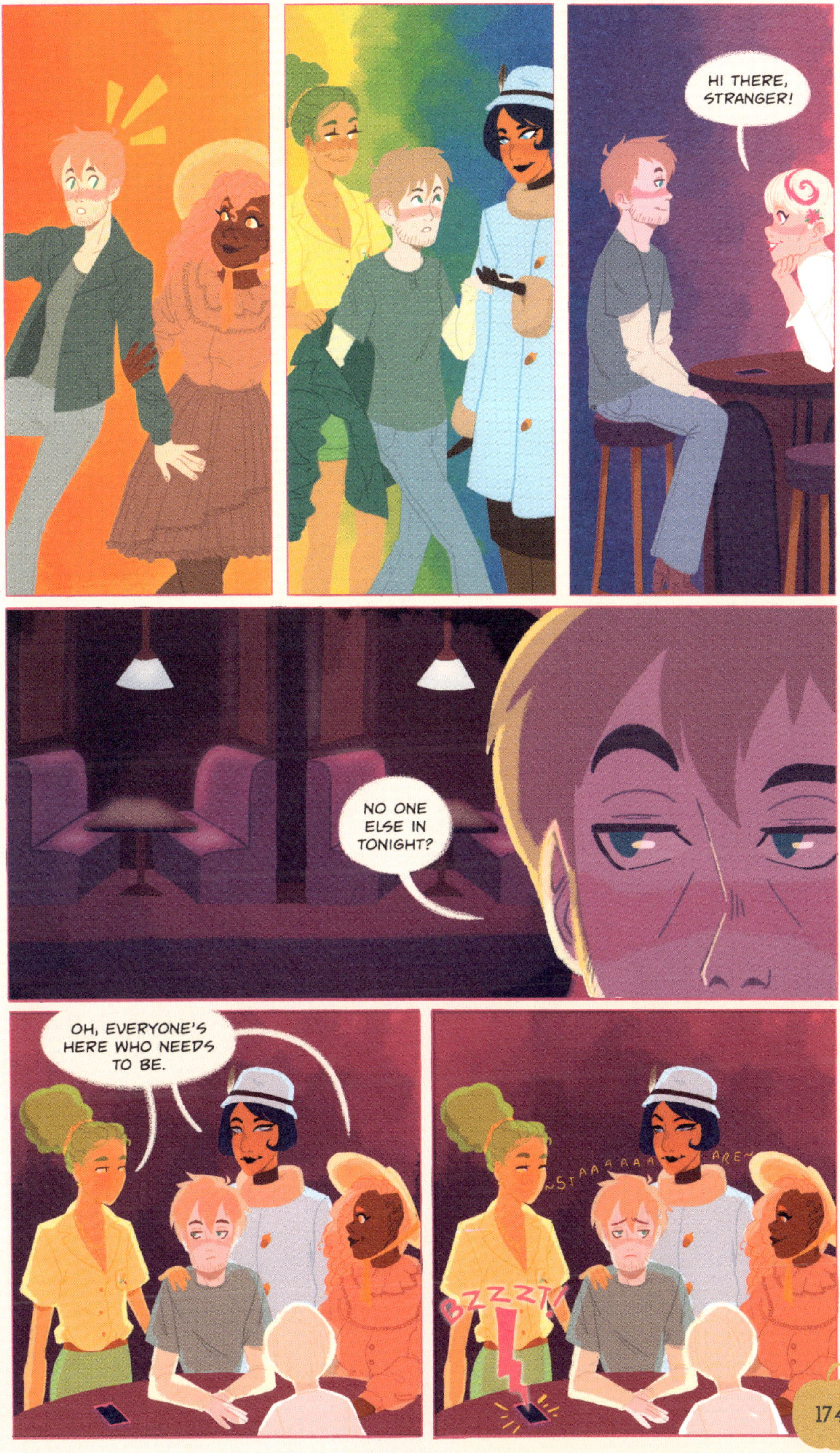
HI THERE, STRANGER!
NO ONE ELSE IN TONIGHT?
OH, EVERYONE'S HERE WHO NEEDS TO BE.
~STAAAAAAAARE~
BZZZT!

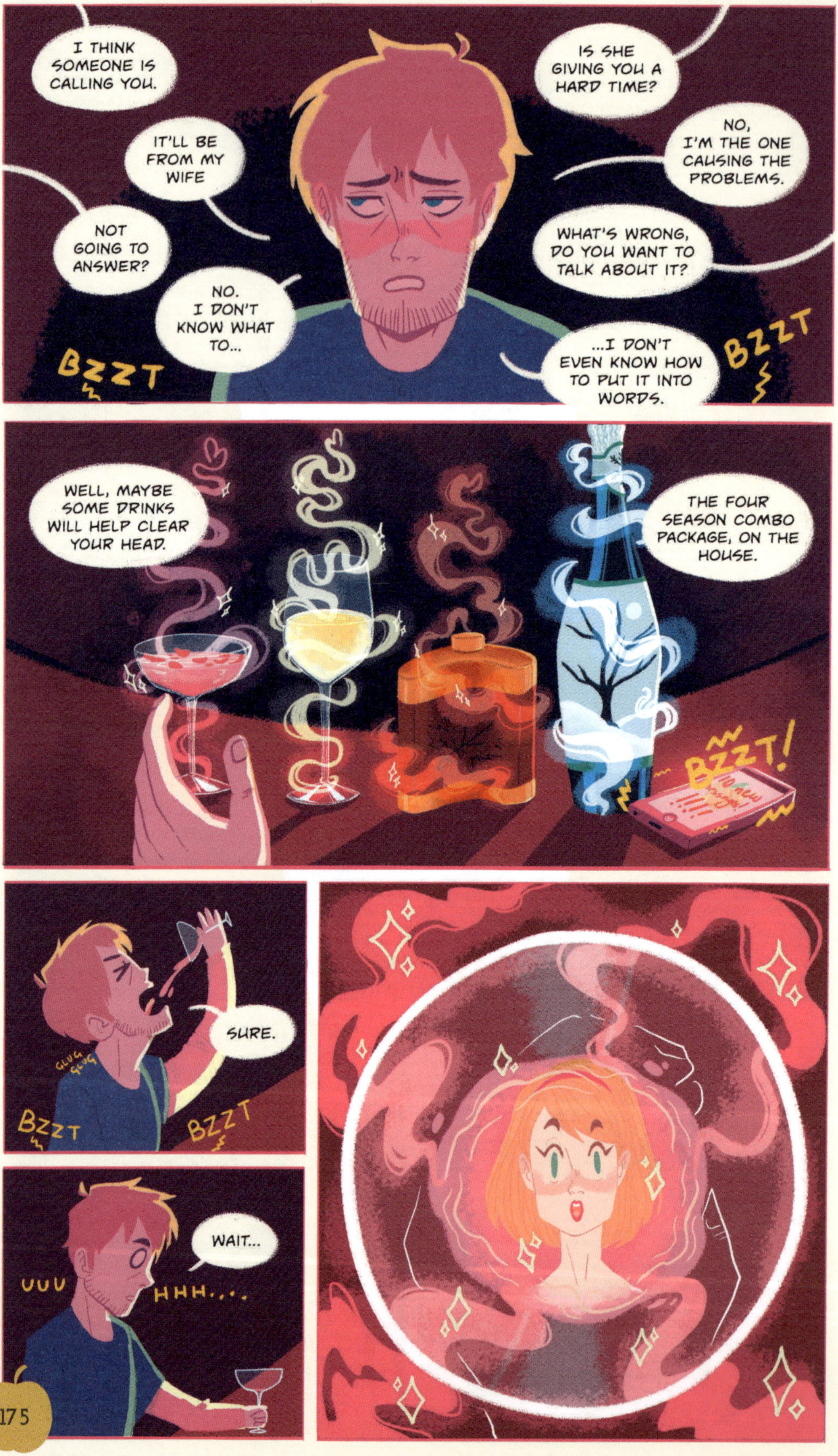
I THINK SOMEONE IS CALLING YOU.
IT'LL BE FROM MY WIFE
NOT GOING TO ANSWER?
NO. I DON'T KNOW WHAT TO...
IS SHE GIVING YOU A HARD TIME?
NO, I'M THE ONE CAUSING THE PROBLEMS.
WHAT'S WRONG, DO YOU WANT TO TALK ABOUT IT?
...I DON'T EVEN KNOW HOW TO PUT IT INTO WORDS.
BZZT
BZZT
WELL, MAYBE SOME DRINKS WILL HELP CLEAR YOUR HEAD.
THE FOUR SEASON COMBO PACKAGE, ON THE HOUSE.
BZZT!
SURE.
GLUG GLUG
BZZT
BZZT
WAIT...
UUU HHH....

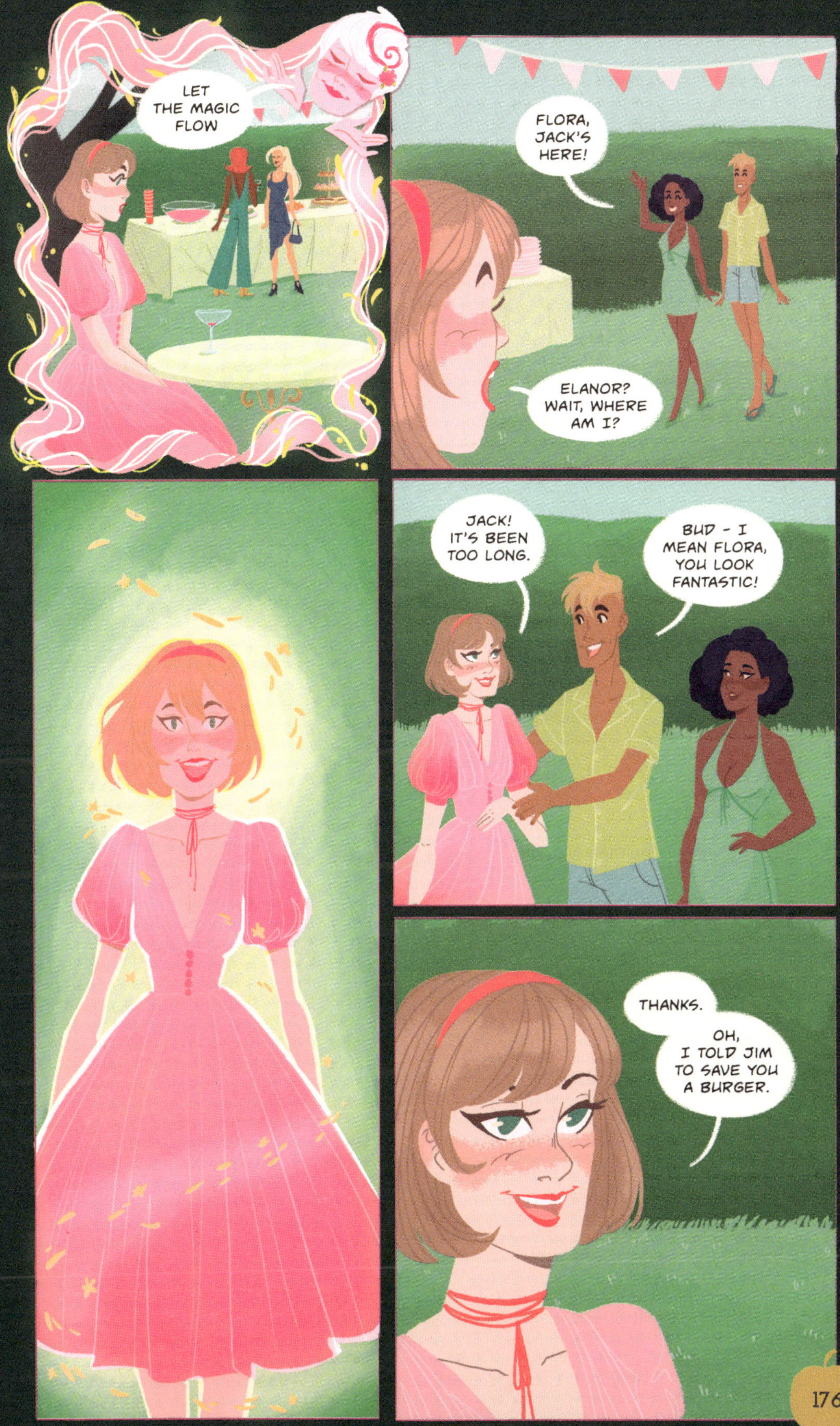
LET THE MAGIC FLOW
FLORA, JACK'S HERE!
ELANOR? WAIT, WHERE AM I?
JACK! IT'S BEEN TOO LONG.
BUD - I MEAN FLORA, YOU LOOK FANTASTIC!
THANKS.
OH, I TOLD JIM TO SAVE YOU A BURGER.

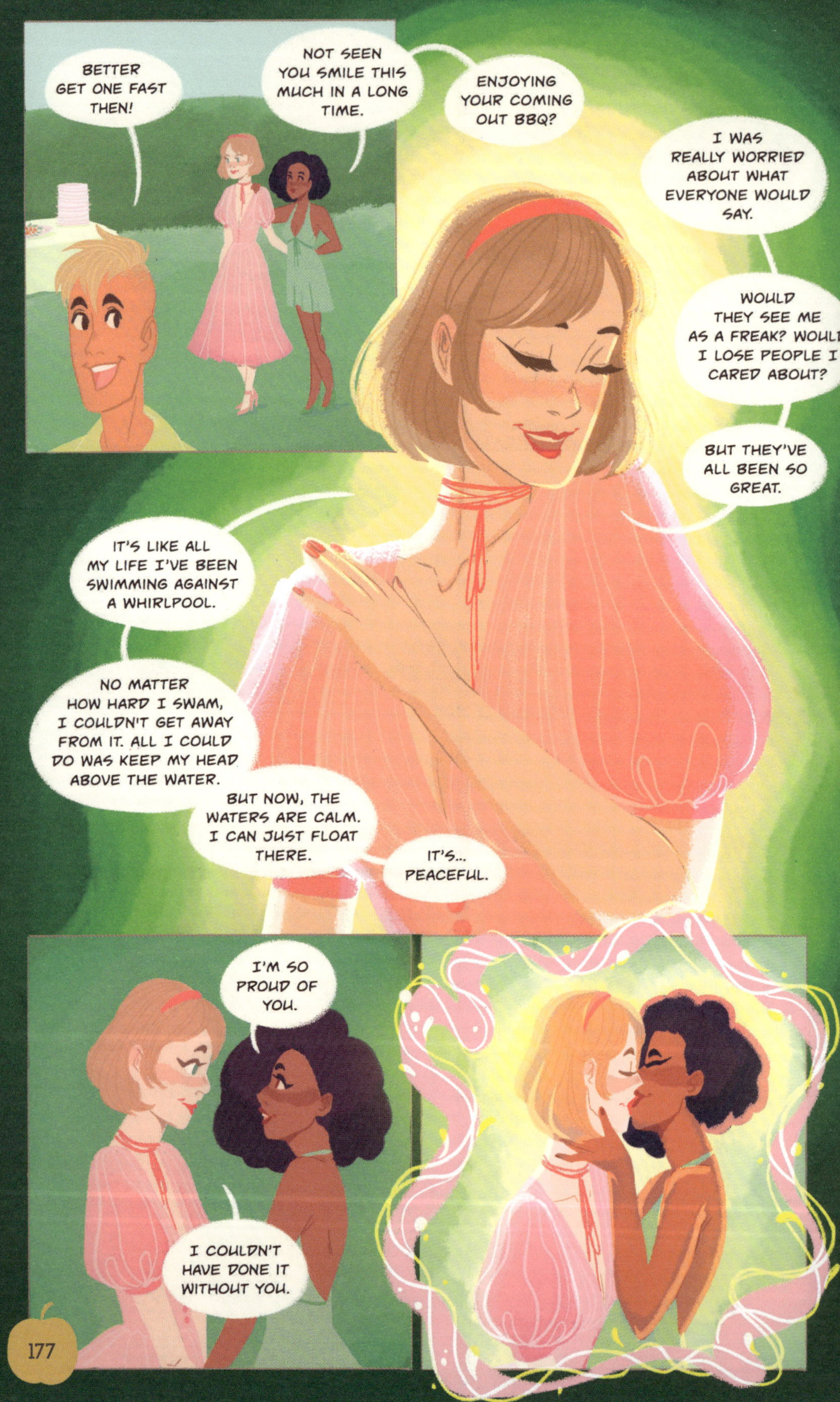
BETTER GET ONE FAST THEN!
NOT SEEN YOU SMILE THIS MUCH IN A LONG TIME.
ENJOYING YOUR COMING OUT BBQ?
I WAS REALLY WORRIED ABOUT WHAT EVERYONE WOULD SAY.
WOULD THEY SEE ME AS A FREAK? WOULD I LOSE PEOPLE I CARED ABOUT?
BUT THEY'VE ALL BEEN SO GREAT.
IT'S LIKE ALL MY LIFE I'VE BEEN SWIMMING AGAINST A WHIRLPOOL.
NO MATTER HOW HARD I SWAM, I COULDN'T GET AWAY FROM IT. ALL I COULD DO WAS KEEP MY HEAD ABOVE THE WATER.
BUT NOW, THE WATERS ARE CALM. I CAN JUST FLOAT THERE.
IT'S... PEACEFUL.
I'M SO PROUD OF YOU.
I COULDN'T HAVE DONE IT WITHOUT YOU.

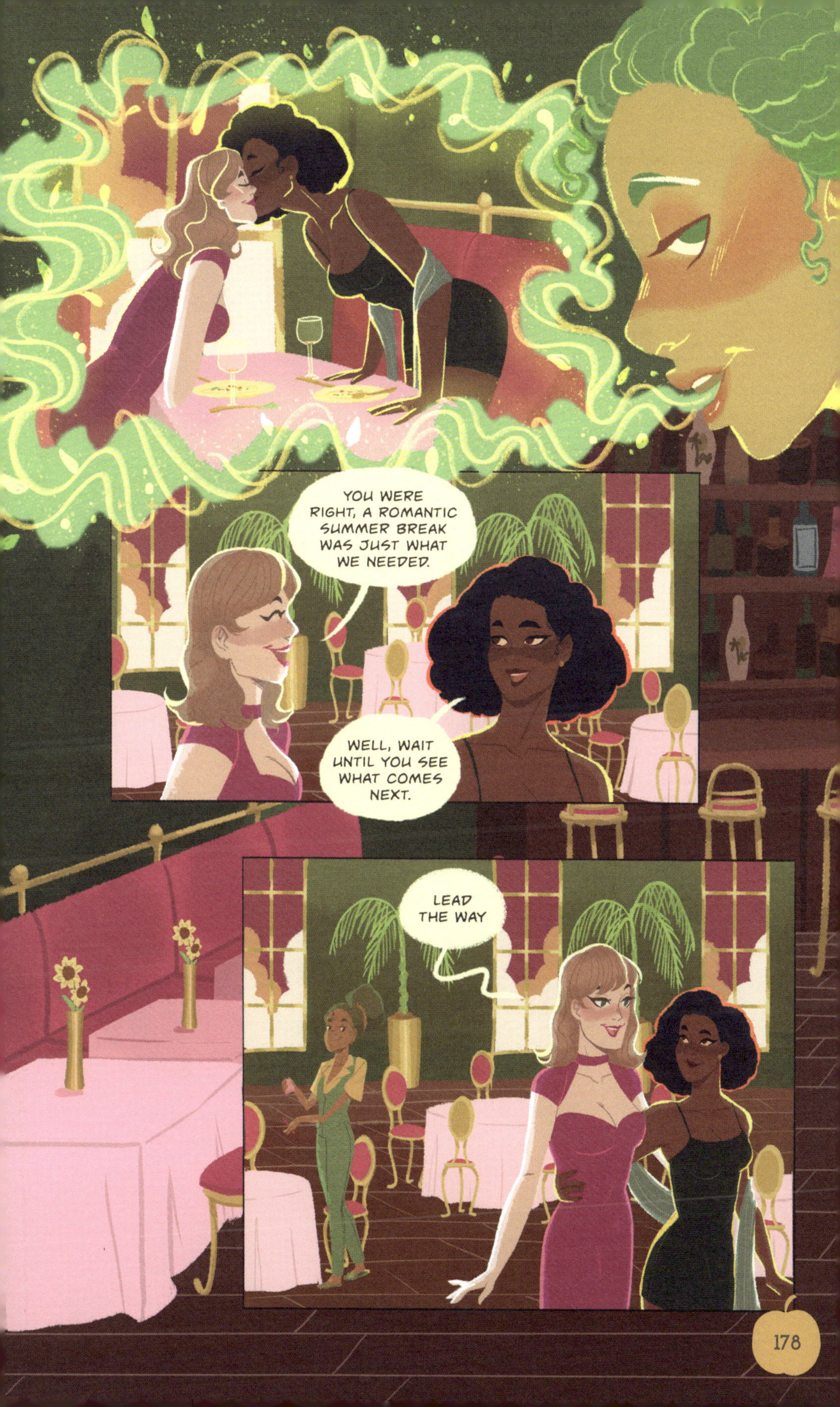
YOU WERE RIGHT, A ROMANTIC SUMMER BREAK WAS JUST WHAT WE NEEDED.
WELL, WAIT UNTIL YOU SEE WHAT COMES NEXT.
LEAD THE WAY

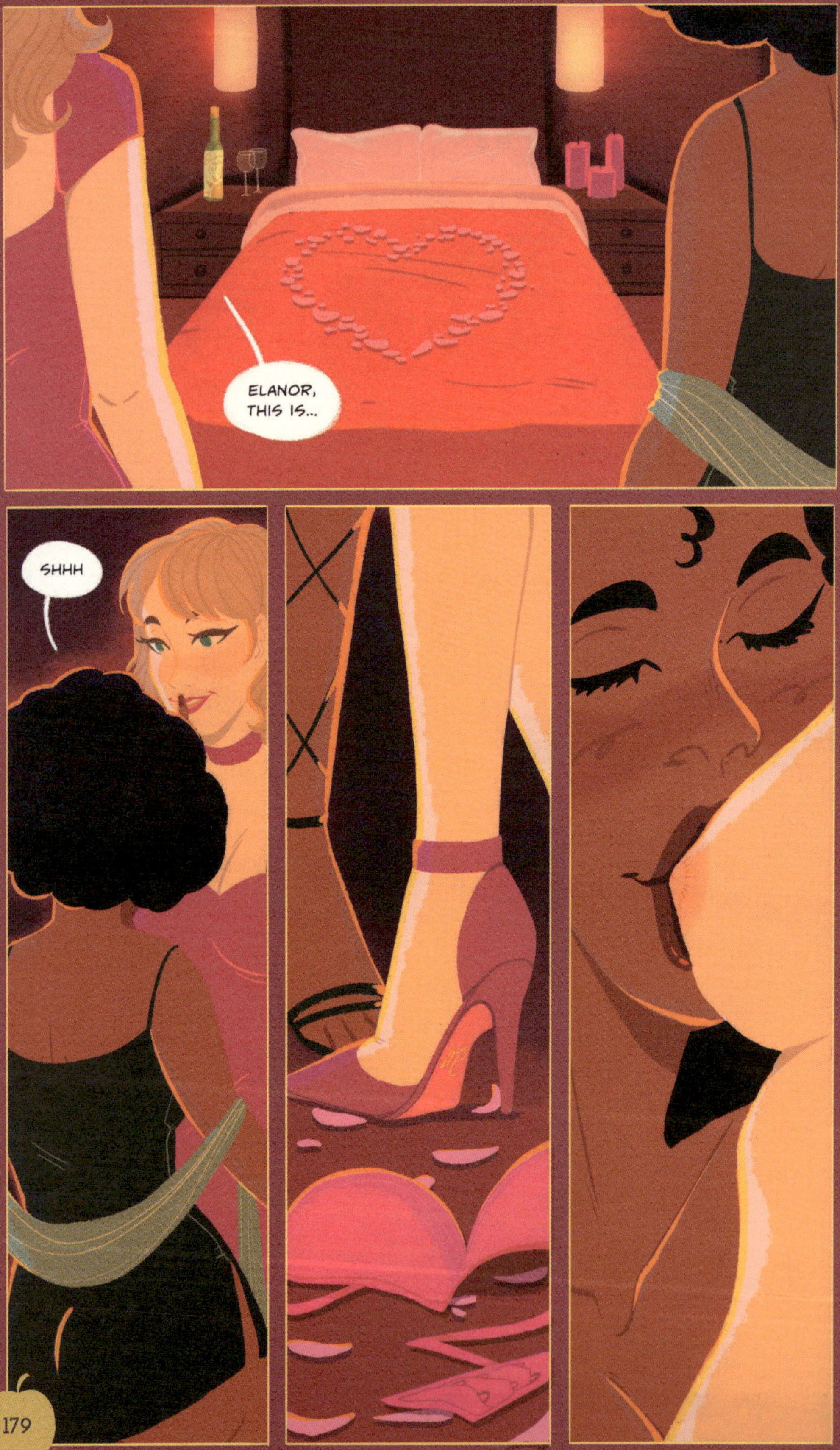
ELANOR, THIS IS...
SHHH

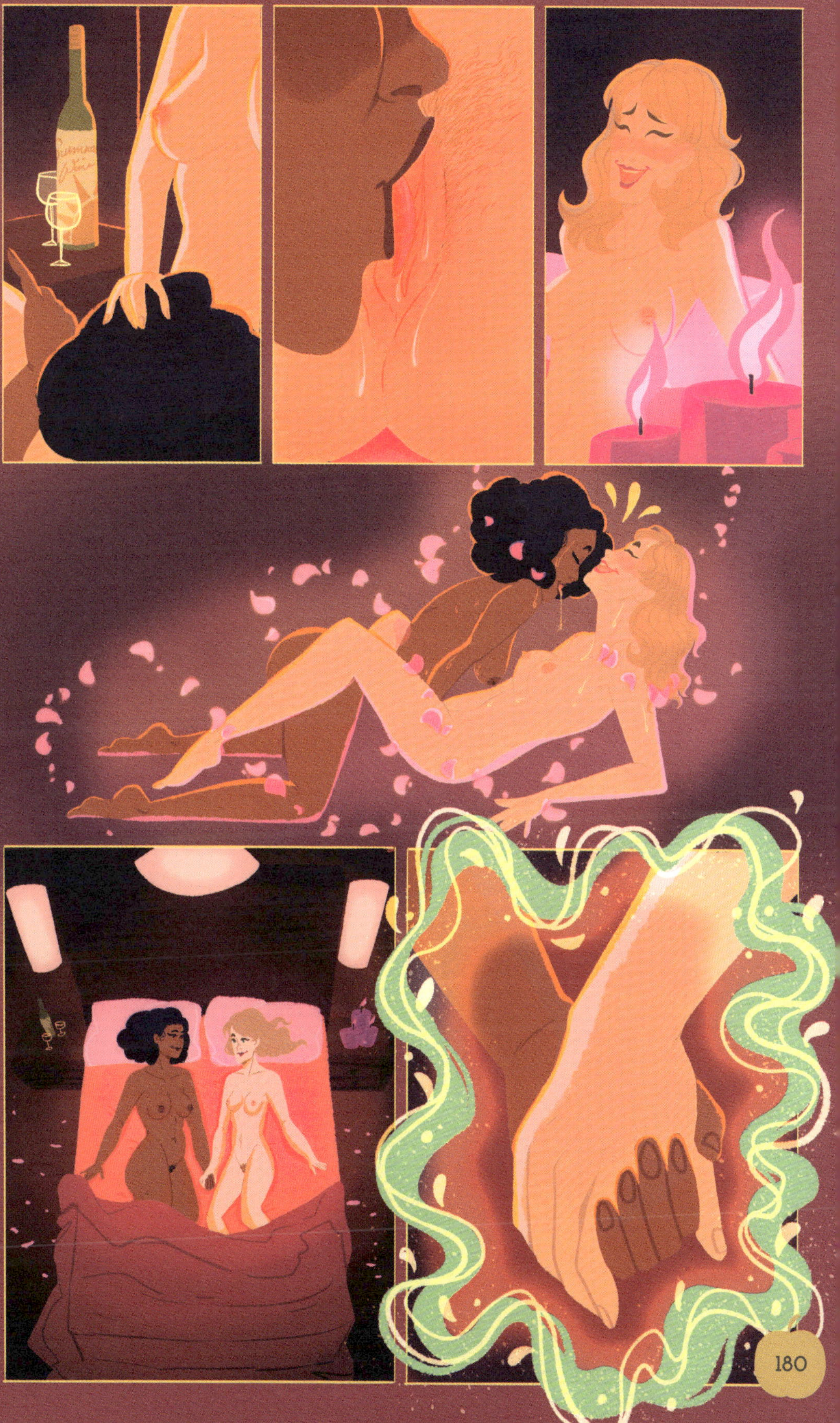

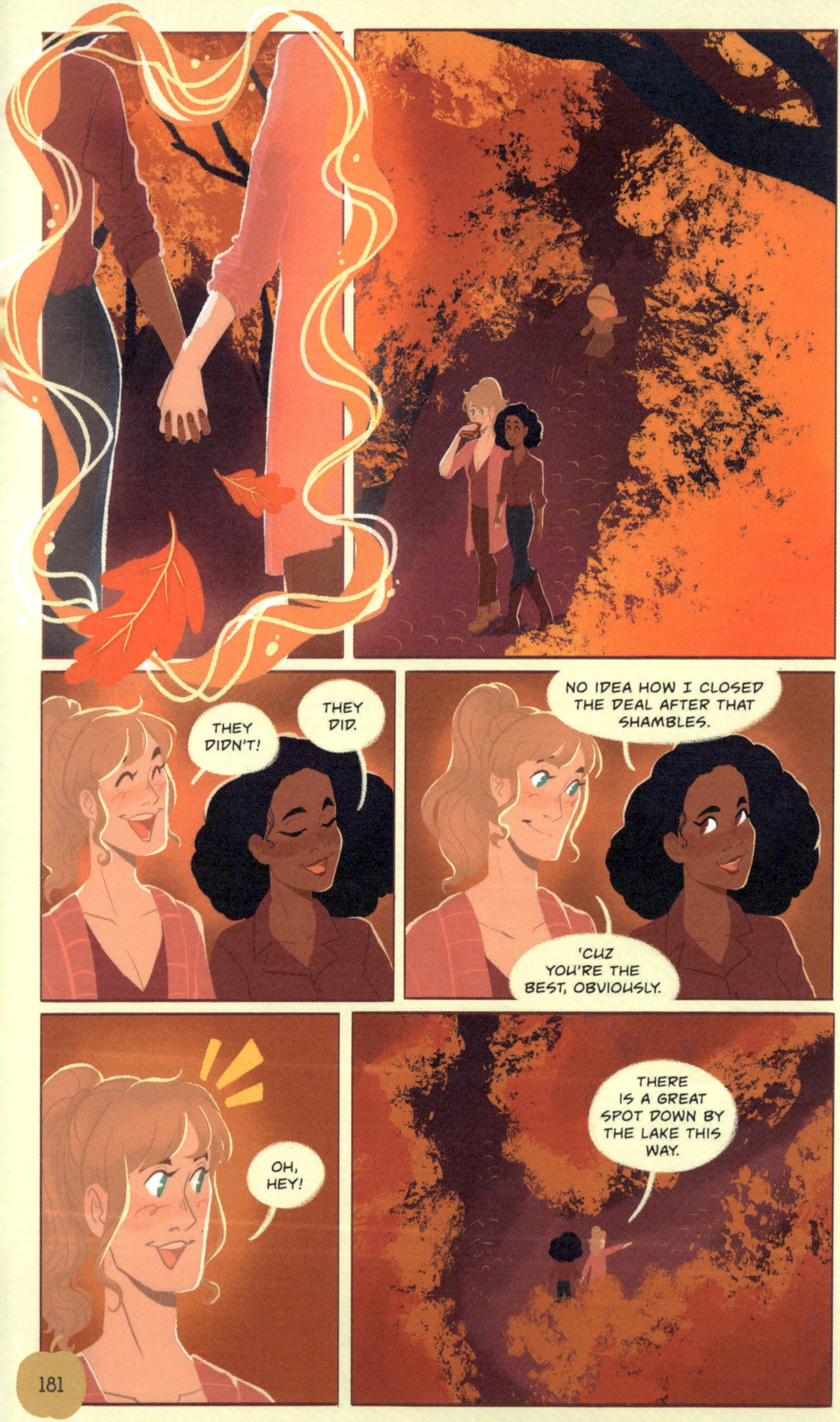
THEY DIDN'T!
THEY DID.
NO IDEA HOW I CLOSED THE DEAL AFTER THAT SHAMBLES.
'CUZ YOU'RE THE BEST, OBVIOUSLY.
OH, HEY!
THERE IS A GREAT SPOT DOWN BY THE LAKE THIS WAY.

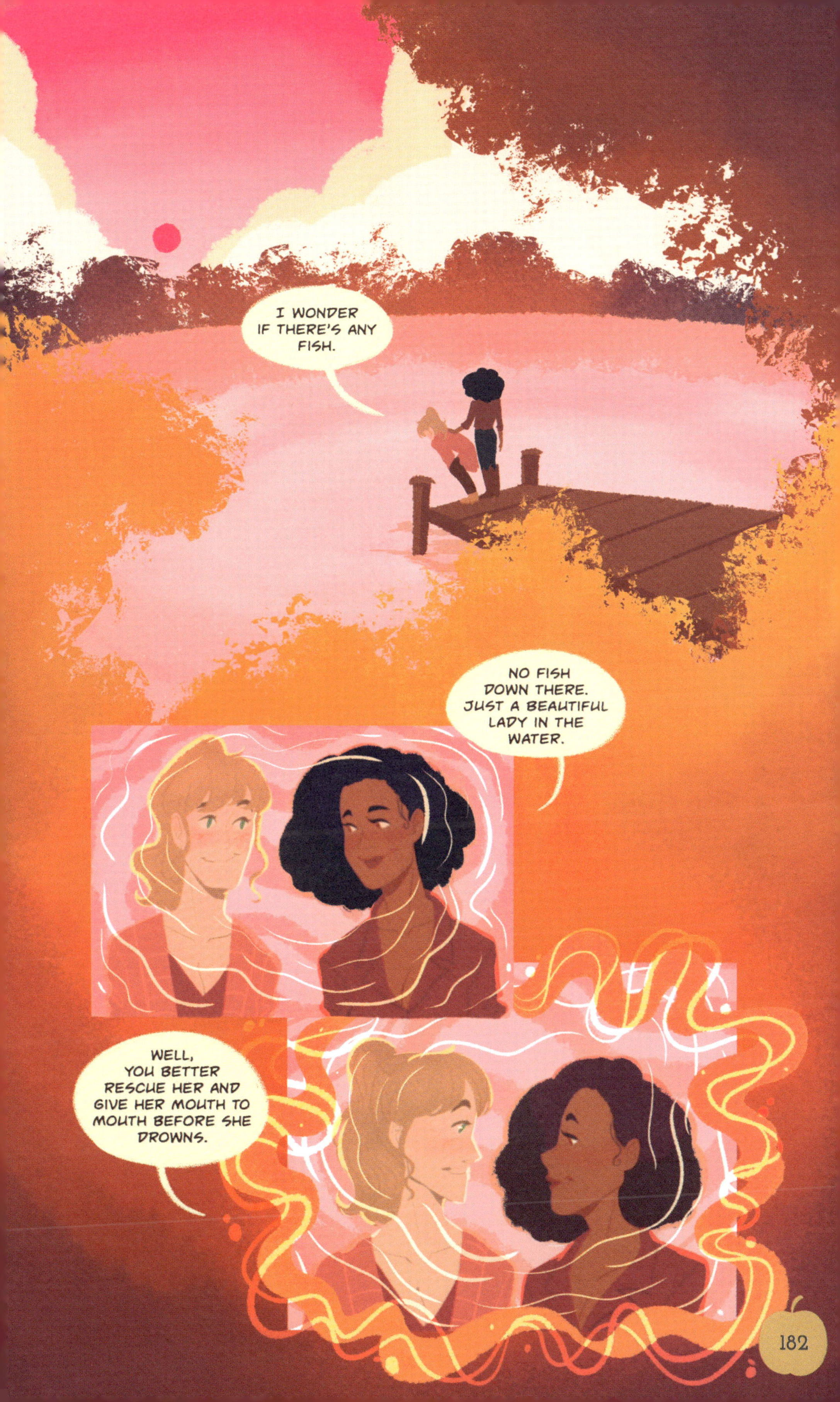
I WONDER IF THERE'S ANY FISH.
NO FISH DOWN THERE. JUST A BEAUTIFUL LADY IN THE WATER.
WELL, YOU BETTER RESCUE HER AND GIVE HER MOUTH TO MOUTH BEFORE SHE DROWNS.

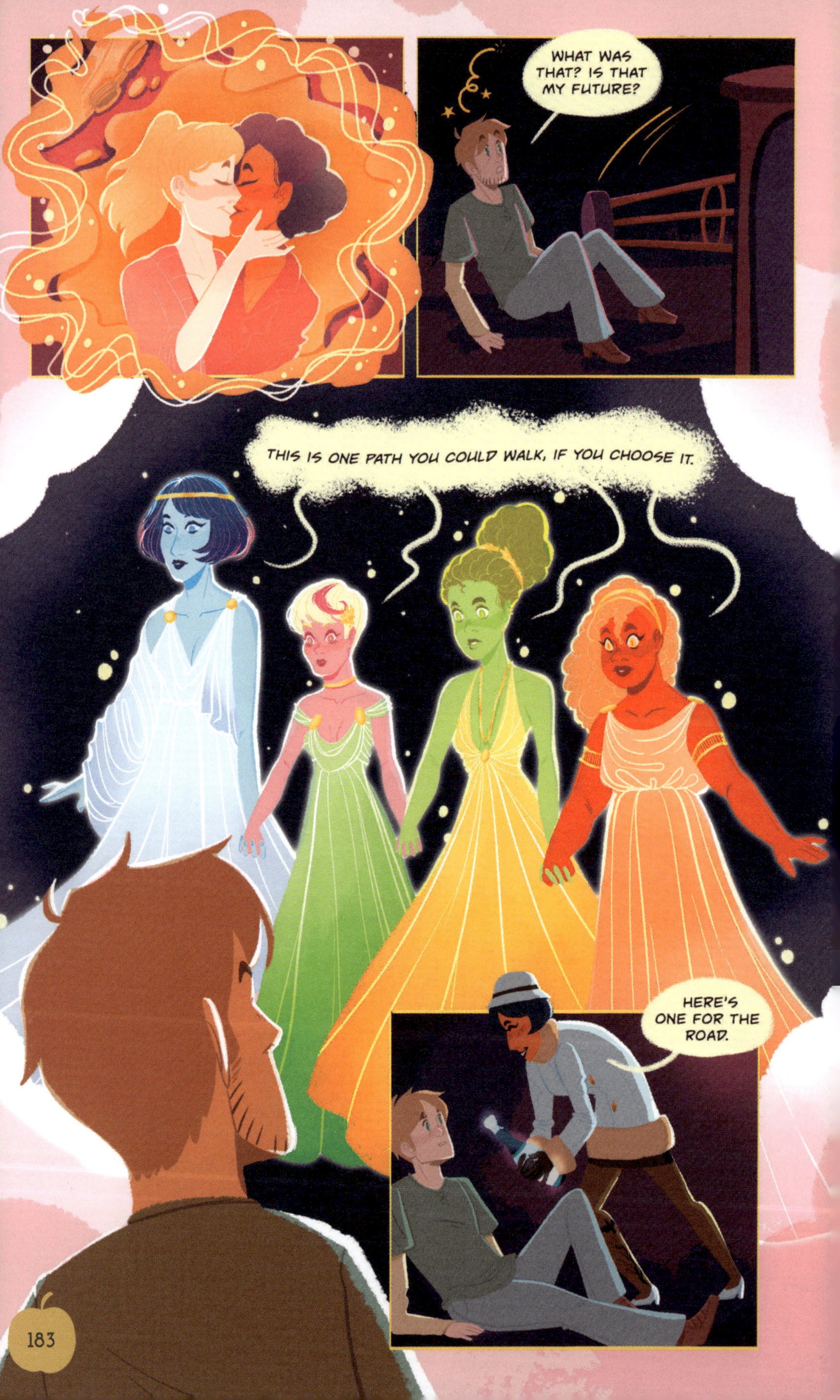
WHAT WAS THAT? IS THAT MY FUTURE?
THIS IS ONE PATH YOU COULD WALK, IF YOU CHOOSE IT.
HERE'S ONE FOR THE ROAD.

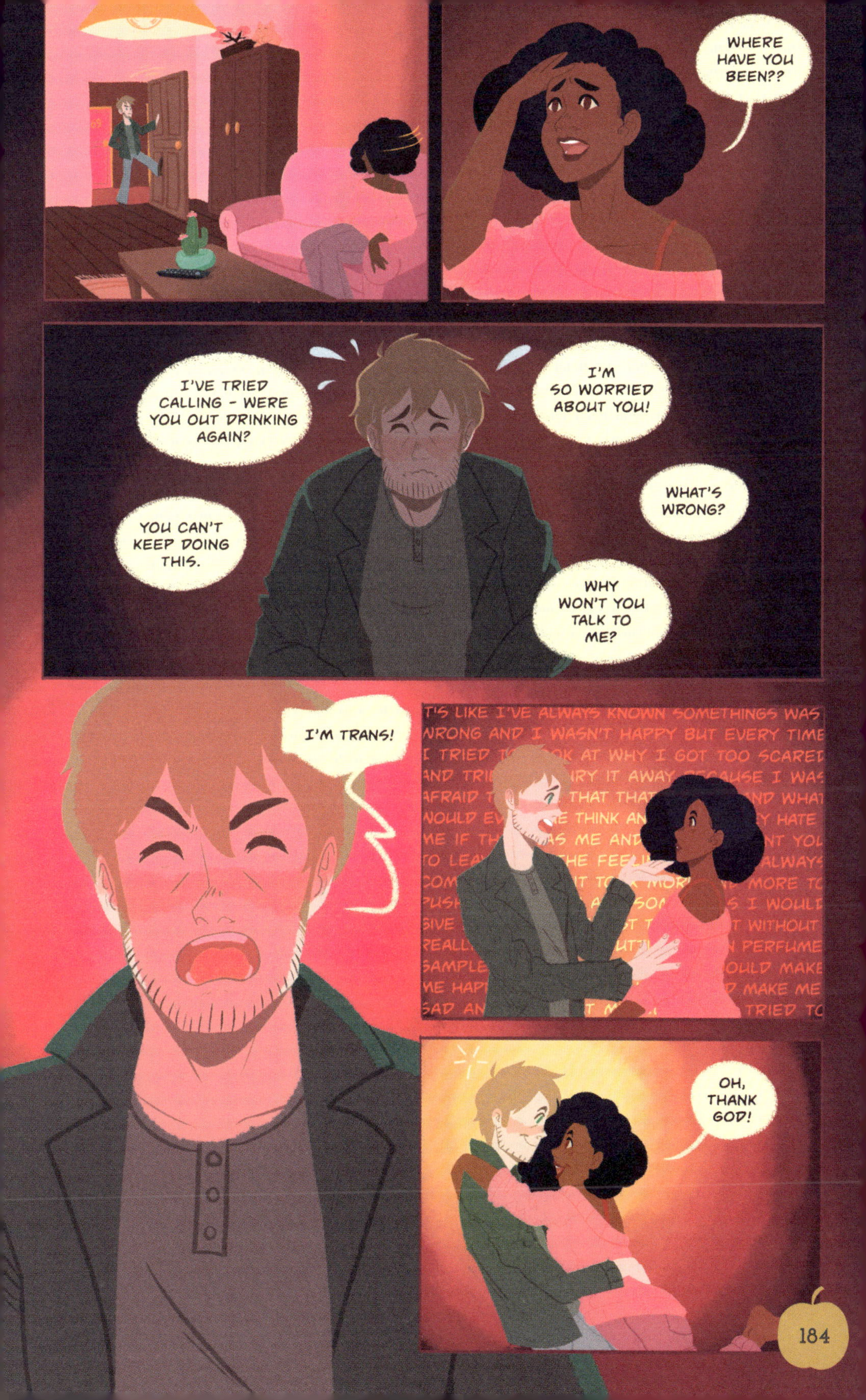
WHERE HAVE YOU BEEN??
I'VE TRIED CALLING - WERE YOU OUT DRINKING AGAIN?
I'M SO WORRIED ABOUT YOU!
WHAT'S WRONG?
YOU CAN'T KEEP DOING THIS.
WHY WON'T YOU TALK TO ME?
I'M TRANS!
IT'S LIKE I'VE ALWAYS KNOWN SOMETHINGS WAS
WRONG AND I WASN'T HAPPY BUT EVERY TIME
OH, THANK GOD!

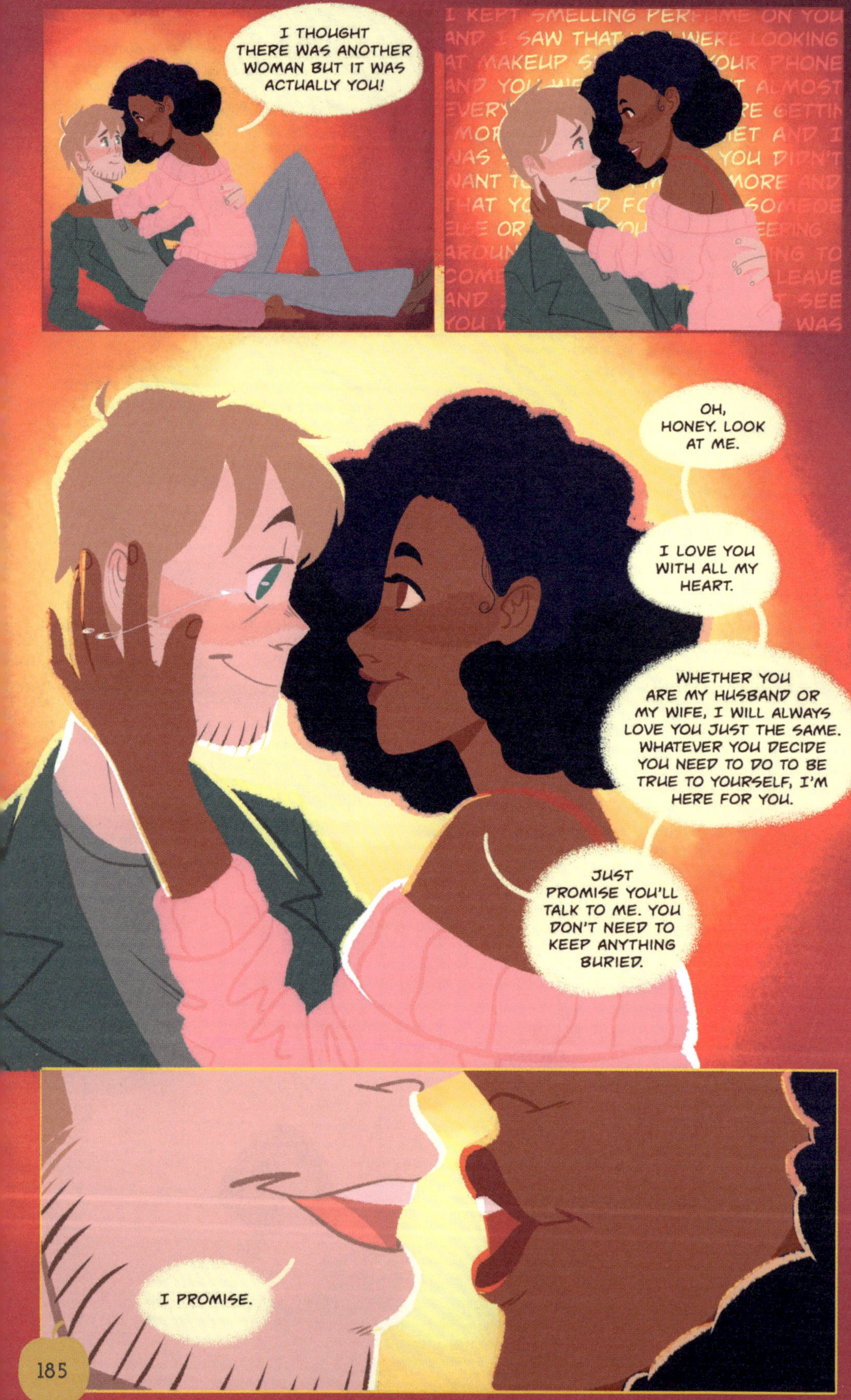
I THOUGHT THERE WAS ANOTHER WOMAN BUT IT WAS ACTUALLY YOU!
OH, HONEY. LOOK AT ME.
I LOVE YOU WITH ALL MY HEART.
WHETHER YOU ARE MY HUSBAND OR MY WIFE, I WILL ALWAYS LOVE YOU JUST THE SAME. WHATEVER YOU DECIDE YOU NEED TO DO TO BE TRUE TO YOURSELF, I'M HERE FOR YOU.
JUST PROMISE YOU'LL TALK TO ME. YOU DON'T NEED TO KEEP ANYTHING BURIED.
I PROMISE.

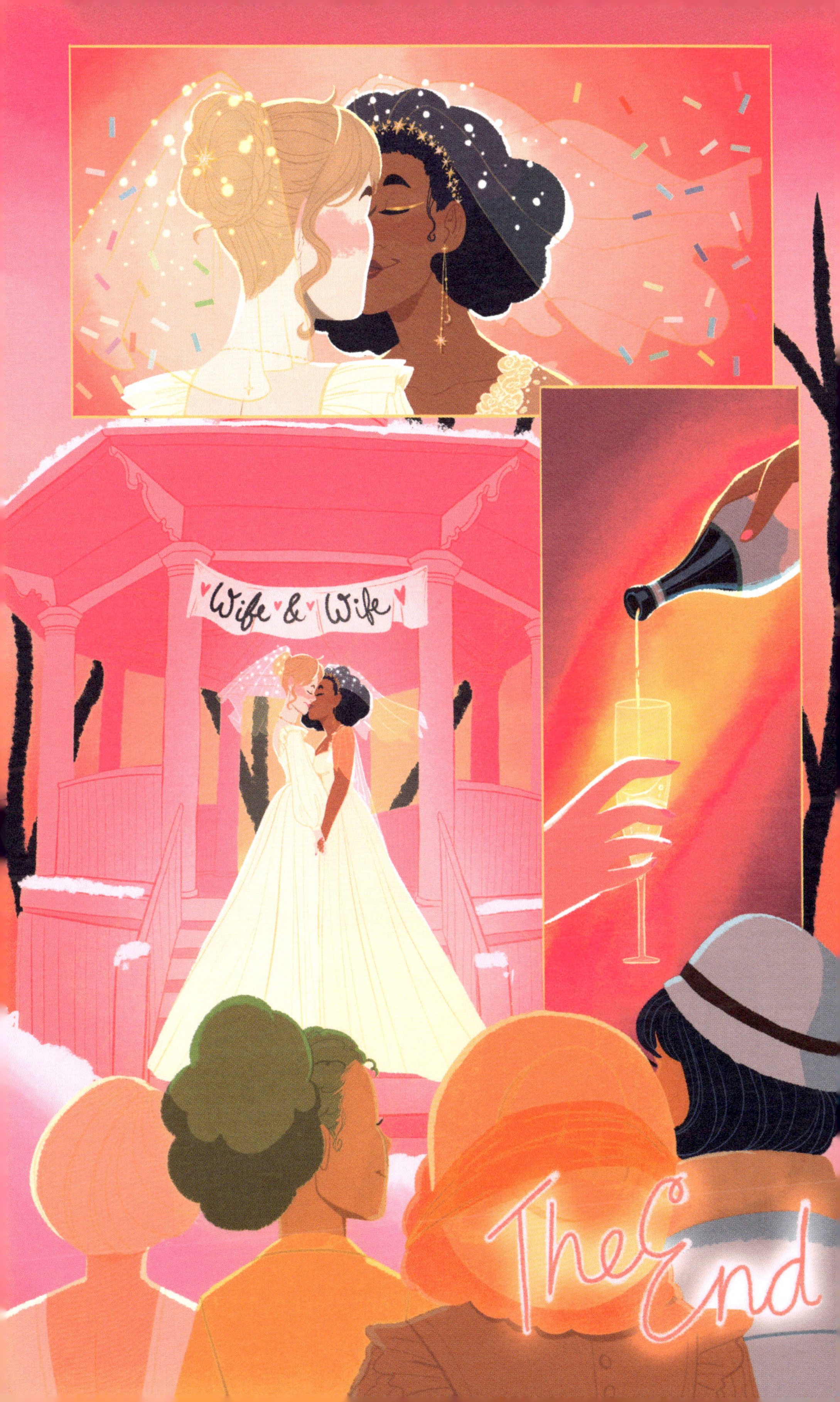
Wife & Wife
The End

Extra Art

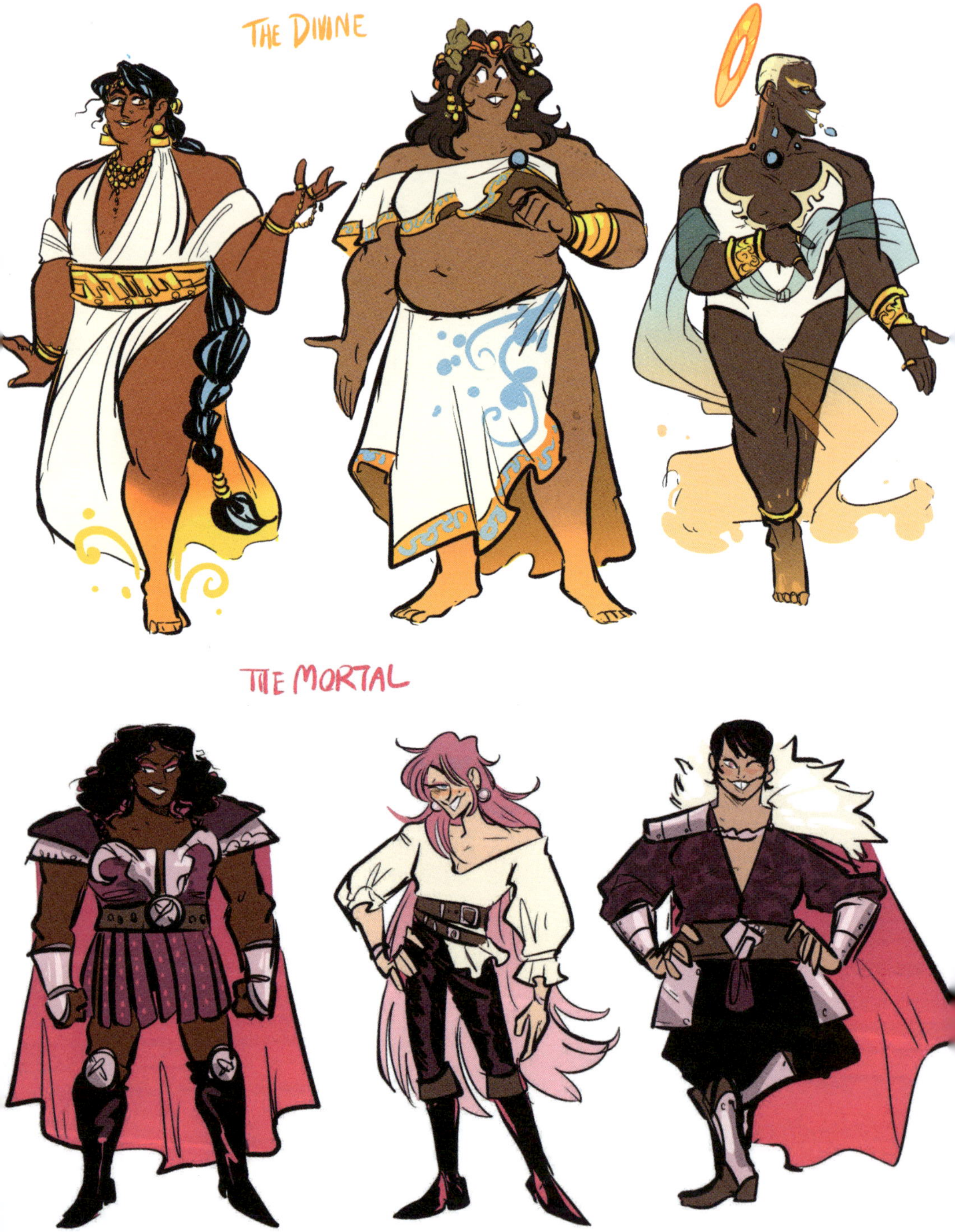

Character concepts for front cover by NJ Barna

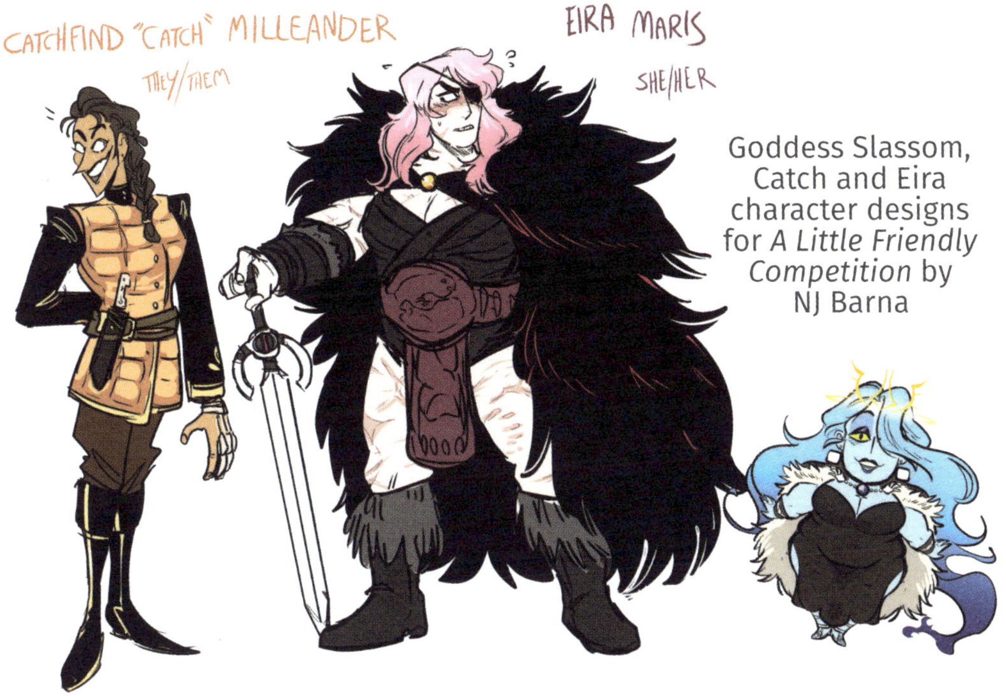

Goddess Slassom, Catch and Eira character designs for *A Little Friendly Competition* by NJ Barna

Galatea, Medusa and Narcissa character designs for *The Cuntsmith*
Story by Harry-Anne Bentley with Art by Phineas Klier

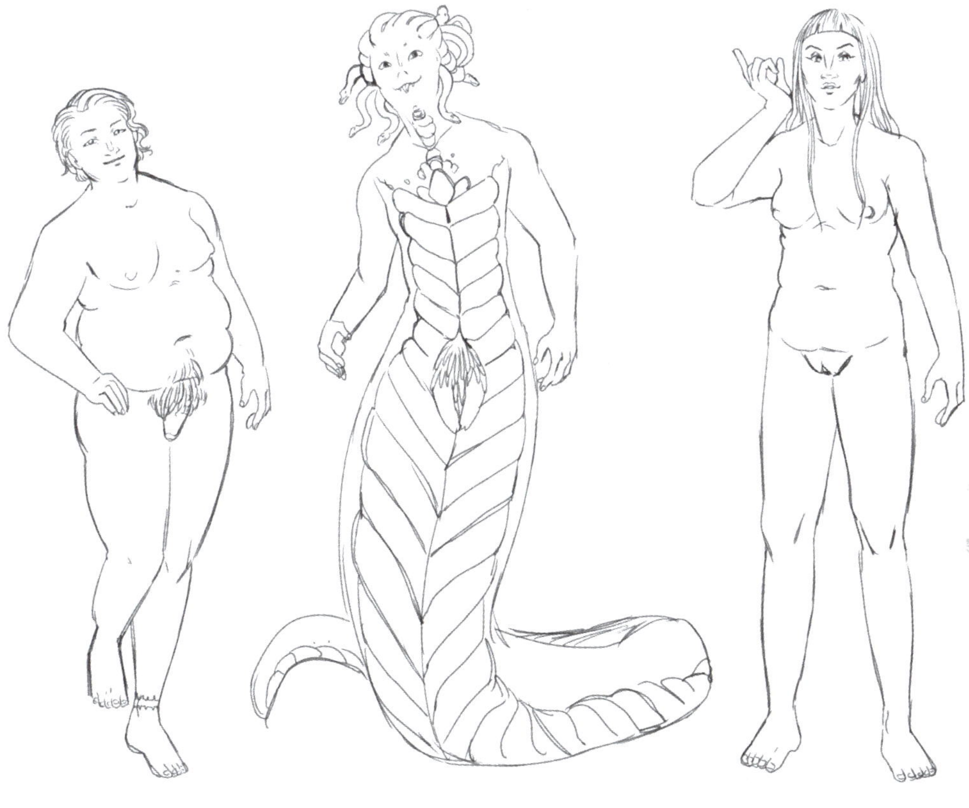

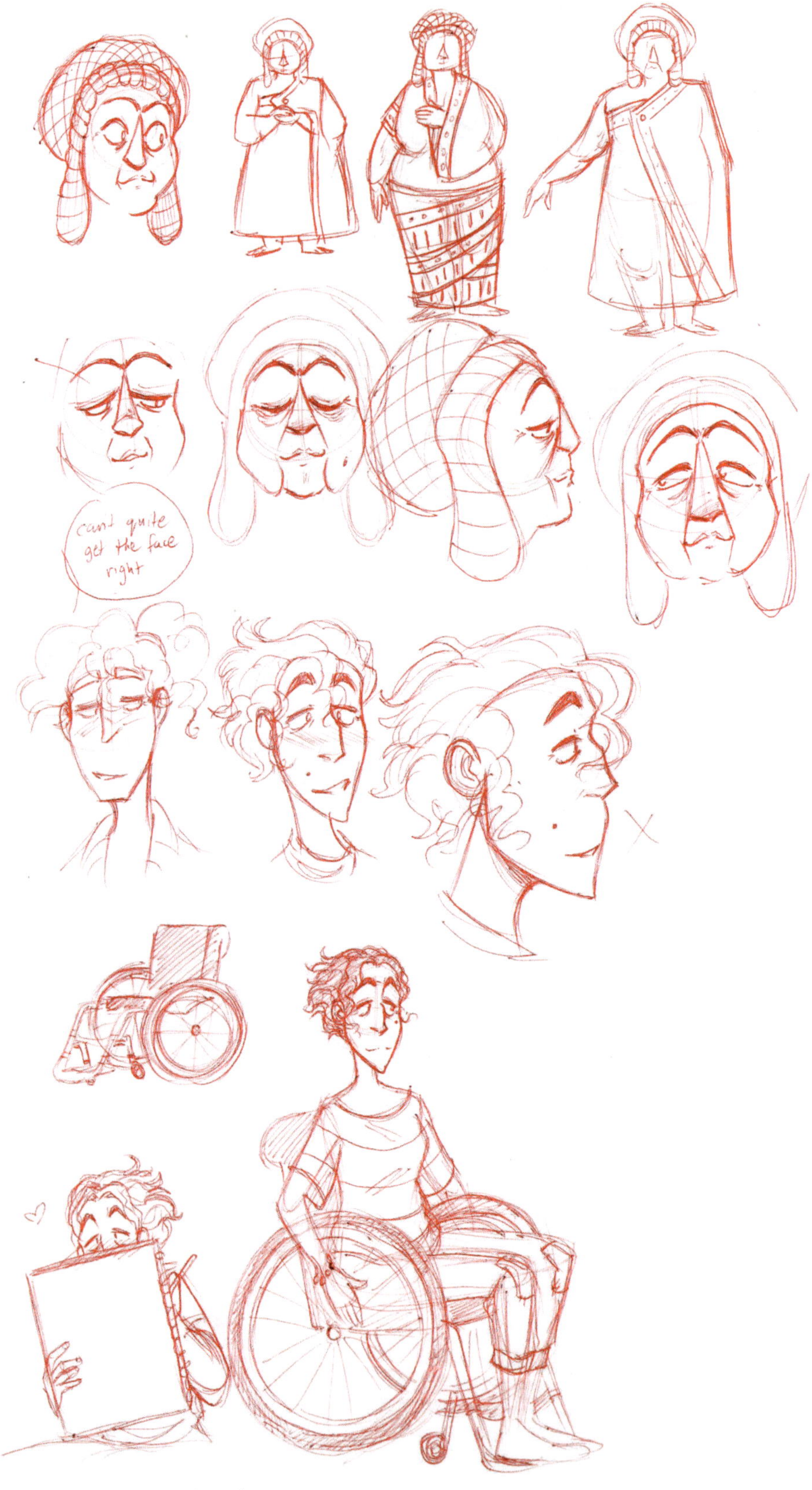

Muse and Painter character designs for *Come Forth My Muse*
Story by Michelle Parker with Art by Jey Pawlik

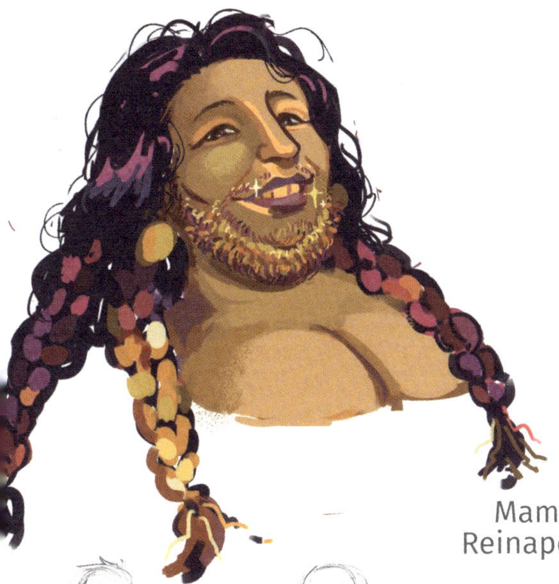

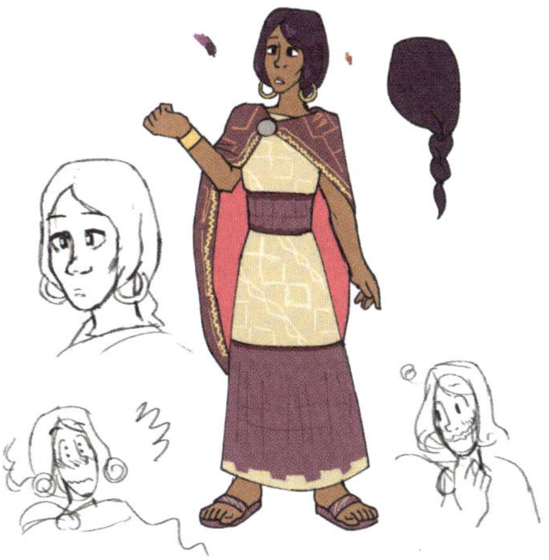

Mama Sorca by Fanfi and Maimará by Reinapepiada for *Cream of the Crop* Story.

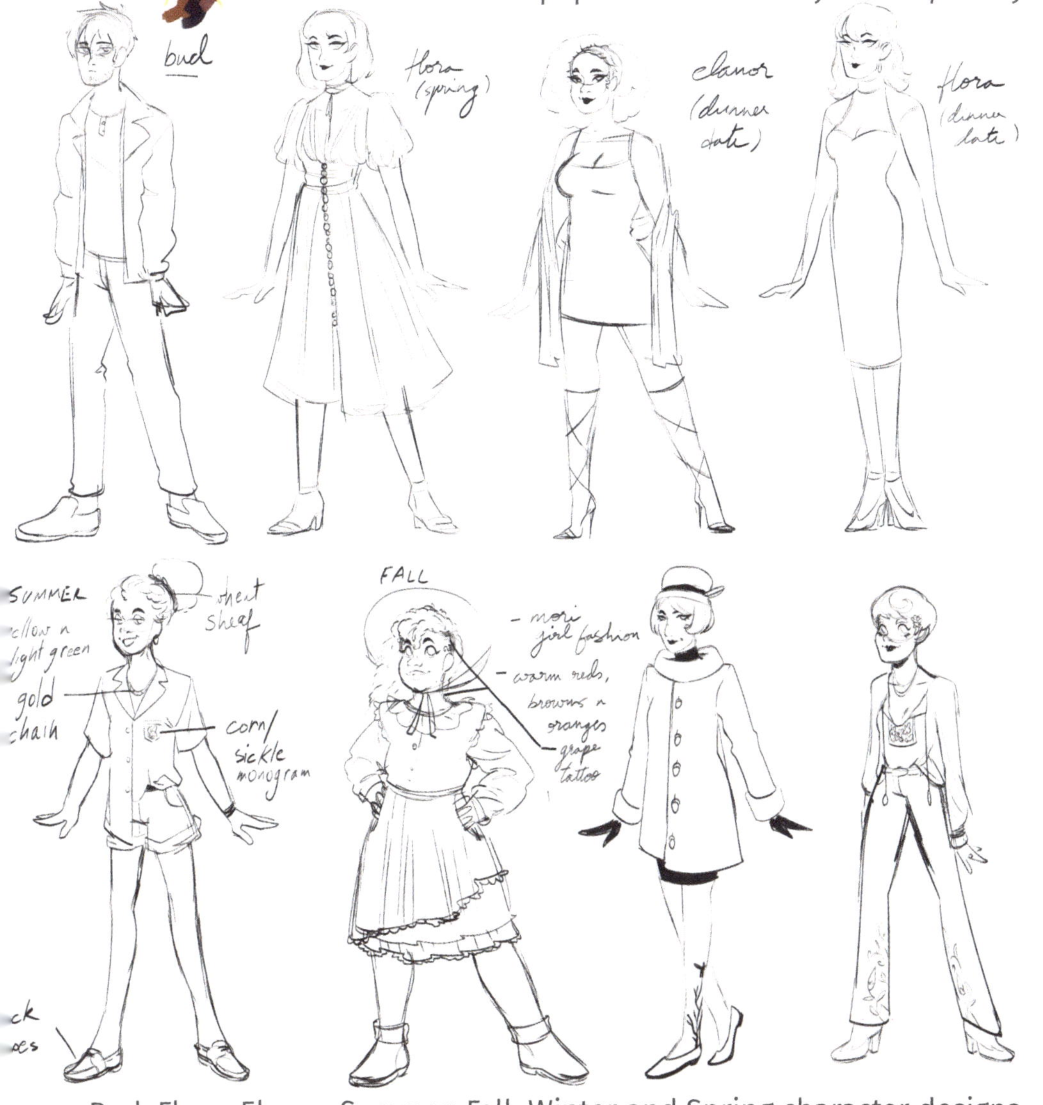

Bud, Flora, Elanor, Summer, Fall, Winter and Spring character designs for *Four Seasons* Story by Mx Andromeda Star with Art by Alina Wahab

Our Back Cover

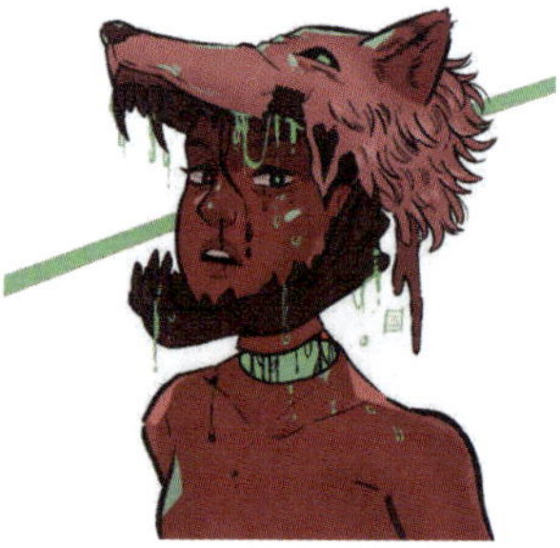

Dylan B. Caleho (They/Them) is a comic artist living and working in Philadelphia. They enjoy bright colors, and telling stories featuring sapphic or queer subjects. They used to work in horror comics but found writing and drawing romance/ erotic/ slice of life stories makes them much more satisfied with their work.

Twitter.com/Dylanbeedoodles